Bond of Union

BUILDING THE ERIE CANAL
and
THE AMERICAN EMPIRE

Gerard Koeppel

DA CAPO PRESS

A Member of the Perseus Books Group

An earlier version of a portion of chapter 9 appeared as "Andrew Bartow and the Cement that Made the Erie Canal," *New-York Journal of American History* 66, no. 1 (Spring–Summer 2005): 52–60.

Designed by Brent Wilcox
Set in 11.5 point Adobe Garamond by The Perseus Books Group

Library of Congress Cataloging-in-Publication Data
Koeppel, Gerard T., 1957-
    Bond of Union : building the Erie Canal and the American empire / Gerard Koeppel. — 1st ed.
        p. cm.
    Includes bibliographical references and index.
    ISBN 978-0-306-81827-1 (alk. paper)
    1. Erie Canal (N.Y.)—History.   I. Title.
    F127.E5K646 2009
    386'.4809747—dc22

                                                            2008048672

Published by Da Capo Press
A Member of the Perseus Books Group
www.dacapopress.com

Da Capo Press books are available at special discounts for bulk purchases in the U.S. by corporations, institutions, and other organizations. For more information, please contact the Special Markets Department at the Perseus Books Group, 2300 Chestnut Street, Suite 200, Philadelphia, PA 19103, or call (800) 810-4145, ext. 5000, or e-mail special.markets@perseusbooks.com.

10 9 8 7 6 5 4 3 2 1

For Diane, Jackson, Harry, Kate, and Scrappy

Pleasure is a shadow, wealth is vanity, and power a pageant; but knowledge is ecstatic in enjoyment, perennial in fame, unlimited in space, and infinite in duration.

—DE WITT CLINTON,
address to Phi Beta Kappa Society, Union College,
Schenectady, New York, July 22, 1823

CONTENTS

ELEVATION PROFILE OF THE ERIE CANAL

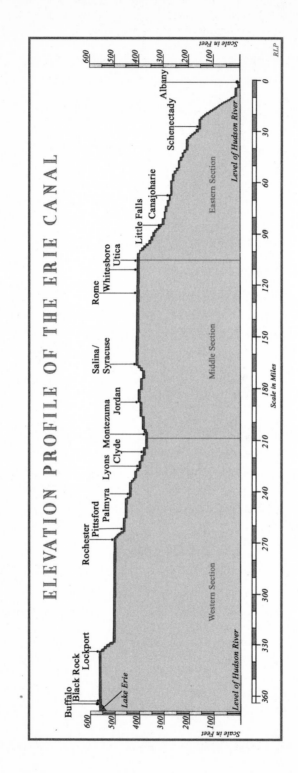

RLP

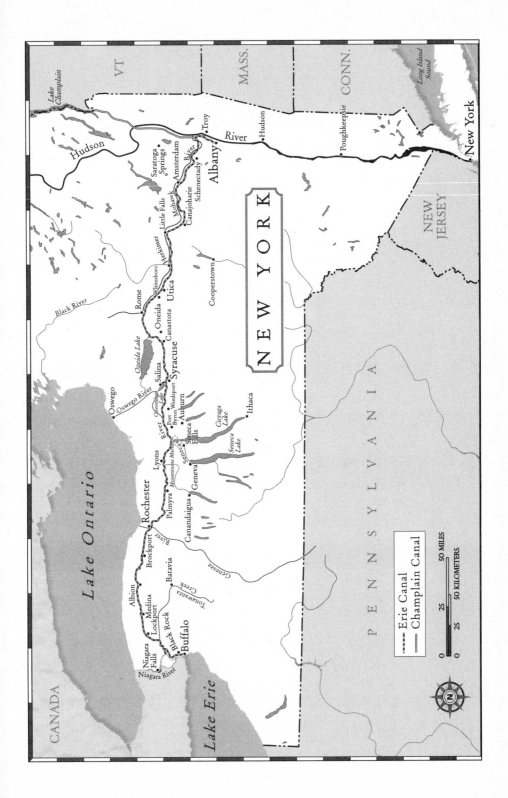

CHAPTER 1

An American Ambition

The building of the Erie Canal was an act of faith, the demonstration of a spirit of enterprise by an organized government that has few parallels in world history.

—George Rogers Taylor,
The Transportation Revolution (1951)

The morning came on cool and bright. A recent frost had just begun to color the surrounding forest autumn. The blue sky and chill air mingled the past with the future, experience with expectation. In the frontier village of Buffalo, possibly even in the whole of New York State, there was no more expectant time than Wednesday, October 26, 1825. The population of just over twenty-four hundred had been swelled by dozens of the state's political and merchant leaders and hundreds of settler families from the surrounding countryside, all eager to celebrate the completion of the great project that would determine their fortunes and those of many others.

Gathered in the Lake Erie port that twenty years earlier had been just a mark on a land developer's map, the leaders of New York betrayed no uncertainties. Their state had just surged past Virginia and Pennsylvania to become the most populous of the United States. New York's namesake city had recently displaced Philadelphia as the nation's largest and was taking control of the young American economy. In fields, drawing rooms, and countinghouses across the Atlantic, the words *New York* were becoming equivalent to economic opportunity for laborers, speculators, and protoindustrialists alike. And yet, until this fall morning, New York was no more assured of becoming The Empire State than was Virginia, Pennsylvania, or even Ohio, South Carolina, or Illinois. Nor was the nation assured of becoming the global empire it remains.

In 1825 the United States were still plural and few: not a singular nation-state but sovereign states with a constitutionally limited federal government. As late as 1855, Walt Whitman proclaimed with verbal plurality, "the United States with veins full of poetical stuff most need poets." Abraham Lincoln, declaring the Union at Gettysburg, finally changed the grammar and perception in the 1860s. In 1825 the sea-to-shining-sea continental nation of patriotic song was still a dream: the land was vast, access to and control of it was limited. The Louisiana Territory had been purchased two decades earlier but remained mostly unorganized. Mexico's north stretched from the Sabine River on the Gulf of Mexico to the 42nd parallel on the Pacific Ocean, encompassing all of what are now Texas, New Mexico, Arizona, Utah, Nevada, and California (as well as parts of Colorado, Oklahoma, Wyoming, and Kansas). The Pacific Northwest was open country. The Appalachian mountain range, guarding the interior from South Carolina to what only recently had become Maine, threatened to confine the great American experiment to the Atlantic seaboard. The allegiance of the several new transmontane states was unproven; their settlers looked west down rolling river valleys toward the mighty Mississippi, not over their shoulders at the mountains that separated them from their political creators. Former vice president Aaron Burr's enigmatic conspiracy of 1805–1806—to make a nation for himself and others in the region opened by the Louisiana Purchase—had come apart but illustrated the limited control exerted by the east over the west, of the national government over its unsettled territory. A continental nation was so uncertain that President Thomas Jefferson had deemed it optional: "Whether we remain in one confederacy, or form into Atlantic and Mississippi confederacies, I believe not very important to the happiness of either part." The coming of the steamboat in 1807 gave hope for connectedness but illustrated the lack of it: soon there were boats on the Hudson and the Mississippi rivers but no true navigation between them.

The War of 1812 proved over its desultory three-year course that the United States remained a shaky nation. The British burned Washington. President James Madison escaped on horseback, separated from his Dolley. The British also burned Buffalo and neighboring Black Rock. The pioneers of Western New York fled east in terror. There was no defending the state's western flank by the effective transportation of arms and supplies. The few roads were "so abominable" that the federal government spent a staggering $60 million on wartime transport, including a dollar a pound for cannonballs that cost a fraction of that to produce. The cost of moving artillery from Albany to the major naval warfront on Lake Erie was more than double its purchase price; transportation of material from Washington to the lake was up to five times the production cost. The British blockade of American ports forced coastal shipping onto primitive land routes: one wagon of war supplies loaded in Worcester, Massachusetts arrived in Charleston, South Carolina, two and a half months later. Nothing had changed dramatically in the decade since peace was restored. Until the Erie Canal opened on a fine fall day in 1825.

The canal was a slender thing: 363 miles across the breadth of New York from Albany to Buffalo, but only forty feet wide and four feet deep. A ribbon of water, the canal traversed by turns malarial swamp, dense forest, rock ridge, steep valley, and arid plateau. For its eastern 125 miles the canal claimed from the Mohawk River a strip of its storied valley, where industry was gaining a foothold amid the rich lore of native, patriot, and settler life. The western two-thirds of the canal passed through sparsely settled territory, a sliver of progress that would convert frontier regions into centers of worldwide commerce. Conceived in the earliest 1800s, the canal was the boldest and biggest American engineering project of its century, with enduring political, social, and economic effect. Two centuries later, the canal remains "probably the outstanding example of a human artifact creating wealth rapidly in the whole of history."

A child clawing a channel through sand at water's edge or flicking a stick to link sidewalk puddles indulges the human instinct to create waterways. Canals are as old as the ingenuity of humans trying to move themselves or their things more quickly and cheaply. Some ancient and medieval canals were of considerable length, but all connected points at the same elevation. How to raise and lower the level of an artificial waterway was unknown. Modern canal engineering was born in the 1480s when Leonardo Da Vinci, famously improving on earlier Dutch designs, designed locks to join existing level canals in Milan. A canal lock is a chamber with gates at each end placed at an elevation change; the sequential opening and closing of the gates raises or lowers a boat that has entered the lock chamber. Although locks were simple in concept, the challenges for early designers were to make them durable, watertight, and practicable, and to find ample water to replace the lock-fulls released to the lower elevation. The earliest lock gates moved vertically, subjecting them to great pressure and friction. Leonardo's innovation was paired mitered lock gates forming a V pointed in the direction of the higher water. Water was deflected to the sides when the gates were swung open, and pressure sealed the lock when the gates were closed. Over half a millennium later, canal locks are still built the same way.

The first great canal of modern Europe was the Languedoc. It effectively connected the Atlantic Ocean and the Mediterranean Sea across southwestern France in 1681, avoiding Spain, Portugal, Gibraltar, and two thousand treacherous sea miles. Pondered by the Romans and proposed by Da Vinci, the canal was finally planned in the early 1660s. It was paid for largely by its promoter and builder, benevolent local baron Pierre-Paul Riquet, who ruined his health and wealth during the construction by eleven thousand workers and died months before the canal was completed. In its 150-mile length and 826 feet of elevation changes through the rugged terrain between Toulouse and Sete (founded as the canal's eastern terminus), Languedoc required over one hundred locks and over twice as many bridges and dams. Among the spectacular and original engineering feats were a 515-foot tunnel through a hill, a staircase of eight locks to surmount a 70-foot rise, a set of nine double locks, and a massive summit-level reservoir system to supply lower elevations. Sixty-four feet wide and six and a half feet deep, Languedoc (now known as the Canal du Midi) was and remains an astounding accomplishment and an inspiration for those who would build New York's grand canal.

Canals were flourishing in France for eighty years before the technology transferred significantly to England, in the form of the Bridgewater Canal. It was only seven miles long but it was as revolutionary as Languedoc. Francis Egerton, the young duke of Bridgewater, was a playboy aristocrat turned spurned suitor and bachelor industrialist who wanted a cheap way to get coal from his mines at Worsley to the power-hungry textile mills at Manchester. The steep, boggy valley of the River Irwell intervened. The duke had been to Languedoc and seen how irregular terrain could yield to a locked canal. To make one for him, in 1759 he hired James Brindley, a local millwright of meager rearing, rudimentary education, and "inexhaustible ingenuity." Brindley, whose eye was mightier than his pen, had his own ideas. After an "ochilor servey or a riconnitoring," the unschooled millwright recommended a canal that could be straight, level, short, and expeditious by *crossing* the valley, instead of going up, down, and around it. The crossing would be on an extraordinary stone aqueduct bridge: six hundred feet long, thirty-six feet wide, with three arches—the middle one with a sixty-three-foot span—carrying the canal forty feet over the Irwell. No structure of that magnitude had been conceived, much less built, in England; an aqueduct carrying boats high above a valley seemed a "castle in the air" to all but the duke of Bridgewater, who endorsed the plan. Without locks, the canal part was easy. Brindley's work on the bridge was archetypal (though he certainly couldn't spell the word). He drained away water to firm up the supporting soil, designed the bridge so its structural loads were suitably distributed, and made the canal trough watertight by extensively "puddling" layers of clay and sand. Canal builders, from younger contemporaries to those in modern times would emulate Brindley's rigor on the Bridgewater Canal and many others. On the issue of whether rivers, always subject to drought and flood, should be used as canal beds or only to provide water to canals, future planners would invoke Brindley's famous answer to a House of Commons inquiry on why potentially navigable rivers were created: "To feed navigable canals." The wisest proponents of Erie would heed Brindley's dictum.

The Bridgewater Canal was just eighteen feet wide and four and a half feet deep, but its opening in 1761 brought coal to Manchester at less than half the previous price by circuitous cart or river route. The duke became the king of coal and Brindley the greatest canal engineer in England: his pioneering works multiplied and his protégés spread, eventually to America and New York. The Bridgewater Canal fed the coal-powered Industrial Revolution the way the Internet facilitates the digital age. It spawned a canal mania in England that Americans would emulate after Erie.

The Erie Canal would be more than twice as long as Languedoc and be laid through regions as primitive as Bridgewater's was industrial. "The building of the Erie Canal was an act of faith," wrote historian George Rogers Taylor, "the demonstration of a spirit of enterprise by an organized government that has few parallels in world history." The canal was sponsored by the state, but thousands of people had a hand in its creation. Pioneers and visionaries conceived and nurtured the idea. Elected representatives drafted and won passage of the necessary laws. Surveyors with little or no engineering education or experience planned and oversaw the construction. Yankee-born farm families and, later, Irish immigrant labor gangs mucked, grubbed, hacked, and blasted a path and fashioned the canal's walls, locks, and bridges with packed earth, timber, and stone. European and American banks and merchant speculators, patrician New Yorkers with deep Dutch and English roots, and even urban working-class savers bought the debt (eventually $8 million) that paid for the work.

Many men claimed, or had claimed for them, the honor of being the single person most responsible for the canal. The debate raged among principals and partisans for years, until the arguments were stilled by death and distraction. Three individuals and one small group were indispensable. Without them, the canal would not have been imagined, approved, designed, built, and efficiently completed. All but one are practically unknown today. The name of De Witt Clinton is, at best, recognizable. The names of Jesse Hawley and Samuel Wilkeson today draw blanks even in the upstate places they pioneered. Benjamin Wright, James Geddes, Canvass White, John Jervis, and Nathan Roberts are known to engineering historians but to few others. But these eight men—dreamers, schemers, and builders—held the keys to the creation of the Erie Canal.

Hawley was a Connecticut carpenter's son and a sixth-generation American. He had failed at becoming Western New York's first grain merchant, defeated by the tenuous network of rivers, lakes, and creeks that led from the state's frontier farms to the eastern market. Imprisoned for debt in 1807, Hawley published a series of essays in a local newspaper proposing and arguing for a canal across New York, effectively joining by water New York City's ocean port with half the continental interior. He wrote under the signature "Hercules," and sought protection wisely because his essays were called "the effusions of a maniac." If readers knew that the writer was a failed merchant jailed for bankruptcy, the essays and the great canal they envisioned might have been dismissed altogether.

For years, people generally assumed that the Hercules essays had been written by surveyors for western land speculators trying to attract attention and sales. Those who knew Hercules's identity—his publisher, certain friends—were sworn to secrecy. Only slowly did influential New Yorkers discover that Hercules was Hawley. He did not reveal himself publicly for nearly two decades, when the canal he had launched from jail was just months from completion and already celebrated on both sides of the Atlantic. He acknowledged then that his essays had been written "when all my private prospects in life were blighted and . . . from a wish to render some use to society for my existence, as well as to divest the mind from painful recollections of the past." His best hopes had been only for "posthumous fame, for no one then believed he would live to see the whole completed."

Obscure now and obscured then, Hawley was recognized as a prophet by his most thoughtful contemporaries. He was "a gentleman of an ingenious and reflecting mind," wrote De Witt Clinton, who was among the first to find Hawley out.

Though he was far from the first person to conceive of or promote the canal, Clinton became and remains the one most associated with it. Even before he made Hawley's acquaintance, Clinton started turning the idea into a political and popular reality. Born into a New York family prominent in politics and commerce, De Witt Clinton at a young age became the supreme leader of early nineteenth-century New York city and state.

His life was politics, as a senator in Washington and Albany, New York City's longtime mayor, and the state's longtime governor. He ran for president in 1812, losing to Madison by one swing state, a crushing defeat for Clinton's ample political ego. Every four years for the rest of his life he fancied himself a contender, but his national star had dimmed. Clinton "was too jealous of all competitors," wrote later presidential New Yorker Theodore Roosevelt, "and at the same time not a great enough man, ever to become an important figure in the national arena." Clinton was an avid philanthropist and an earnest savant, but his intellectual pursuits, like his White House quest, ultimately won just honorable mentions. He is best remembered now for the Erie Canal, otherwise known by his friends and many political foes as Clinton's Ditch.

At a preconstruction estimate of $6 million, the risky project was the most expensive in the United States, equal to a third of all the capital in New York. At 363 miles, it was over thirteen times the length of the country's longest canal and over three times the total length of all American canals, all but three of which were two miles or shorter. With his career in the balance, Clinton committed his substantial ego and influence to winning political and popular approval for a project that few thought could be built.

Few would know it, but Benjamin Wright is the "Father of American Civil Engineering." The posthumous honor was bestowed (in 1969 by the American Society of Civil Engineers) chiefly for his surveying, designs, and managerial skills on the Erie Canal, a reputation that would be burnished subsequently by building canals and railroads from Canada to Cuba, Rhode Island to Illinois. He began merely as a country surveyor at what would become Rome, New York, and not with complete success: at age twenty-three, he was fired by a land developer for failing to lay a thirty-five-mile road through thick forest from what became Utica.

Wright's surveying skills would improve dramatically over the next two decades, but less than ninety days before he and James Geddes were to break ground as the putative chief "engineers" of the Erie Canal, an incredulous assemblyman would ask loudly in Albany, "Who is this James Geddes, and who is this Benjamin Wright, that the [Canal] Commissioners have trusted with this responsibility—what canals have they ever constructed? What great public works have they accomplished?" The answer was none, but neither had any American.

James Geddes was raised on a thriving Pennsylvania farm and educated by Scotch-descended parents and local schoolmasters. He taught school himself, traveling the country, before salt turned his head. The same year (1794) that Wright was flopping as a young surveyor, thirty-year-old Geddes arrived with two iron kettles in the wilderness that would become Syracuse to tap its vast salt springs. Soon he had boiled out good profits and become, like Wright to the east, a leader of his pioneer community: a lawyer, county judge, state assemblyman, and surveyor. Like Wright, Geddes would be in high demand after Erie, engineering state canals for Ohio and Pennsylvania and for the federal government. On the Erie Canal itself, Geddes would make crucial decisions about its route and design, especially in the difficult and disputed western section.

Wright and Geddes were the first deans of the so-called Erie School of Engineering, when the only engineering education in the United States was actually building the Erie Canal. Its brightest graduates were Canvass White, John Jervis, and Nathan Roberts.

Jervis came to his Erie work as a tree-clearing axeman from a struggling family farm at Rome. White came as a prized Wright assistant from nearby Whitestown, the flourishing village founded by his grandfather, the first white settler on the upper Mohawk River. From dissimilar circumstances, Jervis and White would forge complementary pioneering careers, becoming the greatest young American canal and railroad engineers of their time. Frail health would cut down White before middle age; Jervis would remain active for half a century, eventually rivaling Wright's engineering legacy. On Erie, the provincial Jervis would rise Alger-like from axeman to superintending engineer of an eastern section.

White, already a European traveler, would also rise through the Erie ranks. Along the way he would take a patent—in silent partnership with another Erie employee who made the discovery—for the waterproof cement without which the canal could not have been built. The discovery marks the birth of the American cement industry; cement made by

White's heirs and their successors supports the U.S. Capitol, the Brooklyn Bridge, and the Statue of Liberty, and seals the Panama Canal.

Nathan Roberts was the greybeard among his Erie underclassmen. Born in New Jersey three weeks into the American Revolution, which ruined his merchant father, Roberts escaped poverty through mathematics. By age sixteen he was teaching and applying his small earnings to land speculation in New England. Itinerant teaching eventually brought him to Whitestown where he won a reputation educating its many Whites and other children. A month before Roberts turned forty, Benjamin Wright hired him onto the preliminary survey for the canal route from Rome to the Seneca River. The assignment was unlikely and a windfall. The $16-a-month math teacher with little if any surveying experience was suddenly a $4-a-day prospective engineer. The teacher quickly proved a skilled surveyor and a brilliant engineer: his double flight of five locks to surmount a sixty-six-foot limestone ridge at what became Lockport was the greatest piece of engineering on the entire Erie Canal. Like Jervis and White, Roberts would have a lucrative career after Erie, eventually leaving a proper inheritance to his children and his wife, Lavinia, his former student and Canvass White's younger cousin.

Samuel Wilkeson was to Buffalo what De Witt Clinton was to New York generally: singularly identified with its rising fortunes. Clinton convinced skeptical urbanites and upstate pioneers that the canal would make them rich. Wilkeson, a modest farmer in Pennsylvania and Ohio before success as a Buffalo merchant-shipwright, rallied his fellow settlers to build the harbor that made Buffalo the western terminus of the canal. Neither Buffalo on Lake Erie nor rival Black Rock a few miles down the Niagara River had a natural harbor where canal boats could meet Great Lakes ships: Black Rock was swept by current and ice; Buffalo was exposed to violent lake storms. When a hired "engineer" failed, Wilkeson directed Buffalo's harbor project himself, often up to his waist in swirling, frigid waters. When floods and storms destroyed partial works, Wilkeson modified his plans and completed a timber and stone jetty protecting an anchorage for keel draft ships. Wilkeson's gravestone reads "Urbem Condidit," the man who built Buffalo into the gateway to the west.

Ground was broken for the Erie Canal on Independence Day in 1817. Just ten years earlier, it was unlikely that Wilkeson, Roberts, Jervis, White, Geddes, Wright, Clinton, or Hawley would have had anything to do with such a great project. Hawley was not only a failed merchant but also a bail jumper who had fled the state, awaiting a guilty conscience to bring him back for his rebirth as Hercules. Clinton's statesmanship was still confined to the Hudson River valley; he was "a stranger to the western interior of our state [and] had given but little attention to the subject of canal navigation." Geddes was successful in salt and surveying but a stranger to engineering. Wright was an accomplished country surveyor but with limited engineering experience and, like Geddes, little knowledge or experience outside his provincial life. Jervis and White were schoolboys aged eleven and sixteen. Roberts was a schoolteacher. Wilkeson had just turned twenty-six, with a family and farm in Ohio; several ventures stood between him and his destiny in Buffalo. Soon, Hawley's Hercules essays would start the process that made all of these men and others into "Canal Age" pioneers.

The age that Erie spawned was short. It was largely over before the Civil War. Later developments in transportation that are still vital—railroads and interstates—might seem now to have been more important than a canal that passed into irrelevance over a century ago. But the highway was laid next to the railroad, which was laid next to the canal that created the path for the flow of people and manufactures to the west and raw materials and produce to the east. Without the Erie Canal, there would have been no penetration of the Appalachian range before interests inimical to the United States—French, English, Spanish, Russian, and native or discontented American—laid permanent claim to pieces of the continental interior.

For decades, Virginians such as George Washington and Thomas Jefferson sought access to the west (and their speculative landholdings in the Ohio River valley) via the Potomac River. To the Virginians' eternal dismay, however, their river was mountain-choked, too lowly for the navigational task. The Virginians did nothing to help New Yorkers in their own endeavor to reach the west. Denied federal money for the Erie project by presidents Jefferson and Madison, De Witt Clinton and other

New Yorkers made an artificial river with their own money, knowledge, and labor. It was a commercial victory that still pays out.

It also was a nationalist triumph, with deep and mixed geopolitical effect. New York's canal was an "indissoluble bond of union" between east and west, an American ambition since revolutionary times. But although the canal united the nation, it divided it as well. New York's triumph was Virginia's defeat, one of many resentments between North and South that sparked for decades before exploding and will likely outlast the vast nation the Erie Canal helped create.

CHAPTER 2

The Wilderness Years

[T]here is a critical juncture in most undertakings, when the small-est unforeseen discouragement sinks them at least for that age, as the lightest additional assistance would set them afloat.
—Christopher Colles, 1785

Jesse Hawley came to Western New York as many others did: a refugee from eastern disaffection. The merciless soil and notions of New England made new frontiersmen of hundreds and eventually many thousands with a mind for change. Hawley came from a long line of Connecticut Yankees. The Hawleys were comfortable townsmen, so it wasn't poverty or harsh farming that drove Jesse westward, nor was it wealth, business, or the domestic hearth that kept him home. His exodus from Connecticut did not begin until he was thirty, and he went alone. What gnawed at his soul is unknown. In the west, his life had triumph and tragedy. He ultimately thrived as a Rochester federal port officer, prescient land investor, and Clintonian officeholder. But along the way were a discordant, childless marriage and exceptional divorce, as well as disputes with his wife's in-laws and his own sisters. A daughter born on his fifty-eighth birthday to a woman who was not his wife, and a late second marriage to an older woman who was more mother than lover, brought him some measure of joy. He revealed nothing of his emotional life before an asthma attack he suffered one winter night while visiting friends suddenly killed him at age sixty-eight. Just five months later and a few weeks after her eleventh birthday, his daughter Julia died of unknown causes. Viewers of her oil portrait today see deep, round eyes set in an angelic face, but death silenced whatever stories she might have told. With neither husband nor child to care for, the second Mrs. Hawley soon returned to her native Quebec, leaving no one who had shared Jesse Hawley's closest intimacies to tell of them.

In his beliefs and opinions, Hawley was firm, "impatient of contradiction"; in his general comportment, "a dignified gentleman of the old school." Reports of his dry humor are fewer than those about his temper. His stature was robust, his face open, mouth even, cheekbones high, penetrating eyes deep-set below heavy brows, forehead broad below a head of bushy hair that resisted graying until the end of his life. His friends in later years were, like him, among the leaders of Lockport, the city birthed by the canal that his Hercules essays conceived. "He was a sincere and ardent friend," wrote a eulogist, "and singularly sensitive to acts of friendship from others, never forgetting, and frequently mentioning them—though of but trifling importance." His canal essays having been written under a pseudonym and his identity for many years undisclosed, Hawley never obtained full public honors for his efforts. Though he later openly and successfully advocated for the canal's enlargement, he took to his grave "a deep sense of this neglect [which] weighed heavily on [his] sensitive mind." Like most men of action, though, Hawley was not a brooder. When he became the essayist Hercules in 1807, he joined a long line of persons and events that led to the Erie Canal.

New Yorkers of Hawley's time believed that responsibility for the favorable setting to build a great canal rested with the Creator. It was His benevolent design that made New York the place for a break in mountains that otherwise divide the coast from the interior for over a thousand miles. The fact that the Mohawk River ran where mountains didn't was divine guidance for westward Christians, its valley providence for the canal-minded. Science now instructs (most of) us that geology, climatology, and gravity were responsible.

In the dwindling days of Pleistocene North America, a long, slender lake formed along what is now the northwestern border of New York. For a million and a half years, the land as far south as Long Island had felt the heavy march of glaciers, scouring, scraping, and reshaping the landscape under ice a mile thick. Twelve thousand years ago the ice began its most recent northward retreat. As the sun and the warming land liquefied the glacier's thinning southern lobe, the lake of ice-melt grew, bulging on its ends. On the west, it backed up north into what is now Canada. On the south, the lake bottom rose up from a shallow shelf to a rugged shoreline, a great ridge running in a gradual eastward descent from what is now the Niagara River to the Genesee River. On the east, the rapidly expanding lake filled a valley extending southeast to what now is Rome. Seeking an outlet, the frigid, bloated lake first burst through here, gouging a link to what was then a long lake leading south toward the sea—now the Hudson River. This was the first path to the sea for the continent's inland waters, a torrent of ice-clogged water that ripped out a valley through a bleak, barren landscape.

For fifteen hundred years this route gradually narrowed as the land, released from the weight of glacial ice, slowly rebounded upward. The glacial lake, dubbed Lake Iroquois by geologists, refilled with new meltwaters before finding its second path to the sea, a northeastern outlet that finally drained the lake to its present incarnation as Lake Ontario. Only the northern outlet remains, as the St. Lawrence River. Deprived of its natural source, the first path to the sea dwindled into the Mohawk River, with sluggish headwaters near Rome and tumbling falls into the Hudson.

Farther west, the earlier retreat of ice that had reached as far south as what is now Kentucky created an even greater glacial lake, which eventually dwindled into the four other Great Lakes. The easternmost of those is Lake Erie, pouring the waters of the upper four into Lake Ontario through the Niagara River. New York's canal makers of the early 1800s, who knew little about geological history, had to decide if the best route west from the Mohawk River valley was to improve a network of shallow, twisting, and rapids-strewn natural waterways to Lake Ontario or to create a new path overland to Lake Erie.

New York's canal makers were the first humans to substantially change what nature had made. Humans had entered the continent from the northwest, close on the heels of the retreating glaciers, migrating south into its temperate western zones and then turning east and north, following in the newly habitable wake of the melting ice. The region just south of Lake Iroquois as it began to form was cold and wet, with new growths of spruce and fir in the tundra belt at the edge of the ice. As the lake grew, the tundra shrank and the forest transitioned from softwoods to broadleaf hardwoods: oak, birch, and beech. Mastodon, wooly mammoth, and other Ice Age mammals gave way to caribou, elk, deer, and beaver. The marshy region south of the lake became habitable for humans around ten thousand years ago. By nine thousand years ago, across a landscape littered with drumlins, kames, eskers, and other glacial waste, the once cold and bleak climate had warmed and dried to a condition similar to our own.

The first identifiable native culture of what became central New York emerged roughly forty-five hundred years ago, when the local climate was even warmer than today's. Centered on the country between the Genesee River and Oneida Lake—a vestigial puddle of glacial Lake Iroquois—the Lamoka people flourished as hunter-gatherers in dense hardwood and conifer forests. The Lamoka fished the region's abundant shallow lakes, slow streams, and broad marshes—all glacial remnants— for pickerel, bullhead, bass, and perch. They roamed the forests looking for wild vegetables, berries and fruits, and hickory nuts and acorns. They hunted deer, moose, bear, beaver, and turkey. Though they avoided the deeper waters of the Finger Lakes and Lake Ontario, Lamoka in search of new hunting grounds journeyed the web of postglacial waterways in dugout canoes fashioned with rock adzes.

Over succeeding millennia, native peoples developed into waterway wanderers, transitioning from crude dugouts to the remarkably light and swift bark canoes that would later fascinate European arrivistes. By three thousand years ago, the populations of what is now central New York were conducting extensive river-based trading by canoe.

Nearly a thousand years before the arrival of Europeans, rivers and lakes remained essential to native life, but land-oriented culture had emerged. The Owasco people were the first to build villages not exclusively on navigable waterways. Overland trails became the primary link among populations transitioning from regional wandering to provincial, self-sufficient, farm-based, village-oriented life.

Seven hundred years ago, forest-based Iroquois infiltrated from the southwest. These "Native Americans" flourished over the next three hundred years on game, fish, and cultivated grains. Especially in the western portion of their range between Lake Ontario and the Hudson River, the Iroquois population may have been denser than the diverse population of modern times.

As is the tendency of sedentary humans, competition for territory and resources led to warfare between Iroquois groups, ending with a great confederacy among the dominant Iroquois nations: from east to west, the Mohawks, Oneidas, Onondagas, Cayugas, and Senecas. Peace came just a few short years before Europeans did. Caught by fatal timing in the territorial ambitions of Europeans and their American-born offspring, the once-fierce Iroquois were neutralized and decimated, the survivors herded west or contained on reservations. By the time the newest Americans set about building an artificial river between the Hudson River and Lake Erie, the land had been cleared of its prior nations, whose heritage is preserved in the atlas of central New York.

Europeans moved cautiously but inexorably into the native interior. In 1624 the Dutch West India Company established Fort Orange, the Hudson River trading post that now is Albany. The Dutch rarely ventured far from their compound. Instead, Iroquois emerged from the thick forest bearing furs and skins to trade. In late 1634 a precipitous decline in visits suggested interference by the French from Canada, via Lake Ontario and the Oswego and Oneida rivers to Oneida Lake. And so on December 11, Fort Orange barber-surgeon Harmen Meyndertsz van den Bogaert, two companions, and five Mohawk guides were sent west a hundred miles to Oneida Lake to conduct trade negotiations with tribal sachems.

The Dutchmen barely survived their first night in the woods. After traveling inland eight miles, they slept at a hunter's cabin for a few hours, waking to find their guides preparing to abandon them. In the dark, they ate a breakfast of dry bread because their guides' dogs had helped themselves (or been helped) to the party's meat and cheese. Cold and hungry, van den Bogaert and his companions were led to the Mohawk River just west of where Schenectady would be settled a generation later. The river was flooding and choked with ice. The party crossed from the south shore in two-man bark canoes, buffeted by bitter headwinds. "It was so dark," reported their leader, "that we could not see one another without staying close together so that it was not without danger." Without realizing it, the Dutchmen had achieved the first recorded navigation by white men of the Mohawk River. They survived many other adventures and returned safely to Fort Orange six weeks later, having affirmed trade agreements with the Iroquois that, like many afterward, lasted little longer than the negotiators' shadows on the trail home. The trip established a theme in the interior navigation of New York: that it was essential but often harrowing and unreliable.

Travel on the Mohawk River was in places impossible. In the 1680s a Dutch religious pilgrim, Jasper Danckaerts, was the first to write about the terrible power of the falls at Cohoes, over which the Mohawk passes before joining the Hudson just north of Albany. Cohoes is Mohawk for "wrecked canoe." The seventy-foot waterfall was the biggest Danckaerts had ever seen and, he (wrongly) suspected, the biggest on the entire continent. He saw that Cohoes rendered the Mohawk unusable "for carrying goods up or down in yachts or boats" between Albany and Schenectady, recently established twenty miles up the river. As inland settlement increased, Danckaerts predicted (accurately), some means of navigation between the Mohawk and the Hudson would be devised. For many generations to come, however, goods shipped by small boat down the Mohawk would be off-loaded onto carts at Schenectady, carted overland to Albany, and reloaded onto Hudson River sloops (or later, steamboats) bound for New York City. As Jesse Hawley would later discover, this process was expensive, time-consuming, and inconvenient.

In the early 1700s, four decades after Dutch New Netherlands had become English New York, Robert Livingston headed west with the same goal as his earliest Dutch predecessors: to make trade arrangements with the natives. The powerful head of New York's Board of Commissioners for Indian Affairs, Livingston traveled three times deeper into untamed Iroquois territory and was struck by its vast resources. The region where the Onondaga (now Oswego and Oneida) and Seneca rivers met was blessed with abundant salmon and other fish, rich salt deposits, and fertile soil. Making use of all this, Livingston reported to several provincial governors over the years of his service, could be facilitated by improvements to the natural but not easily navigable waterways. None of the governors found the time or resources to act on Livingston's suggestions.

Enter Cadwallader Colden. Like many scientifically inclined provincials, Colden was a dilettante Renaissance man. A serious if not brilliant scholar of medicine, botany, history, and more abstract sciences, Colden in 1724 issued a wide-ranging report on American fur trading. In it he postulated that the headwaters of the Seneca River were very close to Lake Erie. A century earlier, other wise men had believed in a Northwest Passage that proved a myth. Colden, who would serve as New York's surveyor-general for over half a century, did hedge his bet about a Seneca–Erie connection: "[A]s this passage depends upon a further discovery, I shall say nothing more of it at this time." In fact, in his long life he never mentioned it again. Colden soon discovered that the Seneca River originates at Seneca Lake, one hundred very dry miles short of Lake Erie.

Still, Colden was the first to recognize and write about the importance of a water route across New York. Like his Dutch and fellow English predecessors, Colden's inquiry was grounded in commerce. But he looked deeper into the continental crystal ball. A westward race, every bit as exciting and heated as the opening of the "wild west" more than a century later, was beginning. At stake was control—political, territorial, and commercial—of what now seems so inevitably to have become the United States. One hundred eighty-eight years before Arizona completed the Lower 48, the concept of a continental nation had not been born. Knowledge of even the basic geography of the continent ended at the Mississippi River. At the time that Colden wrote, the French aspired to create "New France," from Montreal to the mouth of the Mississippi. This threatened to limit British colonization of North America to the eastern seaboard and severely restrict fur trading with the still-dominant native nations. From the 1690s to the 1760s, France and England (with variable native alliances) would fight four protracted American wars. England eventually would claim Canada from the French, but would not secure the permanent continental hegemony for which its armies suffered. Colden—a royalist to his dying days on the eve of the American

Revolution—was wise to French intentions early on. "The *French*," Colden warned, "have been indefatigable in making Discoveries, and carrying on their Commerce with Nations, of whom the *English* know nothing but what they see in the *French* Maps and Books."

French influence in the unsettled interior had grown steadily, often without much notice in coastal regions, since the times of the Dutch. Originally Europeans had built their settlements near large waterways on or leading to the Atlantic, and natives had come to them to trade. It was a drop off in Indian visits that had inspired the Dutch expedition in 1634 and the English forays into the woods in the early 1700s. In all cases, it turned out that the natives had indeed been induced to trade with the French.

Farsighted provincials like Colden were sensible of the common land, and especially water, borders of English New York and French Canada: the St. Lawrence River, Lake Ontario, and Lake Erie. In a primitive land of thick forests, high mountains, deep valleys, and no roads through them, natural waterways were the obvious and easiest (though by no means always easy) route of travel. Colden was the first to recognize the importance of finding an easily navigable water route through New York's interior that would spread and maintain English influence while bypassing contact with the northern competition. But no such route existed and, in the eleven decades of English colonial control of New York, no one stepped forward with a plan to create one. Colden, who weathered a patriotic mob's threat to hang him from a signpost, died peacefully at his Long Island farm in 1776, two weeks into the English occupation of New York City, which would emerge first as the political capital of a new nation and then, when the Erie Canal was opened a half-century later, as the commercial capital of a rising global power.

Although the English did not discover or create a water route to Lake Erie, they did heavily exploit the natural water route between the Hudson River and Lake Ontario: 125 miles up the often treacherous Mohawk River, a portage of a mile or more—the "Great Carry"—at the future site of Rome, to the aptly named Wood Creek, down the sinuous and shallow creek to windswept Oneida Lake, down the Oneida River to the Oswego River, and down that rapids-strewn river to Lake Ontario. It was an arduous 200-mile journey, measured in unpredictable weeks and undertaken in small boats with limited cargo: small enough to be portaged in numerous places, small enough to navigate narrow or drought-reduced waterways, and small enough to be wrecked easily on flooding rivers and stormy lakes.

By 1728 the route was well enough established that Albany-based merchants opened a trading house at the mouth of the Oswego River on Lake Ontario. This was a major development in the pursuit of trade. A century earlier, native traders had come to Albany; now Albany merchants set up shop deep in the interior. Slowly, the natives ceded their place in the wilderness to white men pursuing trade and territory.

White men began to reshape the wilderness as well. Whereas natives were content to paddle waterways as nature made them, white river boatmen were not. Two years after the trading house opened at Oswego, unnamed men put their shoulders to the first recorded improvement of the Oswego–Albany run. It was a modest effort: a two-hundred-foot cut dug across a narrow neck on the upper Mohawk River. Evidence of the work has been discovered only recently; it was unheralded in its day. The cut eliminated a nearly circular, mile-round meander on the river at what is now Whitestown, just west of Utica: a mile of travel cut to two hundred feet. Presumably the digging was done by self-interested river traders, removing a small but maddening inconvenience among many in the natural interior navigation of New York.

Interior trade grew despite the impediments in New York, as elsewhere on the continent, at a time when being "navigable" required much less of a waterway than now. European-blooded Americans were settling areas farther and farther west. In New York, this first meant up the Mohawk River valley. In the 1720s there came to be a settlement of Palatinate German refugees thirty miles upriver from Schenectady. The Germans eventually spread along another fifty miles, a wilderness Rhineland that survives in towns from Palatine Bridge to Herkimer and Frankfort. Other groups—disillusioned Yankee farmers, frontier merchants and tradesmen, and the kind of people who happen on a place and stay there—also established homesteads and settlements farther upriver, replacing trappers and fur traders as the dominant white presence in the region.

In the mid-1700s tensions between the British and French rose for the final time in American territory. Hostilities broke out in 1754, followed two years later by the start of the fourth and definitive war between the contestants for early continental dominance. In the French and Indian War, the French initially controlled strategic waterways and the English controlled primary land routes, though neither crude roads nor unimproved waterways were suited to the efficient movement of troops and war material. After years of sluggish warfare, the British gained control of Lake Ontario. This came largely through the heroics of "Bradstreet's Boatmen," the rough-and-tumble inland navy of a thousand frontier river men in flat-bottomed boats commanded by plainspoken colonial Captain John Bradstreet. Once Bradstreet cut out Lake Ontario from the supply routes of the French, their war-fighting ability was lost. In 1763 the British at long last claimed victory. The broad control they secured by it, however, would not survive the next decade against a new colonial power.

The lessons of the war were not lost on the victors. Absent good roads, waterways were recognized as essential to the growth and defense of the American colonies. "[T]he only Way of travelling [sic] this Country in its natural State is by the Rivers and Lakes," observed Thomas Pownall, an erudite and wise colonial administrator of Massachusetts and New Jersey. In December 1768 New York governor Henry Moore proposed improvements to the Mohawk River, particularly in creating sluices to raise water levels and eliminate portages around rapids. The Provincial Assembly, however, was in no mood to entertain any of Moore's suggestions. To pay off debts incurred in the recent war, England in 1765 had imposed the Stamp Act on the American colonies, followed by other "taxation without representation." After New York's increasingly rebellious assembly passed resolutions asserting constitutional rights independent of the crown, Moore in January 1769 dissolved the assembly. His river plan dissolved with it.

The unseating of New York's colonial legislature was among the first stirrings that in Massachusetts and elsewhere would lead to the American Revolution. Increasingly, public thought and politics were consumed by rebellion. Until the revolution had been fought and won, almost no one in New York gave much further thought to waterway improvements.

The exception may have been Gouverneur Morris. In 1777 Morris, a member of the New York City gentry and expectant Founding Father, reportedly suggested to two fellow revolutionaries that one day there would be a good waterway between the Great Lakes and the Hudson River. Or so it has been said. His oral prognostication was first reported long after his death. Whether he meant the relatively simple matter of improving the imperfect but existing water connections between the Hudson and Lake Ontario, or creating a wholly original waterway between the Hudson and Lake Erie, is impossible to know. In time, though, Morris would become a leader in the effort to create such a waterway.

Following the Revolution, a new American competition for continental dominance was joined, making rivals of New York and Virginia. George Washington had served as a provincial Virginia militia colonel in the French and Indian War. He had seen the rich lands beyond the Appalachians and made speculative purchases in the Ohio River valley before the Revolution. After independence, Washington hoped that the first water route to western wealth would pass through his state: up the Potomac River, through the Allegheny Mountains, and down the Kanawha River to the Ohio. This was no easy task, starting with the maddening Potomac. An experienced surveyor, Washington had been involved as early as 1773 in unsuccessful attempts to make the river more felicitous to navigation by removing rapids and fashioning short canals around waterfalls. But in late 1783, awaiting the formal British surrender, he toured New York's upstate waterways and recognized—with prescience and resignation—that they, and not Virginia's, might prove better suited to opening the west: "Prompted by these actual observations, I could not help taking a more contemplative and extensive view of the vast inland navigation of these United States, from maps and the information of others." The Father of the Nation was "struck with the immense diffusion and importance of it; and with the goodness of that Providence which has dealt her favors to us with so profuse a hand." By "us," the patriotic Washington meant the new nation, not his Old Dominion. The favors providence dealt New York were not just along the Hudson–Ontario route, but also down the Susquehanna River, flowing from its New York headwaters through Pennsylvania toward tributaries of the

Ohio River, and the Allegheny, a lesser river but a principal tributary of the Ohio. "Would to God," hoped Washington, "we may have wisdom enough to improve them. I shall not rest contented 'till I have explored the Western Country, and traversed those lines (or great part of them) which have given bounds to a New Empire."

Still, Washington remained devoted to Virginia's prospects as the gateway to the west. Fellow Virginian and Potomac promoter Thomas Jefferson—whose American patriotism was thickly gilded with Virginia chauvinism—recognized soon after the war that the North—New York—and the South—Virginia—would likely compete in becoming the path of choice to the lands beyond and gain the prosperity and influence that would flow from it. "The western country is under a competition between the Hudson, the Patomac, and the Missisipi itself," Jefferson wrote Washington in March 1784. "There will . . . be a rivalship between the Hudson and Patowmac for the residue of the commerce of all the country westward of L. Erie." Jefferson was trying to entice the retired general into both supporting congressional extension of Virginia's western border all the way to the Ohio River and serving as superintendent of greater Virginia canalling and river improvement: a Virginia for lovers of river-based empire, with Washington in charge. "This is the moment," Jefferson excitedly pitched to his fellow Ohio land speculator, "for seizing it if ever we mean to have it."

Washington acknowledged the flattering and possibly lucrative offer but parried the seduction. Politics, regional "jealousies," and popular refusal to pay even basic taxes, let alone for remote canals, prevented Jefferson's notions from gaining Washington's serious consideration. At the same time, Washington knew "the Yorkers will delay no time to remove every obstacle in the way" of Mohawk and other waterway improvements.

Washington was the object of many scheming men's desires. Even before the war ended in 1783, he had been approached with the idea of forming a Virginia company to improve navigation on the Ohio River and its tributaries. The proposal came from Christopher Colles, a small man of large ideas.

An Anglo-Irish immigrant, Colles reportedly was, and is often still reputed to have been, a canal engineer in Ireland. In fact, although his family was distinguished—among notable Colleses was nephew Abraham, the greatest surgeon of nineteenth-century Dublin—Christopher's education was limited and his Irish accomplishments minor and few. Washington may have known and taken the measure of Colles during the war, when he served in some uncertain capacity with Washington's army. To Colles's Ohio proposal, Washington replied that "the present juvenile state of the Country" and the scarcity of labor and capital made this "too early a day for accomplishing such great undertakings."

Colles was a master of proposing, and failing at, great undertakings. Before the Revolution, he had designed the first steam engine built in America (it worked poorly and existed only briefly) and attempted to create New York City's first public waterworks (destroyed before completion during British occupation). In the later 1780s he started the first atlas of American roads (abandoned for lack of funds). Colles eventually grew old, impecunious, and philosophical: "He was wont to say," reported one of his many sympathetic friends, that "if he [had] been brought up a hatter, people would have come into the world without heads."

Colles always boldly proposed his ideas to anyone with ears and capital. And so, rebuffed by Washington, he turned his sights back to New York. In late 1784 Colles began efforts to convince the state legislature to charter, and investors to back, a company that would improve the water route between the Hudson and Lake Ontario into a commercial highway for "boats of burthen." His remarkable 1785 pamphlet, *"Proposals for the Speedy Settlement of the Waste and Unappropriated Lands on the Western Frontiers of the State of New-York, and for the Improvement of the Inland Navigation Between Albany and Oswego,"* is a visionary argument for conquering the interior by water:

> By this, the internal trade will be increased; by this also the foreign trade will be promoted; by this, the country will be settled; by this, the frontiers will be secured; by this, a variety of articles, as masts, yards, and ship-timber may be brought to New-York [City], which will not bear the expense of land carriage, and which, notwithstanding, will be a considerable remittance to Europe. By this, in time of War, provisions and military stores may be moved with facility in sufficient quantity to answer

any emergency; and by this, in time of Peace, all the necessaries, conveniences, and if we please, the luxuries of life may be distributed to the remotest parts of the Great Lakes which so beautifully diversify the face of this extensive Continent, and to the smallest branches of the numerous Rivers which shoot from those Lakes upon every point of the compass.

Colles, like Washington, spied a benevolent deity in New York's geography: "Providence, indeed, appears to favour this design; for the Allegany [sic] mountains, which pass thro' all the States, seem to die away as they approach the Mohawk River; and the ground, between the upper part of this River and Wood Creek, is perfectly level, as if designedly to permit us to pass thro' this channel into this extensive inland country."

As English provincial Colden had feared the Canadian French, American pioneer Colles warned of the Canadian English: "It appears highly expedient at this time to promote this undertaking, as the British may, and now are, endeavoring to draw the trade of the inland country towards Quebec; and it is an indubitable fact, that trade is like water, when it once passes in any particular channel, it is not easily diverted or drawn away into another." This idea—that commercial habits are hard to break—would resonate in many other minds during Colles's long life and after his death in late 1816, just months before work began on the great canal that perfected his vision.

Colles's modest proposal of 1785 was for a company, capitalized at a cautious £13,000 ($32,500), with himself as engineer, which would improve the Mohawk with twenty-eight locks and seven miles of canals at Cohoes, Little Falls, and Old Fort Schuyler (later Utica). Investors would be rewarded from lock duties, tolls, and the proceeds from the sale of 250,000 acres of open Western New York land to be granted to the company by the state. Colles imagined all the work completed in three years with just five hundred laborers.

In the early months of 1786, Colles's proposal found its way to an assembly committee, which asked him to draft a bill for its consideration. In March the committee introduced "An act for improving the navigation of the Mohawk River, Wood Creek and the Onondaga [Oswego] River, with a view of opening an inland navigation to Oswego, and for extending the same, if practicable, to Lake Erie." The last bit did not mean that Colles intended to canal to Lake Erie. The implication was that at some point Erie might be reached from Lake Ontario via a canal and locks around Niagara Falls. Still, the bill in support of Colles's proposed company represents the first legislative reference in New York to Lake Erie as a goal of inland navigation.

"[T]here is a critical juncture in most undertakings," Colles had written in his proposal, "when the smallest unforeseen discouragement sinks them at least for that age, as the lightest additional assistance would set them afloat." Perhaps New York's lawmakers glimpsed the impractical in Colles, or perhaps postwar caution or economic recession gave them pause, but after several weeks of committee consideration, Colles's great plan evaporated. There was no vote on it, and the legislative session ended with no further mention of it. Colles, who had conducted only the most preliminary surveys and had drawn no engineering plans, apparently let the matter go, and in his remaining forty years of having novel ideas he never returned to "Mohawk navigation."

None of what Colles envisioned for New York would be worth mentioning, except that it soon inspired another adopted New Yorker to turn similar plans into action, action that eventually drew Jesse Hawley to Western New York and to the idea of an Erie canal. If ego alone were enough to get things built, Elkanah Watson might have made a canal across the continent. As it happened, he succeeded and failed in just the right amounts to put notions in the head of Jesse Hawley.

Watson was of *Mayflower* stock, Rhode Island merchant training, and European business failure. As he had been for Colles and many others, George Washington was a primary target of Watson. One nasty January evening in 1785, Watson arrived by horseback at Mount Vernon, interrupting the Washington family dinner, ostensibly to deliver books (from English abolitionist Granville Sharp). "No pilgrim ever approached Mecca, with deeper enthusiasm," Watson wrote in a diary conceived for public consumption. The pilgrim was uninvited but not unknown; a few years earlier the young merchant had cheered his war-weary fellow Mason with an elaborate Masonic apron sewn under Watson's direction by French nuns. Watson was not entirely unwelcome now, but his host confided to his own private diary a hope that the visit would not interfere with his gardening plans for the morrow.

After the missus retired, the gentlemen repaired to Washington's study to discuss a common interest: canals. Watson knew Europe's canals and the importance of building them in America. Washington presented his long-standing Potomac desires, leaving Watson, "I confess, completely under the influence of the canal mania." His mania may have been heightened by "a severe cold and excessive coughing," which turned the passing visitor into an overnight guest. Watson was awed and easily flattered to be nursed by Washington himself, bearing a midnight bowl of tea to the sickbed. Washington, one supposes, was most interested in the patient's speedy recovery and departure.

In the morning Watson's head had cleared. Urged by Washington to settle along the Potomac, Watson rode upriver to observe the various places where Washington hoped canals might be built. At Great Falls, Watson saw the "whole river rushing down amid rocks and impediments, wave pressing upon wave, like the surging of the ocean in a tempest." Wishing the Virginians well, Watson turned his horse and his canal mania back north. A few years later he moved his family from Rhode Island to Albany, where he emerged as a leading citizen of the future state capital and the proponent of an inspired scheme to make New York the riverine empire that Virginia would never be.

Sevens years after George Washington infected him with canal mania, Watson joined with Philip Schuyler, scion of New York's great Dutch American family, in the formation of two companies: the Western Inland Lock Navigation Company and the Northern Inland Lock Navigation Company. The Western Inland Company was to improve the water route between the Hudson and Lake Ontario along the lines of what Colles had imagined nearly a decade earlier. Not that Watson had anything nice to say about Colles: "wholly incompetent . . . an obscure man, of no consideration." The Northern Inland Company was to join the Hudson to Lake Champlain. Though a smaller and simpler project, the Northern Company venture was of less immediate importance and would die aborning. The Western Company effort would by turns guide and frustrate New York canalling for the next three decades.

Philip Schuyler came to inland navigation in 1792 with some credentials. He had cut his teeth on New York's rivers as a young officer under boat warrior John Bradstreet in the 1750s. In the 1760s Schuyler studied English canals as a sharp-eyed tourist and acquired tens of thousands of Mohawk and upper Hudson River valley acres as a speculator. As a revolutionary general, he had specialized in water transport logistics, run boatbuilding operations in Albany and Schenectady, and commanded river boats for a notable punitive campaign against recalcitrant Iroquois. He also was one of the persons to whom Gouverneur Morris in 1777 reportedly laid out his Hudson–Great Lakes ideas. The father-in-law of Alexander Hamilton, old Federalist Schuyler had lost his U.S. Senate seat in 1791 to rising New York Republican Aaron Burr and, while remaining a state senator, was looking for a new challenge. His influence on New York's legislature remained substantial. His self-admiration rivaled Watson's, making them uneasy partners.

The Western Inland Company was chartered by the legislature in 1792 to improve navigation from the Hudson River west and north to Lake Ontario and west to Seneca Lake. The state charter gave the company fifteen years to clear waterways of natural obstructions and, where needed to pass falls and rapids, construct short canals and erect locks seventy feet long by twenty feet wide, with a minimum water depth of two feet. During the 1793 session Schuyler pushed through a charter amendment that halved the mandated lock width and limited the water depth requirement to only the majority of the anticipated March–November navigation season.

At a coffeehouse on Wall Street and a tavern in Albany, Watson and Schuyler opened their subscription books to well-heeled investors like themselves. Few were truly interested in the nationalist cause of inland navigation. Most were simply willing to chance a few $25 shares for the potential of rising values in speculative lands many of them owned, which good navigation might make more accessible. Among the Western (and Northern) Company investors and directors were enough Van Cortlandts, Livingstons, Van Rensselaers, Gansevoorts, Platts, and Clintons to fill pages of the New York social register and geographical atlas. Little did they know (or most of them deeply care) when they bought their shares that assessments would outstrip dividends for many years to come.

The task facing Watson and Schuyler was larger than it might have seemed at first glance. They needed to build a way around Little Falls, which was little in comparison to Cohoes but, at over forty feet, a considerable hindrance to navigation on the Mohawk above Schenectady. Watson and Schuyler would have to build a canal and locks around rapids at German Flats, which, at nearly twenty feet, weren't so flat. They would need to build a canal joining the upper Mohawk to Wood Creek, the weakest link in the meager chain of waters between the Hudson and Lake Ontario and Western New York. The creek would need to have its numerous necks cut, several significant shallows locked, and its banks and stream cleared of the forest that clutched it. Substantial and unspecified improvements also would be needed leading west out of Oneida Lake—down the Oneida River and especially around the many treacherous falls and rapids on the Oswego River leading into Lake Ontario— and around the falls in the Seneca River, which divided the river's lower section from its headwater lake. For good measure, Watson and eventually Schuyler alone were supposed to make the Mohawk navigable between Schenectady and Albany, by somehow conquering Cohoes Falls, which had disrupted the river since the retreat of the last glacier ten thousand years earlier.

Aside from a promised improvement in the quality of water travel, the Western Inland Company signaled a change in its method. During the generations of white navigation on the rivers of eastern North America, the boat of choice had evolved from native bark and dugout canoes to the battoe, the watercraft employed by frontier traders and militarists like John Bradstreet for the better part of the eighteenth century. Anglicized from the *bateau* of French Canada, where it was first developed, the battoe was flat-bottomed, straight-sided, sharp-ended, and shallow-drafted. A typical boat was thirty feet long and six feet wide, with a cargo or passenger capacity of three thousand pounds and a crew of three. Upstream propulsion was either by poles jammed into the riverbed, rowing oars when the water depth allowed, or a square sail on a single mast when the way was straight and the wind aft, which wasn't often. In all but the best conditions, especially on interior New York's shallow, narrow, twisting, and flood- and drought-prone waterways, making a battoe go was back-breaking labor. Portages and rapids along the route restricted the battoe and its cargo to a size its crew could manage.

The promise of locks and short canals replacing rapids and portages brought a transition from the French battoe to the homegrown Durham boat. It had been developed in the 1730s as an ore carrier from Robert Durham's iron works on the lower Delaware River. Those boats in which Washington famously crossed the river in 1776 were Durhams. As the Western Inland Company started bringing its works into operation, yards in Schenectady began producing Durham boats adapted for New York's interior waterways. They were built largely of white oak, with sharp ends, flat bottoms, soft chines, and nearly vertical sides. Propulsion was the same as with battoes: poles, oars, and the occasional downwind sail, with a crew of five to seven. Dimensions varied, but the typical Durham boat in New York would be fifty feet long and eight feet wide, and would draw only fifteen inches with a full load of sixteen tons, over five times the capacity of a typical battoe. As the native canoe had been dwarfed by the battoe, so in turn was the battoe eclipsed by the Durham boat. Which is not to say that the Western Company made inland boating easy.

The company did achieve some of its objectives. In its first decade, the company built four wooden locks and cut through thirteen necks on Wood Creek, shortening the route by more than seven miles. It joined Wood Creek and the Mohawk at Rome by a 1.75-mile canal, thirty-seven feet wide and four feet deep, with a brickwork lock at each end. German Flats was passed with a 1.1-mile canal, twenty-four feet wide and four feet deep, with two wooden locks. A mile-long canal with five wooden locks and a three-foot-deep channel bypassed Little Falls. On the Mohawk between Little Falls and Schenectady—a fifty-mile run with a relatively moderate hundred-foot descent—the company removed rocks, deepened natural channels, and constructed a series of wing-dams— V-shaped, open-apex stone formations that raised the water level at rapids by channeling the water into a narrow passage.

The company failed to achieve the greater part of its charter obligations. Nothing was done, or even attempted, west of Wood Creek or east of Schenectady: not at Cohoes, on the Oswego, or west up the Seneca River. In short, the Western Inland Company improved the middle but forsook the ends.

Watson and Schuyler learned that making durable, modern things in the wilderness without machines or adequate manpower, engineering skill, or adequate financing was nearly impossible. Schuyler, an unreliable judge of his own abilities, first tried his own hand at lock design and construction oversight but quickly proved overmatched. Other notables followed. William Weston, America's favorite overpaid and underwhelming visiting English engineer of the 1790s, built the wooden or stone locks and canals that were rotting or crumbling long before the yellowing of the substantial receipts for his services (though the lack of proper hydraulic cement and funding for proper masonry structures were not entirely his fault).

After Weston went home, a young upstate surveyor named Benjamin Wright tried his inexperienced hand at building the Wood Creek locks. In 1802 Wright was camped out on Wood Creek under Schuyler's imperious command. At sixty-nine, Schuyler was more than twice Wright's age. Rheumatic and gout-afflicted, he was hardly suited any longer to rough surroundings. Two years later he was dead.

Though it struggled on until the Erie Canal was halfway built, the Western Inland Company undertook no significant construction after Schuyler's death. His partner, Elkanah Watson, had long since abandoned the effort in disgust over Schuyler's tyrannical manner and had taken up agriculture in Massachusetts. "Gen. Schuyler was no friend of mine," Watson wrote many years later, "my enemy in his closing years."

By the year of Schuyler's death, the company had spent nearly $368,000, earned less than $75,000 in tolls, lost many of its original investors, and ceded effective control to the state as a large shareholder and guarantor of its debts. To keep its charter, the company in 1808 voluntarily surrendered its right (and duty) to make any further improvements.

Still, the Western Inland Company claimed certain achievements. Cargo that once cost $100 per ton to ship from Schenectady to Seneca Falls now could be transported for $32. Land values doubled along portions of the route. These at least were the self-serving public claims of

Elkanah Watson in 1820, when the first completed segments of the Erie Canal were bypassing the Western Company's rotting works.

Others who regularly transited the company's works (and paid its tolls) described "extremely dangerous" navigation on the route. Leaky locks and failed canal banks often left boats stranded. The rivers were still turned wild by floods and shallowed by droughts. Uncleared obstructions caused wrecks and occasional fatalities. The most notorious was at the eastern outlet of the Little Falls lockworks, where discharged boats regularly struck a midstream boulder "with more or less peril," lucky to "escape with a violent shock." Simon Desjardins, a Parisian engineer engaged (unsuccessfully) in a northwestern New York land development scheme for aristocratic exiles from the French Revolution, had frequent brushes with death along the route in the late 1790s. The Western Inland Company's crude engineering astounded Desjardins: "[N]o mechanical appliances were used, and everything was done by sheer force of men and animals. They appeared not even to know the use of a ladder, much less of a crane, or of the simplest labor saving power." A sophisticated European, Desjardins scoffed at the company's "pretended canals" and crude hydraulics, "which will render the works passable, but not durable."

If a failure overall, the company nevertheless achieved more success than any of a handful of contemporary navigation projects in the country, including the long-frustrated public and private efforts in Virginia to find a way west via the Potomac. And, just as Colles had transferred inspiration to Watson and Schuyler, their Western Inland Company would lead the way to the Erie Canal. De Witt Clinton, as the righteous young holder of one company share, railed against its fiscal mismanagement and years later smugly condemned its failures as the "most popular and the strongest argument" against building the Erie Canal. But many of the directors, investors, and builders who learned political, financial, and engineering lessons with the Western Company would turn experience into insight for the Erie effort.

Jesse Hawley may have been the person worst served and most inspired by the company. The wheat he collected at Geneva and milled at Seneca Falls would travel east through the locks, short canals, cut necks, and wing-dams fashioned by the Western Inland Company. Unbeknownst to him, just as Hawley was starting his operations in 1804, the company was scaling back its own. Hawley saw the improvements the company made on the Mohawk and Wood Creek. He and most other pioneers of Western New York must have expected that improvements would continue right up the Seneca River, as then still required by the company's charter. But Philip Schuyler's death that year put an end to new construction by the Western Company. Just when Hawley launched his grain-shipping business, the company shifted from building new works and aggressively maintaining built ones to maximizing investor income with increased tolls. Four years later the charter was amended to forsake the Seneca and lower Mohawk.

Before Schuyler's demise, Hawley's idea had seemed a good bet. Grain produced by pioneer farmers in Western New York was plentiful and cheap. It was sought in Albany and New York City, where the supply from Yankee farmers was as uncertain as their weather and soil. A refugee himself from what is now Bridgeport, Connecticut, Hawley was still young at thirty-two and brimming with the agrarian visions of his hero, Thomas Jefferson. With only a schoolboy's education but the practical skills of his carpenter father and the drive of an eldest child, Hawley had come to Geneva, where Seneca Lake feeds the Seneca River, to make his fortune as a grain merchant, Geneva's first of record. His plan was to buy wheat grown in the fertile soil of Western New York by its first generation of farmers, have it ground into flour at the region's only mill at Seneca Falls, and ship it east. Like the Internet investor of our day, western grain merchant Jesse Hawley imagined growing rich quick in a promising new industry.

It seems not to have occurred to Hawley to inquire whether others had attempted sending inland grain to the Atlantic seaboard. The record is clear, at least, that no one had succeeded at it. Hawley was soon to find out that what looks to be a magnificent plan when viewed broadly could easily yield to the hard facts of frontier existence.

The quality that most makes a place a frontier is isolation. For frontier merchant Hawley, the challenge would be transporting his cheap wheat cheaply enough through 250 miles of New York State, from the primitive west where settlers sheltered in log homes to the urbanizing east where a hundred thousand people crowded the southern tip of Manhattan. Hawley had thought that the ongoing improvements to New York's interior waterways would be, literally, his deliverance.

With confidence in his prospects, he built a storehouse in Geneva and began to buy wheat for milling at Seneca Falls ten miles downriver. Apparently beginning with the harvest of 1804, Hawley had the flour loaded on boats, which set off on the challenging journey east to Albany, where Hawley had a partner who was to market the wheat.

Hawley's partner was one Henry Corl. Born Hendrick Carol, the son of a Dutch-descended Schenectady settler, Corl was forty, had married into Albany Dutch society, and was a merchant of fair repute. How Hawley and Corl came to be in business together is unknown. The younger man possibly saw in Corl practical experience, financial merit, and social standing for their enterprise. If so, Hawley miscalculated. In the spring of 1806 Corl disappeared with the company's assets, some $10,000 in cash. A New Yorker then was considered rich if he was worth half that much. In this case, the cash was mostly debt. After Corl took off, Hawley was arrested and jailed in Geneva. A friend posted his bail, and Hawley, in a Henry Corl moment during the autumn of 1806, ran away himself, to the vicinity of a Pennsylvania village called Pittsburgh.

A bad partner didn't help, but Hawley's wheat venture was doomed primarily by "the dreadful conditions of the roads and the uncertain condition of the waterways." Transportation costs and delays along unimproved waterways and those marginally improved by the Western Inland Company had made profits unlikely even before Corl delivered the coup de grace. In the bloom before the doom, though, Hawley had prophesied a better way.

One day in early April 1805, his second spring in Western New York, Hawley got to talking with Wilhelmus Mynderse, who had established the first Seneca Falls mill nine years earlier. In Mynderse's office overlooking the millworks, Hawley mused that what was really needed to make them and other western pioneers rich was a canal "direct into our country," meaning from the Hudson or other major waterway directly to the Seneca River. Mynderse was slightly older and wiser than Hawley,

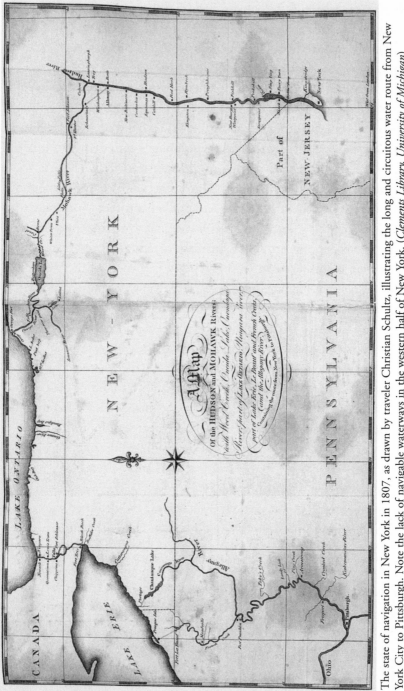

The state of navigation in New York in 1807, as drawn by traveler Christian Schultz, illustrating the long and circuitous water route from New York City to Pittsburgh. Note the lack of navigable waterways in the western half of New York. (*Clements Library, University of Michigan*)

and a good bit better off, having profited from farmers who milled grain for shipment entirely downstream to Montreal and other Canadian ports: down the Seneca and Oswego rivers to Lake Ontario and thence down the broad St. Lawrence, instead of up the Oneida River and Wood Creek toward the Mohawk. The seasoned miller told the striving merchant that although a canal through New York was an interesting idea, there wasn't enough water around to supply one. Hawley "sat in a fit of abstraction for some minutes," then his gaze settled on a map of the state hanging on the office wall. He took down the map, "spread it on the table and sat over it with my head reclined in my hands and my elbows on the table, ruminating over it, for—I cannot tell how long—muttering *a head of water*; at length my eye lit on the falls of Niagara which instantly presented the idea that Lake Erie was *that head of water*." Jabbing his finger at Lake Erie, Hawley yelled out: "*there* is the supply of water!" Mynderse's response is unrecorded. A year later, Hawley was a ruined merchant on the lam in Pennsylvania.

CHAPTER 3

"The Effusions of a Maniac"

[I]t would be a burlesque on civilization and the useful arts, for the inventive and enterprising genius of European Americans, with their large bodies and streams of fresh water for inland navigation, to be contented with navigating farm brooks in bark canoes.

—Jesse Hawley, 1807

[A] canal of 350 miles through the wilderness—it is little short of madness to think of it at this day.

—Thomas Jefferson, 1809

Jesse Hawley jumped bail and fled to western Pennsylvania in the fall of 1806. Whom he met, how he lived, and how miserable he may or may not have been are mostly unknown, but within weeks he was "visited" by Thomas Jefferson, via his sixth annual presidential message.

Hawley was a Yankee engine running on Jeffersonian gas. In October 1803, in his third annual message to Congress, Jefferson had stressed the settlement opportunities offered by the prospective purchase of the Louisiana Territory. Three weeks later Hawley wrote to his president suggesting that the federal government lay out town lots at the head of all navigable waterways; the president did not reply. In his second inaugural address in March 1805, Jefferson asserted that after retirement of the national debt and passage of a constitutional amendment, federal revenues might (in times of peace) be distributed to states for such "great objects" as canals. Exactly one month later, Hawley jabbed his finger at Lake Erie on the map in the mill office at Seneca Falls. In his message of December 1806, Jefferson wrote again of the hopeful day when a flush federal government at peace would be constitutionally empowered to fund such "great purposes" as canals and roads, cementing the states "by new and indissoluble ties." Hawley read these words as a soldier hears a trumpet. The following month "Hercules" was born, in a fervently Jeffersonian weekly called *The Commonwealth*, recently established in the frontier town of Pittsburgh.

"I will presume to suggest [to the president and Congress] that improvement which would afford the most immediate, and consequently the most extensive advantages which any other in the United States can possibly do," wrote this backwoods Hercules: "the connecting [of] the waters of *Lake Erie* and those of the *Mohawk* and *Hudson* rivers by means of a canal." Hawley and others may have thought or spoken of such a wild notion before, but this was the first time anyone had written about it publicly, albeit under the protection of a pseudonym.

Hercules admitted to his readers (likely numbering no more than a few hundred) that he had "no knowledge in the science of canalling," but his brief essay showed a considerable understanding of the distances and elevations involved. He laid out a prospective course to run from the foot of Lake Erie northeast and then east to a crossing of the Genesee River above its falls, along the Mud Creek outlet of Canandaigua Lake, briefly in the Seneca River, then "meandering along between the high and low grounds of Onondaga and Oneida counties, going south of their lakes," and meeting the Mohawk "somewhere above Utica." Starting ten years later, the Erie Canal would be built along incredibly similar lines. Following Jefferson's lead, Hercules proposed that the canal be built with federal money, a concept that would be altered radically only months before construction began.

While Hawley (as Hercules) was writing publicly about a canal across New York to Lake Erie, others had begun to think on it, possibly after reading or hearing about the Hercules essay. James Fenimore Cooper's father was one of them. "The trade of this vast country must be divided between Montreal and New York," wrote Cooperstown founder William

Cooper to a friend, "and the half of it be thus lost to the United States, unless an inland communication can be formed from lake Erie to the Hudson." Cooper imagined a canal large enough for fifty-ton sloops, that is, not a slender canal of locks and levels, but a massive, broad, and deep canal on an inclined plane: "[T]he world has as yet produced no work so noble; nor has the universe such another situation to improve." Cooper's idea was that New York would cede land for the path of the canal to the federal government, which would charter and invest $10 million in a company with substantial enough powers to encourage "the European capitalist to adventure in this magnificent enterprize." Profits would rise quickly from tolls on the canal and an adjoining turnpike that would draw crowds to the falls at Niagara: "No stranger but would make this tour his object, and no traveler of taste would leave it uncelebrated."

Cooper wasn't deeply committed to any of this: "[A]s this speculation lies in the province of fancy, and may be treated as a vision, I leave it to its fate." More concerned with settling his lands around Otsego Lake, Cooper left a visionary canal to others: "Its obvious utility will hereafter challenge more attention, men of great minds will turn their thoughts and devote their energies to its accomplishment, and I doubt not that it will be one day achieved."

Cooper was a well-read man; whether he had read Hercules in Pittsburgh's *Commonwealth* is unknown. It is possible that no one in New York caught wind of Hercules's Erie canal idea, launched in a remote weekly with a small and local circulation. By early 1807, however, great minds were turning to the idea of canals generally. In response to Jefferson's December 1806 message, the U.S. Senate in March 1807 directed Treasury Secretary Albert Gallatin to report in a year on what was being done currently in the states and what might be done presently by the federal government about creating roads and canals.

A Swiss-born aristocrat turned southwestern Pennsylvania farmer, Gallatin was the Republicans' Hamilton. In 1807 he was midway through what remains the longest term of any Treasury secretary. Eager to throw federal support behind roads and canals, Gallatin immediately began soliciting information from important people he knew and via circular queries distributed by customs collectors, port officers, and other Treasury subordinates. The canal circular sought specifics about the many proposed and the few and minor completed canals: dimensions, distances, elevations, construction details, routes, water supply sources, costs, tolls, state legislation, and so on.

As the months passed, Gallatin's office was flooded with information from the owners of small private canals, hopeful canal companies, state governments, surveyors and other professionals, and a bundle of pamphleteers: anybody with information deemed by themselves to be relevant. Practically all of it eventually was included as appendices to the report that Gallatin intended as a blueprint for the internal improvement of the United States.

New York, with its tangle of upstate waterways, was a natural focus for internal improvement. New York City, with its busy ocean port and broad tidal estuaries, was less urgently inclined in that direction. "Agricola" addressed this issue in late January 1807. Apparently a prominent merchant familiar with the country's geography, his identity remains unknown. He wrote his forty-page pamphlet almost certainly without knowledge of Hercules, who had published in Pittsburgh just a week earlier. But the author of "A Letter to the Inhabitants of the City and State of New-York; on the Subject of the Commerce of the Western Waters" was, like Hawley, writing in reaction to Jefferson's fresh pronouncements on canals. "Conversations," wrote this anxious Agricola, "are getting to be fashionable in every mercantile circle" about "what course the current of the surplus of our productions on the western waters would take, and at what point it would probably strike the atlantic [sic]." Unlike Hercules, Agricola had in mind no original canal plan beyond improving the traditional route from the Hudson to Lake Ontario at Oswego. He disparaged Jefferson's dear Potomac and praised the natural supremacy of the Mohawk over all other westward rivers, but Agricola's main purpose was to rouse the fools of Gotham: "[W]hile the large commercial towns to the south are bending their efforts against every impediment which nature has thrown in their way, with a view to a monopoly of the commerce of the western waters, the city of New-York looks on with all the listlessness of a perfect indifference." Agricola had identified a developing theme for his city, a curious truth. Having the most to gain from a navigable connection to the interior, its leaders were doing the least to promote it. Ten years later, none of the city's dozens of state legislators would vote for the bill that authorized construction of the Erie Canal. Not until the canal's first sections were opened and began channeling the promised rewards to the city would its politicians and merchants finally embrace it.

Agricola may not have changed sentiments in his city about a canal, but he was among several pamphleteers responsible in part for arousing political action upstate, where numerous "canal tickets" were formed in advance of the April legislative elections. The winning ticket in predominantly Republican Onondaga County paired an obscure Republican with a rising Federalist named Joshua Forman.

Forman, a downstate native turned upstate pioneer "of wide information and high character," would go on to found Syracuse. Soon he would take a leading role in creating the canal that made Syracuse possible. Later, when he was among the claimants for Erie Canal "projector" honors, Forman asserted that in April 1807 he knew nothing about Hercules or any Erie talk, but that the new federal interest in canals induced him to seek a state assembly seat from which to promote the improvement of the traditional Hudson–Oswego route, which ran through his county. Regardless of his candor on this score, Forman's ideas would gestate significantly during the nine months between his election to the assembly and the opening of its next session.

Forman was the scion of a large extended family. The Formans were among the many migrants responsible for nearly tripling the state's population from Utica west during the first decade of the nineteenth century. In 1800 New York's seven westernmost counties held only one in seven of the state's citizens. By 1810 those seven counties had been divided into eighteen, containing nearly one in four New Yorkers. The westward trend was not invisible. "If you wish New-York to remain, as now, *the Emporium of America*," warned one Yorker, "suffer not the trade with the interior of your state to be carried off triumphantly by the spirited and enterprising citizens of Philadelphia and Baltimore." If its natural water connections to the city remained "neglected and unimproved," the western district's trade would be forced into "a more southerly channel."

Down and out in Greensburg, Pennsylvania, conscience and thoughts of canals were gnawing at Jesse Hawley. In early July 1807, U.S. postmaster-general Gideon Granger passed through Greensburg, where he told several people that New York appeared "best calculated" of all the states to lead the way west by water. Connections between the eastern and western sections were essential, Granger reportedly said, in "preventing a dismemberment" of them. Hawley learned that, as part of Treasury Secretary Gallatin's ongoing researches, Granger's cousin Erastus had been commissioned to take levels of Lake Erie. Erastus Granger was an original settler of Buffalo, a friend of Hawley's, and a more successful merchant. The two had not been in contact since Hawley fled New York the previous year. Granger's Erie assignment was only related to a possible canal around Niagara Falls to join Lake Ontario and Lake Erie, not with a view toward a canal directly to Erie. This limited objective pressed on Hawley the urgency of spreading his "Hercules" vision by confidential letter to Granger.

"I have been in exile for some months past," he explained to his friend, before letting loose: "The favorite idea of mine is to *tap Lake Erie about your place* [Buffalo], *and Canal it to the Mohawk at or about Utica.*" The "stinted waters" of the traditional route could never be sufficiently improved; the "very tedious and laborious passage" for even small boats on upstate waters had made Hawley a failed shipper. The canal he was proposing would be largely in the form of a broad channel arcing north and then east, descending downhill at two feet per mile with "an inexhaustible fountain of water" from Lake Erie. A level canal from Erie would require "the tedious delay" of over forty locks and uncertain local sources of water. Hawley's inclined or "pitched" canal would require as few as five locks to negotiate several major falls and would arrive at Utica with enough surplus water to raise the shallow Mohawk. This unfortunate idea of an inclined plane canal, which William Cooper had privately imagined and canal commissioner Gouverneur Morris later would intractably promote, would plague Erie planning for the next ten years.

Based on his admittedly limited readings on the size, complexity, and cost of major European canals, Hawley predicted that a canal linking Buffalo and Utica would cost $5 million, or roughly $25,000 per mile. Though he got the type of canal wrong, Hawley's financial intuition was right on: construction of the Erie Canal would begin ten years later with the same cost estimate.

In a brief postscript to Granger, Hawley related some details of his failed business and subsequent flight. But guilt over the injustice to the unnamed friend who had bailed him out had convinced Hawley finally to return to New York: "[I] now expect to deposit myself in Canandaigua jail in a few weeks." By early August, Hawley had begun a twenty-month sentence.

Debtor's prison in the seat of Ontario County was not the dungeon experience of urban bankruptcy legend. The Canandaigua lockup was on the second floor of sheriff Elijah Tillotson's hotel, with windows looking out on Main Street. Hawley was confined on the "jail limits," allowing him a certain liberty to circulate about town. Lawman Tillotson, on behalf of the county, provided his prisoner's room; innkeeper Tillotson sold the prisoner his board.

One foul afternoon in the early fall, Hawley came in from his prescribed walking route to find an old friend who was overnighting in Canandaigua on his way by horseback from Albany to his home in Batavia. The two supped together in a public room. The inclement weather and their unexpected meeting "in so remote a place on the borders of civilization" drew them back into their old camaraderie. In the evening, warmed by a fire and a bottle of wine, Hawley discussed his current troubles.

Having last seen him five years earlier in more prosperous circumstances, the surprised friend, William Peacock, counseled Hawley to "not give way to despondency nor indulge in improper habits in order to forget trouble." Hawley assured him he had not and would not. Indeed, he confided, he had begun writing, and was soon to start publishing in the local newspaper, a series of essays under the Hercules signature arguing strenuously for a canal to Lake Erie. Hawley swore his friend to secrecy about the identity of Hercules (who was, after all, a jailed bankrupt) and promised to mail the essays to Batavia as they were published. Peacock was cheered by his old friend Hawley's good spirits but was especially interested in the forthcoming essays. This was because Peacock was the subagent of the Holland Land Company, owner of millions of acres of Western New York through which a canal to Lake Erie might pass, to the company's great benefit.

Born in Pennsylvania, Peacock had begun his long career with the Holland Company several years earlier as a young clerk in its headquarters at Batavia, then nothing more than a half-dozen log houses. Batavia was fifty miles up the Tonawanta Creek from Lake Erie, where the company had established a settlement that it called New Amsterdam and that its homesteaders soon would rename Buffalo. A skilled surveyor, Peacock laid out Buffalo's original street grid in 1804, followed over the next several years by town grids and boundaries throughout the Holland Purchase. Peacock's rise within the Holland Company was helped by marrying the boss's niece. At their 1807 reunion in Canandaigua, Hawley likely heard all about Peacock's October marriage to Alice Ellicott Evans, which secured Peacock's entry into the "Big Family" of Joseph Ellicott, the power broker of Western New York.

During the first two decades of white settlement west of the Genesee River, no person was more important than Joseph Ellicott. He was the great-grandson of a failed English Quaker wool manufacturer who had established a small farm in Pennsylvania's Bucks County. His father was a mechanical genius but an impoverished weaver and struggling miller, until a chance inheritance enabled him and two brothers to build a wilderness mill on Maryland's Patapsco River, where the family soon became prosperous flour manufacturers at what is now the Baltimore suburb of Ellicott City.

Joseph's oldest brother, Andrew, became a renowned surveyor, completing Pierre L'Enfant's plan for the nation's capital city and, among numerous other assignments, determining the southwestern boundary of New York, a survey in which Joseph assisted, exposing him to the territory of his destiny.

In 1794 Joseph Ellicott began survey work in Pennsylvania for the Dutch bankers who would soon form the Holland Land Company. Three years later he was a key member of the company team guiding the Big Tree Treaty talks between the federal government and Seneca sachems, which effectively cleared title to the company's purchase of New York's 3.3 million westernmost acres. The company had already named Ellicott chief of the survey to lay out that vast, unbroken wilderness, an assignment he attacked with passion and ingenuity.

At the time, there was no national standard for the measurement of a foot. Exacting in all aspects of the survey as in his life generally, Ellicott gathered a number of purported one-foot rulers, took an average, and produced a standard foot measure. A brass twelve-inch ruler was attached to the cover of every surveyor's field book. Completed in 1800, Ellicott's "Great Survey" was the reference document by which the company would sell its lands. His excellent maps became the starting point for all discussions about the development of Western New York. Ellicott was named the company's resident agent to promote and oversee land sales, out of his office in Batavia.

Joseph Ellicott was inspired in the field but a terror when confined to business. Six-foot-three and rugged, he was built to command the frontier. He was inexhaustible, meticulous, and with vision as expansive as his shoulders were broad. Ellicott's nature was his downfall; he was quick tempered, intolerant, dismissive, and rude. Many of the settlers he attracted to the Holland Purchase would eventually despise him. His final years in Western New York would be marked by paralyzing depression and isolation, hastening his forced retirement, exile, confinement, and suicide.

It was not really Ellicott's fault that by 1807 little Holland Company land had been sold. It was still an isolated frontier, as Jesse Hawley seventy miles farther east had learned the hard way. But Ellicott had established a control of local affairs that he deemed necessary to future sales. He never married, but in the happier early years of his agency he was the paterfamilias of the "Big Family" that dominated Western New York. Most of its many members had two jobs and one master: they were company surveyors, agents, or clerks employed by and related to Joseph Ellicott, and they were county judges, supervisors, clerks, even congressmen and state senators whose appointments or elections were arranged by Joseph Ellicott. Genesee County itself, with its seat at Batavia, was Ellicott's creation, severed from Ontario County with the help of "gratification" paid by him in the company's name to Republican leaders in Albany. Ellicott himself was the county's largest taxpayer and its first treasurer. He would be deeply interested in the mail received weekly by Peacock from an unnamed sender in Canandaigua.

Days before Jesse Hawley started drafting the arguments for a canal to join Buffalo and Albany, a historic event took place in New York City that drew it closer to Albany. With great fanfare, on August 17 Robert Fulton set out up the Hudson River in his paddle-wheeled steamboat. Not including an overnight layover at Clermont, the riverside estate of his business partner, Robert Livingston, Fulton completed the 150-mile trip between Manhattan and Albany in just over thirty hours. Graceful Hudson River sloops, slaves to wind, weather, and tide, took anywhere from four to ten days, an unpredictability that soon made nostalgia of sailing on large rivers and lakes, and eventually oceans. As the Erie Canal would draw together America's west and east, the steamboat would draw together America and the world. Soon enough, steam pioneers Fulton and Livingston would be attached to the Erie canal effort.

While Fulton celebrated the birth of steam navigation in New York, Jesse Hawley set pen to paper in Canandaigua, "betrayed and defrauded by my partner, broken down and almost destitute in despondency at the thought that hitherto I have lived to no useful purpose." But he had recovered his spirit and "resolved to publish to the world my favorite fanciful project of an overland canal for the benefit of my country, and endure the temporary odium that it would incur." Hawley "secured books and maps" and after "laborious study" penned fifteen thousand words in fourteen essays. "I hope my work will help other businessmen," he privately confided. "Who knows but someday I may be able to take part in an overland waterway!"

Hawley had arranged for the essays to run in the *Genesee Messenger*, an established weekly then published by a respected Canandaigua pioneer. On October 27, 1807, Thomas Jefferson delivered his seventh annual message to Congress, notable for a lack of any direct reference to canals, even though Treasury Secretary Gallatin was then actively investigating them. Instead, Jefferson's text focused almost exclusively on a growing threat to peacetime canal funding: the increasingly hostile relations among the United States, England, and France, which would blossom eventually into the War of 1812. On the same day as Jefferson's gloomy message, the first "Observations on Canals" by Hercules were spread across the front page of the *Messenger*.

"[W]e entertain vast ideas of the destinies of these United States," Hercules began, "but to what are we destined? Servilely to copy the splendid folly of all ancestry, or to borrow wisdom at their expense?" Babel's tower, Egypt's pyramids, Babylon's gardens, Rhodes's Colossus were, to this Hercules, so much "folly and prodigality . . . mere phantoms of glory" distracting nations from the true path to wealth and greatness. In contrast to pacific old China, with its defensive Great Wall and thousand-mile Grand Canal, was modern England, which had nobly spent £5 million on several dozen canals, but ten times that annually on military adventures: "What a satire on wars, navies, and standing armies! . . . So far as nations before us have made the experiment, internal improvements have proved the certain and more speedy road to national greatness." Hercules argued against the European example of "toil, blood, and treasure" wasted on "futile wars for princely domination" and in favor of the spread of American inland navigation by Jefferson's (lately endangered) idea of surplus federal revenue spending. Keenly aware of the "late improvements in the steam-boat," Hercules envisioned a vast Jeffersonian market enabled by cheap water transportation on lakes, rivers, and canals: "By substituting water for land carriage, much of the manual and animal labour would be reserved for the improvement of our forests and the culture of our fields." Hercules saved for his final line what he considered the greatest national improvement and the subject of his future essays: "A CANAL FROM THE FOOT OF LAKE ERIE INTO THE MOHAWK."

While the Erie Canal was being built, De Witt Clinton dated "the first hint" that he saw of such a project to this essay and the subsequent numbers. Elkanah Watson was unable "to trace any measure, public or private, tending towards this great enterprize" before this Hercules essay. Indeed, the series of "invaluable essays . . . are evidently original and display deep research . . . indeed, they may be pronounced prophetic."

As promised, Hawley sent the *Messenger* issue featuring his first essay to his friend Peacock in Batavia. After reading it with great and knowing interest, Peacock wanted "to see how it would strike the mind of Mr. Ellicott." In their office that day, Peacock conspicuously positioned himself with the paper. "What is the news?" asked Ellicott, entering. "Nothing important," said Peacock, "but here is a curious kind of an article over the signature of Hercules." "What about?" "A proposition to construct a canal inland across the country to Lake Erie." Ellicott erupted, "snatched the paper from my hand, looked at it a moment and ran upstairs to read the article over by himself. He read it through once or twice and finally read it to himself aloud, very deliberately, weighing well every proposition. He said nothing about it at that time, but it had evidently made an impression on his mind not soon to be effaced." Peacock "waited impatiently for the next number," careful to hide his "interest and anxiety" on the subject.

Like any good serialist early in the run, Hawley teased out his ideas. His second essay was published on November 3 and offered only a route for the canal; all discussion of size, construction, cost, funding, and commercial prospects was withheld for future essays. The two-hundred-mile route along a four-hundred-foot descent described in the second essay was essentially the same as Hercules had proposed in the more obscure Pittsburgh paper nine months earlier: from the foot of Lake Erie, descending north for enough miles alongside the Niagara River to obtain a sufficient head, northeast to a crossing of the Tonawanta near its mouth, due east along the slowly descending ridge to a crossing of the Genesee River above its upper falls, and on to the west branch of Mud Creek, in the creek's improved channel into and down the Seneca River to Jack's Rift just west of Onondaga Lake, and finally overland to the Mohawk near Utica. "In this proposed canal" Hercules saw "the grand desideratum of nature, viz. an inexhaustible fountain of water . . . which may be pitched and gauged to any dimensions required." With Lake Erie as the headwater and the ridge as a natural inclined plane, it appeared to Hercules "as if the Author of nature . . . had in prospect a large and valuable canal, connecting the Atlantic and the continental seas, to be completed at some period in the history of man, by his ingenuity and industry!" Here for many New Yorkers to read was the design concept that would trouble canal plans for the next ten years. Eventually the planned canal would have to come down from its sloping ridge and take a level approach, with locks to cross the ridge.

In making his projections, Hercules noted that he was relying on elevations given in Ellicott's well-publicized map of the Holland Purchase. Hercules himself had "never seen any part of the route" except the towns at its ends: "My chief object, is to point out a sufficient probability to produce a belief in the propriety of an actual survey."

At the Holland Company office in Batavia, the mapmaker was a believer. Ellicott seized the second essay as soon as the mail brought it and "devoured [it] with greater avidity than the first." When Ellicott asked who was the sender, Peacock said only "a friend of mine at Canandaigua." When Ellicott pressed him about the author or authors of the essays, Peacock replied that he "did not know in such a way as to authorize me in making any positive statement in regard to them." Ellicott let the matter drop. Hawley's several confidantes kept their counsel, and few others learned Hercules's identity until Hawley revealed himself publicly nearly twenty years later.

In essay three and half of essay four, published on November 10 and 17, Hercules offered only hints of the probable size of his canal by quoting extensively from the newly published *Pinkerton's Geography* and the *American Encyclopedia* about the dimensions, construction times, and costs of the canals of modern Europe and medieval China. Finally, at the end of the fourth essay, after noting the failures of the Western Inland Lock Navigation Company and postulating that American canals "should be calculated on a large scale . . . lead[ing] to an entire exclusion of land transport within their range," Hercules pronounced for a "Genesee Canal" one hundred feet wide and ten feet deep. This suggestion—that the America of ancient forest and log-house settlements might build a canal rivaling the largest in civilized Europe clapped maniac's shackles on Hercules.

Few besides Ellicott had been immediately taken with Hercules's notions. In fact, the prisoner of Canandaigua heard his essays described around town as "the effusions of a maniac." His publisher considered withholding the remaining essays to avoid harming the paper's reputation. Opinion was hostile even among Ellicott's Big Family. When asked in the office by Ellicott for his views on the opening essays, trusted clerk James Stevens pronounced the canal idea "visionary and impractical." The only prominent Big Family member not related by blood or marriage, Stevens was a Princeton graduate who had been Ellicott's clerk since 1800 (and Genesee County's first clerk since 1803) and would remain with the company for forty years, until his death. Normally "a man of quiet, unobtrusive habits; possessed of a fine literary taste," Stevens felt compelled to respond to Hercules's essays with a series of his own, "throwing discredit and ridicule on the whole matter."

Ellicott, a man of wider imagination, recognized how the company might benefit from any sort of canal running through company land that had no natural navigable waterway and few settlers. Ellicott continued to absorb Hercules's ideas as they came weekly in the mails, but he had already been convinced. He soon sent to state surveyor-general Simeon De Witt a description of the terrain between Batavia at the head of Tonawanta Creek and the Genesee River—forty miles of unbroken land with which surveyor Ellicott alone was familiar—and a suggested route for a canal through it.

In essay five, Hercules synthesized what he had learned from encyclopedias about the costs of France's Languedoc and Scotland's Clyde canals. Reminding readers of "my ignorance in the art of canalling," Hercules now pronounced his two-hundred-mile Genesee Canal a $6 million venture requiring, even on an inclined plane design, as many as twenty-six locks. This was a million dollars and twenty-one locks more than Hawley had estimated in his private letter to Erastus Granger just four months earlier. A skeptic might conclude that Hawley was at sea with his concept. Others might see a practical visionary adapting to ongoing research.

In the remainder of essay five and all of essay six, Hercules analyzed the canal's commercial utility. The cost of transporting two important products of protoindustrial New York—potash and salt—would be dramatically reduced. Side canals would draw resources from the state's numerous lakes. Trade would be drawn from Canada instead of to it. Indeed, "the trade of almost all the lakes in North America" would be drawn through the canal and down the Hudson to New York City: "In a century its island would be covered with the buildings and population of its city. Albany would . . . cut down her hills and fill her valleys . . . to give spread to her population. The harbour of Buffalo would exchange her forest trees for a thicket of marine spars." It was visions like these that converted Hercules's more thoughtful readers into adherents.

In essays seven and eight, the last before the end of the year, Hercules addressed the possible sources of funding for the canal. Without naming the Western Inland Company, he dismissed private capital as inadequate, monopolistic, and self-interested: "Fifty men associated for a common purpose, can out machinate five hundred unassociated; and one bank association may buy or bribe two-thirds of the representation of the whole state." More objectionable was foreign capital, especially British. Thus, "a patriotic government" with pure intentions of creating an "American empire" was the only option.

Unfortunately, on the day that the Canandaigua newspaper carried Hercules's Jeffersonian ambition for federal funding, Jefferson in Washington signed the Embargo Act, the reckless retaliation for British and French interference with American shipping. Foreign trade was cut off, and the American economy was throttled for the remainder of his presidency. The prospect of federal support for canals dimmed, though it would be a while before that became clear.

In fact, while Hercules's essays were rolling off the presses in Canandaigua, Robert Fulton, whose steamboat success had suddenly established him as the inventive mind of the moment, was lobbying Jefferson and Gallatin heavily in favor of canals. "I hope, indeed," Fulton wrote to Gallatin and Jefferson in December 1807, "that every intelligent American will in a few years, be fully convinced of the necessity of such works to promote the national wealth, and his individual interest." A Pennsylvania native, Fulton had spent the adult half of his forty years failing in Europe before finding instant fame and fortune in New York. He claimed to have little specific information about American canals, but he favored canals generally, especially those that might conquer mountains with steam engines to raise water to elevated sections and move traffic along inclined planes. Aiming directly at the prospective liberation of treasury funds for national improvements (and the improvement of his own commercial prospects), Fulton argued strenuously for canals as "cementing the union" with much lower transportation costs than roads. "[W]hen the United States shall be bound together by canals," Fulton steamed, "by cheap and easy access to markets in all directions, by a sense of mutual interests arising from mutual intercourse and mingled commerce; it will [not be] possible to split them into independent and separate governments, each lining its frontiers with fortifications and troops, to shackle their own exports and imports to and from the neighboring states."

Fulton tactfully mentioned neither his adopted New York nor Jefferson's Virginia and didn't indicate whether he was aware of the Hercules essays thus far published. Jefferson replied that although he was "in favor of the great subject" of canals, the "snail-paced gait for the advance of new ideas on the general mind" might easily stall both the required constitutional amendment broadening federal fiscal powers and legislation authorizing support for specific projects. Embargo and a looming war weighed on Jefferson's mind, and he was now not eager to make any commitments, especially with Gallatin's road and canal report pending.

In the remaining essays, published during the opening months of 1808, Hercules turned his attention to every known navigable river and lake in the Americas. "A marine canal, the most noble work of the kind on this 'ball of earth', would be a cut across the Isthmus of Darien," Hercules suggested, conjuring the next century's Panama Canal. Hercules challenged his fellow Americans closer to home: "[I]t would be a burlesque on civilization and the useful arts, for the inventive and enterprising genius of European Americans, with their large bodies and streams of fresh water for inland navigation, to be contented with navigating farm brooks in bark canoes." Hercules's heart beat hardest for a canal closest to home because New York "is destined to be the brightest star in the American galaxy."

Hercules's final essays were published after the state legislature convened at the end of January. Though he later denied it (to support his claims of primacy), new assemblyman Joshua Forman apparently had read the earlier essays circulated out west and brought the Erie idea east to Albany. Circumstantial evidence and the recollections of neutral parties make clear that Forman and his Albany rooming mate, onetime Western Inland Company surveyor-engineer and fellow assembly freshman Benjamin Wright, arrived in Albany eager to put Erie on the legislative agenda.

In Forman's telling (twenty years later), his inspiration was not Hercules but the "Canal" entry in the latest volume of *Rees' Cyclopaedia*, an authoritative English compendium delivered to Albany by subscription from an American publisher. Written by the Scottish engineering genius Thomas Telford, the illustrated canal essay contained in 140 pages all that was known about the history and technology of making canals. Supposedly thus inspired, Forman had become convinced that "if a canal was ever made to open a communication from the Hudson to the western lakes, it would be worth more than all the extra cost to go directly through the country to Lake Erie." One evening in their shared quarters, according to Forman, he put "his" idea to Wright, who "objected, that it would be a folly to make a canal 150 miles abreast of a good sloop navigation in Lake Ontario." After Forman countered that an inland canal, safe from lake weather, warfare, and Canadian competition, would settle towns and nourish farms along its route, Wright "gave in."

Wright's recollection twenty years later was slightly different. Though the fellow *Rees* subscriber also invoked the canal entry, Wright recalled that he and Forman had discussed publicized plans by Pennsylvania to seek federal funds for the improvement of state roads approaching Western New York from the south. Fearing diversion to Philadelphia of the produce of Western New York—the "Genesee Country"—Wright and Forman agreed that an inland canal built with federal money was a good idea.

They acted quickly. On February 4, 1808, the eighth day of the legislative session, Forman introduced a joint resolution, written by him and seconded by Wright, calling for "an accurate survey to be made of the most eligible and direct route for a canal . . . between the tide waters of the Hudson river and Lake Erie." Regardless of what inspired it, this was the first legislative step toward what became the Erie Canal.

Forman's resolution was everywhere imbued with the promise of federal support, even strangely so. The preamble referred to the use of federal money for canals, recommended by Jefferson in his message to Congress of "October last," though that had been the only annual message of recent years that contained not a word about canals. No matter; the proposed survey was to forward "the end that congress may be enabled to appropriate such sums as may be necessary to the accomplishment of that great national object."

Forman later claimed (perhaps disingenuously) that he actually was "without much confidence" then that the federal government would ever pay for such a canal and had framed the bill that way to induce support for the initial survey, because a survey for a state-funded canal "would not have been listened to at all." Imagine Forman's dismay when the reading of his modest proposal on the assembly floor "produced such expressions of surprise and ridicule as are due to a very wild foolish project." Wright likewise observed the "astonishment of many members . . . by whose look and manner it was easily seen that they considered it a wild, visionary project."

Undaunted, Forman took to the floor in support of the resolution. He suggested a route (very similar to Hercules's) and a cost of $10 million (far above Hercules's),

> which must appear a bagatelle to the value of such a navigation, whether considered in relation to the state, in improving the western district, and enriching the city of New-York by the trade of the rich and growing country bordering on the western lakes; or as respected the United States, whose forty or fifty millions of acres of land, bordering on the lakes, would be enhanced in value beyond the whole expense by causing their rapid settlement, form a dense frontier barrier towards Canada, and by forming an outlet for their trade through our own territory, instead of its flowing down the St. Lawrence, it would be an indissoluble bond of union between the Western and Atlantic states . . . that . . . would chain them to our destinies in any national convulsion.

This was a pretty good performance for a legislator of one week's incumbency. The assembly adopted his resolution, if only on the ground "that it *could do no harm*, and *might* do some good." The same attitude prevailed the next day in the senate, which sent it to a joint committee for further consideration.

The early debate in Albany may have reached the ears of Jefferson a week later when, at a Washington dinner, he remarked to his vice president, former New York governor George Clinton, "I hear it is proposed to divide your state & make the Genesee Country a separate state." This was a recent fantasy of nervous Virginians, about which Washington outsider Clinton honestly replied he was unaware. Jefferson's surprise at Clinton's ignorance gave Clinton the impression that the president "had mentioned what he might have better concealed from me." Three weeks earlier, a Virginia-dominated Republican caucus had rejected the dim but dangerous New Yorker in favor of native son James Madison, Jefferson's longtime secretary of state, to succeed him. Madison's easy election in November over nominal Federalist opposition (with George Clinton returning in the powerless role of vice president) assured a continuation of Jeffersonian government. Whether or not the Virginians were yet aware of it, the New York legislature's consideration of a great canal was added reason to keep the key to the Treasury out of Northern hands. In a year's time, Jefferson would tell Joshua Forman face-to-face what he thought of the New Yorkers' proposed canal.

Forman discovered much sooner what his fellow legislators thought. In late March, his Erie survey resolution emerged from the joint committee substantially modified. Surveyor-General Simeon De Witt was directed to conduct surveys "in the usual route of communication between the Hudson river and lake Erie," that is, via Lake Ontario and around Niagara Falls. Investigation of a direct route to Erie was reduced to "such other contemplated route as [De Witt] may deem proper." The survey report was to be submitted to President Jefferson (as well as in Albany), implying that nothing would come of the survey without federal support. The ensuing debate about survey funding diminished expectations further. The assembly sought $1,000 for the surveying effort, but the senate, loaded with old Western Inland Company directors and shareholders, cinched the purse strings at a meager $600, leaving little room for contemplation of unusual routes. "[I]t was expected that something should be done for nothing," De Witt scoffed privately, "or that a good deal of what ought to be done must be left undone."

De Witt was a Western Inland Company shareholder who nevertheless had warmed to the ideas in the Hercules essays. In June he assigned the survey to his favorite deputy, James Geddes, who openly favored an Erie canal. But as a cautious administrator constrained by budget, De Witt instructed Geddes clearly. Geddes was to survey and take levels for possible routes first for a canal between Oneida Lake and Lake Ontario, and then for a canal between Lake Ontario and Lake Erie. Only afterward, as "the appropriation will probably by this time be exhausted," was Geddes authorized to get "a view of the ground," without formal survey or leveling, in the fifty miles of wilderness between the Seneca River and the Genesee River for a route that might link up with the Genesee–Tonawanta route suggested by Ellicott. A proper survey for an inland canal "must be left as a work by itself, to be undertaken hereafter, should the government deem it necessary." Despite the restrictions of money and scope, Geddes would regard his assignment as "amongst the fortunate occurrences of my life."

Geddes assembled a small survey team, knowing that the national government also had low hopes for Erie. A week before Albany's grudging appropriation, Treasury Secretary Gallatin had delivered his historic report in Washington. It said a lot but was silent on what mattered most.

In the spring of 1808 Jefferson's presidency was foundering on the shoals of embargo, with war clouds gathering. Gallatin's "Report on the Subject of Public Roads & Canals" might have taken its place among the great documents of the early republic. Instead, it was a national improvements blueprint that ultimately would be shelved as peace, surplus, and the prospects for consensus on constitutional amendment drained away. Still, when it was announced "the Gallatin Plan" was exciting, and proponents of roads and canals would selectively invoke its message and specifics for years to come.

Gallatin had done his homework. The plan was as grand as the published volume was long: hundreds of pages presenting Gallatin's recommendations, appended with a full array of locally gathered information on American canal and road projects to date. "Good roads and canals," Gallatin wrote, "will shorten distances, facilitate commercial and personal intercourse, and unite by a still more intimate community of interests, the most remote quarters of the United States." Local capital to accomplish these ends was lacking; only the federal government had the means and the incentive: "No other single operation, within the power of government, can more effectually tend to strengthen and perpetuate that union, which secures external independence, domestic peace, and internal liberty."

Gallatin made the case for federal support of many ongoing and prospective projects throughout the country, from New Hampshire to New Orleans, from Massachusetts to Lake Superior. All told, he recommended an annual investment of $2 million for ten years, or roughly 14 percent of the Treasury's annual revenues.

Of the $20 million total, Gallatin proposed that $4 million be spent in New York, by far the largest single beneficiary of Gallatin's theoretical largess. $2.2 million would make a good boat navigation from the Hudson to Lake Ontario, $1 million would create a deep-water sloop navigation around Niagara, and $800,000 would connect the Hudson to Lake Champlain.

These recommendations sent shivers through Virginians and certain New Yorkers. While he went on at length about various New York projects, Gallatin wrote relatively little about Virginia's thwarted objectives on the Potomac and made no estimate of prospective federal aid. The circle of Erie advocates, meanwhile, searched Gallatin's pages in vain for any mention of their project.

In the end, it was probably best for partisans of the Potomac and Erie that the Gallatin Plan, which slighted both of them, remained on the drawing board. In the short term, however, it was a blow to New Yorkers, who could not yet imagine how to go forward without money from the federal treasury.

Simeon De Witt was disappointed but not alarmed. He was New York's only surveyor-general for its first half-century and tended to take the long view. Even though the state and national governments appeared unenthusiastic about an Erie canal, De Witt saw the future and Joseph Ellicott's pivotal role in it. So, as Geddes headed off into the field for his cut-rate survey, De Witt solicited free advice from the land agent whose company, De Witt pointedly noted, "will doubtless be much benefited" by a canal through its lands.

De Witt needn't have been coy. Joseph Ellicott had been deeply impressed with the full run of Hercules articles and was closely tracking developments as they affected the Holland Company. He informed Paul Busti, the company's chief American officer in Philadelphia, that an interior canal might pass through and drain otherwise worthless company swamp land, a million-dollar windfall. Ellicott then wrote De Witt a characteristically long and detailed reply, rejecting any route via Lake Ontario and favoring only an inland route connecting Tonawanta Creek with Mud Creek.

Ellicott's thoughts were inspired by Hercules, but were significantly different. Whereas Hercules had suggested an inclined plane canal of relatively few locks crossing the Tonawanta near its mouth and continuing north before arcing east, Ellicott envisioned a traditional locked and level canal running directly east, initially in the Tonawanta, for eighty miles to Mud Creek. Hercules's inclined canal would use the descent of the ridge east of Niagara Falls to draw Lake Erie water into his canal. Ellicott's canal would stay south of the ridge until it flattened out naturally near the junction with Mud Creek, drawing water from small intervening streams. Ellicott asserted that "nature seems to have pointed out this route for a canal, not only in consequence of the little labor, comparatively speaking, that would be required in digging it, but because the necessary materials for the construction of locks are close at hand." That was true, but what came to be known as Ellicott's "southern route" also happened to pass squarely through Holland Company land. Hercules's route took the canal largely north of the Holland Purchase.

Future surveys would reveal that the elevations were too great and the local streams too small to supply a canal along the southern route. Much as they would have to get past the inclined plane idea that would be stridently pressed by Gouverneur Morris after even its originator, Hawley, had dropped it, Erie planners would also have to deal with Ellicott and the course of his profound self-interest.

For the time being, Ellicott's informed and influential opinion favoring any inland route over any Ontario route helped convince its supporters, if not yet any detractors, that an Erie canal was at least plausible. Based on his considerable knowledge of excavation costs and the local geology, Ellicott estimated that a canal thirty-three feet wide and four and a half feet deep from the Tonawanta to Mud Creek would cost a very reasonable $700,000. His cost estimate for eighty miles of canal was outrageously (and perhaps disingenuously) low, but Ellicott had brought the canal's dimensions down to a less than maniacal size; the Erie Canal as built would be just seven feet wider and six inches shallower. Always alive to possibilities, Ellicott indicated that he would be willing to go in for $2,500 worth of stock in a private canal company "in case the United States should think the object inexpedient."

De Witt was ecstatic, or at least happy to flatter his important correspondent. He wrote Ellicott that his opinions "will materially change the ideas of the Secretary of the Treasury, in regard to what ought to be done here." The surveyor-general noted that settlement and land values would be promoted along the route traced by Ellicott and "divert to our own seaports, a considerable trade that would otherwise go to Canada." De Witt was not aware yet of the high and dry nature of the southern route, and that the high tide of Gallatin's nationalistic ideas about canals was already ebbing.

Ellicott, meanwhile, saw Western New York more as a local business than a locus of national improvement. By his own hand, he now made himself the middleman in a three-player correspondence: from Batavia he communicated back and forth with Busti in Philadelphia and with De Witt in Albany. There was no communication between Busti and De Witt, and Ellicott was the master of parallel dialogues. To each of his correspondents, Ellicott stressed the importance of abandoning the Ontario route. In November, with Busti's approval, he offered a donation to the state of 18,000 company acres in 160-acre lots along the line of any canal built through company lands. It was a premature and underwhelming offer, but it was a calculated political move that established the company's public posture as pro-canal. As time went on, its support of canal plans would be strongest when the plan was best for the company. Ellicott, who would serve as a state canal commissioner, directed the company's variable support for the canal, endeavoring always to bring canal planning in line with company interests.

Although Ellicott was the single most knowledgeable person about New York's territory west of the Genesee River, he acknowledged knowing relatively little about lands east of the Genesee to Mud Creek. This is where James Geddes came in.

Geddes spent the summer and fall of 1808 leading careful surveys of possible Ontario routes. After spending the $600 appropriation, he returned home to Onondaga to prepare his report. His heart, though, was in finding an inland route. And so, in the snows of early December, he set out west again, to investigate the unexplored, arid tract between the Genesee and Mud Creek. "All knowledge of an interior route was incomplete," he wrote later, "while this piece of country remained unknown." Geddes traveled alone. With neither authorization nor time for detailed surveys or money to employ assistants, he simply walked the unbroken forest from just west of Palmyra (then a mere hamlet) where north-running Mud Creek divides to the west and east. Though he had been told not to, he took levels as he continued west.

It had long been supposed that the ground in this region rose above the level of the Genesee, making a canal through it impossible. Arriving after some days' trek at the Genesee, Geddes to his "great joy and surprise found the level of the river far elevated above the spot where the brooks parted, and no high lands in between."

It was good news and bad that a valley, not a summit, intervened between the Genesee River and Mud Creek. The river could supply a canal, but only if a level was found to cross the valley that the Seneca natives called Irondequoit. Trudging about in the snow-drifted lowlands, Geddes despaired of ever seeing "the Genesee waters" flow east out of the valley, until he found a series of ridges "not surpassed, perhaps, in the world for singularity." These rubbly ridges—which modern geology recognizes as the rocky dump piles of the last glacial retreat ten thousand years ago—were "of just sufficient height and width" to carry and support a canal: "I felt disposed to exclaim, *Eureka* on making this discovery." When the Erie Canal crossed the valley thirteen years later, only one man-made ridge—a spectacular embankment high over Irondequoit Creek—was required to complement the natural embankments that Geddes had found. For the time being, the ridges convinced Geddes that an inland canal was possible. He chalked up $73 in expenses during his explorations in the valley. De Witt later made sure Geddes's bill was paid.

The report that Geddes turned in to De Witt on January 20, 1809, was thorough and illustrated with numerous closely drawn maps. Geddes was careful to avoid an overt argument for the mandated secondary purpose of an inland canal. His preference was indicated, though, by using fully half the report for a section he blandly titled "An Interior Route." And the western component of his primary assignment—surveying around Niagara Falls for an Ontario–Erie connection to go with a Hudson–Ontario route—inadvertently yielded important information about the inland route, which Geddes included in the report.

Getting to and from Niagara, Geddes became familiar with the terrain in the Holland Purchase. He knew about Ellicott's idea to run a canal east in Tonawanta Creek to its summit near Batavia. Geddes, though, reported that he had been deeply impressed with the argument in the *Rees* encyclopedia essay favoring dug canals over improved but unpredictable rivers. Thus, Geddes recommended against using the Tonawanta and for a canal route that might find its way down *through* the ridge stretching east from Niagara and then take up its easterly course along the Lake Ontario coastal plain.

And so Geddes was taking the Erie idea to the next step: moving north not only of Ellicott's locked and level southern route but also north of Hercules's inclined plane *along* the ridge. Geddes had now anticipated more precisely the future course of the Erie Canal, as well as the remarkable locks that would scale the forested ridge at what became Lockport.

Geddes's report accomplished all that interested New Yorkers had hoped for. As Surveyor-General De Witt later wrote, Geddes had shown "that a canal from Lake Erie to Hudson's River was not only practicable, but practicable with uncommon facility." For his part Ellicott, who apparently had not been previously acquainted with Geddes, would question his qualifications and misspell his name—"Geddis"—forever.

Even with Geddes's hopeful report, New York was unprepared to build any canal without the support of the federal government. But the Gallatin Plan was nearly a year old and clearly failing to thrive. So Joshua Forman, sponsor of what Geddes had turned into the first professional report on Erie, was sent to Washington in January 1809 "almost entirely to converse with Mr. Jefferson on the subject."

Forman told Jefferson that New York had explored a cross-state canal route and "found it practicable beyond their most sanguine expectations." Speaking "in as laconic a manner as I could" so as not to arouse Jefferson's Northern phobias, Forman laid out the national benefits: settling the frontier, enhancing land values, channeling the country's western commerce to an American port, providing a safe route for military supplies in wartime, and creating "a bond of union to the states."

Jefferson wasn't buying it. Such a canal was "a fine project, and might be executed a century hence," Forman heard him say. "Why sir," continued the president, temperature rising as he looked out from the presidential mansion at the Potomac, "here is a canal of a few miles, projected by General Washington, which, if completed, would render this a fine commercial city, which has languished for many years because the small sum of 200,000 dollars necessary to complete it, cannot be obtained from the general government, the state government, or from individuals—and you talk of making a canal of 350 miles through the wilderness—it is little short of madness to think of it at this day."

Forman returned to New York, reporting that Jefferson had crushed Hercules, Gallatin, and Geddes. Without federal support, an Erie canal was impossible. The 1809 state legislative session was just getting underway. Jesse Hawley, still jailed, had given his original, handwritten essays to a friend, Ontario County assemblyman Micah Brooks, to distribute among fellow lawmakers in Albany, "but nothing was done." When the session ended, Brooks left the essays in the care of Surveyor-General De Witt for uncertain future consideration.

As with many great things, once the Erie Canal was built, its creation and its effects seemed inevitable. But doubt about the canal was widespread in 1809, not just among those with political or commercial power and interest. Even casual but wise observers saw little prospective connection between Lake Erie and the east.

One wise doubter was Oxford-educated scientist Thomas Cooper. Disillusioned with European civilization after the Terror that followed the French Revolution, Cooper had become a leading American intellectual. A frequent and keen traveler in his adopted country, Cooper toured Western New York in the spring of 1809. He lodged for several days at Buffalo's single tavern, an "indifferent" place but the most substantial of the village's sixteen buildings. He asked about the commerce of the region and learned that its chief market, surprisingly, was New Orleans, a long water route away but requiring just one nine-mile portage. Cooper thought that this was to change: "The future market for the whole western district of Newyork will be Kingston," that is, the English port at the Lake Ontario entry to the St. Lawrence River. Cooper considered a possible cross-state canal as useful only for raising primitive Western New York to "the residence of civilized beings." In 1809 the idea of an Erie canal that would transform New York and the nation had been launched, but few had booked passage.

CHAPTER 4

Apollo Rising

[De Witt Clinton] was not only utterly destitute of intrigue, but he was absolutely defective in that address which, in a popular government, is highly necessary for every man who expects to make a figure in public life.

—Jabez D. Hammond,
The History of Political Parties in the State of New-York (1842)

[His] own aggrandizement has been the only test of his party attachments, and he has, consequently, been a mere man of coalitions.

—John Quincy Adams, 1820

[He] devoted the best powers of his vigorous and capacious mind to [the canal]; and he appeared to grasp and realize it, as an object of the highest public utility, and worthy of his noblest ambition.

—Jonas Platt, 1828

"[A]bout 150 years ago," says Spencer Tracy, narrating the 1962 Cinerama pioneer, *How the West Was Won*, "an idea took shape in the mind of a man named De Witt Clinton. And in the way Americans have of acting out their dreams, it came to be." In the way that the Motion Picture Academy loves sprawling Hollywood epics, the movie won the award for best original screenplay, feeding the popular misconception

65

that De Witt Clinton dreamed up the Erie Canal. Clinton did not conceive the Erie Canal, but he did adopt the idea in its infancy and nurture its development, and it grew to be his proudest achievement. Like interdependent species, Clinton and the canal thrived together. In Clinton, the proposed canal found a tenacious and powerful sponsor; in the canal, Clinton found an issue that solidified his broad but tenuous political base and forged his popular legacy. The canal succeeded in spite of Clinton's habit of working against his own self-interest.

In his personal life Clinton was happy, though often wounded by loss, as many lives were before modern medicine. His first wife, the rich and beautiful Maria Franklin, was raised on New York City's Cherry Street in the home that her family made available to George Washington as president, an office desired but never gained by her husband. In twenty-two relatively tranquil years of marriage, Maria bore Clinton's ten children, of whom six survived him. She sickened after her final delivery and died the following year without recovering, leaving her husband with "an *immedicable vulnus* in my heart." Within a year Clinton had healed the *vulnus* by marrying Catherine Jones, the daughter and niece of prominent physicians, who was as socially adroit and politically astute as Maria had been domestic and maternal. Jones proved an avid hunting partner during the carnivorous later years of Clinton's public life. Of Clinton's adult children, his namesake son was a promising civil engineer but died before age thirty of an undiagnosed illness. Clinton's oldest surviving son, George, became a state judge and Buffalo mayor, whose own son, George, was a promoter of the second and final enlargement of the Erie Canal, completed a hundred years after work started on his grandfather's original. No Clinton, though, before or after De Witt, achieved as much as he did.

Clinton was built for greatness. In his prime, he was an imposing physical specimen: over six feet tall, "of a fine form, and well proportioned. . . . His carriage was elevated; his movements deliberate and dignified, sometimes manifesting great earnestness, but never precipitancy." For his imposing dimensions and commanding (to some, overbearing) presence, as early as his Columbia College days he was called "Magnus Apollo." His lips were thin, fashioned for speech making; his complexion clear; his nose "finely proportioned"; his eyes dark hazel, quick, and expressive; his forehead lofty and broad; his wavy hair brown. He was robust and athletic, a zealous horseman, which proved his physical undoing. Days after Maria's death in 1818, and perhaps distracted by his wounded heart, Clinton fell while riding and fractured a leg. Crutches were his companion during an extended period of healing; forever after he walked with a limp: Apollo with an Achilles leg. Approaching fifty, his previous life of vigorous exercise was over. He put on the weight featured in portraits done at the height of his political power as governor, the same weight and years of his declining health. "[T]o this change in his habits," wrote friend and biographer James Renwick, "from active to sedentary, may be ascribed the gradual approach of that disease, which carried him off in the zenith of his faculties" ten years later.

Jesse Hawley deserved greater contentment than he afforded himself, but De Witt Clinton was more blindly contented with his public life than most believed he had good reason to be. His political life was a great success in his eyes only. From 1800 until his death in 1828, Clinton "was the major issue in New York State politics," wrote the biographer of a devoted opponent, pointedly choosing his singular noun. One of Clinton's closest allies and his longtime personal attorney, Jabez Hammond, who remains the best political historian of the state's first half-century, was openly and brutally critical of his late friend: "On literary subjects, and other grave topics, he was interesting, though not eloquent. His attempts at wit . . . were generally severe and sometimes offensive. . . . [H]e always placed too high an estimate on his own personal influence. He seemed to entertain the notion that all his friends were bound to believe as he believed, and that his supporters were made for him, and not he for his supporters. . . . [A]lthough pure and incorruptible himself, he looked upon corruption in others with too much indifference." Hammond also recognized with deep and generous admiration Clinton's impeccable honesty; tender and affectionate devotion to family; bold action against slavery, poverty, and other social injustice; and unequalled service to New York, which emerged as the Empire State during his long watch.

Hammond identified the source of Clinton's fatal political arrogance: his youthful appointment as private secretary to his uncle, the longtime governor and later vice president, George Clinton. Just eighteen and fresh out of Columbia, De Witt's accession to the inner circle of New York government without effort or proven merit allowed for the rapid development of "a certain coldness and *hauteur* of manner . . . an assumption of superiority and a repulsiveness of manner," which led him to discount the wiser counsel or deeper wisdom even of close friends. Entitlement blinded him to gamesmanship in politics; he was less a strategic player than the owner of a game board that others, like early protégé Martin Van Buren, learned before moving on to bigger games. Though political opponents often charged Clinton with intrigues, "he was not only utterly destitute of intrigue, but he was absolutely defective in that address which, in a popular government, is highly necessary for every man who expects to make a figure in public life." Clinton served his city as mayor for ten years and his state as assemblyman and senator for ten years, governor for nine years, and canal commissioner for fourteen years; on no head did such crowns rest so uneasily.

Joseph Ellicott skillfully managed a "Big Family" in Western New York for nearly twenty years. Clinton had a big family, too, at the seats of state power, but his wasn't nearly as effective or devoted. In 1811 an unfriendly newspaper cataloged Clinton's familial connections by blood or marriage in forty public or prominent (and profitable) offices, including five county clerks, two court clerks, one U.S. senator, three notaries public, the recorders (the chief judicial official) of New York City and Hudson, the postmaster of New York City, the naval officer of the port, the surveyor-general of the state, six state commissioners, three lottery officials, three judges, a district attorney, a sheriff, and two bank presidents. Among them were enough Van Wycks, Van Cortlandts, Clintons, De Witts, Tallmadges, Taylers, and others to dull the pencil of a political genealogist. In many of these relations, though, blood was much thinner than politics, so even among Clinton's relatives were political enemies, such as Ambrose Spencer, chief justice of the state's highest court, who married two of Clinton's sisters (successively) but nonetheless broke very publicly with his brother-in-law for five years over political and banking policies. Clinton's alliances often veered recklessly between factions of the rising Democratic-Republicans and the fading Federalists. He made enemies of yesterday's allies and, with the passage of years, a long enemies list. His closest and most consistent adherents were called Clintonians; their party was over before the dirt cooled on his grave.

Clinton's greatest strength was as a statesman, that is, as a man of his state, for which he labored with great success and always in preference to the interests of his nation, for which his statesmanship was modest. As a U.S. senator, Clinton was the chief proponent of the 12th Amendment to the U. S. Constitution, an essential improvement in the transition of executive power, but his primary target was New York archrival Aaron Burr, whose intriguing for the presidency in 1801 had threatened New York's political order and reputation.

Nothing says less-than-national-stature better than playing a lead in the second most important duel at Weehawken. Two years before the Burr–Hamilton tragedy of 1804, Clinton squared off with John Swartwout, Aaron Burr's bosom friend. Clinton was Hamilton's friend and Burr's political enemy, and had earned Swartwout's challenge by publicly declaring him "a liar, a scoundrel, and a villain," typically impetuous words that breached the creaking code of gentlemen. After five rounds, Swartwout had missed each time, and Clinton, having scored two leg wounds, declared an end to it. A few years later, after Burr's better aim, western adventurism, and national disgrace, Swartwout would make political peace with Clinton and lend early support to his Erie efforts. Had Swartwout's original aim been true, there might well have been no Erie to support.

The presidency was always on Clinton's mind but never in his grasp. Clinton supported John Quincy Adams' presidential ambitions, but the White House aspirant confided to his diary that Clinton's "own aggrandizement has been the only test of his party attachments, and he has, consequently, been a mere man of coalitions." "Most of [Clinton's] political work was mere faction fighting for his own advancement," echoed Theodore Roosevelt in 1891 (then a popular history writer), taking the low measure of his fellow New Yorker's national legacy. With less historical advantage and more geographical distance, freshman state legislator Abraham Lincoln, elected in 1834 on a national improvements platform, declared that his ambition was to be "the De Witt Clinton of Illinois." (Illinois had already named a county for Clinton and would name another one De Witt; six other states would create Clinton counties during the 1830s.) This was Clinton's legacy less than a decade after the opening of the Erie Canal and his death three years later. Lincoln shifted his political course when the Panic of 1837, largely caused by a collapse in stocks for Erie-inspired speculative canal projects, put a damper on so-called national improvements. Lincoln went on to the high office of Clinton's failed ambition and then guided the nation through a civil war brought on in part by the economic dominance that Clinton's canal had delivered to the North. By the time Roosevelt came along, Clinton's star was in permanent eclipse. Today, few Americans and not many New Yorkers have much idea who Clinton was or what he did.

African Americans didn't land on Plymouth Rock, declared Malcolm X in the twentieth century, "Plymouth Rock landed on *us!*" Likewise, the Erie Canal landed on De Witt Clinton (with dissimilar impact) on the morning of March 13, 1810, a snow-drifted Tuesday in Albany. The propitious union of Clinton and Erie was the result of an all-nighter by the treasurer of the troubled Western Inland Lock Navigation Company and the Federalist candidate for governor.

The treasurer was Thomas Eddy, a busted Philadelphia merchant turned wealthy New York City insurance broker and philanthropist. Eddy was a Quaker of unalloyed goodness, his "name a synonym for benevolence." His pioneering humanitarian advocacy included prison and penal code reform, public schools, mental health care, opposition to slavery, support for displaced native tribes, and a savings bank for the working poor that became a major financial backer of the Erie Canal.

The candidate for governor was Jonas Platt, whose stature was inversely related to his chances of elective success in 1810. He was the son of a wealthy lawyer and judge who had been a New York delegate to the Continental Congress and the owner of extensive upstate lands, from Plattsburgh to the Utica area (in partnership with Canvass White's grandfather, Hugh). Jonas was born in Poughkeepsie and was educated at a French academy in Montreal during the Revolution and afterwards at the best law office in New York City. He "had not been trained to a life of ignoble ease." After marrying Helena Livingston, Platt moved with her in 1790 to a log cabin in primitive Whitesboro, started a large family and a successful legal practice, and served as clerk of Herkimer County and then as the first clerk of newly created Oneida County. He served a term in Congress, but his place was upstate New York. Previously an assemblyman, Platt was elected to the state senate in 1809 as a Federalist in the heavily Republican Western District. His election was partly on the coattails of his party's surprising statewide sweep into an assembly majority, and partly testament to his appealing personality: "His morals were perfectly pure, he possessed a high sense of honor and had . . . an entire control over his passions. His address was unobtrusive, modest and conciliatory. He had a high regard to courtesy in respect to political conduct as well as in the private and social concerns of life."

Platt brought this high character to his campaign for governor, but it was a long shot against popular incumbent Daniel Tompkins. Tompkins's election in 1807 had been engineered by state senator De Witt Clinton. Platt was the first Federalist candidate for governor in a decade. In March 1810 his campaign was two months old with one month to go, and withering under Republican press attacks. Clinton himself, freshly turned out of his appointive office as New York City mayor by the newly Federalist-controlled state Council of Appointment, already had dismissed Platt as "the would-be Governor" and anticipated a quick reversal of the Federalists' 1809 surprise.*

What would-be governor Platt desperately needed was an electable issue. He glimpsed it in Thomas Eddy's visit.

Eddy showed up at Platt's Albany lodgings on the evening of March 12 seeking support for a bill to revive the Western Inland Company's dormant rights west of Oneida Lake. Eddy was a dutiful treasurer and nominal Federalist seeking to take advantage of the favorable political environment in Albany. He wanted Platt to push the senate to appoint commissioners to study the route for a canal between Oneida Lake and the Seneca River, to be built by Eddy's Western Company. In an act of corporate self-preservation two years earlier, the company had forfeited

---

*The Council of Appointment named all of the state's thousands of unelected public officials, from the state attorney general to local justices of the peace. Established under the state's 1777 constitution as a check against executive power, the council consisted of the governor plus one senator from each of the state's four senatorial districts, chosen annually by the assembly; thus, the council was effectively controlled by the assembly majority party, which picked senators of its own party. Over the decades, the council became the great font of statewide political patronage; it was abolished under the 1821 constitution, which made most public offices elective.

its long-held monopoly rights (and duty) to make improvements to navigation west of Oneida Lake. Eddy was sensitive to the company's poor reputation: "I had never consulted any person" about this new scheme before proposing it to Platt that evening.

Platt had some reason to hear Eddy out. Concerned citizens had sent numerous memorials to the legislature since the start of the session in January pointing out that the state's frontier trade had been turning dramatically toward Montreal due to the relative ease of water transport in that direction. Governor Tompkins's wavering enforcement of Jefferson's disastrous embargo during 1808 had made Oswego into a favored center of illicit export of salt and potash to Canada. During the so-called Potash Rebellion of 1808, ostensibly illegal potash and pearl ash flowed from upstate New York to Canada in record amounts, and powerless or profiteering customs collectors had little incentive to stop it. When the "Dambargo" was eased the following year, the substantially lower cost of shipping western goods across Lake Ontario and down the St. Lawrence River, rather than east along the traditionally difficult route to Albany, threatened to embed the Canadian trade route. Platt was campaigning for governor on the slogan "Platt and Commerce," and Eddy supposed that his friend might seize on a prospective improvement in the state's commercial prospects to bolster his message.

Platt listened carefully to Eddy's arguments. As the evening wore on, a different idea grew in Platt's imagination, a more "visionary and extravagant" idea than what Eddy was proposing. The idea, the would-be governor told the navigation company treasurer, was a board of commissioners, not to do the Western Inland Company's bidding, but to survey "the whole route from the Hudson to Lake Ontario, and to Lake Erie also." And more: these commissioners should work "with a view to forming a canal, independent of the beds of rivers, and using them as feeders merely." That is, not a canal on an inclined plane running in natural streams where they were available, as suggested by the Hercules essays, with which both Platt and Eddy were familiar, but an entirely man-made canal, with locks and levels, using natural waterways only to supply water. Whether the canal ought to go straight to Lake Erie and bypass Lake Ontario altogether would be determined by the surveys. Platt further startled Eddy's "prudent and excellent" mind with "my decided conviction" that no private company should have anything to do with the project, especially Eddy's, which had so "disappointed public expectation" over the course of nearly two decades. Hard-pressed to argue that point at least, Eddy suggested that the legislature was unlikely even to consider a plan so grand as Platt's.

The two men kept talking past midnight and on into the early morning hours, until Platt brought Eddy around, with a political gambit: the divided legislature might give its support if the plan were backed by the senate Republican leader, De Witt Clinton. Despite Federalist control of the assembly, Clinton remained the state's kingmaker. No man or plan could go forward without him. And Platt, although a Federalist looking for votes, was also an upstate pioneer aware of the commercial benefits that a canal would deliver, regardless of who delivered the canal. Eddy, meanwhile, characteristically recognized that the cause was larger than his narrow corporate interests.

As the night ebbed away, Platt and Eddy agreed to solicit Clinton in the senate chambers at the morning session. Platt drew up a resolution for the appointment of commissioners and, with dawn breaking, he and Eddy assembled a bipartisan list of commissioners, "men of wealth and public spirit" who would give their time and services without compensation.

Later that morning Eddy met Platt in the senate, and they "called out" to Clinton. The Republican leader approached and "listened to us with intense interest." He acknowledged that he knew little about canalling or Western New York, but the plan struck him with such "great force" that he agreed to second and support Platt's resolution, with one provision: that the names of the proposed commissioners be left blank on the resolution so it would not seem as if Clinton had participated in selecting Federalists for the list. Platt immediately sought out friends in the assembly, who indicated that they would guide support for the measure when it got to the lower house.

Confident of support in the assembly, Platt presented his resolution to the senate. It had two main points: that the state's agricultural and commercial interests required improvement of inland navigation "from Hudson's river to lake Ontario and lake Erie," and that it was doubtful that the Western Inland Company could accomplish this. Platt wisely favored neither Erie nor Ontario, alienating partisans of neither. The resolution sought only the naming of commissioners to explore "the whole route" and report to the legislature in a year's time.

As promised, Clinton seconded the resolution, and the senate, following his lead, voted unanimously in favor. Two days later Platt inserted the agreed-upon names of the commissioners, and the lineup was presented to the assembly. It was a model of political pragmatism, social acceptability, and practical knowledge.

The Federalists proposed Gouverneur Morris, Assemblyman Stephen Van Rensselaer, assembly speaker William North, and Thomas Eddy himself. The fact that Platt and Eddy named the latter to their lineup might seem a crass quid pro quo for his cooperation in Platt's plan, but Eddy was only nominally political, utterly ethical, and highly qualified. Morris was then a venerable Founding Father, and still actively engaged in civic good works, such as heading another state commission that was then planning the street grid for Manhattan. Van Rensselaer, the reigning scion of one of New York's oldest Dutch families, was the country's largest landholder and admired for enlightened liberality with his tenants, a perennial officeholder whose integrity was unchallenged by Republican opponents, and a genial gentleman scientist who would found the country's first engineering school. North, a Maine native and Revolutionary War veteran, was married to a daughter of Federalist New York City mayor James Duane; had a large family with her; and presided over a salon for presidents, royalty, and celebrated travelers on a Duane family estate near Schenectady. "[A] man of strong prejudices who combined in rare fashion joviality of temper with zeal in the performance of duty," North was a regular in the state legislature; at the opening of the 1810 legislative session, he had been voted assembly speaker for a third time.

The Republican commissioners would be Clinton, his elder cousin Simeon De Witt, and western pioneer Peter Buell Porter. Though canals and Western New York had commanded little of his attention until days earlier, Clinton was a natural and essential choice. So also was De Witt, midway through his half-century as New York's first surveyor-general. Porter was a more complex choice.

Porter represented the virulent anti-Clintonian, Burrite wing of the Republican Party, headquartered in New York City's increasingly potent Tammany Hall and with outposts around the state. He was also the dominant citizen of Black Rock, the village vying with neighboring Buffalo for supremacy as the western gateway to New York. Porter also owned (with partners) the monopoly portage rights around Niagara Falls, making him significantly interested in how the state pursued canalling.

Porter was no provincial. He was Western New York's influential representative in Congress, where as a leader of the "war hawks" he would help seduce Madison into the ill-conceived conquest of Canada known as the War of 1812 (and not unforeseeably profit by it). In 1818, Porter (at age forty-five) would marry Kentucky power widow Letitia Breckenridge, whose father had been Jefferson's attorney general. In early 1810 Porter was pursuing New York's canal interests in Washington. He was the sponsor of a bill to revive the possibility of federal funding for road and canal projects, from land sale proceeds instead of Treasury surpluses, as proposed under the dormant Gallatin Plan. In a February 1810 speech on the U.S. House floor, widely reprinted and circulated afterward, Porter had argued passionately for "opening a great navigable canal from the Atlantic to the Western States." He had not suggested a canal directly to Lake Erie—which would harm his Niagara portage interests—but rather one along the traditional route to Lake Ontario—which would improve his portage interests. But as to the eastern portion of the route, Porter had recognized that the Mohawk River itself was unacceptable: "A canal of any extent may be made along the margin of this river, and supplied with its waters, as high as Rome." This mix of progressive and regressive thinking would mark Porter's tenure as a canal commissioner. When Platt and Eddy chose him, his House bill had died; a companion U.S. Senate bill was being mortally wounded by a coalition of senators wary of New York's western ambitions. As canal commissioners, both Porter and Morris would prove divisive and contentious, Morris for his insistence on an inclined plane canal, Porter more enigmatically for his unresolved conflict between personal and public interest.

The list of commissioners assembled by Platt and Eddy had someone for many factions and no one who was incurably objectionable. The assembly, like the senate, gave its unanimous approval. "[T]he violence of party feelings," observed Clinton, "yielded to great considerations of national policy." "Be assured Sir," Platt confided years later to his political opponent and canal collaborator, "it will ever be to me a subject of just pride . . . that I had the honor of cooperating with You [cq] in initiating and promoting our great system of internal navigation." Writing publicly after Clinton's death, Platt noted that from the passage of the 1810 law, Clinton "devoted the best powers of his vigorous and capacious mind to this subject; and he appeared to grasp and realize it, as an object of the highest public utility, and worthy of his noblest ambition."

On April 5, the next to last day of its session, the legislature appropriated $3,000 for the commissioners' work, five times the niggardly allowance made in 1808 to surveyor James Geddes. Three weeks later Platt led his Federalists to a crushing defeat in the state elections: Tompkins dispatched the would-be governor by a nearly 9 percent margin, and Republicans took back the assembly by nearly two to one and increased their majority in the senate.

Jonas Platt retained his Senate seat (until 1814) but his fleeting moment in the statewide sun had passed. He had left his mark, though. There was no time, other than during the Federalists' brief re-ascendancy in early 1810, that Platt could have successfully proposed and lobbied for the creation of a commission to explore the possibility of a canal to Lake Erie. With the commission formed and his Federalists put to rout, Platt quickly recognized that the canal was likeliest to become a reality not through his leadership, but under the guidance of De Witt Clinton. And so, quite by the accident of electoral politics, Clinton and the canal became partners.

CHAPTER 5

Erie Rise and Fall

The commissioners must . . . have the hardihood to brave the sneers and sarcasms of men, who, with too much pride to study, and too much wit to think, undervalue what they do not understand, and condemn what they cannot comprehend.

—Gouverneur Morris, 1812

Mr. Morris [was] a man of elevated genius, but too much under the influence of a sublimated imagination.

—De Witt Clinton, 1821

Most of the men named as New York's canal commissioners in April 1810 were already familiar with the topic. Some had even read the promotional literature, which consisted primarily of the Hercules essays published over two years earlier. Since then, few if any copies of the essays as printed in the *Genesee Messenger* had found their way to Albany. In January 1809 Jesse Hawley, still jailed and anonymous in Canandaigua, had given a sheaf of his original drafts to a friend, an Albany-bound assemblyman, to drum up support during the 1809 legislative session. But James Geddes's promising survey had been followed by Jefferson's presidential rebuff, and canalling was dropped from the legislative agenda. Hawley's friend left the Hercules essays with Surveyor-General Simeon De Witt "to investigate the subject." A year later, De Witt was a canal commissioner and in a position to do so.

In the early 1800s New York lawmakers made laws for less than four months a year. They were elected in mid-April after the close of that year's legislative session and weren't seated until the following January. Albany's long off-season meant that in any given year more than twice as much time could be employed actually doing things as debating the whether and why. Office holders—outgoing, incoming, or returning—spent most of their lives at home, tending to family, field, and business.

New York's new canal commissioners started work in 1810 largely free from Albany politics and with the blessings of the press. "[W]e have formed sanguine expectations concerning the benefits which the state and city of New-York may derive from inland navigation," wrote the editors of the *American Medical and Philosophical Register*; "the business . . . is committed, as all national matters should be, to men of capacity and public spirit, without regard to their political sentiments." The commissioners set out on their major order of business at the end of June: a summer tour across the breadth of the state.

Feeling very much in his element as a hearty traveler and an amateur botanist, De Witt Clinton in particular relished the adventure into the western frontier. He would record the pilgrims' progress in a candid private journal, complete with comic flourishes. If Hollywood had discovered the manuscript, it could have been a Hope-Crosby road movie, with a cast of supporting characters and rivers as well as roads.

Near midday on June 30, 1810, a blazing hot Saturday, Clinton raced through the crooked, cobbled streets of lower Manhattan toward a Hudson River pier where one of Robert Fulton's crowded riverboats was getting up steam for Albany. Clinton had lingered at home vainly waiting for a new servant, who had the travel disincentive of a month's advance wages. Finally the political leader of the city and state realized he had been ditched. Like any of tens of thousands of Gothamites, he hoofed his way alone. Still robust, Clinton made the boat, joining his older and less sprightly friend Thomas Eddy, who had made more careful arrangements: Eddy traveled with his son John, a budding geographer but deaf for half his twenty-six years. Safely aboard, Clinton and the Eddys settled in for the thirty-hour voyage up the Hudson.

In Albany on July 2, Clinton and Eddy met up with fellow commissioners Peter Porter and De Witt. The surveyor-general informed them that he had hired James Geddes, who had conducted the "Eureka" survey two years earlier, to conduct surveys on this tour. The four commissioners would go by road to Schenectady to meet river transport. Geddes and commissioner William North would come aboard at Utica. The two remaining commissioners, the patricians Gouverneur Morris and Stephen Van Rensselaer, were to forgo boating altogether, traveling entirely by proper land carriage, Van Rensselaer with a brother-in-law, Morris with a scandalous bride and an English painter who had just completed wedding portraits of the outrageous couple.

In deference to his senior years, his fellow commissioners had voted Morris their president. He had been pondering canals longer than any of them. For all the trouble he later caused the Erie effort, Morris brought to the 1810 summer tour a posture and style that elevated the event to the extraordinary.

Morris was a man to be reckoned with. Connecticut patriot and puritan Roger Sherman had considered Morris "an irreligious and profane man," and George Washington had warned his devoted follower that "the promptitude, with which your lively and brilliant imagination is displayed, allows too little time for deliberation and correction." Yet it was Morris's imagination, deliberation, and correction in 1787 at the Constitutional Convention in Philadelphia that had drafted the essential document of the American nation.

Morris served his country with distinction for many decades and in many places, notably as an ambassador in revolutionary France, where he was as successful in diplomacy as he was with the mesdames et mademoiselles. "Gouverneur is daily employed in making oblations to Venus," John Jay once observed. Morris's wooden left leg, the result of an earlier and typically impetuous carriage accident, had distinguished his performances in all activities. Despite the amputated appendage, Morris always mixed his pleasure with the country's business, tempting Jay "to wish he had lost *something* else."

On Christmas Day 1809, Morris had tossed off decades of active bachelorhood by marrying his housekeeper, a bitter celebration for

Morris relatives counting on inheriting aging Gouverneur's substantial estate. He was fifty-eight; Anne Cary Randolph was thirty-five and no mere housekeeper. She was a "reduced gentlewoman" with a past. Morris had first met "Nancy" in the 1780s when she was a carefree girl being properly reared on a Virginia plantation, surrounded by Randolphs and Jeffersons (Thomas was her brother's father-in-law). But Nancy was presently orphaned and, after the notorious but unproven killing of a newborn allegedly fathered by her sister's husband (a Randolph cousin), she was cast out of her family, penniless. Over the years she found her way to Connecticut and then a New York City boardinghouse, to which Morris was drawn in 1808 by a letter from the "Jezebel of Virginia." Charmed by her frankness about the reduction in her circumstances, Morris took her into his home and then, shockingly, made her his wife. Hounded in the courts by vindictive Randolphs and irate Morrises, Nancy soon delivered an heir, Gouverneur Jr., who in memory of his beloved mother would erect St. Ann's Church, still standing on the former family estate, which is now the Morrisania section of the Bronx. Contrary to the hopes and allegations of their detractors, Gouverneur Morris and Nancy Randolph were a very happy couple.

In the blushing dawn of marital love, the couple came to the 1810 commissioners' tour prepared, hitting the rugged roads in two deluxe phaetons, one carrying a retinue of servants and a French chef. This very American power couple would show their vigor at the western end of the trip. An advance scout for a touring British official and his wife had booked the only double bedroom in the "mean village" of Chippeway on the Canadian side of Niagara Falls, but the timelier Morrises laid claim to it and, after lusty discussion following the Britons' arrival, forced the latecomers into separate beds in an adjacent house.

In honor of their well-equipped president, the canal commissioners traveling west up the Mohawk River dubbed their baggage boat the *Morris*. It was loaded with a ton and a half of supplies, including such proper gentlemen's accessories as wine, cigars, and a library trunk. Among the reading material was a special folder of papers brought by Surveyor-General De Witt: the handwritten Hercules essays. These would be well thumbed by tour's end when De Witt, who had learned but would protect their author's identity, returned them directly to Jesse Hawley "with the compliments of the commissioners for their use."

The commissioners, with the younger Eddy and two of his friends, traveled in the lead boat, christened the *Eddy* and under the command of "the Commodore," as Clinton dubbed the boat's namesake. Comforts were minimal. Each passenger was allotted a mattress, a blanket, and a pillow. In a provisioning lapse, camp stools and large tents were absent, a serious deficiency in the malarial wilderness toward which the gentlemen were headed.

The commissioners' boatmen—a captain and three crew members for each boat—were fully typical of their breed. When a pitchfork was tossed at the *Eddy* by a group of prankish farm boys making hay along the Mohawk just west of Schenectady, the "enraged boatmen" immediately landed, chased the boys off, and smashed all of their remaining tools. Two weeks later, on the Seneca River, the crew of the *Morris* "evinced a mutinous spirit," complained of being pushed too hard, and threatened to quit. "On being treated with proper spirit," noted Clinton, "they took wisdom for their counselor." At Seneca Falls two days later, the crews of both boats were dismissed and the *Morris* was sent back east. The commissioners had had no particular trouble with the *Eddy*'s crew, until it was discovered after their departure that they had helped themselves to various favored items, including a trumpet. The *Eddy*'s new crew was a quintet of "sagacious" New England coopers "who understood nothing about boating." Hired only to deliver the commissioners the ten miles from above the falls to the head of Seneca navigation at Geneva, these boatmen promptly proved their skill by "continually running the boat zigzag from one side of the river to the other." This, one of them explained, "was to give the Commissioners the most ample opportunity of exploring and examining the river." The coopers may have been suspect boatmen, but they proved savvy bargainers: demanding $15 for services that normally cost $10, they happily settled for $12.50.

The experience ashore was no less challenging. Bedbugs, fleas, mosquitoes, sickness, and crude or drunken frontiersmen accosted the commissioners throughout. A "dirty and unaccommodating, although much frequented" river house near Canajoharie was a typical lodging. Served amid "swarms of flies," a breakfast custard there "exhibited the marks of that insect as a substitute for the grating of nutmeg." Most horrifying was the entertainment at a tavern near the upper falls of the Oswego River, where a country dance was broken up by a local boatman who cut the tail off a dog and let it loose among the ladies, splattering them with blood.

For all their travails, the commissioners got along remarkably well, largely displacing their personal agendas with camaraderie in rough surroundings. As a man of varied interests would, Clinton enjoyed the tour the most. At every stop he observed and recorded the flora, fauna, geology, and natural surroundings of the wilderness. The naming years later of the lily genus *Clintonia* (by eccentric botanist Rafinesque in honor of his contemporary) followed from Clinton's descriptions of a previously unknown white and yellow lily along the Seneca River.

Clinton wrote freely in his journal. He disparaged the Western Inland Lock Navigation Company works wherever they were encountered, especially the "unnecessary expense" of their fruitless wing-dams on the Mohawk: "[T]he next freshet or rise of the river has either swept away their erections or changed the current." He recognized that it was not the river but its "admirably calculated" valley that held the greatest promise for canal making: "The river is good only as a feeder," he concluded, in agreement with commissioner Porter.

Clinton was not in agreement with Morris's pronouncement at Rome on July 12 in favor of an immense inclined plane canal across the state: "[T]he Senior Commissioner was for breaking down the mound of Lake Erie, and letting out the waters to follow the level of the country, so as to form a sloop navigation with the Hudson, and without any aid from any other water." Morris alone would insist on this notion for years, long after even Jesse Hawley had realized the impracticality of the concept that he as Hercules had launched. Morris's inflexibility would alienate his fellow commissioners and embolden the project's many detractors.

Continuing by land west of Geneva, all the commissioners but Morris paid close attention passing through the Irondequoit Valley, "where Mr. Geddes proposes a great embankment for his canal, from the Genesee River to the head waters of Mud Creek." Here Geddes showed off to the commissioners and reexamined the "Eureka" place of nineteen months earlier, where he had discovered among the snowdrifts a series of natural ridges across the long valley that could support a canal with the addition of man-made embanking.

The commissioners consulted with every prominent local between Albany, Oswego, and Buffalo. No visit was more important than their stop on August 7 in Batavia, headquarters of Holland Land Company agent Joseph Ellicott. Clinton admired the "great intelligence and talents for business" exhibited by Ellicott and his men. Ellicott and Clinton talked in particular about the great limestone ridge that ran laterally through westernmost New York, between the Niagara and Genesee rivers. Morris imagined a canal riding the ridge east. The others would come to understand that the great but irregular elevations of the ridge were unsuitable, and a canal would have to cross or entirely avoid that glacier-made barrier between the low Lake Ontario plain and the higher and drier interior.

Clinton did not record the substance of their canal discussions. Ellicott may not have revealed his latest thinking. Three years earlier he had been thrilled by the Hercules essays and imagined a canal route that would pass through company lands. But two months before the commissioners' visit, Ellicott had decided that a canal by any route through Western New York giving access to New York City wouldn't matter to the company and its settler farmers: "I am pursuaded [sic] that it will be more advantage at once to make Montreal our market," he had written to his boss, Paul Busti; "the great object is to go to such a Place where we can make the most profits." Two Canadian firms had just set up produce-purchasing posts at Great Sodus Bay and at the mouth of the Genesee River, and more were expected farther west. Land developer Ellicott saw no reason to commit any company interest to domestic canalling. Four days after the commissioners left, he wrote again to Busti, "Montreal will be our market."

Ellicott's market awareness was not unique. At Utica, Clinton discovered that the town had been the depot for thirteen hundred barrels of potash from Black River merchants the previous year: "This year not one—it has all gone to Montreal." At Ithaca, established at the southern end of Cayuga Lake a few years earlier by Simeon De Witt, Clinton reckoned mileages via road and water to various cities and concluded that

Ithaca flour "will probably seek Montreal as the most certain market." He was uncertain what to make of it:

> Does it make any essential difference to the community where its produce is sold, if sold to profit? If a bushel of wheat can be carried to Baltimore for six shillings less than the expense to Albany, ought not this to be encouraged? Here the profit to the farmer competes with that of the merchant. But the importing merchant is not injured; the money is carried to New York and expended in merchandize, and more is expended in consequence of the increased price of the commodity. How does this doctrine bear on the Montreal trade? This idea deserves further reflection.

Here at the very top of the emerging canal hierarchy was a measure of the ambivalence that would mark the opening years of the Erie effort.

As the commissioners made their way back to Albany in mid-August, reflecting on what they had learned, all but one had been convinced that there was no reason to think any more about the so-called lake (or Ontario) route, which would involve canalling only by the traditional trade route to Oswego on Lake Ontario, with lake travel to points west. It was evident to all but one that the so-called inland route was preferred, even if the manner—inclined plane or locks and levels—and specific course were not yet clear. The holdout for the lake route was Porter. He and Clinton had recognized that on the east the canal should run along the Mohawk River valley, using the unpredictable river for canal water only. Yet Porter knew that on the west a canal to Lake Erie would wreck the bottom line of his Niagara Falls portage business. Still, in the coming years Clinton would have trouble deciphering the "singular inconsistency" of Porter's conduct: "While in conversation he earnestly urged the Ontario route, he did not hesitate to unite with the other members of the board in recommending the Erie canal."

The commissioners minus Porter returned east from their six-week summer adventure to favorable notices. De Witt received a letter, later published, stating that the canal project was "by far the most important that has heretofore been presented to any of the United States," and would turn New York City into "the largest commercial city in the world." A long communication by "An Observer," published in the October issue of the *American Medical and Philosophical Register*, argued strenuously for the inland route: "If our produce once gets into lake Ontario, I deem it certain that it will never return to the United States [and] must be expected to be landed in Montreal." A subsequent correspondent, signing as "Mercator," warned in January 1811 that the only way to keep New York's western and northern produce out of Canada was to build "an extensive western canal" *and* a canal linking the Hudson with Lake Champlain. Mercator noted that it was only since the embargo that Americans had engaged in extensive (initially illegal) trade through Canada, the province of "bad farmers and worse merchants." Internal navigation was becoming essential because certain voices in Congress, Porter's among them, had started calling for American military adventurism into lower Canada, a "sickening" prospect that could only alienate France and England and make reliance on Canadian trading routes quixotic.

The concerns about Montreal, in private and public, were not posturing. It is easy to forget in our Atlantic-to-Pacific nation of global domination that uncertainty and instability worried many American generations. The Observer and Mercator essays, widely distributed and discussed, helped put "[p]ublic expectation . . . on tip toe" as Geddes prepared his surveys for the commissioners and they prepared their report to the legislature.

Although all the commissioners including Porter had agreed to recommend the inland rather than the Ontario route, their president held fast to the notion of a broad, inclined plane, ship canal instead of a locked and level, narrow and shallow, boat canal. Unfortunately the drafting of the commissioners' report was committed to Morris, the eloquent draftsman of the U.S. Constitution.

"Mr. Morris," Clinton wrote after his death, was "a man of elevated genius, but too much under the influence of a sublimated imagination." Thomas Eddy also carped about the late Morris: "[W]ith all the greatness of mind he possessed, he was in many of his opinions at times visionary—he was not a practical man." But Morris was a force majeure. His fellow commissioners, to their (later) admitted discredit, discounted their own best judgment and "vested much confidence in the opinions" of the great patriot. And so the first report of the Canal Commission of New York State, presented to lawmakers on March 2, 1811, was a very mixed bag.

Morris's lively pen "exploded" the use of rivers instead of artificial canals. Rivers not only were subject to flood and drought, but "in the navigation of rivers, reliance must be had principally on the labour of men; whereas, along canals, the force employed is generally that of horses." In frontier New York, labor was dear and feed cheap. The Ontario route was rejected as difficult to build; the elevations on the Oswego River were "peculiarly unfavourable; so much so, that an intelligent, practical man (Mr. Weston) formerly pronounced it impossible." (Former Western Inland Company engineer and long repatriated Englishman William Weston later denied making any such pronouncement.) Regardless, Morris warned against opening a canal to Lake Ontario, which New York shared with Canada: "The eyes of a rich, enterprising, commercial rival are open."

Morris's report envisioned an Erie canal built in three sections: an eastern division along the length of the Mohawk; a middle or "lake" division from Rome through the Finger Lakes region to Canandaigua; and a western or "dry" division from there to Lake Erie. This partitioning anticipated the eventual construction arrangement of the Erie Canal. Basic geography dictated the proposed divisions in 1810; eventually the demarcation points would shift and a modified set of canal commissioners would propose building the middle first, because it was the easiest and its success would win support for construction of the more difficult ends.

Morris projected the total cost of an Erie canal at $5 million, far too much for private enterprise to attempt: "Too great a national interest is at stake. It must not become the subject of a job, or a fund for speculation." The question was whether the state or "the Union" should undertake it. New York "might deem it . . . advisable, to make the canal at her own expense" and charge tolls for its use. This anticipated the scenario that eventually would be forced on the state, but in 1810 Founding Father Morris preferred federal support on the Gallatin model: "[W]e are connected by a bond, which, if the prayers of good men are favorably heard, will be indissoluble. It becomes proper, therefore, to resort for the solution of the present question, to principles of distributive justice. That which presents itself, is the trite adage, that those who participate in the benefit, should contribute to the expense."

The trouble with Morris's report, though, was its central argument: the canal should be built on an inclined plane. Flood- and drought-prone rivers were unreliable for navigation but, Morris claimed, also as feeders of water to canals. Thus, "that inexhaustible stream of limpid water which flows out of lake Erie, with little variation of height to endanger the canal, is a strong temptation to use it exclusively." There was no good reason for canals to "be made on a perfect level" requiring expensive locks when the slope of an inclined canal could be readily maintained with "mounds and aqueducts . . . over intervening vallies." The report unfortunately offered estimates of some of the elevations necessary to maintain a sloping canal: 83 feet to cross the mouth of Seneca Lake, 130 feet to cross Cayuga's mouth, 80 feet above the Mohawk at Little Falls, and some 150 feet over the river at Schoharie Creek. Morris argued that "instead of depriving the country of water, every drop of which is needed by inhabitants, they will gain a great addition from the canal; and as to the navigation, singly considered, there can be no doubt but it must in that way be superior to a waving course ascending and descending by locks." A reasonable person might wonder, though, about the prospect of a canal atop a towering linear mound bisecting a countryside of ancient forests, new farms, and nascent villages and towns.

The other commissioners had only themselves to blame. When they convened to consider Morris's draft, Clinton later recalled, "they, from motives of delicacy, did not insist upon striking out [the] long exposition" on the inclined plane. They signed the report, Eddy later explained, "without proper care and deliberation, believing that [Morris] knew much more than he really did, and distrusting, perhaps too scrupulously, their own judgment."

The report contained many good recommendations, but when copies were printed and distributed "and read by sensible men throughout the Union, they were disappointed, and condemned it on account of the proposed plan of an inclined plane canal. The rare project of a canal on so extensive a scale, connected with the idea proposed of the inclined plane, caused much opposition to the whole undertaking." Clinton lamented that if the report had been confined "to its natural and appropriate objects—the practicability and expense of the Erie canal—much ridicule would have been averted, and many prejudices prevented." Ridicule and prejudice would thrive for half a generation, hampering but also challenging advocates of the canal. It would take two decades—when portions of the canal, built with locks and levels, were actually functioning—before all critics of the project were finally silenced.

The Holland Company, pondering its role in any canal project, had the most illuminating reaction to the commissioners' report. "I can perceive but vague plans which leave ample room to doubts," Paul Busti wrote to Joseph Ellicott, ordering his land agent to monitor the situation as "it must naturally afford a vast field of conversation . . . not only among the community but even among the best and most influential class of the gentry."

Despite his anger at Morris, Clinton also took a longer view. Excepting Morris's "gratuitous suggestion" of an inclined plane, the report "was every way worthy of the pen of its author. It established the practicability of an inland canal, and illustrated its advantages in a masterly manner." The report was wrongly skewed, but it was backed by "the best and most influential" people, and it produced the first law aimed at creating an Erie canal.

Along with their report, the commissioners had drafted a bill, which Clinton introduced on the senate floor right after Morris formally delivered the report. With the bipartisan support of senators Platt and Clinton, "An Act to provide for the Improvement of the Internal Navigation of the State" passed the legislature on April 8, the next to last day of the 1811 session. Whereas the give and take over the drafting of the report had not separated the bad from the good, a month of lobbying produced a very good law.

In an attempt to broaden the popular appeal of the commissioners, the 1811 law enlarged their cast by two: Robert Fulton and Robert Livingston. Fulton was a leading advocate of canals in America, while he and Livingston were thriving in the steamboat business, with five boats operating on the Hudson, another on the Mississippi, and others under construction for service on waterways from Long Island Sound to the Ohio River. In the same week that the steamboat partners were named canal commissioners, the Livingston-friendly legislature enhanced their Hudson River steamboat monopoly with a new law that allowed them to take possession of any rival boat the moment one was put into service. Neither Livingston nor Fulton would exert great influence on canal policy before their deaths, but they added stature to New York's canal effort.

The substance of the 1811 law empowered the commissioners both to seek financial support from Congress and interested states or territories and to explore whether New York could borrow money to pay for the project itself. On the home front, the commissioners were authorized to seek land grants from owners along the prospective canal route and begin negotiations for a buyout of the Western Inland Company, a legislative acknowledgment that the company's days were numbered. To finance these activities, hire an engineering staff for a round of more detailed surveys, and prepare a report to be delivered in a year's time, the commissioners were given $15,000, five times the previous year's appropriation and a clear indication of the legislature's encouragement.

Though Morris remained the official head of the board of commissioners, Clinton had emerged during their 1810 tour and in the months after as the leader of the project. Morris, clinging to impractical notions, was in the dimming twilight of a life formed in patriotic times. Clinton was the Republican leader of the state, using the canal to nurture his political goals, and vice versa. In February 1811, as a senatorial member of the once again Republican-controlled Council of Appointment, Clinton had returned himself to the New York City mayor's office. In the April state elections, held just after the close of the legislative session, Clinton was elected lieutenant governor, a post akin in its largely ceremonial power to that of the vice presidency, then held by Clinton's patron uncle, George.

But the polls reflected Clinton's paradoxical political situation. In the city in which he resided and which he long served as mayor, he was outvoted more than three-to-one by the Federalist candidate and polled lower than the anti-Clinton candidate backed by Tammany Hall and Governor

Daniel Tompkins. But he won the office handily on the strength of pro-canal Republican voters upstate. At the same time, in a portentous blow to Clinton's rising presidential aspirations, a Tammany candidate backed by anti-Clintonian Republican forces in the city and Washington forced Clinton out of his state senate seat. According to contemporary political historian Jabez Hammond, longtime New York City district attorney Nathan Sanford would not have challenged Clinton's powerful state senate seat without the tacit approval of a wary President Madison.

So, just as Clinton was emerging as the leader of the canal project, his political capital was shrinking in the state and nation. It is not coincidental that the canal project, so closely identified with Clinton, would never find support in Washington, and would find support only in New York City after it was half-completed and pouring money into the hands of the city's merchants.

Regardless of their underlying politics, most of the commissioners were eager to build a canal. In the first week of May they met in New York City to divide up their new responsibilities. Clinton and Fulton were to handle the Western Inland Company, De Witt and Van Rensselaer the land grants, Clinton and Livingston a plan for federal and other state aid, Morris and North loans to the state, and Eddy and Fulton the hiring of a lead engineer. Only Porter took no individual responsibility just yet.

Morris quickly wrote to European friends about the possibility of obtaining $5 million in loans. Copies of the commissioners' report and Geddes's survey and maps were sent across the Atlantic to William Weston, soliciting his opinions about New York's plans. His less-than-stellar work for the Western Company over a decade earlier was suddenly less relevant than his unique status as a trained engineer familiar with the state's waterways. In the meantime, De Witt sent the state's homegrown protoengineers into the field to survey what officially was supposed to be an inclined plane canal, Geddes again focusing on the area west of Rome and Benjamin Wright detailing the lay of the land between Rome and the Hudson River along the north side of the Mohawk River. This was Wright's first assignment on the project that he would come to lead—more famously than fellow chief Geddes—and that would make him the "Father of American Civil Engineering."

Wright was well aware that a competition was emerging between New York's surveyors and the English engineer with an American past, whose professional opinions and service the commissioners seemed intent on having. As a young upstate surveyor, Wright had observed Weston's Western Inland Company work and pointedly remarked years later that he had taken "no part in any of the operations going on under the direction of Mr. Weston." In his November 1811 surveying report to the commissioners, Wright would note trenchantly that he had fixed the fall in elevation from Schenectady to the mouth of Mohawk at 197 feet, some 30 feet higher than given in the benchmark Gallatin report, which had relied on Weston's apparently "erroneous" earlier levels.

Their surveyor's low opinion of the engineer they coveted was the least of the commissioners' concerns. Their efforts aimed at gaining federal and other state support were fatally sagging. In early October, while Geddes and Wright were still in the field, Clinton, Morris, and Livingston sent a solicitation letter, signed by all the commissioners, to the score of state and territorial governments. Noting the "special benefit" to New York but stressing the "general advantage to the whole nation" of a canal linking the Hudson to the Great Lakes, the New Yorkers had sought either "pecuniary appropriations" paid directly to New York to build the canal on its own or, preferably, "the exercise of your state influence in the public councils of our country" to win federal money for the project. The appeal did not play well in the country's legislatures. Connecticut replied quickly that it would be "inexpedient" to cooperate, while Vermont put off a decision indefinitely. In November New Jersey "saw nothing to warrant" its congressional representatives supporting New York's cause, though Tennessee did enlist. The Michigan territory eventually indicated it would only support the Ontario route. Most legislatures chose not to reply at all.

In late December Clinton and Morris were designated a committee by their fellow commissioners to go to Washington to plead New York's case. They had for allies at that point only the senators and representatives of Tennessee. A stopover at the Pennsylvania statehouse in Lancaster yielded no further support.

The prospects for the wise men journeying to the nation's capital were not favorable. "The characters of the two men are pretty well known," wrote a Federalist senator to a Republican friend, "and it is rather supposed they mean to open a road to the presidency than a Canal to the lakes." The rising forces of New York City's Tammany Hall, who opposed Clinton and his "visionary and absurd" canal project, spoke openly of his Washington trip as a cover for presidential "electioneering purposes" aimed at forging cross-party political alliances.

Clinton and Morris arrived in Washington seeking something better than the summary dismissal given Joshua Forman by Jefferson three years earlier. In that time the stakes had risen considerably. In January 1809 it had been an informal discussion between a provincial New Yorker and a lame duck president about the most prospective of state projects. In December 1811 New York's most influential Federalist and most powerful Republican were state emissaries on a mission to create and shape national policy and return with millions of dollars for the most fantastic thing in America.

Congressman Peter Porter had handled the Washington advance work for his fellow commissioners. Porter was both a rising Tammany-affiliated Republican with political distaste for Clinton and a canal commissioner ambivalent at best about the commission's preferred inland route. After consultations in November with Madison and Treasury Secretary Gallatin, Porter had finally advised his fellow New Yorkers that late December was the best time for them to come to make their pitch. Clinton and especially Morris would come to rue their reliance on Porter.

The commissioners had sent a solicitation letter to Madison back in October. It was notably subtler in its arguments for a New York canal than the letter to the various state and territorial legislatures: "We do not assign reasons in its support, because they will not escape your penetration; neither do we solicit your patronage, because we rely on your patriotism." Morris and Clinton's audience with Madison on December 21 started inauspiciously. They found him to be "an enthusiast as to the advantage of interior navigation, by means of canals," but a president "embarrassed by scruples derived from his interpretation of the constitution." In other words, he made the standard Virginian retreat behind the limits of federal authority to allocate Treasury largesse, especially when sought by Yorkers.

By the end of the interview, though, Madison "was in a better disposition," and three days later he delivered to Congress a message that gave New York's envoys some reason for hope. Madison commended New York's "honorable spirit of enterprise" and noted the national "as well as more limited" objects. Without naming Gallatin but invoking "the signal advantages to be derived to the United States, from a general system of internal communication and conveyance," the president called on Congress to take "whatever steps may be proper on their part, towards its introduction and accomplishment." A dance of many steps ensued.

On the day that Madison gave his message to Congress, the New Yorkers met at the Treasury Department with Gallatin. They found him, in the tenth of his record thirteen years as Treasury secretary, still eager to implement his 1808 national improvements plan. He had devised a new financing scheme: not dollars directly from a Treasury surplus that had evaporated, but federal land grants that states, upon completion of a canal or road project, could redeem for cash when the Treasury was "in a more prosperous condition."

This concept was a modification of Porter's land-based financing proposal of the previous year and struck Morris and Clinton more favorably than other ideas they heard directly or indirectly during the early days of their Washington visit. One idea in circulation was a constitutional amendment allowing the federal government to make canals and roads and incorporate banks without the consent of states. Promoted by supporters of a new national bank, this proposal was "worse than useless" in the view of the New Yorkers, who "felt it a duty to declare, on all proper occasions, a decided opinion" against it. Linking canals and banks was dangerous business, and strict constructionist Madison was clearly averse to expanding the Constitution to facilitate it.

More troubling were whispers heard by Clinton and Morris that the proposed New York canal would benefit no state but itself. This talk, "seldom and cautiously expressed [but] sedulously inculcated," was "operating with baleful effect" among senators and representatives "whose minds are imbued with state jealousy." Morris and Clinton had "reason to fear" that this idea "will have but too much influence in every consideration of the subject."

Immediately following Madison's message on December 24, the issue of New York's canal was committed to a House canal committee already considering proposals for canals by two private companies in other states. Porter sat on this committee, but his fellow New Yorkers and canal commissioners had to wait for over two weeks before the committee summoned them. Morris and Clinton were put out by the delay, but the committee was not dallying. It had sent a series of questions to Gallatin on December 28, and he had not submitted replies until January 6. He informed the committee that the federal government had no money but plenty of open land adjoining the western Great Lakes to give in the cause of canals, and that the value of those lands would be greatly enhanced by a canal linking the Hudson River and Lake Erie.

On January 8 Morris and Clinton finally sat down with the committee; "marks of reluctance were perceptible" at the outset. Over the course of the discussion it became "evident that [our] object . . . would not be separately attended to," but the New Yorkers succeeded in keeping the committee from dropping the matter altogether. The committee demanded that Morris and Clinton draft a bill for "a general system" of canals. Knowing from prior confidences that the whole House would not vote its support "unless something was done for many of the states," the New Yorkers agreed to the committee's demand.

Morris and Clinton rushed out to Gallatin's office, and the three men settled on a nearly ten-million-acre tract of open land in the Michigan and Indiana territories that would be available for appropriation for canal-building states. Then the New Yorkers drew up a "land for canals" bill, and on the evening of January 10 presented it to the committee.

Clinton and Morris loaded their bill with something for nearly every state in the Union: the Gallatin Plan reimagined as an unprecedented partnership between the states and their federal government. Massachusetts would get a million of the western acres if it opened a canal linking Boston and Providence or breaching Cape Cod, Georgia would get a million acres for linking the Tennessee and Savannah rivers, Pennsylvania 800,000 acres for linking the Susquehanna to the Schuylkill and the Schuylkill to the Delaware, and so on down the line of original Gallatin projects in New Jersey, North Carolina, South Carolina, Kentucky,

Delaware, Ohio, Tennessee, and Virginia. The private Potomac Company was promised 200,000 acres if it ever accomplished its purpose.

The greatest beneficiary, of course, would be New York. It stood to claim nearly half of the offered land: four million acres if it built a canal sixty-three feet wide at the surface, forty-five at the bottom, and five feet deep—"if practicable, along an inclined plane"—between the Hudson and Lake Erie, and another 400,000 acres for a traditional locked canal linking the Hudson and Lake Champlain. The bill specified that states would get not their promised lands but the cash proceeds after the sale of their lands by the federal government at a minimum of $2 per acre. Thus, for its cross-state canal New York could anticipate receiving at least $8 million to pay off principal and interest on loans secured by the proffered federal lands. This would have been a most ample arrangement for a canal project that Morris and Clinton as canal commissioners had estimated as costing $5 million.

It was a bold scheme overall and seemed to have the favor of the House committee. Five days later it appointed a subcommittee to write a report recommending the bill's passage. With "good ground to believe" that the subcommittee report would "be brought speedily before the House," Clinton headed back to his many other responsibilities in New York, leaving Morris "to accelerate" the legislative wheels. Instead, the wheels came off.

"[N]otwithstanding the solicitations" of Morris, the subcommittee, "for reasons which, though unknown, are presumed to be weighty," was still toying with the matter eleven days later. Morris gave up and headed for home. The subcommittee presently reported favorably, but the full committee rejected the report by a vote of nine to four. On February 20 it reported to the House that it would be "inexpedient for the Congress of the United States to make a donation in land or money" for canals. Though the committee "felt the strongest disposition" to report favorably, its single stated reason for killing the bill was "the inauspicious situation of the United States, in regard to our foreign relations." That is, the looming War of 1812.

Why after sixty days did New York fail to get a canal out of Washington? The written record, public and private, says little. If there was a villain, it was most likely Peter Porter. After Clinton had returned to New York, Morris reported from Washington that Porter "hangs back" rather than pressing their case with his many allies. On the face of it, he failed as a member of the House canal committee to gain the result sought by his fellow commissioners.

But Porter was also the chairman of the House Foreign Relations Committee and a leader of Madison's "War Hawks," who were openly advocating hostilities with Britain over Canada. Porter himself never revealed whether patriotism or profiteering drove his war urges. His Niagara portage monopoly promised great rewards. While he had been agitating for war as a congressman starting in late 1811, he was also a lawyer negotiating with the War Department a military supply contract for his freight forwarding company. After all was lost for New York in Washington by the end of February, Morris would note that in the decisive days and weeks Porter's dominant trait had been equivocation. In late March Porter left Washington for Western New York, bypassing New York City and Albany, where his fellow commissioners were working on their annual report to the legislature. Porter would spend the war in command of various militia and regular corps, earning major-general's bars from the state, a gold medal from Congress, and substantial returns on his military contract. His signature would not appear on the commissioners' 1812 report.

Back in New York, Morris and Clinton explained the Washington failure to the rest of the commissioners. They labeled plausible the denial of any direct appropriation for their canal in the face of war, but they attributed the rejection of the land grant scheme to unnamed men of limited vision. "These men console themselves," Morris wrote in his characteristic style, "with a hope that the envied state of New York will continue a supplicant for the favor and a dependant on the generosity of the Union, instead of making a manly and dignified appeal to her own power. It remains to be proved, whether they judge justly who judge so meanly of our councils."

The rejection in Washington did not mean that New York's canal plans were dead, only that no federal funding could be counted on for the time being. The commissioners' annual report to the New York legislature in mid-March carried a defiant spirit, with Morrissanian eloquence:

[T]here can be no doubt that those microcosmic minds which, habitually occupied in the consideration of what is little, are incapable of discerning what is great, and who already stigmatise the proposed canal as a romantic scheme, will, not unsparingly, distribute the epithets, absurd, ridiculous, chimerical, on the estimate of what it may produce. The commissioners must, nevertheless, have the hardihood to brave the sneers and sarcasms of men, who, with too much pride to study, and too much wit to think, undervalue what they do not understand, and condemn what they cannot comprehend.

If great works could be built with words, Morris would have been the American Claudius. But in March 1812 he was sixty years old, four years from his grave, and seemingly aware that his life, the genteel federal government he helped create, and the canal he hoped to create might be slipping away:

The life of an individual is short. The time is not distant when those who make this report will have passed away. But no term is fixed to the existence of a state; and the first wish of a patriot's heart is, that his own may be immortal. But whatever limit may have been assigned to the duration of New York, by those eternal decrees which established the heavens and the earth, it is hardly to be expected that she will be blotted from the list of political societies before the effects here stated, shall have been sensibly felt. And even when, by the flow of that perpetual stream which bears all human institutions away, our constitution shall be dissolved and our laws be lost, still the descendants of our children's children will remain. The mountains will stand, the same rivers run. New moral combinations will be formed on the old physical foundations, and the extended line of remote posterity, after a lapse of two thousand years, and the ravage of repeated revolutions, when the records of history shall have been obliterated, and the tongue of tradition have converted (as in China) the shadowy remembrance of ancient events into childish tales of miracle, this national work shall remain. It shall bear testimony to the genius, the learning, the industry and intelligence of the present age.

It is easy to see how Morris enthralled his contemporaries. But while his fellow commissioners were happy to let his flowing pen conjure heroic imagery, they made sure this time to rein in his most cherished notion. "[A]s the other commissioners had gained some experience on the subject generally," eminently practical Thomas Eddy later wrote, "more care was taken, and the errors contained in the first Report avoided." Specifically, in the commissioners' report of 1812 the heart was taken out of Morris's massive inclined plane.

The surveys conducted by Geddes and Wright during the summer of 1811 had proven that the lake or middle section dipped to a lower elevation than previously measured. This compelled Morris to acknowledge in the report that "the course by an inclined plane cannot be pursued throughout" the canal's route. Now an inclined plane was only possible at the westernmost end—from Lake Erie to the outlet of Seneca Lake—and on the east from some unspecified place in the lower Mohawk River valley to the Hudson. The greatest portion of the canal, the commissioners all now agreed, would consist of locks and levels. His fellow commissioners had insisted that Morris include this information in his report before they would sign it. They had divided and begun to conquer the inclined plane.

That was one issue set on a forward course, but the commissioners had to look backward on another. The project as a whole was immense but had no authoritative engineering opinion supporting it. There was no such thing as an American engineer. Robert Fulton was designing the "Steam Age," but as a canalist he was an advocate without practical experience or training, and as a canal commissioner he was proving to be so minimally involved that he missed the signing of the report. So the other commissioners were forced to recycle old standby William Weston. He had analyzed the commissioners' 1811 report in a lengthy and largely favorable letter. That letter was now quoted extensively, more than one might think prudent given Weston's Western Inland Company associations and his postmark from the country with which Americans were preparing to go to war. Yet the report cited only Weston as an external authority.

Weston had questioned the commissioners' 1811 cost estimates for soil excavation, tree and root removal, masonry, and locks. The commissioners now dutifully reconfigured their estimates and arrived at a construction cost of $10,000 per mile of canal, plus another $2.5 million for locks, embankments, culverts, and aqueduct bridges, for a total cost of $6 million. That was a million dollars more than their official estimate of the previous year. "The expense, be it what it may," Weston had advised the commissioners, "is no object when compared with the incalculable benefit." Quoting him, the commissioners hoped the opinion was broadly shared.

The commissioners hailed Weston as an engineer of "unquestioned" ability and "great and acknowledged talents and experience." Strong arguments against these characterizations could be made by many people familiar with Weston's work, including several of the commissioners and their surveyor, Benjamin Wright. But Weston was at the least a trained engineer, and the only one whose convenient opinions were available. He had declared the Oswego route "impracticable" and the St. Lawrence the preferred natural route. "However," he had written, and the commissioners happily quoted, "should your noble plan, of uniting lake Erie with the Hudson, be carried into effect, you have to fear no rivalry. The commerce of the enourmous [sic] extent of country bordering on the upper lakes, is yours forever; and to such an incalculable amount as would baffle all conjecture to conceive."

Anybody paying close attention would have noticed that the noble plan that Weston had "without hesitation . . . strongly recommend[ed]" was "the canal with an uniform descent, in preference to the usual mode of carrying it on a level." Weston had written in response to the 1811 report, which had only considered an inclined plane canal. The commissioners had now largely discarded the inclined plane but regardless were quoting Weston in support of a locked and level canal that he had never considered. It seems that Morris in his report draft had quoted Weston in support of the inclined plane; the rest of the commissioners, after they edited Morris toward the level canal, left Weston in because they had nobody else. This was an indication of the dimming prospects for any sort of canal in the weeks before war.

As they made the best of the expert at their disposal, the commissioners' report also put the best light possible on the matter of funding. Washington would not help, but New York should go forward on its own: "[T]he maxims of policy . . . seem imperatively to demand that the canal be made by her, and for her own account, as soon as circumstances will permit; . . . there would be a want of wisdom, and almost of piety, not to employ for public advantage those means which Divine Providence has placed so completely within our power."

There actually was good news from Europe. Despite Napoleonic warring, $5 million in loans reportedly were available from unnamed continental bankers at the prevailing 6 percent interest rate for up to fifteen years. But there was financial bad news on the domestic front: no landowners, including the Holland Company, had agreed yet to cede any land for the canal, and the Western Inland Company was not going easily. The company president had informed Clinton and Fulton in February that the company wanted $190,000 to surrender its rights to the state, a "sacrifice" on its total investment of some $450,000. The commissioners, company treasurer Eddy included, considered the demand "too much" and were leaving the matter open to further negotiation.

As to who should be employed to engineer the canal, the commissioners again resorted to Weston. He had written that "the utmost skill of the professional engineer" would be required, by which he meant a European such as himself, because there were no professionals in America. The commissioners reported that they would "employ a capable engineer as soon as a suitable character can be employed. None but a man of the first talents, tried integrity, and approved experience, can be relied on." In the meantime, "surveyors" Geddes and Wright would "continue their search [for] the best possible route."

The commissioners called their canal "a monument of national magnificence, unequaled by any thing on earth." But in all, their report had better questions than answers:

> Shall it be done now, or shall it be postponed to a future day? Those who wish to postpone are respectfully asked, whether they suppose time will render the matter easier? Will it alter the shape of the country? Will the land to be used for the canal cost less when it shall be planted as an orchard, tilled as a garden, or covered by a house, than in its present condition? Will timber and lime be cheaper when wood, now worth

nothing, shall have grown dear? Is it certain that the state of public affairs will be as favorable then as now? Will not a fertile imagination invent as good reasons for postponement than as now? And to what day shall it be postponed? Must it be to the day when a legislature shall have *that* patriotism which the idea of postponement pre-supposes the present legislature to want?

As it happened, the legislature would be forced into a postponement having nothing to do with patriotism. Twelve days after the commissioners turned in their report, Clinton protégé turned rival Tompkins prorogued the legislature for two months. The governor's unprecedented maneuver, employing a vestigial royal power in the state's revolutionary-era constitution, was ostensibly to shut down the legislature's imminent incorporation of the gigantic Bank of America, amid accusations of rampant vote buying by the bank's largely Federalist backers. Clinton had alienated many influential longtime Republican allies, including his brother-in-law Ambrose Spencer and senator and future governor John Tayler, by only mildly criticizing the proposed bank. It posed a threat to the Bank of the Manhattan Company (now JPMorgan Chase), which Clinton as a director over the past decade had skillfully nurtured as an instrument of Republican commercial and political power. Wary Republicans detected in Clinton's relative silence a forging of Federalist bonds for his presidential aspirations. Tompkins dismissed the legislature to prevent its Clintonian Republicans from pushing his endorsement for president before Madison gained the endorsement of congressional Republicans in Washington. The canal was not yet superior to politics.

When the legislature went into suspended animation, Joseph Ellicott took the measure—accurately as he often would—of the canal and its commissioners. "[T]hese people" had been after him in Albany for a commitment on how much of its land the Holland Company would be willing to cede for the canal. Ellicott had told the commissioners he would have to ask Busti, to whom he now confided that the project seemed "in embrio [sic] and that from present appearances there was nothing like certainty that the object would go into effect for many years." Busti replied that any deal making over the size, location, and legal and tax status of a land grant seemed premature because he had "so little expectation of the Canal ever being undertaken."

The legislature was still out when Clinton suffered a blow: on April 20 his uncle George became the first vice president to die in office. De Witt lost the mentor who had introduced him to politics twenty-five years earlier and had continued to serve as a friend (if an ineffective ally) in Washington.

The presidential race proceeded apace. Four weeks later the Republican congressional caucus endorsed Madison for president, following the lead of state caucuses in Virginia and Pennsylvania. Three days after that Tompkins called New York's legislature back into special session, but if his intention had been to weaken Clinton's position, it failed. New York congressmen arrived in Albany bearing tales of waning support for Madison as he let the country drift toward war, and ninety of ninety-five members in the Republican legislative caucus quickly endorsed Clinton, either as the principled opponent of war or as a likely decisive executive should war come. Thus, when canalling resurfaced on the state legislative agenda in early June, its most influential Republican advocate was also positioned for a run at becoming the first president from New York.

On June 5 Jonas Platt introduced a senate canal bill prepared by the commissioners. Over the next two weeks close votes were taken in the senate and assembly on many provisions, until the bill won final approval on the last day of the session. The law provided the commissioners with far less than they had sought, but enough to keep them in operation.

The commissioners were given authority to obtain voluntary land cessions. They were authorized to purchase the rights of the Western Inland Company, but only after first receiving "satisfactory information from some experienced engineer, by an actual examination" that the intended cross-state canal was "practicable," and then the passage of another law authorizing its construction. They were authorized to secure $5 million in 6 percent, fifteen-year loans they claimed were available, and to manage the money until the state decided to go forward with the canal, which it would not do until a "full examination by a competent and practical engineer."

New York's lawmakers had recognized the major problem facing the canal commissioners. They would have to find an engineer who could pass the legislature's muster for experience, competence, and practicality; that is, nobody American. And the obvious difficulty with meeting that requirement was that the day before the canal law of 1812 was passed in Albany, Washington declared war on England.

The commissioners actually wrote "to England for one of the first Engineers there." They did not name him but, based on subsequent years of appeals to him, it was probably Weston. They unrealistically hoped for his arrival in the fall of 1812. By then western and northern New York had become the front line for military control of lakes Erie, Ontario, and Champlain.

During the summer, before the war heated up, there was no choice but to move forward with available and familiar surveyor Benjamin Wright. Working against the war clock, Wright examined over two hundred miles between Seneca Lake and Albany, shifting his Mohawk investigations from the north to the south side of the river. Wright made significant determinations. He concluded that a single level between Rome and the Seneca River would be "too crooked and serpentine" to be practical. A straighter line, with locks, would be necessary. He also calculated that the plain between Schenectady and Albany was elevated anywhere from 130 to 200 feet above the Mohawk at Schenectady. This effectively ended any possibility of an inclined plane canal in that section, the latest blow to a dying but persistent notion.

As to the western end, Morris and Eddy wrote to Ellicott in June requesting a survey of the Holland Company's favored route, through prime company land up Tonawanta Creek to the Genesee River valley. This eighty-mile run past Batavia and along Black Creek to the Genesee would come to be called "the southern route." The commissioners "apprehend a want of water, fatal to the Enterprise," but they flattered Ellicott with "[r]espect for your Intelligence, and . . . local knowledge" in order to keep him interested in the canal and his company willing to offer land. The survey did not happen. In late July Ellicott wrote back that "the late declaration of war occasioned some disorder in our affairs here and other objects occupied the most of my leisure moments."

The war did not interfere with negotiations over a company land grant, on which Eddy, Ellicott, and Busti conducted an extensive correspondence through the summer. Eddy advised his "most trusted friend" Ellicott why his company's cooperation was essential:

> The amount in Land that other large proprietors may be induced to grant to the State, will depend very much on what your Company may agree to contribute. If *the whole* should amount to something considerable, there is no doubt the Legislature would agree to commence the work—but it is, in truth, so materially and decidedly your interest to make a handsome & liberal offer, that there can be no doubt of your doing equal to our expectation—if unfortunately *you should fall short of what might reasonably be expected from you, the whole plan would be frustrated.*

A deal was worked out in principle by August (though not officially accepted until the end of 1813). The state would receive a 100,632-acre grant, of the company's worst land: a mountainous tract wedged between the Allegany River and the Pennsylvania border. Busti had initially suggested a tract of prime land a tenth the size, but wily agent Ellicott had privately advised his boss, "It would . . . appear to the public vastly more liberal because the quantity of land is so much greater, and neither the Commissioners nor the public have any knowledge of the difference in quality."

It is unclear when Ellicott's "trusted friend" Eddy and the other commissioners came to understand that the larger plot, at 25 cents an unmarketable acre, was less valuable than the smaller tract, worth at least $2.50 a prime acre. In any case, the terms were set, with the state to assume tax payments on the granted land, which would revert to the company if the canal were not operating within twenty-five years. When the time came for the commissioners to proudly announce the deal and other smaller cessions inspired by it, only the public remained unaware of its true insignificance.

While Eddy was running the negotiations with the Holland Company, De Witt Clinton's political life was undergoing the sea change that would make him an icon of no certain or substantial constituency. With the young nation now at war, Clinton was challenging the incumbent commander-in-chief. This could play as unpatriotic or even treasonous. By August, however, the quick and embarrassing loss of Detroit and the failure to launch a promised Canadian invasion had exposed Madison's deficient war preparations and management. Meanwhile Clinton, using the then-broad judicial powers of his New York City mayor's office, had meted out stiff jail sentences to anti-Federalist, prowar rioters, and had conducted private consultations with assorted Federalists. In mid-September the leaders of the antiwar, New England–based Federalists held a secret, three-day meeting in the city that concluded after vigorous debate with an agreement to support lifelong Republican Clinton as the Federalist nominee for president.

A dominant figure in this Federalist gambit was fellow canal commissioner Gouverneur Morris. Morris was the leading advocate of secession by the pacific Northern states from the war-making, Virginia-dominated national government, a seed of civil war that would flower a half-century later.

The Federalist prototype of the modern nominating convention took care to not openly name Clinton for fear of alienating anti-Clinton Federalists and pro-Clinton Republicans. But word soon leaked out and was used in the press mercilessly by Clinton's Republican enemies, especially in the "swing state" of Pennsylvania.

Endorsed for president by his own state as a Republican, Clinton went to the national polls in November as a Federalist and nearly pulled off his fusion candidacy. When all the electoral votes were counted (there was no popular vote tally in those days), Clinton had won every Northern state but Vermont, for a total of 89 electoral votes. Pennsylvania, on the edge of the North–South divide and hotly contested, awarded its 25 electoral votes to Madison, giving him a total of 128 and the presidency. If Clinton had taken Pennsylvania he would have been the fifth American president and the first from New York. In losing, Clinton lost more than the presidency. He had forsaken his Republican party and would never again dominate it in New York. He had courted the aging Federalists, who henceforth had nearly as little use for Clinton as national politics had for them.

The cap on Clinton's year of loss came a few days before Christmas, when his father died. James Clinton had been a heroic Revolutionary War general; it was a small irony that the elder Clinton had served on the postwar commission that settled the boundary between New York and Pennsylvania. James Clinton died eight months after his brother George, the mentor uncle who had initiated De Witt's political life.

The fortunes of New York's would-be canal were also suffering. No surveys were planned for 1813, on account of "military operations which are not favourable to internal improvement." In early February anticanal forces in the senate tried to force an immediate report from the commissioners on their progress over the past eight months, knowing full well that, apart from the pending Holland Company land cession, little had or could have been accomplished. Jonas Platt led a narrow defeat of the resolution. In late February commissioner Livingston died, prompting a maneuver by assembly opponents to void the 1812 law empowering the commissioners as a board. In March Clintonian attorney general Abraham Van Vechten ruled that the powers of the commissioners generally did not expire with the life of one of them.

Clinton's national political career was effectively ended, but he did reap certain dividends from his dalliance with the Federalists. Antiwar sentiment had delivered a narrow majority to the Federalists in the April 1812 assembly elections and thereby control of state appointments in 1813. The party repaid Clinton's presidential efforts by retaining him in his lucrative mayoral post. For the November state elections, though, anti-Clinton Republicans named John Tayler to replace Clinton as lieutenant governor, running with incumbent governor Tompkins. The Republican ticket cruised to victory, and Clinton entered 1814 with no elected office in Albany.

Just two weeks into the 1814 legislative session, canal opponents in the senate organized quick passage of a bill to strip the commissioners of their fund-raising authority under the 1812 law. Without the leadership of Jonas Platt, who had left the senate after four years to begin his long tenure as a state supreme court justice, no canal supporters rose against the measure in the senate.

The issue, though, was practically moot. In the predawn hours of the next to last day of 1813, British forces had burned to the ground the settlements at Buffalo and neighboring Black Rock, killing men, women, and children, and filling "the Inhabitants of the two Counties of Genesee & Niagara with terror, consternation, and dismay." Joseph Ellicott and his people at Batavia joined twelve thousand refugees fleeing to safety east of the Genesee River. Meanwhile, the loan market had succumbed to war on two continents and dried up.

The commissioners were under no legal obligation to make a report in 1814, but they issued one in early March. It was an effort to stay the daggers they saw before them in the senate and assembly. The report was brief, dispiriting, and probably harmful to their interests. The commissioners reported the Holland Company's pending "free gift," plus two other commitments totaling just six thousand acres, but noted "it would be doing injustice to [the grantors'] intelligence, should it be doubted, that a prudent regard to their own interest had its proper share in their determinations." The commissioners had learned the true value of Ellicott's land. They also claimed that an English engineer, presumably William Weston, had been "appointed" to build the canal when the legislature should signal its approval, but they failed to say who he was, what his terms were, or when he was due: "He would probably have arrived before the present hour," if there hadn't been a war going on. Under the circumstances, there would be no further surveys for the second year in a row. The commissioners lamented that they were still "much misunderstood" as exclusively favoring an inclined plane canal. Without offering any specifics, they reminded the legislature that "the nature of the country" must determine what form the canal should take. The report concluded, pathetically, with a long quote from their presumed English hire, Weston. It was a block extract from his 1811 comments on their 1810 report, a quote that the commissioners had already used in portions in their 1812 report!

Smelling blood, in late March assembly anticanal forces attempted to repeal the entire 1812 law authorizing the commissioners' existence, but eventually settled for the senate-sponsored annulment of the commissioners' fiscal authority. "The commissioners were thus frittered down into a board of consideration," Clinton wrote bitterly. "They had indeed power to make surveys, but no means of defraying the expense—and as they never had the authority to commence any work, and were now deprived of the means of doing when authorized, they were stripped of all substantial power, and were now a mere nominal board."

In principle, Clinton had reason to complain, but in practice he didn't. War had pushed canalling far off the state and national agendas, and only peace would bring it back. On the other hand, war had forestalled the hiring of an English engineer of questionable skills, while the abilities and experience of American surveyors matured. The loss of power to borrow money ostensibly from abroad helped assure that when the project did go forward, the funding would be substantially American.

Clinton may have been upset by the legislature's anticanal action, but there was worse news ahead. The Federalists had held the assembly for a final session in 1814 and had once again reappointed their new friend Clinton as mayor. But in the state legislative elections in late April, Republicans reclaimed the assembly (to go with their longtime senate majority) and thereby gained control of appointments in 1815. The Federalists receded from power in all but the oldest and wealthiest wards of New York City. The mayor's office awaited a faithful politician.

In the meantime, the enfeebled canal commission lost its most famous member when Robert Fulton died. He had attained wealth and fame in his last years from steamboats, but his four-year tenure as a New York canal commissioner had been largely symbolic. Fulton had been "absent" for the signing of the commissioners' 1812 report, and "numerous engagements" had prevented his paying any attention to the 1814 report until he put his signature on it. His final year had largely been spent peddling a patented steam frigate to the U.S. Navy. The bare hull of the monstrous warship *Fulton I* was christened four months before its inventor's death in February 1815. Two weeks before his death news came to New York of the Treaty of Ghent, which had been signed in Europe in December.

In early March 1815 Clinton met his political fate. He had served as New York's mayor for all but two annual terms since 1803. The Council of Appointment now put an inglorious and permanent end to his tenure. In a dark arrangement, the Republicans gave the office to Tammany grand sachem John Ferguson, who dutifully resigned three months later to take over the lucrative patronage plum of port surveyor. The mayoral vacancy was then filled by Federalist Jacob Radcliff. The Federalists had given him the mayor's office in 1810, replacing then-Republican Clinton, but they had favored Clinton over Radcliff since 1811. In 1815 and thereafter, neither party cared to give the office to Clinton.

For the first time since he won election to the assembly in 1797, De Witt Clinton held no position in national, state, or local government. His only office was an unpaid post on a powerless commission for a canal with few prospects of being built. For a man whose only business had been politics, Clinton's future seemed bleak. That he now retreated to a recently inherited Long Island farm for a bout of seclusion and "strong drink" is alleged but unproven. What was certain was that all Erie bets were off. "The canal bubble," concluded Joseph Ellicott in August 1815, "has at length exploded."

CHAPTER 6

The Cause Uncrowned

It remains for a free state to create a new era in history, and to erect a work more stupendous, more magnificent, and more beneficial than has hitherto been achieved by the human race.

—De Witt Clinton, December 1815

By late 1815 the nations of the Atlantic had put away swords for ploughs and market shares, the weapons of war for the battlefield of commerce. New Yorkers had learned the news from Ghent back in February. Napoleon had met his Waterloo in June. Likewise, a new sort of political peace was breaking out in the United States. In the long twilight of the Federalists was the coming dawn of one-party rule, the "Era of Good Feelings." For a decade of not always such good feelings, Democratic-Republicans—otherwise known as Republicans and, eventually, as Democrats—ruled the country until Federalist embers sparked up Whigs and, from them, today's Republicans.

The final war of the revolutionary generation had been fought to a draw. In New York, the old landed gentry of Dutch and English roots was withering, and a class of merchant men born with the rights and freedoms of American citizenship was on the rise, bidding for wealth, power, and fame. New York's aspiring merchants, betwixt royal Canada to the north and plantation America to the south, shouldered past the doddering patroons and contented patentees of New York toward a wider western destiny.

When New York titans Aaron Burr and Alexander Hamilton had met fatally in 1804, the victory of the nation's Republican vice president over the formerly glorious Federalist Treasury secretary was rich with symbolism. But an earlier and more obscure Burr–Hamilton conflict had a greater significance. In 1799 Burr had skillfully connived from the state legislature a liberal charter for a Manhattan water company that enabled him to start a bank, a direct challenge to the local monopoly of Hamilton's Bank of New York. The Bank of the Manhattan Company, with an unprecedented $2 million of authorized capital, financed the rise of Republican merchants shut out from Hamilton's bank.

Burr manipulated the creation and determined the earliest policies of his bank, but its rapid growth into a dominant financial institution (thriving now as JPMorgan Chase) was orchestrated by longtime bank director De Witt Clinton. Thanks in large part to the bank and Clinton's involvement in it, by 1815 New York's commerce, like politics and governance before it, was falling under Republican control.

Political and international peace allowed Washington to refocus its domestic attentions. In his first six annual presidential messages and two inaugural speeches, James Madison had ignored internal improvements. Now the stakes were rising. "[T]he occasion is a proper one," Madison acknowledged in his early December 1815 message, "for recalling the attention of Congress to the great importance of establishing throughout our country the roads and canals which can best be executed under the national authority." The president saw the lack of bonds between "the various parts of our extended confederacy" as a national issue: "Whilst the States individually, with a laudable enterprise and emulation, avail themselves of their local advantages by new roads, by navigable canals, and by improving the streams susceptible of navigation, the General Government is the more urged to similar undertakings, requiring a national jurisdiction and national means, by the prospect of thus systematically completing so inestimable a work." Madison appeared to invite the required constitutional amendment to broaden federal spending authority: "[I]t is a happy reflection that any defect of constitutional authority which may be encountered can be supplied in a mode which the Constitution itself has providently pointed out." Committees in the House and

Senate, chaired by canal-minded Ohioans, began work on the executive's directive, a prospective rebirth of the dusty Gallatin Plan. The Senate even authorized the reprinting of eight hundred copies of the eight-year-old plan; only twelve hundred copies had been printed originally.

At the same time that Washington was starting anew on pathways west, familiar characters were doing the same in New York. On a late autumn day in 1815, Thomas Eddy sent a note inviting his friend Jonas Platt to breakfast the next morning in Manhattan. Six winters earlier, in Albany, Eddy had sought out then senator and gubernatorial hopeful Platt on behalf of Eddy's Western Inland Lock Navigation Company, and Platt had countered with a plan to build a canal to Lake Erie. A shortage of engineering knowledge, popular support, and political will, plus a war, had entirely discouraged the notion half a decade later. In 1815 Eddy was still the treasurer of the navigation company but felt a higher calling as a member of the dormant state canal commission that had tried and thus far failed to build an Erie canal: "I could not thus resign a favourite project, and it appeared to me that one more effort should be made." The effort for which Eddy wanted the support of Platt, now a state judge riding circuit in the city, was a public meeting of leading citizens to renew, unify, and loudly proclaim support for the canal.

For several months, Eddy had been quietly gauging support for an Erie revival. He corresponded as far west as Ohio with its major pioneers and state officials, who wanted nothing more than for New York to build a canal that would directly link Ohio with the Atlantic. Closer to home, Eddy sounded out fellow Western Inland Company directors who might stand in the way of a canal project that would doom their company.

In fact, the much-maligned Western Company was finally, and literally, paying dividends. The company was as unpopular and its works as deplorable as ever, but war and peace had suddenly made it modestly profitable. Hampered by few and often impassable roads to transport war supplies, the federal government had paid enough of the company's high tolls by 1813 that it was able to issue a 3.5 percent dividend, its second ever and the first in fifteen years. Through the end of the war and into the first years of peace, long-suffering investors received an average of 4.5 percent annual dividends, as a surge of new commercial activity generated toll revenues that were applied more to shareholders than to maintenance and construction.

Eddy wanted an indication that influential New Yorkers who were also Western Inland Company men would promote an Erie canal with broad long-term benefits over a company with an incidental burst of profitability. "I am perfectly satisfied," Eddy wrote to longtime director and original investor Robert Troup, "that unless you in the western country will come forward . . . we shall not be likely to get any thing done." Troup, an English-born, Manhattan-bred patriot colonel, postwar lawyer, state assemblyman, and federal judge, had grown rich as an upstate land speculator, based at Geneva on Seneca Lake. He saw that although some western trade was moving east through company tolls to the Hudson, peace had restored and threatened to make permanent greater trade through Canada. "I place no confidence whatever," Troup replied to a gratified Eddy, "in the power of any company, incorporated on the basis of private credit, to rescue us from the criminal act of permitting the British to sever from the body of our commerce what may truly be called its right arm. I conceive that the stream of our western trade can only be forced into the Hudson by the mighty power of our legislature." Troup saw that "the British have their eyes wide open, to the importance of the trade of this country, and are adopting measures to secure it." With its armies at rest, England was focusing on its remaining North American prospects. The cost of sending a barrel of flour from Troup's Geneva to Montreal was already 30 percent lower than the $2.50 cost to Albany, and the British were building steamboats for Lake Ontario and canals around rapids on the St. Lawrence River that threatened to widen the gap: "[I]t behooves our state to wake from its slumber—to be active, and to strain every sinew of its ability, to counteract it." This validated Eddy's decision to go forward.

Over breakfast with Platt, Eddy proposed a great public meeting that would introduce a memorial to the legislature "pressing them to prosecute the canal from Erie to the Hudson." Platt readily agreed and offered to give the meeting's keynote speech.

Eddy next visited De Witt Clinton. A politician without paid public office since the beginning of the year, Clinton may briefly have sought refuge in distilled spirits, but he had maintained ample civic virtue. In 1815 he was the president of three institutions (the American Academy of the Arts, the Free School Society, and the Literary and Philosophical Society), a vice president (and soon president) of the New-York Historical Society, a director of the Humane Society, and a manager of New York Hospital, all of which he had been active, with Eddy, in founding or promoting. Among numerous other charitable, intellectual, and fraternal involvements, Clinton was currently working with Eddy on the creation of the Bloomingdale Asylum for the Insane, a model medical facility soon established in bucolic upper Manhattan. The asylum's most notable early resident would be a fatally deranged Joseph Ellicott.

Clinton was keeping busy with civic duties, but he had not stopped thinking about the canal. In 1812 he had borrowed the Hercules drafts that had gone along on the commissioners' tour two years earlier. (Clinton obtained the essays through Elijah Hawley, whom Clinton knew as a fellow Mason and business associate but not apparently as the discreet brother of the still anonymous Hercules.) Clinton would hold on to the drafts for eight years. Over time he sifted their ideas with his own. Clinton had discarded, even as Gouverneur Morris still cherished, Hercules's notion of an inclined plane ship canal, but the wide-ranging and deeply reasoned essays remained the Erie codex and required reading.

In 1810 Eddy and Platt had sought Clinton's support in Albany for a law establishing a canal commission. Clinton, then a powerful senator, had responded decisively. Now, little more than a private citizen, Clinton instantly signed on to the new idea for convening canal supporters in New York City. Just as they had once made up a list of canal commissioners, Eddy, Platt, and Clinton enrolled other prominent men as organizers of the big event: chairman William Bayard, secretary John Pintard, Cadwallader D. Colden, and John Swartwout.

The seven organizers compiled a list of their hundred most important and influential friends and sent them invitations to gather at seven in the evening on Saturday, December 30, in the large assembly hall of the elegant City Hotel, the Broadway landmark a block above Wall Street. Colden, Eddy, Swartwout, and Clinton were designated a committee to write the memorial to be introduced at the meeting. The memorial then would be copied and circulated throughout the state, to be signed by supporters and forwarded to the 1816 legislature. It would be, in effect, a populist campaign to revive a project that the politicized, wartime legislature had effectively put on hold two years earlier by stripping the canal commissioners of their financial authority. In the days leading up to the City Hotel gathering, Clinton emerged as the draftsman and guiding spirit of New York's most important canal document since the Hercules essays.

Clinton and his fellow organizers later proclaimed, and dutiful commentators ever since have portrayed, the meeting as a massive public demonstration of procanal spirit. But the only public invitation was a small notice in the *Evening Post*, published a few hours before the meeting convened. The hall was filled with a select crowd of invited supporters. None of Clinton's many enemies was on hand to interrupt the preaching to a receptive and well-heeled choir.

In his keynote speech, Platt argued broadly that a canal to Lake Erie was in the best interests of the state and the city. Wary of inciting new ridicule over the inclined plane idea "which had been unfortunately proposed" in the commissioners' first report back in 1811, Platt "urged the expediency of a formal and public abandonment of that plan, for the simple mode . . . of following the general surface of the country in its undulations;" that is, a traditional canal with levels and locks. Future developments would indicate, however, that the inclined plane was not yet fully consigned to the dustbin of New York's canal prehistory.

The defining business of the meeting was Clinton's presentation. His memorial was written in a "masterly manner," thought Eddy, and demonstrated its author's "uncommon talents" and "complete knowledge of the subject." The memorial displayed "a sagacious discernment" of the canal's "beneficial results to the state and to the nation," echoed Platt: "If Mr. Clinton had left no other evidence, that memorial alone is sufficient to entitle him to the character of an accomplished writer, an enlightened statesman, and a zealous patriot."

Emotions were high as Clinton rose to speak. Three years and a day earlier, Clinton as mayor had presided in the same ornate hall at a banquet celebrating the spectacular naval victories of Captains Decatur,

Hull, and Jones in the giddy early days of the war. A year and a day later, the British burned and terrorized Buffalo and Black Rock. With that two-year anniversary fresh in wounded memories, ex-mayor Clinton unfolded his text—in fact, a rough draft instead of his mislaid fair copy—and grasped destiny.

"It may be confidently asserted," Clinton confidently asserted, "that this canal, as to the extent of its route, as to the countries which it connects, and as to the consequences which it will produce, is without a parallel in the history of mankind." Clinton's seventy-seven-hundred-word manifesto presented the entire argument for the canal, with equal doses of fact and hyperbole.

For those who had been keeping up with the public discourse on the canal since the Hercules essays were published, the memorial revisited many familiar themes. Canals from ancient Egypt to modern England proved that artificial waterways were cheaper, quicker, more certain, and safer than roads, and the keys to national prosperity and greatness. The unique break in the Appalachian mountain chain revealed divine intentions for temperate, centrally located New York, and not frigid, "inconvenient" Montreal or distant, "insalubrious" New Orleans (or unmentioned Virginia), to reap the west's bounty: "[T]he superiority of New-York is founded in nature, and if improved by the wisdom of government, must always soar above competition." Clinton conjured visions of farms, factories, and warehouses in new villages, towns, and cities lining artificial and natural shores from Lake Erie to the Atlantic, rendering New York City "the great depot . . . of the western world." For the faithful, the future American Bible Society vice president quoted (without citation) Isaiah 35:1, about the wilderness and solitary places becoming glad, and the desert rejoicing and blossoming like a rose.

On the Erie versus Ontario issue, which remained "the subject of controversy," Clinton declared the Erie route preferable to the Ontario route in terms of time, distance, safety, and practicality. The inland route to Erie would pass through the state's fertile western territory; the Ontario route would bypass it on a "boisterous and . . . dangerous" inland sea, and require five costly and time-consuming loadings and reloadings of cargo to different types of vessels between Lake Erie and New York City.

"We are so fully persuaded of the superiority of the Erie canal," Clinton intoned, "that although we should greatly regret so useless an expenditure of public money as making a canal round the cataract of Niagara, yet we should not apprehend any danger from the competition of Montreal, if the former were established." In this, Clinton was anticipating how the Welland Canal, opened on Canada's side of the falls four years after the Erie Canal, would fail to loose New York's grasp on the continent's commerce. The brilliance of Clinton's memorial was its distillation of a strong argument from elements that hadn't changed dramatically since Jefferson's embargo, when the market-seeking pioneer farmers of Western New York first looked at Canada with licentious intent.

To be sure, there were weaknesses in Clinton's presentation. American engineering was still such a blank that he inserted into his memorial William Weston's obsolete blessing of the "noble but stupendous plan." Anyone familiar with Weston's 1811 judgment knew that he was talking about an inclined plane canal. Clinton's lengthy reprise of Weston's dubious opinions risked rousing bad memories of the Englishman's Western Inland Company work. Presumably it was meant to reach the flattered ears of that "celebrated civil engineer," whom Clinton had decided to woo back to upstate New York.

As he resuscitated a distant engineer, Clinton was not above dissembling about land donations. He claimed that 106,000 acres with a potential value of over a million dollars had been granted to the state. He was well aware that the deal for the Holland Company's 100,000 inferior acres had been undone in 1814.

Clinton was sober about time and expense. Reviewing the actual and estimated cost of European canals and some small American projects, Clinton hoped for a $6 million canal but conceded that the project could cost double that and take as much as fifteen years to build. He had little to say about financing and construction. The state itself might build the canal or incorporate private companies to undertake the work in sections. If the latter, "great care ought to be taken to guard against high tolls, which will certainly injure, if not ruin the whole enterprise." If the former, not more than $500,000 should be spent in any given year, requiring the payment only of 6 percent bond interest, which could be easily raised from increasing state land sale prices and salt sales. Clinton deemed repayment of principal unnecessary.

If he was less than definite on these particulars, Clinton was adamant on the broader issues. The necessity for the canal was demonstrated by the "injurious" transportation expenses of the late war and the "destructive and ruinous" postwar encroachment of British commerce. In the state's western territory, goods from Montreal were priced 15 percent lower than similar items from New York City. The "most imminent danger" was separation between the old Atlantic states and the lengthening roster of western states: "The commerce of the ocean, and the trade of the lakes, passing through one channel, supplying the wants, increasing the wealth, and reciprocating the benefits of each great section of the empire, will form an imperishable cement of connexion, and an indissoluble bond of union." New York, Clinton observed, was "both Atlantic and western," the only such state: "Standing on this exalted eminence, with power to prevent a train of the most extensive and afflicting calamities that ever visited the world, (for such a train will inevitably follow a dissolution of the Union,) she will justly be considered an enemy to the human race, if she does not exert for this purpose the high faculties which the Almighty has put in her hands."

The memorial served as a blueprint for Clinton's coming takeover of the canal commission from Gouverneur Morris, who did not participate in the City Hotel proceedings. The old visionary's inclined plane was largely dispatched in Platt's speech. Clinton took care not to specify how the canal should be built, but allusions to locks, deep cuttings, valley-crossing aqueducts, and rivers that could supply water at different elevations clearly envisioned a traditional level canal. At the same time, he showed Morrisian flash: "Delays are the refuge of weak minds, and to procrastinate on this occasion is to show a culpable inattention to the bounties of Nature; a total insensibility to the blessings of Providence, and an inexcusable neglect of the interests of society."

In 1815 Clinton held no position in Albany, which made it easy to tweak his former peers: "If it be important that the inhabitants of the same country should be bound together by a community of interests, and a reciprocation of benefits; that agriculture should find a sale for its productions; manufacturers a vent for their fabrics; and commerce a market for its commodities; it is your incumbent duty, to open, facilitate, and improve internal navigation." After that warning shot to a possibly reluctant legislature, he concluded triumphantly, "It remains for a free state to create a new era in history, and to erect a work more stupendous, more magnificent, and more beneficial than has hitherto been achieved by the human race."

The City Hotel meeting itself could not have been a greater success. Before the meeting broke up, the attendees voted to print and circulate a thousand copies of the memorial. A committee composed of Clinton, Eddy, Swartwout, Colden, and Bayard would oversee signature gathering in the city and urge communities throughout the state to communicate their own support to Albany.

Unlike a canal commission report, signed by a few appointees and read and debated mostly in Albany, Clinton's memorial would be subscribed to by tens of thousands of citizens. It became a de facto public referendum on the canal to Lake Erie as envisioned by De Witt Clinton. To one modern historian, Clinton's memorial was "the greatest single factor in mobilizing public opinion on the subject of canals." In the immodest but not invalid opinion of Clinton himself—thinly disguised as pamphleteer "Tacitus" when the canal was under construction—his memorial became "the foundation of the present system of internal navigation; as it effectually exploded the Ontario route, and silenced forever its advocates; and as it produced an electrical effect throughout the whole country."

A wave of local canal meetings swept the state from east to west. Clinton knew that opposition would coalesce rapidly in regions remote from the line of the canal and in persons remote from his political allegiance. He rushed a copy of his memorial to Joseph Ellicott, warning that it was "highly important that the west should second the efforts of [New York City] on this great question." Meetings at Buffalo and throughout the Holland Purchase were convened within weeks.

At Ellicott's suggestion, the leaders of the thousand pioneers of Buffalo who had returned to rebuild their burned settlement also organized a committee to improve their exposed and undeveloped harbor. This inaugurated the long and fierce competition with Peter Porter's neighboring Black Rock over which of the rival villages would become the western terminus of the canal.

Geneva villagers, led by Robert Troup, agreed in early January to petition the legislature in support of a canal and promoted similar action in other Ontario County towns: "I think we shall, by our proceedings," Troup informed Eddy, "put this county in motion." In Utica, the local newspaper reprinted the memorial and editorialized in favor of the canal, and the leading citizens signed a supportive petition to the legislature. By the time Governor Daniel Tompkins opened the legislature in early February, and continuing throughout the session, Albany was deluged with memorials, petitions, and resolutions from dozens of villages and towns.

The New York City Common Council officially signaled its important support, but its action proved to be a geographic and portentous anomaly. No other community south of Albany would communicate any support for the canal. As Clinton had feared, the opposition in regions not directly connected to the prospective canal—the Hudson River valley, Long Island, and the southern tier of the state out to Chautauqua County—was forming. Hudson Valley and Long Island grain farmers properly feared the wrecking of their local markets by abundant and cheaper grain (though they would shift successfully to dairy and vegetables, respectively). Southern tier settlers who traded south down the Delaware, Susquehanna, and Allegheny rivers correctly feared that Erie would bypass and marginalize them (their fortunes would remain mixed).

The problem was not just the geography of the canal; it was also the promoter: Clinton was out of office, short on money, and, as one opponent put it, "determined to seize on the canal project as a ladder to climb into power." Sides were being formed.

From the west, Joseph Ellicott warned Clinton in mid-January of "much anxiety" that Governor Tompkins was intending to open the legislature with a speech favoring the Ontario route. Ellicott gave assurances that such a move would be met by "a remonstrance" against it.

On February 2 Tompkins disappointed the worst expectations but maddened canal supporters nevertheless with equivocation: "It will rest with the Legislature," he declared, "whether the prospect of connecting the waters of the Hudson with those of the western lakes and of Champlain, is not sufficiently important to demand the appropriation of some part of the revenues of the state to its accomplishment, without imposing too great a burthen upon our constituents."

Tompkins was a respected and popular governor, a man of substantial good looks, "gracious manner, affability, and broad human sympathy." He was on the brink of becoming, as James Monroe's irrelevant vice president, bitter, broken, intemperate, and prematurely burnt out. Clinton had orchestrated Tompkins' successful run for governor in 1807, but after he failed to support Clinton for the presidency in 1812 the relationship turned ugly. Spurned patron Clinton considered Tompkins "a tool and a dupe . . . the insidious enemy of the Erie canal," and much worse:

> He had not mind to conceive, nor ability to execute any extensive plan for the public good. His strength consisted in the little details of office— in the formal drudgeries of business. His mind was disciplined in the petty chicaneries of the bar—without power to elevate itself to any eminence of greatness, and without strength to sustain itself after being elevated by others. He was great in little things, and little in great things—a courtier of the populace—skilled in the arts of diminutive intrigue— equally destitute of literature, science, and magnanimity—a mere creature of accident and chance, without an iota of real greatness.

This assault was not written privately about a late enemy but for publication in 1820 when Clinton was New York's governor and Tompkins the nation's vice president!

In early 1816 the canal was still a dream, and Clinton was out of office and less overt. Furious at Tompkins's insipid message to the legislature, Clinton wrote to Ellicott the next day in a letter marked "Confidential" that Tompkins was "profoundly ignorant of the subject . . . not worthy of respect but . . . opposition." Clinton needed Ellicott's support and his confidence that the canal struggle could be won. Clinton advised his western friend that Tompkins had been "infused" with the "heresy" of Ontario-oriented commissioner Porter, who was in league with the Martling Men, the most rabid Clinton-hating Republicans of New York City. Clinton was endeavoring to soften Porter's stance: "I presume that he will not be a dangerous opponent in a case so clear." Except for the Martlings, Clinton assured Ellicott, the city was united on "the Grand Canal." In Albany, anticanal lieutenant governor John Tayler and the "decidedly hostile" Ambrose Spencer would be mere "Cyphers if we make exertions worthy of the cause." Clinton was then on the verge of reconciling with his politically estranged in-law, Spencer. "You & all your friends who are influential ought to be at Albany," Clinton urged Ellicott. "I shall be there." Ellicott, as would prove his habit, stayed away from Albany, but Clinton's own presence there over the next two and a half months would prove both decisive and, to many, strange.

Before much had happened in Albany, Congress indicated that its help was unlikely. Four days after Tompkins's speech, the Senate committee working on Madison's internal improvements directive issued its report. It proposed that roads and canals be funded by annual $600,000 allocations from federal budget surplus for the purchase of stock in designated state projects. Inexplicably, at least to New Yorkers, the proposed first beneficiary of this federal largess was to be a then-dormant private project to make a canal linking the Chesapeake and Delaware bays. Incredibly, the committee report didn't mention New York's canal plans at all. Fatally, the report also said nothing about Madison's requirement of a constitutional amendment empowering Congress to start handing out money. Two months later, the Senate committee report was tabled. The House committee never wrote its own full report.

"We have a good cause," Clinton had written Ellicott after Tompkins's speech, "& let it not be our fault if it is not crowned with success." If Clinton were to make the canal king in 1816 it would be by holding sway with the joint committee of the legislature that was named to act on Tompkins's directive. The committee was a politically and geographically mixed bag of seven assemblymen and four senators. Several were notable. Federalist senator George Tibbits was a wealthy retired merchant and longtime political and civic leader of Troy; he was opposed to Clinton but supported the canal, for which he later would devise a sophisticated financing plan. Peter R. Livingston was an anti-Clintonian Republican senator from Dutchess County in the Hudson River valley south of

Albany; he would drive the opposition. Myron Holley, a Federalist assemblyman from Canandaigua, was devoted to Clinton and the canal; he would rise high with them and eventually fall hard alone. The chairmanship of the committee fell initially to assemblyman Thomas J. Oakley, a Dutchess County Federalist who had opposed Madison and his war in the previous Congress; he was pro-Clinton but uncertain about the canal. In short order, Livingston and others in Oakley's predominantly Republican county successfully pressured him to quit the committee, but his place was taken by Jacob R. Van Rensselaer, from neighboring Columbia County. A Federalist and ardent friend of the canal and Clinton, Van Rensselaer was a cultivated and popular lawyer, a substantial landowner, and an enduring force in state politics. A skilled politician during long years in office, he spent "many days and nights in Albany in an unofficial way" when he was out of office. Few might have had a better chance than Jacob Van Rensselaer of steering the 1816 canal committee in a favorable direction. Which is not to say that he did.

Prospects for success were uncertain early on. "[I]f the legislature should not be able to rise so far above paltry considerations of party spirit, and local interests, as to come to a level with the magnanimous policy of undertaking the canal, as a state work," a nervous Robert Troup confided to Eddy, "we may bid adieu to the object, and most probably forever!" Troup had reassured Clinton that the Western Inland Company was "a broken reed" that would not stand in the way of "this great state project," but he also feared that "too much apathy every where [sic]" was creating a lack of consensus in the legislature. Under Troup's management, numerous procanal petitions had been sent to the legislature from Ontario County, but expense prohibited a county delegation from traveling to Albany to "act as lobby members." This seeming ambivalence added to the uncertainty in the capital.

Politics and personality drove the opposition to the canal, but geography, economics, technology, and timing were legitimate concerns. The people (and their chosen representatives) in a triangle from below Albany southwest to Chautauqua and southeast to Long Island quite reasonably feared that opening the west on a line from Albany to Lake Erie would doom their farms and nascent industries. And the people of the upper Hudson Valley and northeast counties feared that an Erie canal would curtail their natural trade with Canada; they were willing to pledge support only if the legislature, as it had done in incorporating the Northern Inland Lock Navigation Company along with the Western Inland Company a quarter-century earlier, committed to a short Hudson–Champlain canal as well. Even in regions that stood to benefit directly from an Erie canal, there was fear of the project's magnitude and its stress on an untested economy just shaking off eight years of embargo and war. Many New York City merchants still saw the upstate project as a greater chance for taxation than for economic benefit. There was doubt statewide about either the ability of frontier surveyors or the availability of imported engineers to build a canal across the breadth of the state. Even "sound and intelligent men, and accomplished legislators" who favored the project in principle and politics, admitted influential Clintonian editor William Leete Stone, "paused and hesitated."

The canal commissioners themselves gave pause. In early 1816 Gouverneur Morris was a contented husband, excited father of a three-year-old heir, and largely confined to his estate along the Harlem River opposite rural upper Manhattan. His left leg stump was pained with gout and his body hurt with fatal aches, but Morris had lost little of his verbal skill. He railed to various correspondents against Madison, the chartering of the Second Bank of the United States, the subsidization of "Hot-bed Manufactures" by pending congressional extension of wartime import tariffs, and the industrialization of children at the "Spinning Jenny, till they are old enough to become Drunkards and Prostitutes." Morris was also still the head of the dormant canal commission that was now reasserting itself.

As their president, Morris began drafting the commissioners' fourth report to the legislature in early March. Clinton and Simeon De Witt, poised in Albany, bid fellow commissioners Eddy, North, and Stephen Van Rensselaer to travel from the city on lower Manhattan to Morrisania to have a look at the draft. By Eddy's later account, the dozen miles of winter roads out to Morris's estate were deemed so bad that the commissioners sent a messenger instead, with a promise to Morris that if the report met with their approval they would send it on to Clinton for presentation to the legislature.

The draft did not meet with their approval. They sent it back by messenger to the inclined plane champion "with respectful observations proposing amendments." What they wanted to amend is unknown, because Morris's draft has not survived. Morris pondered the amendments for a few days and then folded. On March 9 he sent back a note saying that the rest of the commissioners could do as they wished: "I pray you to be persuaded that I have not the slightest desire to exercise authority."

Persuasion, in fact, was unnecessary. While the old aristocrat was stewing out at Morrisania, Eddy, North, and Van Rensselaer had drafted their own brief report and sent it up to Clinton and De Witt who, with time only for minor changes, presented it to the assembly the day before Morris formally washed his hands of canalling.

The final report of the commissioners first appointed in 1810 was neither written nor signed by the wordsmith of the revolutionary generation. The absence of his signature from the report of the board of which he was still president automatically made it suspect to some in Albany. An Erie canal was coming before the legislature for the most serious consideration it had ever had. The report backing it wanted flourish and forceful argument. Instead, it was tentative, flat, ineloquent, and just seven paragraphs long.

No surveys had been done during the war, or since the previous commissioners' report in 1814. Clinton's memorial had spun old news into something bold. The report he presented to the assembly did not. Existing plans should be examined and a precise route fixed preferably by "our own countrymen . . . if the requisite scientific and practical knowledge can be found." Clinton's memorial had praised "celebrated civil engineer" William Weston. The report questioned European engineers who "cause the useless expenditure of vast sums of money" but, paradoxically, also questioned whether American surveyors would do. The report suggested that the legislature might only see fit to authorize a portion of an Erie canal—from Rome to the Seneca River—and only if this lesser authorization was "judged expedient." Financing should come initially from a million dollar loan at 6 percent interest, though "better means may be devised."

The report was devoid of any urgency or even an indication of what type of canal was preferred. The commissioners, now effectively led by Clinton, had been willing to ditch Morris but not, at least in their official report, his inclined plane. Possibly they wanted to avoid public debate just yet on the nagging issue, or perhaps they just weren't sure enough yet as a group whether an inclined plane might have some part in their great canal. Whatever they were thinking, their report nowhere expressly called for work to begin. "[A]n immediate commencement and vigorous prosecution of this great national work" was called for in the many "applications now before the legislature" but not by the commissioners themselves.

To some, the commissioners' report could have been read as a challenge to the 1816 legislature to do nothing about canals. In fact, the report reflected a subtle game being played by Clinton.

Few contemporaries were aware that Clinton had been taking direct and indirect guidance from Joseph Ellicott. Ellicott had declined Clinton's invitation to sojourn in Albany lobbies, but he was exerting his influence on Clinton both by hand-delivered correspondence and through intermediaries, such as Western District senator Chauncey Loomis, a Big Family nephew. In mid-February Ellicott had written to Loomis in Albany that although a canal on "the waving plan" (that is, with locks and levels following the contours of the countryside) would likely be cheaper and easier to build than an inclined plane, "I think it might be well to lay out the canal on both principles . . . and cause an estimate to be made of each route." A week later Ellicott had written to Clinton directly that informed opinion was deeply divided on how to build an Erie canal. This is one explanation for the seeming ambivalence of the commissioners' report.

Likewise, in his letter to Loomis Ellicott had advised "neither to send to France or England for Engineers, have no foreigners in the Business; they make everything cost double what it ought, and really have not as much knowledge of constructing objects of this nature as many Americans that may be obtained." A week later, he wrote to Clinton: "I would recommend employing Americans solely, and avoiding foreigners; they know very little about the management and conducting of business economically in this country; and the truth is, the laying out a path for a canal, requires neither conjurers nor wizzards [sic]; practical nature is every thing that is necessary." Two weeks later, the commissioners' report disparaged foreign engineers who "cause the useless expenditure of vast sums of money."

Ellicott's advice to Clinton was not limited to how and who; he also had a strong opinion about when. Authority to begin building a canal, he wrote to Clinton, should not be sought from the 1816 legislature. Instead, the legislature should appoint a new canal commission with the power and funding to make detailed surveys, maps, and profiles reflecting a specific route; the number and location of bridges and locks; excavation depths; and numerous test shafts to determine "whether clay, loam, sand, gravel, stone or rock" was to be excavated and what the costs would be. This knowledge was required, in Ellicott's view, before "a succeeding legislature could judge, whether the ability of the state was competent to the undertaking." Clinton wrote back that "the Erie canal . . . subject is in a fair way; I hope it will receive the support it deserves." As far as Ellicott was concerned in 1816, the canal deserved to be studied, not approved. If Clinton was of like mind, the commissioners' report is explained, as is Clinton's subsequent behavior at Albany.

Following the report, Jacob Van Rensselaer's joint committee required a high degree of cooperation from Clinton. Widely perceived as the canal's motive force, the longtime commissioner had the most information to impart and the strongest arguments to make. Instead, he reined them and let ambivalence run free. Members of the committee found Clinton "reserved, mysterious, and apparently incapable of affording any essential information." "Their interviews," wrote a close observer,

> were, by no means, productive of the benefits expected from them. He was either unable or unwilling to afford them any assistance; nor did he present them with levels, maps, or surveys that had been made under the direction of the commissioners. The committee requested to be provided with those documents, and he promised to procure them. After considerable delay, the committee were furnished with maps and papers relating solely to the plan of an *inclined plane*;—the other maps and surveys, though repeatedly called for, were not produced during the session.

This appeared curious behavior, indeed.

Instead of getting detailed materials relating to the locked and level canal that Clinton supposedly favored, the committee were given only brief statements from surveyors Geddes and Wright. Each provided only a "general view of the difficulties and obstacles" involved. In a few paragraphs, Geddes described his preferred route from Erie to the outlet of Cayuga Lake and made no cost estimate, while Wright estimated a cost of just over $4 million from Cayuga to the Hudson and gave slightly more detail. No one reading the surveyors' brief statements could imagine them justifying a canal. It is unclear what effect Clinton had had on his surveyors' behavior.

Most in Albany did not fully comprehend that, as one observer later put it, Clinton "had a delicate and difficult game to play." Clinton was staking his political rebirth on the canal, but overtly supporting it was "extremely problematical," especially because of wild rumors of costs in the tens of millions of dollars and staggering taxes needed to cover them. Clinton "found it therefore expedient to be particularly circumspect, not to offend its friends by too much caution in his capacity of commissioner, and yet not to hazard too much zeal. In this dilemma, he trimmed his sails . . . avoiding with dexterous steerage the shoals . . . with which he was encompassed, keeping steadily in view his main object. This conduct was palpably obvious to every member of the canal committee, and to all the legislature."

The *conduct* may have been obvious to all, but the *object* was evident to few. Though Clinton was undeniably active in Albany—in mid-March he was "put[ting] down the terror about heavy taxation"—his mysterious refusal to hand over documents was highlighted in the joint committee's report to the assembly. "The committee have investigated the subject with patience," wrote confounded chairman Van Rensselaer on March 21, but "regret that they have not been able to procure the reports heretofore prepared by the surveyors [which] would have afforded the committee and the legislature, better means of forming a correct opinion of this important subject, than those presented." The effect of these words on legislators preparing for debate on whether to start building the canal was deadly.

Van Rensselaer's committee report was nearly as brief and unsatisfying as the commissioners' report that preceded it by two weeks. The strongest statement regarding canal navigation between the Hudson River and Lake Erie was only that it "can be improved and completed" at "moderate" cost. As with the commissioners' report, there was no explicit statement that work should begin. As for a Hudson–Champlain canal, the committee merely asserted that it "ought to claim the early attention" of the state. Though admitting that there was no reliable information about the cost of a Champlain canal, the committee claimed without discussion that both projects together would cost $6 million. The report spent its greatest energy reeling off a list of terror-inducing taxes to pay off construction loans: trebled duties on Western District salt; a $100,000 diversion of existing auction sales duties; a 14 percent tax on steamboat fares; and assorted taxes on bank stock, official seals, and court records. Poorly positioned, at the bottom of the list, were "moderate and reasonable tolls" which, as it happened, would be the revenue item that made the canal a stunning economic success.

After presenting his report, Van Rensselaer introduced a bill entitled "an act *for improving the internal legislation of this state.*" The language of the draft legislation was bolder than the committee and commission reports that informed it, but much change lay ahead. The bill was immediately assigned to a committee of the whole house. After Van Rensselaer lost a motion to begin debate right away, formal consideration was delayed until early April. This provided ample time for public and private discourse.

Many New York City merchants imagined the canal a bottomless ditch into which their earnings would be tossed by taxation. Tammany forces churned out handbills targeting Clinton as the ditch digger:

> Oh a ditch he would dig from the lakes to the sea,
> The Eighth of the World's Matchless wonders to be,
> Good Land! how absurd! But why should you grin?
> It will do to bury its mad author in.

The national media were more hopeful. Under the headline "The Lakes with the Ocean!," *Niles' Weekly Register* ran the commissioners' and committee reports and declared the proposed canal "one of the grandest objects . . . that ever entered the heart of man." The nation's leading apolitical journal called on the "dispassionate gentlemen" of New York to leave politics out of their deliberations.

Joseph Ellicott may have advised Clinton not to start building the canal in 1816, but he knew that no time should be lost calming fears about financing and taxation. In late March Ellicott sent Clinton a broad plan of indirect taxation. It was a provocative counterpoint to the plan in the pending bill. Ellicott wrote that it would be necessary to raise annually only enough money to pay for a given year's construction work, just under half a million dollars by his estimation. To do this, he suggested that tolls would be unnecessary and, while salt and auction duties and steam travel taxes should be considerable, the largest single contribution—$150,000 a year—should come from a graduated tax on bachelors and childless husbands and widows, from a dollar for unmarried men over age twenty-five to five dollars for the childless with net worth over $10,000 (then a very high net worth). The proposal might "wear the appearance of levity," but Ellicott was serious. As a rich old bachelor of Western New York, he at least was willing to pay the price of his curious proposal. Clinton wasn't sure what to make of it. In another confidential reply, he noted that the "interesting" plan might be adopted "either on this or a future occasion."

Ellicott had other ideas as well. Two days before debate finally began on the canal bill, Ellicott sent notes to Senator Loomis and friendly perennial state comptroller Archibald McIntyre urging that Black Rock protagonist Peter Porter be dropped from any newly constituted canal commission, in favor of longtime Holland Company clerk James Stevens. Ellicott would get more than he asked for on this matter.

By the time the 125 members of the assembly began consideration of the canal bill on April 3, Albany was crowded with lobbyists on all sides of the issue, from all points of the state. Legislators were the targets of varied arguments and attentions.

William A. Duer was named chairman of the assembly proceedings. A Dutchess County Federalist, Duer was the son of the late financier whose land speculations had ruined John Pintard when he was a young merchant. Duer *fils* was an arch anti-Clintonian but also a canal supporter, who wasn't convinced its time had come. A fiscal conservative, Duer was concerned about the ambiguities of expense and funding, as well as the absence of comprehensive surveys.

With the dubious Duer seated, Jacob Van Rensselaer rose to speak in favor of his bill, "directly and eloquently," to the ears of a supportive observer. Discoursing at length on the great benefits of the canal, Van Rensselaer "admitted frankly" that the grain farmers of Hudson River counties such as his own Columbia would be challenged by the cheap and abundant produce of the west, but that increased supply would inevitably create new demand. Van Rensselaer could not have imagined how quickly the Erie Canal would transform his lower Hudson Valley from the breadbasket of New York to its dairy. "[C]ourteous and dignified . . . frank [and] fearless," Van Rensselaer's manner nonetheless "betrayed the strongest anxiety for the success of the bill."

The action came on fast and furious. On April 5 Duer lost by a wide margin a motion to strike out the bill's clauses authorizing the commissioners to start construction when and where they chose. Five days later he introduced a substitute bill authorizing only further surveys and applications for money or land grants from Washington, other states, and any willing individuals or corporations, with progress to be reported by the canal commissioners to the next legislature. The motion was extensively debated and lost by just nine votes. Thomas Oakley then moved an amendment that would allow the commissioners to start work, but not for another year. When this motion came up short by three votes, the canal's supporters "began to tremble."

Sensing the tide was with him, Duer moved the next day for reconsideration of his substitute bill and gained a three-vote majority, but that did not end the matter. Given the narrow margins and shifting votes—canal supporter Myron Holley had voted strategically for the latest Duer motion—the bill was referred to a select committee. Five assemblymen were given twenty-four hours to come up with a bill that the entire assembly could support broadly and send to the senate.

All five members of the select committee were from ostensibly anti-canal Hudson Valley or southern counties, but it was roughly split between those who wanted the canal to go forward and those who didn't.

Peter A. Jay, a Manhattan lawyer, tipped the balance. By "the wisdom of his remarks, and the affability and courtesy of his demeanour," Jay prevailed on his select committeemen to return Duer's bill to the full assembly on April 12 substantially amended to favor immediate construction authority for the canal commissioners.

At this point Clinton left Albany and returned to New York City. This was the latest action in his seemingly strange behavior with the legislature. Did he depart presuming a pending victory for the canal, or to avoid connection with an ultimate (and secretly desired) defeat? According to one detractor, lawmakers had been seeking information from Clinton during the April debates "with no better success" than had Van Rensselaer's joint committee the previous month. The supposed champion of the canal "evinced no solicitude whatever for the fate of the bill" as it moved through the assembly, doing "little or nothing to aid it." Likewise, a supporter with whom Clinton spent a lot of time "felt assured from his manner that he was not at Albany for the purpose of using his influence in favor of internal navigation."

Clinton was gone, and the end of the legislative session was four days away. After "animated debate" during the morning session on Saturday, April 13, the assembly voted by a comfortable margin for an amendment directing that thirteen commissioners be named to build Erie and Champlain canals, with the date of commencement to be specified elsewhere in the bill. At the evening session, select committee member Thomas Oakley proposed a new clause empowering the commissioners to raise $250,000, for the construction of the Champlain canal and an Erie portion from Rome to the Seneca River, by taxing owners of land lying within twenty-five miles of the prospective routes. Evidently devised in the select committee discussions, this burdening of the likeliest canal beneficiaries softened regional opposition to the canals. It passed by eight votes. "From this moment," noted one observer, "things once more assumed a brighter aspect."

After further debate, a comprehensive bill emerged late on Saturday. It had nearly everything canal supporters wanted. The thirteen commissioners would have a $2 million spending authority at a maximum of $250,000 per year, initially to be applied to the Rome–Seneca and

Hudson–Champlain work. The local land tax revenue would be augmented with a variety of duties: up to ten cents per bushel on Western District salt, plus $100,000 annually from statewide auction duties. The commissioners were further authorized to seek land or cash from any willing donor or loaner.

The long roster of commissioners named in the bill was a political masterwork. The only original commissioners designated to remain were Clinton and Stephen Van Rensselaer. The leading anti-Clintonian nominee was Saratoga lawyer Samuel Young, the 1815 assembly speaker who had been defeated for reelection by a fellow Republican. No longer on the commission after six years would be Morris, Eddy, De Witt, North, and, as Joseph Ellicott wished, his rival, Porter. Most notable among the nominees on the assembly list was a presence that had been strongly felt in absentia at Albany: Joseph Ellicott himself.

Finally, enough assembly interests had been served. In Saturday's final hours, a wearied but large majority signaled its support of the bill. On Monday the assembly voted overwhelmingly to send the bill on to the senate. The naysayers were roughly split between Federalists and Republicans, but nearly all hailed from Long Island and the lower Hudson Valley. Few were political heavyweights; even William Duer had thrown in with the procanal majority.

On April 16 Martin Van Buren took over. In contrast to towering "Magnus Apollo" Clinton, "Little Magician" Van Buren was a toy soldier, though one of impeccable dress and comportment. Congenial and discreet where Clinton was domineering and careless, Van Buren was then conjuring his way past his former mentor to the center of New York politics. Van Buren was a future president, Clinton a national never-was. The 23–9 Republican majority in the Senate would largely follow Van Buren's lead on Clinton's canal.

In a long speech, Van Buren argued that the legislature had far too little information to approve a grand project that "might be prejudiced in the public mind by inconsiderate legislation." He moved to strike out all parts of the assembly bill authorizing construction and funding. The motion passed by a 2–1 margin. This returned the bill to the limits initially proposed by Duer and widely rejected by the assembly.

The next day was the last of the 1816 legislature. Senate debate began with a series of votes slashing and remaking the proposed board of commissioners, which would have the privilege only of making surveys and a report. From the assembly's thirteen commissioners, the senate first cut to seven and then settled on just five. Finally, the names and a one-year appropriation of $20,000 were inserted and overwhelmingly approved. The senate clerk was dispatched with the bill across the hall to the assembly chamber.

De Witt Clinton may have left Albany after showing apparent indifference to the doings there, but the senate could not have named a set of canal commissioners better suited to his broader purposes. Former assembly speaker Samuel Young was the only anti-Clintonian. Joseph Ellicott and joint committee member Myron Holley were emphatic Clintonians, joining incumbents Stephen Van Rensselaer and Clinton himself.

It was not at all clear, though, whether they would serve. After several readings of the drastically amended senate bill, the assembly voted its nonconcurrence and sent the bill back to the senate, which promptly resolved not to change a thing and returned it to the assembly, presumably to die in the waning hours of the legislative session. Suddenly realizing that the canal game either was entirely lost or could be partially won, joint committee Republican James Lynch, supported by Federalists Jay and Duer, pleaded from the assembly floor to keep alive the possibility of a canal. After much debate Lynch moved for votes to accept the five commissioners as named by the senate, as well as its $20,000 appropriation for a year's survey work.

With Livingston leading the opposition and many assemblymen already gone, the roll calls came down. The five-member commission passed by 43–34, and the appropriation by 43–35. By these slender margins, the assembly rescinded its nonconcurrence and "An act to provide for the improvement of the internal navigation of this state" became law.

For Van Buren, it won his Republican allies a year to see if a canal was what the people really wanted. But this proved a Pyrrhic victory. For Clinton, the 1816 law was the first legislative step toward crowning him the creator of the Erie Canal, with which he would rule New York as governor for most of his remaining years.

Clinton rarely achieved subtlety in his political life, but the state legislative session of 1816 was one of those occasions. It was Clinton who quietly did not want the canal to be approved that year, but it was Van Buren who emerged as the scapegoat. The 1816 law was "hope deferred," as James Geddes wrote to Clinton a few days later, but responsibility for the deferral settled on Van Buren's head. "The Grand Canal DEFEATED, By a Democratic Senate," screamed a widely plastered Federalist broadside directed especially at Western District voters. Van Buren had "destroyed" the assembly bill, allowed only a "pitiful" appropriation, and made a law that was "a disgrace to the state" beyond its borders: "The eyes of the whole United States have been directed towards this canal. What is the result? The cities, towns and villages and individuals, who have petitioned that it might be undertaken, are disgraced, and the interests of the Western District sacrificed by its own Senators, as well as others, to mean party spirit."

The broadside and other Federalist strategies didn't work politically—in the late April state election, no Western District Republican lost his senate seat—but Van Buren would be tagged forever as an opponent of the Erie Canal.

In the governor's race, Clinton maintained his Republican alliances by supporting Tompkins—described privately to Ellicott, "not as a positive good, but as a less evil"—over Federalist Rufus King. King's broad loss and Tompkins's prior nomination as running mate of Madison's presidential heir apparent, James Monroe, paved the way for Clinton's election as governor the following year. At the same time, in "one of those political revolutions which sometimes sweep suddenly over our city," a slate of Tammany-backed New York City candidates "as strongly opposed to the canal project, as their predecessors had been in its favour" was elected to serve in the 1817 legislature. This was another of those spasms of antipathy for Clinton in his own city, and for the canal in the city that did not yet understand the supremacy the canal would deliver.

Once the electoral season had passed, the new canal commission settled down to its business of 1816: obtaining the definitive surveys that would make construction authority unavoidable the following year. If there was any question about Clinton's interest and role in the canal, it was settled on May 17 during the commissioners' first meeting in New

York City. Clinton was chosen by his fellow commissioners as their president, formalizing the transfer of executive authority from Gouverneur Morris. Samuel Young was chosen secretary, and Myron Holley, in a role that would later haunt him, treasurer. Though politically aligned with Holley and opposed to Young, Clinton later observed that "to the judicious and indefatigable efforts of those gentlemen, too much credit cannot be ascribed."

Only four of the five commissioners attended the May meeting. New commissioner Ellicott stayed home. To Clinton earlier in the month, Ellicott had written that he was unlikely to be "an active commissioner" on account of Holland Company duties and "an indisposed state of health," an early acknowledgment of the fatal melancholia gradually overtaking him. As yet, it was manifested only in more frequent bouts of his familiar incivility with frontier associates and settlers, without clouding his keen insight into the linked futures of Western New York and the canal. Ellicott gave his proxy to Clinton, along with a long exposition to Eddy on how the commissioners should proceed.

Ellicott's main idea was that only one commissioner, preferably Clinton due to "the great interest he has taken in the canal," should take active control of the season's operations, making it his only business and consulting the other commissioners only on the broadest issues: "The acting commissioner ought to be amply compensated for his laborious services, because . . . this canal will pass a considerable distance through a wilderness country, and of course a personal superintendence will not be so comfortable as reclining on a Sopha."

Ellicott was a poor humorist, but he did have vision. The acting commissioner "ought to have a private markee . . . in order that . . . he might have his accommodation separate and apart from the engineers, when he would receive information and make out his instructions and directions." Ellicott managed Western New York as a not-so-benign dictator and recommended the same ruthless management for the canal: "[U]nless the business is methodized in this . . . way . . . it never will be effected judicially."

Ellicott's greatest wisdom and success was in the field. He proposed two initial survey parties, one laying a canal line from Rome to the

Seneca River, the other from the Seneca to Lake Erie. "They ought as it were to be a community by themselves, without having in any manner to depend either for lodging or on receiving any accommodations from the Inhabitants where the line of canal would pass." In a largely uncharted wilderness, each party should have tents, ample provisions, "and men or boys to prepare the victuals." Each party should consist of an "Engineer" at $5 per day; a surveyor at $4; two pole bearers at $1.50 each; and two chainmen, two axemen, a "Packhorse man" to run camp, and a cook at $1 each. Provisioning would cost $6 a day. Ellicott estimated a combined cost of $7,350 for the two parties over a five-month survey period.

He suggested nobody in particular to head the two surveying parties, but expressed little confidence in James "Geddis," as he invariably misspelled the name of the western pioneer whose original survey was a major reason the canal project had come this far. Though Geddes had never claimed for his early surveys a professional caliber, Ellicott pointed out that Geddes's unsystematic methods "would never answer for engineers to lay out a canal." His work in Ellicott territory had always been in such haste and without proper markers and field notes that "all his labour as it regards applying it to actually laying out a canal is useless." Of course, if Ellicott's fellow commissioners opted against a single acting commissioner as he suggested, Ellicott offered to organize the Lake Erie to Seneca River survey himself, provided he was furnished with leveling instruments and "could prevail upon one of my assistants to undertake" the field work. The head of the Big Family would have to do little persuading in that regard. In effect, at Geddes's expense, Ellicott was trying to gain control of the canal's western course.

No commissioner cared less about the canal than Ellicott. Back in February, Ellicott's Philadelphia-based boss Paul Busti coyly had advised support of any government-funded improvement, "provided the Company has not to pay the piper you shall never oppose the pleasure of the settlers of running a race over a new Road, and having a rowe Match on a Canal or pond." Ellicott now wrote back that he had not had "the most distant expectation" of being named a commissioner, but it couldn't hurt their cause: any money locally spent attempting to make the canal a reality would be a windfall to Holland Purchase settlers even if it "should never be completed."

At their May meeting, the other four commissioners acknowledged Ellicott's guidance regarding survey party organization but discounted much of the rest of his advice. Each of the commissioners took on active roles in examining prospective routes for the Champlain and Erie canals, dividing the latter into three sections. Erie surveys were assigned logically based on local expertise. Geddes was given the Erie–Seneca western section where he lived and worked. Rome-based Benjamin Wright took the Seneca–Rome survey. In the Mohawk Valley, Utica-based Charles Brodhead was given the Rome–Schoharie Creek segment of the eastern section. The fifty miles from Schoharie Creek to the Hudson, featuring the daunting Cohoes Falls, was left unassigned.

For Geddes and Wright, the 1816 assignments were a natural increase in their long-term involvement with the canal. For Brodhead, it was a great boost to a surveying career that had started in the early 1790s. In 1794 he had completed a difficult survey north of Utica for a French land company that had fired his overmatched predecessor, twenty-three-year-old Benjamin Wright. Since 1800, when he was appointed Oneida County sheriff, Brodhead had been a prominent Utica resident. A lifelong bachelor, he had accumulated some wealth before the War of 1812 in partnership with a local merchant, lost it in the postwar depression, and was recovering it through real estate holdings when he got the eastern section survey job in 1816.

The Geddes assignment displeased Ellicott. Claiming overwhelming company duties, he advised Myron Holley before a June visit "to take upon yourself the task of furnishing the Engineer with a surveyor to attend him." Ellicott's extraordinary failure to show courtesy to Geddes and respect for the choices of his fellow commissioners would characterize his years on the commission. On the other hand, Clinton and the other three commissioners recognized the importance of Ellicott's support of the overall effort and did not make an issue of his obduracy.

Clinton oversaw the commission's applications to Congress, other states, and estate holders for donations of money or land. William Bayard was asked to investigate the European loan market. Friendly newspaper publishers were enlisted to promote the canal in their editorials and run in their columns the commissioners' own pseudonymous writings. Barely disguised as "Atticus" in *Evening Post* essays, Clinton cast the canal as the "child of the people"; New York would be "unrivalled by any city on the face of the earth" and further delay a disaster: "by neglecting to execute the proposed canal, we shall in fact surrender to Great Britain all the northern and western parts of the United States, as far as the river Missisippi [sic], and we shall surrender no small part of the State of New-York."

Holley and Young traveled to Massachusetts and examined the Middlesex Canal. At twenty-seven miles, the country's longest and only significant canal had finally started operations in 1803 after a decade of expensive surveys (including one by William Weston), construction difficulties, and cost overruns. It wouldn't become profitable for its corporate investors until significant improvements into the 1820s, when it finally shed comparisons to New York's similarly troubled Western Inland Company. The particulars of the canal, which joined Boston and the Merrimac River, were of great interest to New York's canal commissioners: its twenty locks, eight major aqueducts, $20,000-per-mile construction cost, and especially its dimensions—thirty feet wide at the surface, narrowing to twenty at a three-foot depth. The commissioners also solicited construction and cost details from the proprietors of several short private canals in New York.

All four active commissioners traveled the faint lines of the canals being traced by their so-called engineers. The first survey party organized was Wright's, for the middle section. By the end of June he had assembled a thirteen-man team, slightly larger than but very similar in organization to that suggested by Ellicott. Under Wright were a surveyor, an assistant engineer, two rodmen, two chainmen, three axemen, a packman, a cook, and a teamster. Wright's fifteen-year-old son Benjamin was one of the "men" in command of a tree-clearing axe. One of the rodmen was Benjamin's senior by a year, William C. Young. Young was a grandson of Hugh White, a son of the founder of the Ohio town (now city) that bears his name, and a cousin of Canvass White. The most unlikely novice in Wright's crew was a forty-year-old itinerant math teacher named Nathan Roberts.

Roberts was descended from New England Puritans and raised without material comforts in rural southwestern New Jersey. Unlucky as a young man in small land speculations and livestock farming in central New York, and dulled by accounting and sales work at early cotton factories in Oneida and Whitestown, Roberts had found a measure of happiness and respect teaching school. Equipped with only a common school education, but having a gift for mathematics and an easy intellectual curiosity that he spread around his classes, Roberts had become a favored instructor at Oneida area schools beginning in 1804. The local gentry sought his instruction for their children, among them Hugh White's grandchildren, including William Young, Canvass White, and their younger cousin Lavinia. In time she would become Roberts's wife, and Canvass would become his comrade in the top ranks of America's first civil engineers. In June 1816 Roberts' mathematical skills and a bit of local surveying, done to supplement his meager teaching salary, led Benjamin Wright to employ him at a windfall of $4 a day on the first survey party for the Erie Canal.

Nobody was more delighted with Roberts's appointment than William Young. As a Whitestown youth, he had taken geometry and other instruction from his "stout built, quick spoken and cheerful" teacher and had sorted yarn "hank by hank" in Roberts's cotton factory office. As a teacher, Roberts had "punished severely with the ferule, and rewarded with pictures of birds and animals, drawn and painted to please the youthful eye." Young recalled fifty years later that his engineer in-law's "plottings and maps of land surveys were accurate, plainly and neatly drawn and written."

On July 1, 1816, the Wrights, Roberts, and Young set out with their party on a grueling three-month enterprise. In the eighty miles of swamp, marsh, and virgin forest, Wright *fils* counted the number of cultivated tracts "upon the fingers of one hand."

The daily routine, as Young recalled, went like this. Through "swamp and swale" or "woods of hemlock, cedar, alder bushes and weeds," the surveyor would scan a course of probable water level, sight an object and note its compass bearing, and march toward it with outstretched arms bearing compass and staff. Hard on the surveyor's heels, one axeman chopped bark from trees (when available) along the line of march, while the other two axemen cleared a four-foot-wide path of all obstacles to sighting. The chainmen followed, driving stakes four chains (264 feet) apart and, next to each stake, a flat-topped peg level to the surface of the ground. With the two rodmen resting graduated poles vertically on consecutive pegs, the assistant engineer placed a leveling instrument equidistant between them, and the chief stepped in to sight the poles. The difference, if any, between the two readings was the change in elevation. During all this, the surveyor would record the location of watercourses and property lines and details of topography and geology, as well as sketching prominent landmarks, all for the purpose of mapping the terrain and estimating the costs of excavation and construction.

This was how things worked when they went according to plan. As often as not, they didn't. Ridges, valleys, and streams forced the survey team far afield in pursuit of a level. Staked stations often proved far off level, bringing an angry hail for the surveyor and "retrograde steps taken to a station of suitable level and a course pursued as experimental as before . . . feeling the way."

Trailing the experts were the packman "with dinner sack on his back, and water can at his side" and, passing by day from the rear forward to the next night's camp, "the nucleus of the party": teamster, cook, and two-horse covered wagon loaded with gear and provisions. Rounding out the equipage were "[a] dog, a gun, two tin horns, camp kettles and frying pans; and for tables and furniture, a fallen tree, or a log, a hillock, a fresh-hewn chip for the plate, a pointed or forked stick for roasting spit; and a pocket jack-knife carried by each one of the party."

The menu was unrelenting monotonous, to Roberts's taste: "breakfast— chocolate, a piece of pork, salt and hard, hard bread. Dinner: boiled or frizzed pork, hard bread, whiskey and swamp water. Supper: hard bread and milk if we could get it—scarcely any." In Young's reminiscence, early on meals featured fresh fish and small game exchanged for pork with Oneida natives; it "occasionally gave savory odors from camp fires." But the situation deteriorated as the survey party moved west to lower regions avoided by the natives: "[P]ools of stagnant water were often drank from by the laboring men of the party, violently exercising in the foul, moist air of a dense forest in July and August heat, though so shaded from the sun."

Proper camp life was an acquired skill. Early on, Wright taught the cook and teamster how to judge where to make camp so the surveying crew would just reach it at day's end. More often than not, the crew had to trudge backward to camp or Wright would order it reset to the forward position. Responsive calling with the tin horns guided the weary crew to camp. Requisite for a good camp, though not always available, were dry ground, fresh water, and hemlock trees: their boughs offered shelter and shade while their "odorous and fresh" cut foliage was spread in the tents as matting "for sleep and rest and waking dreams of the great work undertaken."

On many days the great work was a waking nightmare. Old windfalls of tangled trunks and roots overgrown with bush, brier, and noxious weeds clogged the survey path. The occasional logged field was a thick nest of underbrush "abandoned to the rattlesnake, by whose rattle our steps were arrested." Severed with an axe blow, the vipers' tails were turned into trophies. In swamps and thickets, mosquitoes made a bacchanal of Caucasian blood. Hands "fixed upon instruments requiring a steady purpose gave no weapon of defense to crush or brush off the blood-sucking insect." Birch bark cylinders stuffed with moss, bark, leaves, and twigs, "ignited to a smoking state" and hung around the neck, offered limited deterrence.

There were occasional distractions. A "country woman" encountered along the way "expressed joy at the prospect of soft Lake Erie water for washing-days," still under the popular impression that an inclined plane canal would be spilling the lake eastward across the state. At another spot beside the line, the entire survey party got inside the hollowed trunk of a massive buttonwood tree, "elbow to elbow, facing inward, with backs against its inner side [and] room for more." At Salina, "the novices of the party" played tourist at a saltworks.

Despite their travails, Wright's crew found a relatively direct level for forty-five miles from Rome west to Salina, and confirmed that the outflows of lakes Onondaga, Skaneateles, and Owasco would provide plenty of water for a minimally locked thirty-mile stretch of canal leading on to the Seneca River. "I feel much pleased with the rout [sic] I have passed over," Wright wrote to Holley. "[T]he more critical the examination the more easy and practicable the great route of Canal thro this part of the Country and in time I believe I can say that no country in the world presents so few obstacles to the execution of a work of this nature as the rout thro which I have passed." Wright collected "a considerable handsome bundle" of cession deeds from settlers along the route. He also encountered "those penurious, illiberal, avaricious beings" anxious for and likely to be benefited by the canal who withheld their deed signatures in the hopes of later collecting damages.

While Wright was in the field, the commissioners were busy. In July they met at Utica, typically without Ellicott, who stayed home claiming illness. Using all the information they had gathered about canals great and small, far and near, from books and personal inspection, Clinton, Holley, Young, and Van Rensselaer settled on the trapezoidal dimensions of their Erie canal: forty feet wide at the surface, four feet deep, and twenty-eight feet wide at the bottom, or a third larger than the Middlesex Canal. They also settled on a standard lock size of ninety feet by twelve (the Middlesex locks were eighty by ten or eleven). After making these essential decisions, Clinton, Holley, and Young headed overland to Buffalo, arriving at the prospective western terminus at the end of the month.

Weary but exhilarated, Clinton gazed at "the magnificent scenery of the lake" through the open window of his lodging room: "The wind northerly, and the surface of this sea gently ruffled—a square-rigged vessel sailing up the lake—a sail-boat passing to Canada, and a British vessel of war in sight." Most people still doubted that a canal could join the Hudson to the Great Lakes, but Clinton was sure "that these immense seas will in a few years be whitened with commerce—that they will be connected by inland navigation with the ocean, and that the place where I now write will, in all human probability, before the passing away of the present generation, be the second city in the State—the mind is lost in wonder and perplexed and confounded with the immensity of the ideas which press upon it."

Joseph Ellicott, recovered from his latest (probably imaginary) indisposition, welcomed his fellow commissioners to Buffalo. He had a new idea to press on Clinton's confounded mind. Ellicott the land agent had long been concerned about the limited benefit to the Holland Company from the canal route long favored and currently being surveyed by Geddes: the flat arc from the middle of Tonawanta Creek north through the great ridge, then east in its diminishing shadow to the Genesee, and on to the Seneca River. Commissioner Ellicott now suggested surveying the "southern route": from the headwaters of the Tonawanta through swamps and marshes bordering the company's Batavia base to Black Creek, which drained east into the Genesee. This route would remain south of the ridge—"the great Slope" in Ellicott's parlance—and avoid a worrisome amount of engineering and blasting powder to penetrate its dense limestone. In 1812, then-commissioners Morris and Eddy had requested such a survey of Ellicott, but the outbreak of war had prevented it. Now a commissioner himself, Ellicott was eager to prove it practicable.

Always a "Geddis" detractor, Ellicott proposed for the job his nephew and clerk-turned-surveyor, William Peacock, Jesse Hawley's old friend. Ellicott offered to employ Peacock at Holland Company expense. "[A]s to passing over extended surface my Engineer will not bear a comparison with Engineer Geddis," Ellicott later conceded grudgingly to commissioner Young; "However I have the satisfaction to believe that [Peacock's] level and work will bear the test of scrutiny and will be found faithful, precise, and such as to deserve the public confidence."

It was an offer Ellicott's fellow commissioners couldn't easily refuse. By accepting it, they kept the mercurial power broker happy and got a free and nonbinding option against any doubts about Geddes's "northern" route. Ellicott's bid to oversee all western section surveying had been rejected by the other commissioners in May; now he kept a hand in the evolving two-pronged western game. What mattered wasn't just *how* the canal made its way west, but *where* it got to: Ellicott's Buffalo on the lake or Peter Porter's Black Rock just down the Niagara River and outside Ellicott's fiefdom. Even though Clinton already imagined Buffalo as New York's second city, the long and bitter contest between the two settlements to be named the canal's western terminus lay on the distant horizon, and all parties knew it. Ellicott's southern strategy would lead the canal away from Black Rock.

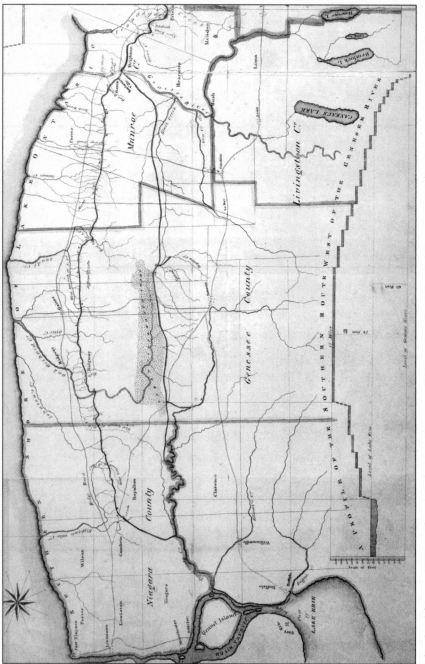

This detail from an 1821 canal commission map shows so-called "northern" and "southern" route options for the western portion of the canal, from Rochesterville to different points on Tonawanta Creek and down to Lake Erie. Joseph Ellicott eventually acknowledged that a southern route through Holland Company land was too high and dry, and the commissioners opted for the northern route originally proposed by James Geddes. (*The Lionel Pincus and Princess Firyal Map Division, The New York Public Library, Astor, Lenox and Tilden Foundations*)

Leaving the simmering rivalries of the west, Clinton, Holley, and Young headed back east, "examining the land and the water with a scrutinizing eye, superintending our operations, and exploring all our facilities and embarrassments." At Pittsford, then a tiny settlement just east of the Genesee, they met up with Geddes, who had been working his way west from the Seneca. The commissioners and their primary western surveyor examined his proposed site for the canal's Genesee River crossing and walked "the difficult grounds" of the Irondequoit Valley, where nearly eight years earlier Geddes had shouted "Eureka" across the snow-drifted ridges. Now, even as they authorized Ellicott to look south, Clinton and the others were "entirely satisfied that the impediments will fall short of anticipation" on the north.

Continuing east, the commissioners converged on Wright's party at Manlius, a hamlet three-quarters of the way along his long level to Salina. "He will experience no embarrassments from swamps or deep cuttings, and the supply of water will be exuberant" all the way to the Seneca, Clinton wrote confidently to Ellicott.

By mid-August Ellicott's southern man Peacock had been busy along his survey line, though not without trouble. He had not tested the accuracy of his favorite leveling instrument in a long time and was chagrined to find that, "owing to the loss of one of the small screws, I suppose," the instrument was "very much out of true." To Ellicott, he confessed privately "little confidence" in a good portion of his survey. Still, Peacock preened that the survey overall was "a more particular examination of the country than ever had been made before." Under the strict orders and occasionally severe eye of his boss, Peacock spent weeks gauging flows in a dozen brooks and creeks that were essential to the feasibility of the southern route. Ellicott understood that "without a sufficient supply of water the canal itself if formed would be even worse than useless." Fortunately the region was experiencing a drought greater "than ever before observed by the Indians," making for easier work and worst-case measurements.

The question of the western terminus would grow heated and hostile, but Clinton returned east in mid-August personally convinced that Buffalo, burned to the ground thirty-two months earlier and struggling to recover its prewar population of fifteen hundred, would prevail: "[I]n 50 years it will be next to N. York in wealth and population."

The general excitement Clinton felt back in Buffalo had deepened: "We have looked at all the difficult points, ascended the mountains, penetrated forests, descended into wide-spreading and deeply excavated ravines, and have, upon the whole, encountered more fatigue than I thought I could bear." All that he found in the west was "most satisfactory. The work can be easily effected, and the utmost cost will not exceed our calculations." The commissioners had been warmly received and found opinion about the canal uniformly favorable throughout the west, with "scarcely a dissentient in this vast country."

A man of broad interests, Clinton also had made satisfying observations during his trip on natural history, geology, and "antiquities." It does not appear, though, that Ellicott ever passed along Clinton's request that Peacock, in "service to the cause of science," collect rare plants and minerals, the plants to be "inserted between leaves of paper and kept dry as possible." Ellicott's narrow interests did not include this sort of fieldwork.

In company with commissioner Young, Clinton headed north from Albany in late August to examine the route for the Champlain canal. He found "its practicability beyond all manner of doubt," and the people there both "very desirous" to see it built and "that the Western Canal shall proceed *pari passu*." By the time all the commissioners (that is, all but Ellicott) regrouped in September, their president was indisputably the most informed of them all.

While Peacock and Geddes continued into the fall tracing opposing ellipses across the west, Charles Brodhead was struggling through his difficult eastern survey. By early October his party had descended the Mohawk Valley from Rome just thirty-one miles to an encampment opposite the village of Herkimer.

Unlike the virgin western wilderness, the upper Mohawk was a region of merchants, travelers, and crude boatmen, raucous riverside taverns and public houses, with the comforts and discomforts of rough progress. The survey crew matted their tents with farmyard oat straw instead of fresh-cut hemlock, but the cook was able to serve a full board of fare fresh from harvest fields. Butternut and shag-barked walnut "afforded good pickings during leisure moments." The rock-ribbed, forest-crowded gorge of the Mohawk at Little Falls presented a natural beauty not yet eroded by development. The valley's rich alluvial flats hosted grand brick homes of "high-toned families," but their luxuriant fields were worked more by slaves than free farmhands.

Brodhead's party featured as surveyor Canvass White, beginning to glimpse his engineering destiny at twenty-six. For a young upstater, he had already traveled far and wide. After his schooling as a boy under Nathan Roberts, White had studied mathematics, astronomy, chemistry, mineralogy, and surveying at a Herkimer County academy and then with a private instructor. During a clerkship with a local merchant following the completion of his studies, White's health had faltered. Advised of the curative powers of salt air, he shipped out in the spring of 1811 as super-cargo on an American merchantman bound for Russia. On the return voyage during wartime the following year, the ship was briefly seized in England, then driven ashore by a storm. An inspection of the beached ship's bottom revealed rotten planking that otherwise might have caused it to sink during the Atlantic crossing. The captain pondered abandoning the ship on the English beach, but its young commercial officer, who had shown a genius for innovation since childhood, advised replacing the bad planking and then digging a channel a thousand feet through the sand to float the ship at high tide. This the crew did, and the ship sailed into New York a few weeks later, its health and that of its savior, White, materially restored.

The former prisoner had his revenge on the English at the end of the war. With a company of volunteers and a commission as a lieutenant, White took part in the seizure of Fort Erie on the British side of the Niagara River. He was severely wounded by a shell during the occupation, but recovered, and then captured a British reconnoitering party, killing or wounding several of its members and taking the rest prisoner. Canvass White was the rare young man of upstate New York in 1816 who knew war and the world.

Sprung from Wright's completed survey, William Young joined Brodhead's party in early October. He was thrilled to be in the field with his older cousin Canvass, who was "kind, quiet, and considerate in all his ways." The teen was considerably less taken with Brodhead, whom he found "cross, crabbed, petulant and uncongenial, but with his set associates, Utica exclusives." This may have been youthful impudence filtered through a reminiscence of fifty years, but it was a caution about the soon to become reclusive Brodhead, who would gain "no prominent and lasting stand as a civil engineer." A month after they teamed up on the upper Mohawk survey, White and Young celebrated the addition of Nathan Roberts to the extended White family, when cousin Lavinia married their old schoolteacher and new Erie surveying comrade.

As the summer of 1816 turned to fall, the perception of the public generally was that all the survey parties were doing remarkable jobs and bringing the canal closer to reality. "The Grand Canal," an eleven-stanza poem by one William Ray, was printed in many western newspapers:

> *Let* Clinton's *mental pow'rs unfold;*
> *Who first conceiv'd the project bold,*
> *To bid the western floods*
> *Revolt from nature's long control,*
> *Freely through new-mark'd regions roll,*
> *And leave th' astonish'd woods.*
>
> *Immortal be the statesman's name,*
> *Eternal be the patriot's fame,*
> *Who shall mature the plan!*
> *And draw those oceans from the west,*
> *To bathe th' Atlantic's heaving breast,*
> *A monument to man!*
>
> *"Bold is th' attempt, and wise the scheme;*
> *August the work, sublime the theme,*
> *May list'ning millions hear . . .*

This was just the sort of propaganda that Clinton knew was needed to unite the people behind the canal so that "its easy and cheap execution will be placed beyond the reach of cavil." Ellicott did his part with good news about Peacock's survey for the Batavia *Advocate*; its supportive editorial was picked up for the national readership of *Niles' Weekly Register*: "We are convinced that the undertaking is perfectly within the capacity of the state to undertake and complete."

Survey parties arrayed across New York from lakes Champlain to Erie were everywhere finding hard work but few troubles, but Paul Busti was not impressed. Mulling a renewal of the Holland Company's 100,000-acre offer, Busti wrote to Ellicott on All Hallows' Eve that "the magnitude of the undertaking of the Canal is so great that it is impossible for me to believe the work will ever be perfected." As the country surveyors masquerading as canal engineers turned from the lengthening shadows of the field to desks and drafting tables to prepare favorable accounts, there remained no general consensus that a canal would materialize from those surveys.

There was mischief making over governor Tompkins's brief speech on November 5. Opening a weeklong special session of the legislature to choose presidential electors, Tompkins suggested that state prisoners might be employed to assist in various state construction works, including canals. Clinton deemed this "a full exposure of the cloven foot of hostility." He affected horror at Tompkins's "sneer of contempt" for canal navigation, which if "effected at all it is to be the work of convicts." Anti-Clintonians saw less devil in the details. Tompkins's speech, which raised subjects only of "pressing and indispensable importance" during a largely single-issue session, actually was focused on the overcrowding of the state's single prison, at the Hudson River foot of Christopher Street in Manhattan. The governor was merely suggesting that rather than ease overcrowding with mild or reduced sentences, it might be better to legalize convict labor, especially for ongoing construction of a new upstate penitentiary at Auburn, just a few miles from the line of the prospective canal, which would logically be a proximate convict labor site. Whether provocative or naive, observed a Clintonian editor, Tompkins's "chilling" proposal was immediately "construed into a settled hostility" against the canal in advance of the main legislative seasons in Washington and Albany.

When Clinton met with his fellow commissioners a few days later in Albany, he brought word of the painful but curiously poetic demise of Gouverneur Morris. In September Morris, as the new president of the New-York Historical Society, had given a robust keynote address at a City Hall celebration. He had written recently to a friend that at age sixty-four he could still feel "the gayety of inexperience and the frolic of youth." A measure of frolic, though, had been curtailed by trouble with his penis.

Some years earlier in a backwoods setting, Morris of necessity had employed "a flexible piece of hickory" to successfully clear a urinary blockage. Beset anew, at Morrisania, the aging frolicker had less skillfully "forced a piece of whale bone thro' the Canal," causing lacerations, inflammation, and necrosis. It was, cruel observers might note, the second canal job he had botched. The final result, after what the newspapers discreetly called "a short but distressing illness," was death, at five in the morning on November 6, 1816, with Nancy by his side in the room of his birth overlooking the Harlem River, the wooded hills of upper Manhattan still dark before the dawn. The revolutionary generation and the salons (and boudoirs) of Europe and America lost a great member. The canal visionary was gone, but the canal maker was more than ready to take up the quest.

CHAPTER 7

"The Most Gigantic Undertaking"

[I]f this canal is to be a shower of gold, it will fall upon New-York [City]—if a river of gold it will run into her lap.

—Elisha Williams, April 8, 1817

[T]he man who will enter into this project, must be a madman, a fool, or a knave.

—Peter Livingston, April 14, 1817

If we must have war, or have a canal, I am in favour of the canal, and I vote for the bill.

—James Kent, April 15, 1817

Gouverneur Morris "filled a large space in the political history of this country," observed the New York *Evening Post* upon the death of the Constitution draftsman and Erie Canal dreamer. De Witt Clinton paused, along with fellow New Yorkers, for the funeral, and then resumed the quest for the canal that Morris had failed to create.

In January 1809 Joshua Forman had traveled to Washington seeking support for New York's cross-state canal. President Jefferson told Forman it was "madness" and sent him home. In December 1811 Morris and Clinton had sought support in Washington but found President Madison ambivalent and Congress interested but ultimately unwilling. Now, five Decembers later and a few weeks after Morris's demise, Clinton headed south alone into the hostile territory of the Virginia Dynasty. It was to be a brief visit, to deliver a formal application for federal aid. Again, the portents were unfavorable.

On December 3, 1816, Madison had issued his eighth and final annual message to Congress. It included a directive on canals but, compared with his strong statement a year earlier, this one contained ambiguity: "I particularly invite again [Congress'] attention to the expediency of exercising their *existing powers*, and, *where necessary*, of resorting to the prescribed mode of enlarging them, in order to effectuate a comprehensive system of roads and canals" (emphasis added).

In 1787 at Philadelphia, Madison had failed to convince his fellow conventioneers to write broad internal improvement powers into the Constitution. A few weeks later, in the fourteenth *Federalist*, he wrote expansively of the new nation's many rivers as natural "canals . . . which art finds it so little difficult to connect and complete." Now, only months from the end of his long political career, Madison leaned hard on constitutional amendment before federal support of the canalling arts, though it was not absolutely clear what he meant by the *existing powers* of Congress and *where* it was *necessary* to enlarge them.

The day after Madison's message, his secretary of state and fellow Virginian James Monroe crushed New York's senior senator Rufus King's bid for the White House, winning all but three states. The Federalists had sent their final national candidate to a humiliating defeat. Virginia had another winner. With Monroe—and vice president elect Daniel Tompkins—waiting in the wings, select committees in the House and Senate were formed to deal with Madison's canal policy.

Clinton arrived at the capital a few days after the election, bearing the application from New York's canal commissioners for federal support. It was presented in the House on December 11 by freshman Micah Brooks, who eight years earlier as a state assemblyman had brought to Albany the "Hercules" essays of jailed Jesse Hawley. The commissioners' appeal to Congress for land or money employed the familiar political, economic, and social arguments in favor of nation-unifying works. But there was something new now, a tone of independence and impatience, veiled in condescension: "The state of New-York is not unaware of her interests, nor disinclined to prosecute them; but where those of the general government are united with hers, and seem to be paramount, she deems it her duty to ask for their assistance." The application was referred to the House select committee on roads and canals, of which Brooks was a member.

In case Congress didn't get New York's more aggressive position, canal commissioner Joseph Ellicott made it clear to his Washington representatives. Writing to Brooks, Ellicott ranted that "if the State shall accomplish the navigation unaided by the national Legislature the State will unquestionably retain the jurisdiction, police, and supreme control over it, and may exercise that control in such manner as to be extremely injurious to the U.S. territories, and exclusively beneficial to the State." Ellicott intended for Brooks to make this attitude understood around Congress.

A few days later, Ellicott sent a long rant to another disciple, Archibald Clarke, a Buffalo pioneer who held the House seat vacated in mid-term by former canal commissioner Peter B. Porter to become New York's secretary of state. Ellicott vilified James "Geddis" as an adherent of Morris's "visionary projects" like the inclined plane (even though Geddes had always favored a level and locked canal and scorned the "canal notions" of Morris: "his ignorance of the country to be passed, and his pertinacity was such, that it was almost impossible to call his attention to the impracticability of such a thing."). For his part, Ellicott admitted that he knew nothing about the route east of his territory, but claimed that the entire canal could be built on levels in less than five years for less than $6.5 million if "some visionary theorist" didn't get involved.

For all his impertinence, Ellicott had accurately gauged congressional uncertainty. Brooks reported back that the lingering belief that New York still favored an inclined plane design "has had a tendency to produce doubts of the practicability of the Erie canal." Brooks had discovered that South Carolina Republican John Calhoun favored New York's project but was anxious for "correct surveys" showing it really could and would be built with locks and levels: "[I]f he could be convinced that it could be effected by any reasonable sum he would give it all the support in his power." Calhoun's power was considerable. He was already trying to legislate a national improvements system of his own design.

A future vice president and perennial cabinet secretary and congressional leader, Calhoun is chiefly remembered today as the "Great Nullifier," after his early national statesmanship curdled into a Southern parochialism that would have allowed states to declare null and void certain acts of Congress. Calhoun's states' rights defense of slavery helped bring on the Civil War after his death in 1850. In the second session of the 14th Congress, though, John Calhoun was a still young and idealistic advocate of union-binding improvements.

Calhoun had been dismayed by early quibbling in the House and Senate select committees. So he bypassed them by gaining the appointment of a committee "to inquire into the expediency of setting apart the bonus, and the net annual proceeds of the National Bank, as a permanent fund for internal improvement." Just before Christmas, Calhoun introduced what became known as the Bonus Bill, a bill that effectively aimed to revive the Gallatin Plan under Calhoun's leadership.

Compared with earlier contrivances to fund internal improvements with federal monies, using the new Second Bank of the United States as a revenue source was straightforward. The fund for national improvements would consist of the $1.5 million bonus just paid to the federal government by the bank to obtain its charter, plus future dividends on the government's $7 million worth of stock in the bank, which was opening for business in January 1817. The Treasury secretary would manage the fund, with an estimated annual yield of $650,000, and invest the balance in U.S. stock; Congress would appropriate funds for road and canal projects specifically requested by states. Calhoun had led the successful effort to charter the bank. Treasury Secretary William Crawford of Georgia and his Treasury predecessor, Gallatin, were avid supporters of Calhoun's bank and bill.

Six weeks after introducing the Bonus Bill, Calhoun got it up for debate before the full House. His speech on February 4, 1817, sought to draw a bold line directly from Madison's fourteenth *Federalist* of 1787, through the Gallatin Plan of 1808, to the peaceful and flourishing nation of 1817.

Calhoun was tall and imposing, an elegant speaker with graceful gestures and persuasive manner. He naturally commanded the attentions of the House. "To legislate for our country requires not only the most enlarged views, but a species of self-devotion not exacted in any other. . . . It must be submitted to as the condition of our greatness." It was imperative that networks of roads and canals increase with the nation's territory: "Whatever impedes the intercourse of the extremes with this, the centre of the Republic, weakens the Union." Calhoun spread open the map of needed national communications: between Maine and Louisiana, the Atlantic seaboard cities and the western states, New Orleans and the uncharted west, the Hudson and the Great Lakes. Having been assured by Micah Brooks and others that New York indeed intended to build a level and locked canal, Calhoun placed New York's project near the top of his long list: "In a political, commercial, and military point of view, few objects could be more important." Virginians cringed.

Sensitive to Madison's constitutional issues, Calhoun addressed the question of Congress's right to be the nation's communications maker. Admittedly "no advocate for refined arguments on the Constitution," Calhoun pronounced it an "instrument . . . not intended as a thesis for the logician to exercise his ingenuity on. It ought to be construed with plain, good sense." His sense of Article I, Section 8 was that its failure to include canals and (non-post) roads was irrelevant in this case because the language of the Bonus Bill didn't sanction particular national works through possibly nonconsenting states. The bill merely provided money for future projects that states wanted.

The "general welfare" clause leading off Section 8 was a bit trickier. By Calhoun's interpretation, the power of Congress "To lay and collect Taxes, Duties, Imposts and Excises, to pay the Debts and provide for the common Defence and general Welfare of the United States" was not limited to establishing post roads and the other powers *enumerated* in the section's seventeen succeeding clauses but only *outlined* by them. If the use of money was restricted to the enumerated powers, Calhoun asked, how could one justify previous congressional appropriations for distressed refugee populations, the Louisiana Purchase, or the ongoing National Road?

The National Road was the nearest thing to the canals and roads envisioned by Calhoun, but a portentous precedent. Otherwise known as the Cumberland Road because of its starting point in Cumberland, Maryland, the macadam highway west had been ordered by Jefferson, promoted by Gallatin, initially funded by Congress in 1806, and finally begun in 1811. In 1817 the embryonic interstate had nearly reached the Ohio River at Wheeling. There, however, its progress would soon be halted, first by the financial Panic of 1819, and then by Monroe's 1822 veto on constitutional grounds of a bill for further financing. When individual states finally took over repairs and new work starting in the 1830s, the road was no longer national.

Calhoun could not foresee this in early 1817. But in placing greater value on nation-binding improvements than on strict constitutional interpretation, the Republican leader was lurching up the highway of implied powers hacked through the constitutional wilderness by Hamilton but little traveled by Madison.

Heedless, Calhoun proclaimed: "Let us . . . bind the Republic together with a perfect system of roads and canals. . . . Let us conquer space." Before closing, he warned that if his plan for internal improvements did not win approval at a time of peace and growing prosperity in 1817 "it is certainly very doubtful whether it ever will." He was more right than he imagined.

Back in New York, Clinton and the canal commissioners were watching closely. The week before Calhoun introduced the Bonus Bill in the House, the commissioners sent a letter to the state's congressional delegation. Bearing Clinton's signature, it was guidance—what might now be called talking points—for the legislators to help them debate and vote on Bonus Bill provisions in New York's best interests. As Clinton saw it, population was the "fair and unexceptionable standard" on which to make bonus funds available. This would be a convenient standard: New York was just then finally overtaking Virginia as the most populous state. Clinton estimated that New York alone should be entitled annually to $85,000. If the entitlements of Ohio and Vermont, which Clinton argued stood to benefit directly from the Erie and Champlain canals, were allocated to New York, the state should be entitled to $140,000 a year.

This, by Clinton's calculations, would pay for construction of the two canals, newly repriced by the commissioners at $6 million and $1 million, respectively.

Clinton explained how. If construction were funded entirely with loans at the prevailing 6 percent rate, total interest would be $420,000. The state's only obligation would be to service the debt, not pay off the principal. Because loans would be taken only as needed over years of construction, an annual federal contribution of $140,000 would form "an accumulating fund, which . . . would enable us to execute these great works without imposing any taxes." Thus, the federal government through the Bonus Bill would pay to build New York's canals.

Clinton had a warning for delegation members who might question his plan or oppose the canals generally: do not "be hostile to the appropriation of an adequate revenue, which will promote the object, without any inconvenience to your constituents." Elected New Yorkers who closed the tap in Washington, Clinton implied, might drink political poison back home.

One hostile representative was Erastus Root, the Republican leader of Delaware County. An erstwhile Clinton supporter turned implacable foe, Root was a perennial officeholder in Albany and Washington. He was "a little uncouth in his manner, and rough . . . sometimes rude in his expressions," wrote one of his peers, but "his wit was keen and his sarcasms severe and biting . . . his illustrations were exceedingly clear and well chosen, and his attacks upon his opponents were severe almost to ferocity." Clinton called him "the Root of all evil."

Moments after Calhoun asked the House "to conquer space," Root rose to conquer Calhoun. He argued that all road projects should be excluded from the Bonus Bill: "A South Carolinian or Georgian may find a trip to Congress more easy and pleasant, but is it fair to tax the industrious and the provident to make roads for the negligent?" And he objected broadly to the entire concept of federal funding for state or local projects: promises of money "would either be broken in cases of emergency, or embarrass the fiscal operations of Government."

Over several days of intense debate, Root found few adherents among his fellow New Yorkers. Oneida County Federalist Thomas Gold argued that funds were due New York because its port "yields to the Government nearly one-third of the commercial revenue of the Union," more in a year than the entire anticipated cost of the Erie canal. John B. Yates, a Schenectady Republican and no friend of Clinton's, nevertheless offered fresh details of Canadian inroads into American commerce and vowed that if Congress failed to act, New York would build its canals "without such assistance."

Sectional, rather than political or constitutional, concerns drove the House debate. Massachusetts Federalist Cyrus King argued furiously that a federally supported Erie canal would "build up the already overgrown State of New York." Across two houses, Calhoun's bill divided half-brothers; New York's pro-Bonus Rufus King was waiting in the Senate.

On February 8 the Bonus Bill passed the House by the slimmest of margins: 86–84. "When the Clerk announced the vote a buz [sic] was heard thro' the house: 'New York has carried it'." Calhoun's plan may have been national, but the smart money knew that New York, with its well-publicized plans and superior population, stood to benefit most. Newspapers across the state reported that the House had "passed the bill to aid in the opening of the Canal from Lake Erie to the Hudson."

New England, with old Federalists fearful of the country's western movement, voted overwhelmingly against the bill. The smaller Middle Atlantic states were substantially opposed. The Southern states, with varied geographic blessings, were narrowly opposed. The westernmost states, some bordering and some isolated from navigable rivers, were narrowly in favor. The victory was delivered by Pennsylvania and New York, with a quarter of the country's population and congressmen. Pennsylvania approved by 17–6, New York by 25–2; only a minor Westchester Republican joined irascible Root in the nay column. Virginia voted 15–8 against. All Virginia's nays were Republicans, but three Republicans voted yes. Had just one of them toed the party line, the Bonus Bill would not have made it out of the House.

The Senate debate focused more on constitutional issues, but the results three weeks later were slightly more favorable. On February 28 the Bonus Bill passed, with minor amendments, by 20–15. New York's canals were as good as funded.

Two days later Calhoun and others paid a Sunday call at the White House to offer their regards to Madison, whose presidency was ending the next day. On the visitors' way out, the "father of the Constitution" took aside the Carolina statesman half his age. Calhoun was astounded at what Madison calmly said. In the morning, in his final hours as president, Madison would not be signing the Bonus Bill. In fact, he would be vetoing it. "[N]ot even an earthquake that should have swallowed up one half of this city, could have excited more surprise," declared House speaker Henry Clay, who, with the rest of the congressional majority, had assumed they were doing Madison's bidding with Calhoun's national plan. Fifteen months after he had set Congress in motion on national improvements, and just as New York was set to gain an advantage on his Old Dominion, Madison swung his constitutional crutch and toppled everything.

For Madison, who had built the Constitution when Calhoun was a boy, the veto decision was sudden, but easy and inescapable. Congress, the president decided after all, had no "existing powers" to fund roads and canals. To construe such authority from the Constitution's general welfare clause would be contrary to "established and consistent" interpretation. It would render "nugatory and improper" the "special and careful" enumerated powers following the clause. As he explained further in later writings, Madison's commitment to the progress of the nation required strict adherence to the protections from tyranny embedded in its Constitution. He never directly acknowledged that, in the case of the Bonus Bill, restricting federal power also served a more parochial purpose: hindering New York from getting a westward leg up on Virginia.

New Yorkers were outraged. In his last three days in office, wrote one city paper, Madison had approved a bill that gave federal money for public roads and canals in Mississippi, but to the Bonus Bill, which would have benefited New York, "he gave a Parthian, parting blow, and retired to Virginia—pleased with his last act." Faced with the prospect of funding a canal that might elevate New York to "the most exalted station in the union . . . Mr. Madison [had] suddenly become wonderfully delicate and squeamish upon the provisions of the constitution," observed an Albany paper. "[T]he chosen ones of the south might still strive to make her move in a secondary sphere . . . New York must therefore depend solely on herself." "If she wishes to attain that rank in the union," echoed another editor, "to which she is entitled by her wealth, population, territory and natural advantages, she must burst the shackles of Virginia—cast off her allegiance to the 'RICHMOND CLUB,'—and advance boldly to the work."

The terms of the fourth president and Fourteenth Congress came to an end, and with them the prospects for a network of nation-binding roads and canals. Internal improvements as a federal activity would remain blocked through two Monroe administrations, until John Quincy Adams—and his vice president John Calhoun—brought different constitutional scruples to the executive branch in 1825. By then New York was preparing to celebrate the completion of its Erie Canal.

"After swallowing the National Bank and the Cumberland Road," a stunned De Witt Clinton wondered to Rufus King, "it was not to be supposed that Mr. Madison would strain at canals; but so it is." Clinton later railed at Madison's "reprehensible conduct" and his "totally indefensible" constitutional objection to canals but not to a national bank or road, or even coastal lighthouses: a "miserable sophism."

Clinton and other New York canalists had been looking to Washington no less for federal money than for validation of their ongoing efforts in the state legislature to pass a law authorizing construction. In 1816 Congress's restraint had compounded Albany's. Would Madison's veto have a similar effect in 1817? New York's lawmakers had no constitutional anxiety, but the latest rejection in Washington could send either a chill or a challenge up the Hudson. The legislature had opened in Albany in mid-January with no certainty of favorable action on canals. Indeed, the large delegation of senators and assemblyman sent to Albany by New York City in 1817 was to a man opposed to all things Clinton.

As the legislature took up its first items of business, Clinton and fellow canal commissioners Samuel Young and Myron Holley met in Albany to organize for the battle ahead. They studied the latest surveys from Geddes, Wright, Brodhead, and William Peacock; all were thorough, and essential to the report the commissioners were preparing. The commissioners also sent solicitations for information from the builders of the several short private canals in New York and to the superintendent of the Middlesex Canal in Massachusetts. Clinton, Young, Holley, and Stephen Van Rensselaer each wrote to fellow commissioner Ellicott, asking that he bring his "intelligence and influence" and "extensive knowledge" to Albany. Ellicott replied with the usual excuse of "indispensable duties" preventing any travel east.

In his stead, Ellicott sent maps and a detailed account of the Peacock survey party's findings (and a bill for $1,500 in expenses). Ellicott put the cost of a sixty-two-mile southern route at a very modest $450,000, with ten locks accounting for a quarter of the total. He took pains to show how Peacock's meticulous stream gaugings indicated the supply of enough canal water for the daily passage of exactly 168.39 thirty-ton boats in an eight-month season. "[T]here cannot be a question," Ellicott sought to assure his fellow commissioners, "but that the supply of water for the use of a canal navigation this route is fully commensurate with any extent that may be required." Absent their own explorations of the southern route and any direct dialogue with Ellicott or Peacock, the commissioners at Albany for the time being did not dispute their distant colleague's deductions. But they were newly suspicious of a route that Ellicott now acknowledged had a summit nearly seventy-five feet above the level of Lake Erie. Watering the southern route could only be difficult at best.

The commissioners' January meeting produced Clinton's directive to the state's congressional delegation about the Bonus Bill, with the cost estimate of $6 million for the Erie project. The number was little changed from what Hercules had suggested a decade earlier. Now that the canal was edging closer to becoming a reality, and farther from the effusions of a maniac, however, the expense loomed large. In January 1817 there was barely $20 million in banking and insurance capital in New York State. But a broader economy was emerging. Within a few months of its opening in early 1817, the Manhattan branch of the new Bank of the United States would take in over $5 million in cash deposits and nearly $3 million more in securities.

Among the matters that remained unsettled after the commissioners' January meeting was a land donation by the Holland Company. In a three-way correspondence through January and well into February, company boss Paul Busti in Philadelphia, canal commissioner Clinton in Albany, and Ellicott out west—acting more as company land agent than state canal commissioner—performed a delicate ballet. Busti dangled but avoided a commitment with Clinton, while confiding to Ellicott, "I cannot divest myself of my old opinion that if ever begun [the canal] will in no age be completed."

The legislature did not take up canals until mid-February, a month into the session. All the while, Clinton, Young, and Holley remained in Albany "not idle in regard to their high trust"—that is, lobbying—while preparing their report. Back in December, Young had agreed to prepare and anonymously publish a "plain and practical treatise, of trifling expense" to sway the minds of "the common reader" about canals. The pamphlet was to lay out the steps in the creation of a canal, from surveys through operation and management. "A Treatise on Inland Navigation" emerged from an Albany-area press at the beginning of February. The 150-page primer was little more than the canal article and other relevant articles from *Rees' Encyclopaedia*, abridged and "divided into chapters, merely for the readers' convenience." It was the equivalent of a campaign biography. Appended for good measure and without comment was the Gallatin Plan, in its latest published resuscitation.

The commissioners drafted their report with Clinton's political prospects on the rise. Governor Tompkins had floated the notion of remaining in office beyond his March accession to the vice presidency, but opponents and indignant supporters were shortly to prevail on him to quit as state executive. In late February lieutenant governor John Tayler was to assume Tompkins's duties until a new governor was chosen in the May state elections. The new governor would be a Republican, because the sagging Federalists were not expected to field a candidate. The choice of Tammany, and especially Clinton protégé turned nemesis Van Buren, to be Tompkins's elected successor was secretary of state Peter Porter. Porter, however, was perceived by many Republicans to be a likely loser in a nomination battle with Clinton. To Van Buren, Porter confessed privately that he did "not possess the requisite talents & qualifications for [the] office." John Pintard predicted, "Clinton will certainly be . . .

elected Governor, notwithstanding the howlings of the Panther Tribe in Tammanys [sic] Den."

Pintard was writing on February 15, the same Saturday that Clinton, Holley, Young, and Van Rensselaer met to complete their report and sign it. Ellicott was not present at Albany and did not sign the report. When it was delivered to the assembly on Monday, the report noted in a post-script that the missing commissioner "was not consulted on the details" but "approves its general principles."

It had been six years since New York's canal commissioners had written a substantial report. The report of 1811, exuberantly written by Gouverneur Morris, was essential but preliminary; it was short on details—of which there were few on which to expand—but Morris's gravitas gave it substance. The exhaustive 1817 report, seventy-five printed pages long, was a construction blueprint. It synthesized a vast array of information with little of the rhetorical flourish or empty bluster of earlier reports. The 1817 report was a compelling, if imperfect, document.

The commissioners' report reflected the painstaking efforts of their surveyors. The bulk of the canal route had been "carefully designated by bench marks, level pegs, and other fixtures." In each of their sections, Wright, Geddes, Brodhead, and Peacock reported sinking deep shafts at regular intervals to determine the nature of the ground, enabling "a just estimation of the labor required, and the expense to be incurred" in laying the canal. In all, "great pains have been taken to collect all the facts which might be requisite to elucidate the facilities in favor, and the impediments in the way, of this great undertaking." This was a moderately verbose way of saying that not every fact had been collected.

The main feature of the report was an analysis of the Erie route from the Mohawk at Schoharie Creek to the western Genesee Valley, and from there to Lake Erie by either Geddes's northern route or Peacock's southern route. The report reeled off mile-by-mile details of terrain and soil, and named the materials required to lay a canal through them. There were expense projections for grubbing, clearing, and excavation, and for embankments, culverts, deep cuttings, locks, dams, aqueducts, waste weirs, bridges, and feeder canals, to be fashioned of stone, iron, or wood. Calculations filled columned pages: grubbing at $500 per mile through easy terrain; soft earth excavation at twelve and a half cents per cubic yard; an aqueduct over the Oriskany Creek along the upper Mohawk River for $15,000; dozens of masonry locks at $10,000 apiece; engineering services at $1,000 per mile; and so forth. The report was a verbal atlas of the geography, topology, and geology of the breadth of the state, albeit in a narrow band: rivers, creeks, brooks, springs, swamps, marshes, mud flats, meadows, and forests; ridges, hills, valleys, and ravines; and granite, limestone, yellow slate gravel, red sandstone, marl, "stiff brown clay," sand, and loam. Canal structures would have to tame several "mad streams" of the Mohawk Valley. If Geddes's northern route were chosen, conquering the "mountain ridge" would require as many as eight locks.

The commissioners reported their intention to employ and manage the builders. They budgeted such details as $40,000 for carts, plows, scrapers, wheelbarrows, iron bars, pickaxes, shovels, chains, and other tools; $20,000 for workers' barracks; $10,000 for clerk and lock keeper houses; and $5,000 for temporary workshops for carpenters, smiths, and stone cutters. The commissioners had not yet embraced the idea of contracting out the work in small sections as the Middlesex Canal proprietors had done to avoid the direct costs and other headaches of supplying and overseeing a large labor force, a practice that would become standard in American civil engineering.

In all, the report priced the Erie canal at $4.85 million. This was substantially less than the $6 million that Clinton had estimated in his letter to New York's congressional delegation just four weeks earlier. Then, Clinton had been looking for as much federal money as might be available. Now he was trying to make the project palatable to his state legislature.

The bulk of the canal—the 250 miles from the Mohawk Valley at Schoharie to the Genesee Valley—presented relatively few major issues. The commissioners dealt carefully with the uncertainties of the sixty westernmost miles and the forty easternmost miles.

On the west, the commissioners had "determined that it would be expedient" to connect the canal to Lake Erie at Buffalo. Ellicott's man Peacock had started his survey from the Holland Company village, but it was unclear if Peacock's southern route would work: "[T]he canal should certainly take" the southern route if "every doubt" about its water supply was removed. There was much doubt, but none was expressed in the report. The report omitted any mention of Peter Porter's Black Rock, as well as the emerging differences of opinion among the commissioners and the surveyor-engineers that would make neither Buffalo nor Black Rock a sure thing for many more years.

On the east, the commissioners downplayed the Schoharie–Albany segment and the daunting Cohoes Falls. There had been no survey of this section because, the commissioners briefly noted, none of their surveyors "had time." No explanation was offered for why another surveyor with a freer schedule wasn't hired. Instead, the commissioners asserted that a route from Schoharie along the south bank of the Mohawk River and turning south before Cohoes to meet the Hudson near Albany was "practicable without a very serious expense." For this assertion, they relied on their "personal knowledge," the decades-old Western Inland Lock Navigation Company surveys done by Benjamin Wright, and, yet again, the favorable but creaky opinions of long-repatriated Englishman William Weston. The report noted without comment that these forty-two miles, which accounted for less than 12 percent of the canal's total length, featured 40 percent—286 of 661 feet—of aggregate level changes, requiring thirty of the anticipated seventy-seven locks. The commissioners estimated the Schoharie–Albany segment at $1.1 million, the same amount as for the twice-longer upper segment of the eastern section. For those who did math, the commissioners were projecting the Schoharie–Albany segment to cost $26,000 per mile. That was nearly triple the rate of the western and middle sections, and far beyond the rates of the greatest European canals and the small and scattered private works in America.

There were other negatives. Back in January, the commissioners had sent applications for financial assistance to the governors of Ohio, Kentucky, and Vermont over Clinton's signature. Vermont and Kentucky had not bothered to reply, and Ohio's legislature had responded only with a request for more information. A year's worth of inquiries in European loan markets had come up empty. The Holland Company had yet to renew its land offer. The commissioners simply asserted that "a munificent spirit" on land donations would arise once the project was approved and that "as much money" as needed could be borrowed within the country. And, if no aid was forthcoming from other states or Congress, New York had the power to levy high duties on goods transported to and from other states and territories "and thereby secure, eventually, a greater fund than can possibly arise from any present contributions from those quarters."

This is what distinguished the 1817 commissioners' report: overwhelming detail about what was certain, measured optimism about what was not, short shrift given to uncertainties that opponents might seize on. The report concluded with a dire warning about failing to build a canal across the state: "[U]nless it is established, the greater part of the trade, which does not descend the Mississippi, from all those vast and fertile regions west of the Seneca lake, will be lost to the United States."

Five hundred copies of the report were printed as a thick pamphlet for sale and distribution. "I cannot but believe that when our report is read and understood," Holley wrote to Ellicott the next day, "the Legislature will be disposed to take efficient measures for the accomplishment of this great work." When he had read the report on which he had avoided putting his name, Ellicott gushed to Clinton that he and the other three commissioners "have immortalized their names by their unparalleled industry, enterprise & perseverance."

A joint committee was named to review the report and recommend a course of action. The committee's agenda was largely empty while the Bonus Bill worked its way through Congress. In the meantime, Ellicott's boss finally gave at least the appearance of supporting the canal. Although privately still "incredulous of its ever be[ing] perfected if begun," Paul Busti formally renewed the offer of 100,000 acres of company land on the Pennsylvania border. This was the land that had been offered back in 1811 and withdrawn in 1814. In the company's calculated interest, Busti also threw in a sixty-six-foot-wide right-of-way for the canal wherever it might pass through company land, conditioned on the state building "a good and safe harbor" at Buffalo, the company town on Lake Erie. Busti confided to Ellicott that this condition might stir "the jealousy of the Black Rock partizans." Leading Black Rock partisan Peter Porter was already steaming over the preference shown for Buffalo in the commissioners' report. Busti's harbor-for-land gambit was another slap at Porter's ample cheek that would not go unanswered.

The following week, Tompkins resigned as governor and the Bonus Bill passed the U.S. Senate. A few days later, Madison's veto hit Albany "in the very crisis" of the legislative season. Suddenly the viability the Erie project was at risk. There would be no federal funds to pay for construction. There would be no national plan, with New York's canal as the key piece. After a decade of hope, interrupted by war, the bold Gallatin model was finally dead. If it were to be built, the longest canal in the world would be a remote, wilderness project of a state with limited financial resources and the elected representatives of its major city opposed to it.

Clinton and the other commissioners at Albany were indignant at the rejection from Washington, but immediately set about to control the damage. They countered first with what passed for a celebrity in the limited world of American canalling. By the end of the veto week, they had brought to Albany John Langdon Sullivan, superintendent of Massachusetts's Middlesex Canal. In ten years on the job, John Sullivan had turned the country's most substantial canal from a notorious failure into a singular success.

Sullivan's father James had been the main developer of the project that sought to link the Merrimack and Charles rivers. Begun in the early 1790s, with accurate but expensive surveys by William Weston, the canal was not completed until 1803. The Middlesex was only twenty-seven miles long but required twenty locks and eight aqueducts. It cost a staggering $528,000. Repairs, uncollected tolls, and sluggish traffic hampered operations and stifled profits until the death of the elder Sullivan (then the Massachusetts governor) in 1808, when his thirty-year-old son took over as superintendent.

A student of European canals, John Sullivan quickly began transforming Middlesex from a drain on its prominent, oft-assessed investors (John Adams among them) into an efficient and profitable operation. The canal became an important conduit of manufactured goods from Boston to the New England interior, and of coal, granite, produce, and especially timber from New Hampshire to Boston. During the war New

Hampshire timber traveled the canal to the Boston Navy Yard to repair the U.S.S. *Constitution* and build the U.S.S. *Independence*. By 1817, under Sullivan's superintendence, annual toll receipts had quintupled, to $32,000. His compensation was generous—$1,500 salary plus 5 percent of tolls—but complaints were few and the company paid its first dividends two years later.

In its early years Middlesex had been widely perceived as the Massachusetts twin of New York's hapless Western Inland Company: paragons of unvirtuous private enterprise. By 1817 John Sullivan was transforming Middlesex into an exemplary model for the proponents of the Erie canal. Though only a fraction of the length of New York's proposed canal, the Middlesex was proving that canal transportation could be practical and economical. And its basic dimensions—a width of thirty feet on the surface narrowing to twenty at a three-foot depth—made it a nearly perfect three-quarter scale model for Erie.

Unlike Englishman William Weston, whose degree of favorable opinion about early American engineering projects tended to increase in proportion with his compensation, Sullivan gave his professional opinions freely but with moderation. Commissioners Holley and Young, who had consulted with Sullivan during their examination of his canal in 1816, had found him "very intelligent" and obliging in all respects. Now Sullivan told New York's lawmakers that the geography of the Erie route was "peculiarly favorable" and the commissioners' cost estimate "high enough." He deemed sufficient the cost estimates for the middle and western sections, and for locks and aqueducts. He doubted whether the cost projection for the unsurveyed Schoharie–Albany segment "has been sufficiently considered," but the route appeared to him no more difficult than the worst of the nearly lock-per-mile Middlesex. In sum, Sullivan saw nothing to prevent New York from accomplishing its "great object."

Sullivan was the commissioners' star witness, but they were also pleased to publicize a letter solicited from Canandaigua mill owner Philetus Swift. Overseeing the construction in 1806 of a short canal feeding his mills on the outlet of Canandaigua Lake, Swift had carefully calculated the expenses for grubbing and excavation. His cost ratios were substantially in line with the commissioners' Erie projections. Though

Swift's canal was less than a mile long, its dimensions—forty feet wide at the surface narrowing to thirty at a four-foot average depth—were nearly identical to what the commissioners had proposed for Erie. Swift's knowledge and opinions were important. In 1817 he was the president of the state senate and, as he had been the year before, a member of the joint committee deciding whether Erie should move forward. Swift was politically opposed to Clinton, but his enthusiasm for canals was greater.

The chairman of the joint committee was William Ford, the only returning assemblyman from the 1816 committee. "[T]hough little of a rhetorician," Ford was "a plain, sensible man, of solid understanding [and] manifest and unquestioned integrity." He was a Clintonian Republican, a Herkimer County native and lawyer who wanted nothing more than a canal running through his Mohawk Valley.

On the Senate side of the committee with Philetus Swift were two other returning members, Peter Livingston and George Tibbits. They were a trio of anti-Clintonians, but Tibbits, like Swift, was an upstater eager for the canal.

Even before arriving in the state senate in 1815, Tibbits had been thinking hard about how to finance a great state canal. Since the formation of the first canal commission in 1810, the successful Troy merchant turned civic benefactor had been concerned about an expensive project prospectively financed in a relatively unsophisticated manner: millions of dollars borrowed by politically appointed commissioners on the general credit of the state and "vested in some sort of stock at their discretion, to be from time to time sold and applied to . . . construction." In advance of the 1817 legislative session, Tibbits had carefully put together an elaborate and conservative "projét of finance."

Central to Tibbits's plan was separating canal construction from canal financing. While the appointed canal commissioners should oversee planning and construction, a separate set of elected officials should control the purse strings. Tibbits envisioned the state comptroller, secretary of state, attorney general, surveyor-general, and treasurer—all of the state's top officials but the governor—serving as a board to control and invest canal funds and dispense them to the canal commissioners. The canal fund board would have power over a very tightly regulated pot.

There would be specific duties on salt and auction sales, taxes on steamboat passengers, taxes on localities contiguous to or otherwise directly benefiting from the canals, state lottery and land sale proceeds, and canal tolls. Tibbits calculated that, with interest, the fund ought to generate a maximum of just under $600,000 a year to cover annual construction costs. Over what Tibbits anticipated would be twelve years of construction, the fund would generate an ample $7 million.

Many of the revenue sources were familiar. What would be new was their role in a capped, interest-earning fund dedicated to the canals and administered by the state's top officials. The plan, noted Assemblyman Wheeler Barnes, Tibbits's Albany boardinghouse mate, "would complete the canals without impoverishing the treasury, exhausting the funds of the state, burthening the people with taxes, or placing the canals subject to the influence of party views, or local prejudices."

Tibbits's conservative financial vision was obstructed by Clinton. As longtime head of the canal commission, Clinton wanted a freer fiscal hand. As incoming governor, he would be excluded from the financial control board that Tibbits had conjured up. In the opening days of the legislative session, Tibbits sought out Clinton, and they spoke several times about canal funding. In mid-February, shortly after the formation of the joint committee, Tibbits showed his "unavoidably voluminous" plan to Clinton. A couple of weeks later, Tibbits gave Clinton a copy of the plan and the outline for a canal law encompassing it. He asked Clinton to "give to them the most deliberate investigation and consideration" and, as commission president, draft a bill "conformable to them," which the joint committee would present with its recommendations to the assembly. Clinton took Tibbits's plan, "saying that he would examine it as soon as he had leisure." Tibbits then made his plan and his arrangements with Clinton known to the rest of the joint committee. The committee agreed that, rather than writing its own bill, it was proper to wait for one drafted by the head of the commission that would build the canals.

The joint committee arranged a meeting in early March to receive and consider Clinton's draft bill. The date came, the committee assembled, and Clinton failed to show. He sent no emissary to deliver a draft or any other communication. This recalled Clinton's evasive behavior at the 1816 session, when canal legislation failed due to his (probably intentional) inattention. The committee decided that Tibbits's materials should be taken by chairman Ford to draw a bill under his own name, to be submitted with a report to the committee for consideration at its next meeting.

This is what Clinton wanted. Now he made his move. Before the joint committee next met, Clinton sent a draft bill directly to Ford. Ford, a Clinton ally, proceeded to work the draft into the materials he was now preparing. Thus, Clinton had effectively bypassed the committee, and his opponents on it. But Clinton and Ford would learn that they had underestimated Tibbits.

Before Tibbits played his cards, Clinton received an astounding proposal from Jacob Van Rensselaer. Van Rensselaer had been the chairman of the 1816 joint committee, but he was not a member of the 1817 assembly. Nevertheless, he "was much of the time at Albany" during the session. In a brief letter to Clinton, Van Rensselaer now offered to build the Erie canal himself.

To undertake "the object [that] lay so near to his heart," the landowner offered to form a private company that would give the state a $1 million security, get a $500,000 advance, and build the canal largely as laid out in the commissioners' report. Van Rensselaer proposed that his company be paid in one of several ways: $10 million outright from the state; or $7.5 million outright plus twenty years' worth of tolls at a maximum two cents per ton per mile; or $5 million outright with the same twenty-year toll arrangement and, thereafter, either at half that rate or at a flat $5 per ton, for which the company would pay the state either a 3 percent annual premium on the half million dollar advance or over time $2.5 million plus 6 percent interest. Van Rensselaer clearly was thinking long term: it would take 166 years of $15,000 premiums on the advance to equal the $2.5 million option. Under any of the proposed arrangements, given the phenomenal financial success of the canal, Van Rensselaer would have broadly compounded his existing fortune.

Was Van Rensselaer cleverly calculating in his own financial interest, or making a calculated statement on the canal's expected profitability, to be duly noticed by canal doubters? It was unlikely that New York would suddenly opt for a privately owned canal, given the Western Inland Company debacle and the popular preference for a state-owned canal. Clinton, who had made sure to submit his draft bill only to committee chairman Ford, happily passed on Van Rensselaer's immodest proposal to the entire joint committee.

On March 18 Ford presented his report and draft bill to the full assembly, without first presenting it to his full committee. Just who among his committee was actually involved in the preparation of the report and bill is unknown. The bill had its issues, but the report, nevertheless, was in many ways a compelling document. Although its particular recommendations with regard to financing would arouse controversy that nearly sank the whole effort, the report's lengthy front matter was an inspired leap forward from the previous year's tepid report by the Van Rensselaer committee.

Ford's report expressed the "settled conviction" that the legislature should act for the "immediate commencement" of the Hudson–Champlain canal and the Rome–Seneca River section of the Hudson–Erie canal, with an anticipated opening of those initial works within three years. The "minute and copious details" in the commissioners' report were "very satisfactory," especially information about the Middlesex and small New York canals. They showed that "actual experiment . . . is far more extensively furnished by our own country than is generally imagined." Attempting to stifle regional opposition, the report patiently explained how the benefits of the fully completed canals would "in no parsimonious measure, reach and enrich every part of the state." The rapidly populating eastern, northern, and western districts would gain safer and surer markets for their minerals, lumber, and produce than could ever be offered by the hostile "foreign power" commanding "the frozen outlet of the St. Lawrence." The rich southern and middle districts, "replete with inhabitants," would gain these cheaper goods as well as new and diverse paths to wealth beyond "the bounties which nature has spread out before them." New York City, as often promised, would become "the greatest commercial emporium in the world," radiating its wealth: "Experience shows, in all the rich cities of Europe, that as the means of communication with the interior are rendered easier, better and more extensive from those cities, the value of property has uniformly increased in their vicinity." Beyond the rhetoric, it was a fact that transporting a ton of goods between Buffalo and New York City cost $100 and took twenty days, while the average costs and times between Buffalo and Montreal were less than half that. "Make the western canal," Ford promised, and shipping from Buffalo to New York City (with "reasonable tolls") would drop to as little as $10, average less time than to Montreal, and avoid the regular loss of vessels and lives on the "dangerous" waters of Lake Ontario and the St. Lawrence River.

For once the name of William Weston was absent from a major New York canal document. Instead, "a perspicacious statesman of our country" was quoted anonymously, at length:

[I]n proportion as the mind is accustomed to trace the intimate connexion of interest, which subsists between all the parts of a society united under the same government; the infinite variety of channels which serve to circulate the prosperity of each to and through the rest; in that proportion will it be unapt to be disturbed by solicitudes and apprehensions which originate in local discriminations. It is a truth as important as it is agreeable, and one to which it is not easy to imagine exceptions, that every thing tending to establish substantial and permanent order in the affairs of a country; to increase the total mass of industry and opulence, is ultimately beneficial to every part of it. On the credit of this great truth, an acquiescence may safely be accorded, from every quarter, to all institutions and arrangements, which promise a confirmation of public order and an augmentation of public Resource.

This was weightier stuff than commonly appeared in committee reports out of Albany. It had nothing to do with canals. The words had been written way back in 1791 in the "Report on Manufactures" to Congress by Alexander Hamilton. Congress had asked the nation's first Treasury secretary for a plan to stimulate American industry. Hamilton proposed broad federal support for new domestic manufactures; tariffs on imported goods; and incentives for mechanical invention, artisan immigration, and the employment of women and (unfortunately) children. A prescient vision of economic nationalism that has since gone global (for better and worse), it seemed in the early 1790s to be a New Yorker's protectionist scheme for American industry that threatened the agrarian visions of Jefferson and Madison. Now considered his most innovative report, it was Hamilton's only major state paper to fall flat in Congress. Under the deepening spell of Virginians, Congress had laid aside Hamilton's industrial plan, to which Southern ears were presently deafened by Eli Whitney's cotton gin.

How did the martyred Hamilton find his way into Ford's report? The likeliest agent was committee member and Hamilton comrade Nathaniel Pendleton, an indication that Ford was not completely alone in preparing his report. Invoking iconic New Yorker Hamilton was a way of saying to Albany legislators who might oppose the canal that the time had come for "an augmentation of public Resource."

The lofty words of Hamilton also served to draw some cover over certain bad news. Ford's report disingenuously noted the "concurrent" interests of "several of our sister states and of the union generally," without acknowledging that neither states nor union had actually pitched in for New York. Ohio's legislature supposedly had "expressed their zealous approbation" and pledged their "effective cooperation," but communications from Ohio presented in the senate the day before Ford's report was read in the assembly contained nothing more than the request for more information.

The report concluded with the full text of Van Rensselaer's odd proposal and an emphatic rejection of it: "[T]he state should retain the perfect control of this canal, in every period of its construction and future regulation." Thus did Van Rensselaer, with purpose or not, help the state declare the policy of public works that would make New York the leading state of the canal age and far beyond.

Not every committee member was happy with Ford's "committee" report and the accompanying bill. George Tibbits appears not to have been consulted at all. The financing plan was not to his liking.

Ford proposed a set of fund commissioners comprising the state's highest officials (except for the governor), who would oversee all financing. That much was Tibbits's idea. From there, as Tibbits saw it, things went awry. The fund commissioners would be empowered to borrow immediately $1.5 million, to Tibbits an unacceptably high number. The fund commissioners would pay out money to the canal-building commissioners, purchase the Western Inland Company, and establish and receive tolls as canal sections opened, but they would not be required to report a comprehensive finance plan until the next year's legislative session. In the meantime and possibly beyond, principal and interest would be paid from the appropriation of new salt taxes, a portion of existing auction duties, the entire proceeds of state land sales, and, should these not be enough, further loans or surplus money in the state treasury. The latter was a not insignificant pot: with annual revenues of $924,000 and expenses of just $547,000, the state that year had a budget surplus of $377,000. Numerous additional sources of future revenue were mentioned: a tax on real and personal property in counties, cities, and towns "particularly benefited" by the canals; a steamboat passenger tax; lotteries; the long-sought but never proffered contributions from the federal and other state governments; and private land donations, including the newly reoffered but not yet deeded Holland Company tract. However construction financing was accomplished, only "light tolls" and the leasing of surplus waters for mills along the completed canals would be needed to generate "a great revenue . . . which will speedily extinguish the whole debt."

In none of this were Tibbits's restrictions both on the size of the fund and the fund commissioners' power to enlarge it. The open-ended financial and loan powers of the fund commissioners and the one-year delay in reporting a comprehensive financing plan were ideas that Clinton had introduced to Ford.

The day after submitting it, Ford's bill was read in the assembly. No senate member of the joint committee had previously seen what supposedly was the product of their efforts. "It was thought most strange that Mr. Ford should report a bill" in that way, a perfectly restrained Tibbits later observed. "But the gentlemen of the committee, all I believe except myself, fearing lest any interference of theirs might prevent the passage of some bill, remained silent." Tibbits did not remain silent, but he spoke softly. "I did no more than to give Mr. Ford, and the gentlemen of our committee, notice that I should not vote for the bill; that if his bill ever came to the Senate, which I thought it would not, I should offer a substitute."

Tibbits was widely regarded in the legislature for "sound judgment [and] practical knowledge upon many subjects." A negative vote from such a respected member of the sponsoring committee would, as he knew, doom the bill and possibly the whole project. Tibbits wanted a canal, but only with what he considered the proper financial safeguards. Still, Tibbits sat tight amid another major development, the Republican state convention, on March 25, 1817.

Just months earlier, Clinton had been a pariah among the state Republican leadership. But the stains of his cozy political relations with Federalist factions and his opposition to Madison and Tompkins were washing out in a tide of popular opinion in favor of the canal and its "patron saint." In Albany and New York City, Clinton was the toast of St. Patrick's Day dinners. Since February, a Clintonian newspaper campaign had tarred Tammany as anti-Irish and opposed to the canal, which promised mass employment for the first waves of immigrants from the ancestral land of the Clintons. Martin Van Buren received reports that western districts of the state that until recently had been anti-Clinton but were now in line for the canal's benefits had suddenly thrown their support to Clinton for governor.

At the Republican convention in Albany, the anti-Clintonians backed Secretary of State Porter as the party nominee for governor, though six weeks earlier Porter had confessed to Van Buren his unsuitability for the office. Clinton's supporters effectively determined the outcome with a procedural maneuver. They charged that the custom of allowing caucus delegates only from counties represented in the assembly by Republicans was undemocratic. Applied to the forty-one assembly districts, that rule would exclude the ten districts then represented exclusively by Federalists; abandoning the rule would allow into the caucus Clinton supporters from those conservative districts. Party leader Van Buren inhaled the populist wind and, for the avowed sake of party unity, opted to run with it. The Clintonian caucus numbers swelled. In a midnight vote after eight hours of caucusing, Clinton prevailed over Porter, 85 to 41. After March 25, anyone opposing the canal was opposing the presumptive next governor.

Three days later assembly debate began on Ford's canal bill. The *National Advocate*, an influential Tammany mouthpiece, cautioned that "no law was ever introduced to any legislature in this country of so much consequence to the people. . . . we hope and trust, before it receives legislative sanction, that it will meet every inquiry its magnitude is susceptible of, for it is of too much importance to be acted on without the greatest caution and deliberation." The paper called particular attention to the bill's fourth section, which gave to the fund commissioners "any unappropriated moneys in the treasury, to make good any deficiency" in the fund.

As Tibbits expected, the bill "met with vigorous opposition from all sides of the house," but chiefly from the Tammany men of New York City and other virulent anti-Clintonians. That evening in their quarters, Wheeler Barnes told his roommate Tibbits that the assembly "would never pass" the bill. And so together they drafted a bill featuring the senator's financial plan. The next morning Barnes took it to the assembly. Ford, a pragmatist, stood aside.

Like infants switched at birth, the "essentially different" bill was quietly substituted for the original that Saturday morning. No notice of the switch was entered in the official assembly journal. When the assembly next considered canals three days later, the bill up for debate was the one featuring Tibbits's "efficient and durable plan of finance." If De Witt Clinton objected, there is no record. Apparently he had recognized either the greater wisdom or political viability of Tibbits's financial plan or both and, without losing any public face, accepted it. And so Tibbits and Clinton—political antagonists and canal bedfellows—had united for the greater legislative battling ahead.

Despite the better bill and the political rebirth of the state's greatest canal advocate, the next two weeks of debate were a fierce struggle, with the outcome uncertain. Most of the ferocity came from the Tammany men of New York City. Freshman Samuel Romaine wondered what all the rush was to "tax the people before the Canal is completed [and] they have actually received some of these great advantages to which gentlemen have so often called our attention?" Romaine's fellow Manhattanite and Tammany leader Peter Sharpe argued against the diversion of city auction duties at a time when the city had already been drained by taxation and the "most respectable and opulent of her merchants are daily becoming bankrupts." Sharpe was one of those supposedly threatened merchants. The city would "sink under" the canal debt, the costs were "too great for the state," and the project's "magnitude [was] beyond what has ever been accomplished by any nation."

Wheeler Barnes parried Sharpe and Romaine with a speech laying out the economic advantages to be gained throughout the state. William Duer, the assembly's top Federalist, then spoke at length in favor of the bill, but he surprised fellow supporters by suddenly asserting that the first work ought to be the difficult Mohawk–Hudson link. Unfortunately, he noted, the commissioners' report was defective in that regard. Indeed, Duer continued while canal supporters blanched, the bill was so "materially defective" in this area that he proposed naming a select committee to redraft it. His friend Barnes, "indefatigable" on the floor and "out of the house" in support of the bill, jumped up to assure Duer that the bill could be improved in regular debate.

Poughkeepsie Federalist James Emott spoke next, with the same level of hostility toward the bill and the canal project generally as he had shown as a congressman five years earlier toward Madison's war. Barnes, Ford, and others rose in turn to defend the bill and the canal.

On April 7, a few days into the floor debate, Ford began strategic warfare. He introduced a motion to strike out the bill's clause calling for taxes on canal-benefited towns, cities, and counties. As hoped, this roused anti-Clintonian Republican William B. Rochester, sitting in his first legislature. He was the twenty-eight-year-old son of the founder of the Genesee River settlement then called Rochesterville. Its seven hundred people needed nothing so much as a canal. Young Rochester responded to Ford with a speech favoring the bill but opposing the motion that might strip the project of necessary construction funding. It was important for detractors to see that Rochester was willing to pay for the canal that would enrich his village.

Poughkeepsie's Emott was unswayed. A canal that linked New York City to the west would make a scenic byway of his Lower Hudson Valley. Rising to his feet "in a more formidable and determined manner" than before, he presented "appalling" financial predictions about the "visionary" project. His passionate speech cast a cloud over the assembly chamber. "The prospect began now for a moment to darken," noted a close observer, "and serious doubts were again entertained as to the fate of this bill."

It was entirely unclear if there was to be any canalling in New York, when Nathaniel Pendleton's turn came. As a member of the canal committee, he presumably favored the canal bill, but he had revealed his position neither publicly nor privately on the legislation that committee chairman Ford had largely written. Like Emott, Pendleton was rich, a distinguished attorney, and a Federalist representing anticanal Dutchess County. Pendleton, however, at age sixty, was a seasoned statesman who could look more deeply at things.

A Virginia-born Revolutionary War veteran, Pendleton had been a close friend of Alexander Hamilton. As Hamilton's second in the fatal encounter with Burr in 1804, Pendleton had conducted a scrupulous postmortem inspection of the grounds and proved that the only shot fired by his mortally wounded friend had been involuntary, the bullet passing wild through a cedar tree limb that Pendleton sawed off to preserve as evidence. Pendleton was known as a man of "sterling character, and high and honourable principles." In the spring of 1817 he was serving his single term in the state assembly. Did the canal and the bill that would authorize it meet his high standards? During early debate the previous week, he had given the impression to some observers that he was "hostile to the entire project, and would oppose the bill throughout." Pendleton was an ineloquent debater, but when he spoke, the assembly listened.

"It [is] a principle of equity," Pendleton addressed the chamber, "that those who [are] to receive the benefits of the measure should bear some additional part of the expense." Those eastern (and mostly Federalist) speculators in Western New York lands, like himself, might balk at what seemed like double taxation; they would be taxed both on their as yet unprofitable western holdings in the canal region and as easterners who disbelieved that the distant canal would benefit them as well. But there should be no doubt of the pending benefit to the city in which many of them did business: "[I]t would be the emporium not only of our own products, but for the northern part of the western states and territories, and this would increase with the increase of their population." For the landed, like Pendleton himself, to reap reward without obligation was "so partial, so selfish, so grossly inequitable" he was "surprized any honorable man would support it." Pendleton, as he finally revealed, had been turned into an avid canal supporter only after closely examining the surveys contained in the commissioners' report. These detailed surveys had convinced him that the canal could and should be built.

Pendleton's speech brightened the canal's prospects, but not conclusively. The same surveys that so impressed Pendleton struck others differently. In the chamber and lobbies of the assembly, the prospect of country surveyors engineering the nation's greatest construction project brought ridicule and alarm. "Who is this James Geddes, and who is this Benjamin Wright, that the Commissioners have trusted with this responsibility?" taunted one member from the Assembly floor. "What canals have they ever constructed? What great public works have they accomplished?" In truth, none. But neither had any American.

Even as the assembly debated, the commissioners themselves were unsure that their surveyors could become engineers. Clinton had even sought once again to entice William Weston back to New York. Weston, then in his mid-sixties, sent word from England that not even the astounding offer of $7,000 a year—a thousand dollars more than the governor's salary—could convince him to return. This left the commissioners "in great doubt as to the best course to pursue."

Geddes and Wright were aware of the commissioners' anxiety. A meeting in Albany was quietly arranged that proved a defining professional moment. The would-be engineers "expressed their confidence in their ability to locate and construct the canal." They stated their "strong desire that the Commissioners should feel a like confidence" if Geddes and Wright "were to be entrusted with the responsibility." This plain appeal won the day. The commissioners ceased looking to Europe. There would be no regrets that Weston or any other foreign engineer was not employed. As assembly debate continued, commissioners Clinton, Holley, and Young privately assured certain assembly members that Wright and Geddes were up to their task.

While the prospective engineers gained stature behind closed doors, Ford's motion to scrap taxes on benefited areas was put to a vote, the first of many. The tally came down 52–51 in favor. The proposal split major factions: canal supporters, canal detractors, even the New York City delegation were unsure exactly what their votes meant. But without a replacement revenue source, the bill would eventually fail. In the remaining hours of that day's session, Duer worked the floor and found enough support for the 1816 proposal to tax lands lying within twenty-five miles of the canals. This effectively shifted the burden of direct taxation away from New York City, which still would be making a substantial but indirect contribution through the partial appropriation of auction duties.

The following morning Duer took the floor in support of his motion, speaking in "language . . . at once persuasive and powerful." Rumblings still were heard from the representatives of Gotham. Finally an assemblyman not previously outspoken on the bill had had enough.

Federalist Elisha Williams was a member of the so-called junto that controlled Columbia County. He was an oratorical force. Oliver Wendell Holmes considered Williams "the most notable personage" among his legal contemporaries. Thomas Addis Emmet, the exiled Irish nationalist turned New York lawyer, had "listened to the great men of Europe and America, but never to one who could enchain the attention and captivate the judgment like Elisha Williams."

Furious at the course of the debate, Williams rose to defend the bill, section by section, extolling the broad merits of the western canal and laying waste to the provincialism opposing it. "Will not all the productions of this vast and fertile territory, go to New-York?" he intoned, glaring at a city delegation leader. "Sir, if this canal is to be a shower of gold, it will fall upon New-York—if a river of gold it will run into her lap. . . . Are we to give her the means of enriching herself, beyond all former example, and of monopolizing the trade of the whole world, and she pay nothing in return?" Williams's argument was given greater weight because two years earlier he had founded the Seneca County town of Waterloo, well within the twenty-five mile range of proposed taxation. "We have been called on by every principle of policy and patriotism, to construct these canals—to improve the choice blessings which heaven has lavished upon us—to secure our own internal commerce, and to preserve the commerce of N. Y."

When the great orator sat down, the battle had been won. The ensuing vote on Duer's motion passed 61–45, followed by a decisive 70–30 against a motion rejecting the bill entirely. Other important votes monetized the annual land tax at $250,000 and the salt tax at twelve and a half cents per bushel. On April 10 the entire bill was approved 64–36.

Federalists—many of them with western interests—voted overwhelmingly for the bill, 25–7, with four not voting. Republicans, many torn between the canal and Clinton, more narrowly gave their support, 39–29; twenty-two avoided the issue by not voting. In the end the vote, like politics, was local. Among the assemblymen from the fifteen legislative districts along the prospective canal route, the Republican vote was 26–0 (thirteen didn't vote), and the Federalist vote was 9–1. In the six districts of the Lower Hudson Valley, Republicans split eight votes, while Federalists voted 16–5 against, with Pendleton, Duer, and Williams in that minority. In the eight New York City area districts, all seventeen recorded votes were against the canal, including all three Federalists and fourteen Republicans.

To appearances, it is a stunning irony sometimes noted by historians that all of New York City's assemblymen voted against the canal that assured their city's rise to greatness. But the unanimous negativity is not the whole story. Seventeen of the city's assemblymen voted no, but seven other assemblymen, all Republicans, didn't vote. That is, nearly a third of the city's Republican assembly delegation did not vote against the canal and Clinton, as they were supposed to. Leading the nonvoters was strident canal opponent Peter Sharpe. He had done Tammany's bidding during the debate but managed to avoid voting against his interests as a merchant who stood to benefit greatly from the canal. Sharpe and his fellow voting absentees, notably including East River shipbuilder Henry Eckford, who had served briefly on the canal committee, were able to look beyond personality, sidestep politics, and see the prosperity ahead.

Immediately ahead was senate consideration of the canal bill. Opposition more to Clinton than the canal had characterized most of the no votes in the assembly, as much from personal animosity as political principle. The senate was more sophisticated, but the debate was no less contentious.

"[T]he man who will enter into this project, must be a *madman, a fool, or a knave*," blustered Peter Livingston, in a long and raving speech on Monday April 14, the penultimate day of the 1817 legislative session. Livingston argued that the senate was taking too little time to consider a bill of such importance and that the longstanding failure to effectuate the Gallatin Plan proved that "the project of canals in this country is visionary." He recalled the "splendid schemes" of Philip Schuyler's Western Inland Company, but also warned that a successful canal to Lake Erie would flood the west with cheap English goods, smothering nascent American industry. The city and state were already suffering "oppressive" levels of taxation and escalating labor costs. To embark on a public project of unprecedented financing would invite disaster, because there are "no worse managers of money than the public." But if financing were to be secured by a limited but untested canal fund, and not the unfettered state treasury, the project would become an object of speculation, "from the diggers up." No matter the contrivances for planning and paying for the canal, "you will find it a ditch that will bury you all. It will make paupers of the state."

A year earlier, Livingston's similar stridency had played favorably in the senate. "Now the scene is entirely changed," Martin Van Buren told his fellow senators. After an Ulster County senator had made a long speech along the familiar lines of Lower Hudson Valley opposition, and "master spirit" George Tibbits had countered briefly in support of the bill, Van Buren made the "great speech of the session."

A year earlier he had asked for more time and information. Now he had "great confidence" in what the canal commissioners and their surveyors had discovered: "[W]e have arrived at the point, when if this bill do not pass, the project must for many years be abandoned." Tracing the progress of legislation since 1810, he now found an obligation to act: "We are now to say that all our former proceedings have been insincere, or we must go on with the work." Satisfied that the conservative financial plan would provide ample revenue to complete the canals, he noted both the willingness of the canal districts to shoulder the load of taxation and the overwhelming support of the general population: "For six years we have been engaged upon this business. During this time our tables have groaned with the petitions of the people from every section of our country in favour of it." For the second year in a row, a bill to start construction had passed the assembly, the legislature's popular house: "After so much has been done and said upon this subject, it would be discreditable to the state to abandon it." Van Buren "considered it the most important vote" he was to make, "but the project, if executed, would raise the state to the highest possible pitch of fame and grandeur."

When the Little Magician sat down, his former political mentor, "breaking through that reserve which political collisions had created," approached him. At worst, Clinton considered Van Buren "a scoundrel of the first magnitude . . . without fixture of principle or reality of virtue." At best, their "personal intercourse was very reserved." Just weeks earlier Van Buren had "zealously opposed" Clinton's nomination for governor. But now for all in the senate chamber to see, Clinton approached the stunned Van Buren and "shook hands with me, and expressed his gratification in the strongest terms." It was a scene between the state's two greatest political rivals never to be repeated.

The tender moment concluded, a chorus of Republican extremists led by Livingston rose in opposition, but a vote immediately thereafter on the bill's enacting clause passed 21–8. All six senators of the Southern District, comprising New York City and surrounding counties, voted against.

For the rest of the day, a sequence of votes on various motions made senate passage of the bill inevitable, largely in the form approved by the assembly. Toward the end Van Buren succeeded in a strategic ploy to make the state and not the canal fund itself the guarantor of canal loans, a modification calculated to earn him and his party a share of the credit for the canal. It was accepted by all of the bill's supporters and opposed only by the diehards, including even Livingston, who had supported the idea in his speech just hours earlier.

On the morning of April 15 the senate voted 18–9 in favor of the bill as amended. The minority were all Republicans: the six Southern District senators and three from the Middle District, comprising the Lower Hudson Valley. Five Republicans, including canal committee member Swift and fellow anti-Clintonian Henry Seymour, avoided overt support for Clinton's canal by not voting, as seven of their assembly brethren had done. In the majority were the handful of Federalists, a group of moderate Republicans like former canal committee member William Ross, and five usually rabid anti-Clintonians whose votes Van Buren later took great credit for securing.

In memoirs written many years later when he was vice president, Van Buren painted his support of the canal as a sudden, dramatic thing, a bold decision risking terrible political consequences for him and the five otherwise unremarkable anti-Clintonians. "I believe our adverse votes would have caused [the bill's] failure," he claimed, "quite certain that we could, if so inclined, have defeated it with the greatest ease."

In fact, his actions were politics at its most pragmatic. In the year's worth of reflection that he had earned for himself and his party at the 1816 session, Van Buren had seen that the canal and Clinton had grown enormously in popularity, while the party leadership had only grown more anti-Clintonian. Tompkins, Tayler, Livingston, and others had closed their eyes to the convincing surveys and saw only the dark image of the despised governor-to-be. Van Buren, a future president, closed his eyes and saw more clearly.

After going back and forth a few times between the senate and assembly chambers to work out relatively minor differences, "An Act respecting Navigable Communications, between the great western and northern lakes, and the Atlantic ocean" was sent down the hall for its final test before becoming law. With just hours left in the session, the decision on whether New York would start leading the nation west in 1817 came down to the Council of Revision, the creakiest and most capricious organ of state power.

Established during wartime by the state constitution of 1777 on principles originating with the veto power of the English king's Privy Council, the Council of Revision was designed as a check on the executive and legislative branches. The council consisted of the governor (as council president), the chancellor of the Chancery Court, and the chief justice and four judges of the state supreme court; the six judicial members, initially appointed by the Council of Appointment, served during "good behavior" until age sixty. A bill passed by the legislature was sent automatically to the council for a ruling on whether it was "inconsistent with the spirit" of the constitution or "with the public good." It became law either with the consent of a council majority or, if the council vetoed it, by the override of two-third majorities in the assembly and the senate. The vast majority of bills did not raise substantial issues and passed as a formality through the council and into law; such, for example, was the case with the 1816 law that merely reconstituted the canal commissioners and gave them $20,000 for surveys.*

Much more was at stake in the 1817 legislation.

There were many troubles with the Council of Revision. Aside from denying a veto to the governor, it involved its judicial members in politics and legislation and gave veto power to appointed judges not responsible to popular opinion. By the time it was abolished in 1821 (and the governor given veto power), the council had come to be seen as an antidemocratic super-legislature, an anachronistic repository of Federalist power: of the council's six judicial members, four were long-serving Federalists, long after the party had legislative clout. On scores of council vetoes with heavy political overtones, the legislature had managed only a handful of overrides; since 1806, not one override of forty-two vetoes.

---

*From 1777 until the council was eliminated under the state constitution of 1821, the legislature passed 6,590 bills and the council vetoed 169; the legislature ultimately overrode 51 vetoes, but only six after 1800. See Alfred Billings Street, *The Council of Revision of the State of New York* (Albany: W. Gould, 1859).

The influence of a council veto on the 64–36 and 18–9 margins for the canal bill made an override practically impossible.

What the council had in store for the bill on the afternoon of April 15, 1817, was unclear. Two of the four judges—Clinton in-law Ambrose Spencer and Columbia County Federalist leader William Van Ness—were not in Albany, leaving the bill's fate to just five council members. Acting governor John Tayler "had ever been distinguished as one of the ablest and most formidable opponents of the canal." That was the opinion of Judge Jonas Platt, one of the project's original and greatest proponents. Fellow judge, Schenectady Federalist leader, and future governor Joseph C. Yates was allied with Platt as "a decided friend of the canal." Allied with Tayler was chief justice and fellow anti-Clintonian Republican Smith Thompson. A future U.S. Supreme Court justice, Thompson "cherished no hostility to the canal" (though he was a native of anticanal Dutchess County), but opposed the bill because it "gave arbitrary powers to the commissioners over private rights" without adequate safeguards. Thus, the fifth and deciding vote on the canal bill would fall to the chancellor: eminent jurist, unrivaled legal scholar, and ardent Federalist James Kent.

Kent's position on the canal bill was unknown, but his qualifications to judge wisely were legendary. Since transitioning in 1814 from state chief justice to chancellor, Kent had been reforming the Court of Chancery from the insignificant institution it had been for its entire four decades. By initiating the practices of written opinions by supreme court judges, compilation by a reporter of decisions and opinions, and annotation and publication of them, Kent practically created American equity jurisdiction. His opinions—legal and otherwise—were firm; he wrote plainly that his predecessor as chancellor was stupid.

The five men took some moments to read through the canal bill, before Tayler began the deliberations by asking Kent for his impressions. He had "given very little attention" to the canal subject, Kent confessed, but it seemed "a gigantic project, which would require the wealth of the United States to accomplish." The bill, he noted, had passed the legislature "after a desperate struggle" without overwhelming majorities. It seemed to Kent, at least at the outset of the council's discussions, "inexpedient to commit the State, in such a vast undertaking, until public opinion could be better united in its favor."

As expected, Thompson then spoke in opposition, and Yates and Platt in support, and Tayler "panted with honest zeal to strangle the infant Hercules at its birth." It seemed to Platt that the canal measure had come to "a fatal crisis." After "warm and animated" discussion, "a more temperate and deliberate examination of the bill" ensued that seemed to soften the objections of Tayler and Kent, though not enough to change their positions as the debate wound down. A 3–2 decision against the canal appeared likely.

Then, like a Roman god clumsily descending, Daniel Tompkins appeared. Having remained substantially more involved with matters at Albany than as vice president in Washington, Tompkins was welcomed into the "informal and desultory" discussions in the council chamber. Aiming to bolster his fellow canal opponents, Tompkins began declaiming against the bill. The still fresh peace with Great Britain was "a mere truce," he said. War "undoubtedly" would soon be renewed and, instead of wasting the state's resources on "this chimerical project," all of New York's revenues and credit ought to be employed immediately "in providing arsenals, arming the militia, erecting fortifications, and preparing for war."

"Do you think so, sir?" asked Kent, for whom the recent war had been an abomination perpetrated by Republicans like Tompkins. "Yes, sir," Tompkins replied, blind to his argument's effect on Kent: "England will never forgive us for our victories on the land, and on the ocean and the lakes; and my word for it, we shall have another war with her within two years." Enlightened now by his lesser and witless adversary, Chancellor Kent sprang to his feet, exclaiming: "If we must have war, or have a canal, I am in favour of the canal, and I vote for the bill." Just like that, the three council Federalists were suddenly united in a majority, and the 1817 canal bill became law.

Would Kent have come around without Tompkins's overreach? He never said. Perhaps Tompkins gave strident voice to the anticanal position that Kent was trying to find a reason to reject. Possibly it was just Kent's revulsion at politicians like Tompkins who mistook warmongering for statesmanship.

No one in New York felt greater vindication than Jonas Platt, who had conceived Erie as a legislative project on a snowy Albany night seven years earlier:

> At no future period could the work have been accomplished at so small an expense of land, of water, and hydraulic privileges. Rival routes, and local interests, were daily increasing and combining against the project; and in my estimation it was one of the chief grounds of merit in the advocates of the Erie canal, that they seized on the very moment most proper and auspicious for that immortal work.

☆   ☆   ☆

"In our America we are turning to public improvements," wrote Thomas Jefferson that June, with a mix of pride and nostalgia. "Schools, roads, and canals are everywhere either in operation or contemplation." The Monticello retiree was describing the changing American landscape to Prussian geographer Alexander von Humboldt, scientific explorer of ocean currents and remote territories. "The most gigantic undertaking yet is that of New York, for drawing the waters of Lake Erie into the Hudson. . . . The expense will be great, but its effect incalculably powerful in favor of the Atlantic States." One particular Atlantic state, the old Virginian might have written.

The former president had kept up on New York's progress with copies of the commissioners' reports and other materials. Clinton had forwarded them, seeking "the powerful weight" of Jefferson's opinions. With no hint of regret for his failure to support "these great and honorable enterprizes," Jefferson assured Clinton that "the conception is bold and great, and the accomplishment will be equally useful. The works of Europe in that line shrink into insignificance in comparison." The misguided embargoist and disinclined national planner turned sage of

Monticello saw how the glory would go to younger men like Clinton: "the prospect of the future face of America is magnificent indeed, but for the whole revolutionary generation it is to be enjoyed in contemplation only."

Clinton's own prospects were pretty good as well. In May he ran unopposed for governor and won all but some write-in votes for Tompkins. In little over a year's time, Clinton had been transformed from unemployed politician and powerless canal commissioner to herald of the Empire State.

CHAPTER 8

Laying the Groundwork

The whole project hangs upon an attenuated thread which will break and cause our destruction, if we do not exercise the utmost care, caution and vigilance.

—Canal Commissioner Samuel Young, 1817

Cannon fire shook the flat earth around Rome before the dawn of Independence Day 1817. The explosions roused few of the twenty-five hundred townspeople; most had been up all night celebrating the event of the coming morning. Rejuvenated by the artillery and armed with spades, Romans set off southwest by horseback, wagon, and foot through birch and hemlock woods to the north bank of Wood Creek, where a butternut stake had been driven into the muddy ground and marked in red chalk: "No. 1, True Canal Line." Two months earlier, James Geddes had placed the stake as the starting point for the first section of what would become the Erie Canal.

Villagers gathered in a ring around the morning's dignitaries: canal commissioner Samuel Young, Rome village president and canal contractor Joshua Hathaway, and John Richardson, a Cayuga Lake settler and contractor for the short canal section beginning at stake No. 1. As the sun lit the treetops to the sound of more artillery, Hathaway took charge of a plow-tethered team of oxen and, for a few ceremonial moments, they toiled through the furrow.

"[W]e [have] the honor of commencing one of the grandest objects that ever has and perhaps ever will grace our nation," said Hathaway in a brief speech. Young spoke at greater length. "The work . . . will diffuse the benefits of internal navigation over . . . a tract of country capable of sustaining more human beings than were ever accommodated by any work of the kind. By this great highway, unborn millions will easily transport their surplus productions to the shores of the Atlantic, procure their supplies, and hold a useful and profitable intercourse with all the marine nations of the earth . . . Let us then proceed to the work, animated by the prospect of its speedy accomplishment, and cheered with the anticipated benedictions of a grateful posterity." Richardson took a spade and drove it into the new-furrowed earth, and everyone with a spade followed his example.

Such were the lead performers at the groundbreaking for the Erie Canal: two local contractors and a canal commissioner, all good but now long obscure men. There were representatives of neither the nation destined for unprecedented benefit from the canal, nor the state that would rise by the canal to become the commercial seat of national empire, nor the city that would lead the global economy. Even De Witt Clinton was absent. Inaugurated as governor three days earlier, he was in New York City for gala celebrations of the national holiday.

No city paper covered the groundbreaking, other than to reprint the only original account, eleven days after the fact, in Utica's paper (Rome had none), which put Young's words in Hathaway's mouth. *Niles' Weekly Register*, the authoritative national paper published at Baltimore, eventually proclaimed "the great and glorious undertaking" but, in reprinting the Utica item, compounded the misreportage by placing the groundbreaking at Utica. Fifteen days later the anti-Clintonian *National Advocate* issued its opinion: "[E]ach citizen turned up a clod or two, and the whole party then adjourned to dinner, which was, by far, the most important part of the ceremony, as the time and expense to be employed on that object might be safely calculated."

The relative obscurity of the groundbreaking was such that before his death a decade later Clinton was credited with turning the first dirt. "Very likely he did," asserted the keynote speaker at the centennial celebration in 1917, and no one bothered to disturb the myth. In 1817 Rome was a remote place, and the canal project not so sure a thing that notables felt compelled to attend opening day. Within a couple of years that attitude would change. The groundbreaking was to be the first and last Erie milestone modestly celebrated.

✯ ✯ ✯

A lot had happened in the nearly three months since Daniel Tompkins inadvertently talked James Kent into approving the Erie and Champlain canals. The day after the Council of Revision voted for the canal law on April 15, the canal commissioners (as always minus Joseph Ellicott) had met in Albany. Their first decision was to abandon the idea "derived from the best English engineers" of employing and equipping laborers to build the canals. Instead, they adopted the "more economical course" of letting out the work in short sections by competitive bid to contractors who would supply their own tools and labor and be paid stipulated prices for excavation and construction under guidelines established by the state-employed engineer corps. Often as not, the easy winner of a section contract would simply be the farmer or landowner whose property was to be crossed by the canal path. Unremarkable now when practically all government construction is done by contract, construction by men with limited or no experience in canal building was a risk the commissioners in a state with limited resources and bureaucracy and no public works experience wisely took in 1817.

In their April meeting, the commissioners had also enlarged their mandate, by taking advantage of some legal ambiguity. The law authorized the commissioners to begin work on "canals and locks between the Mohawk and Seneca rivers," encompassing what the commissioners had designated as the Erie's middle section. The law did not specify a starting point on either river. Thus the commissioners "believed themselves vested with a discretionary power" to size the middle section at what "would most conduce to the public good." They decided to extend the eastern end of the middle section from the presumed starting point at Rome to Utica, fifteen miles farther east. From an engineering point of view, this made perfect sense. The upper Mohawk Valley is practically level between Rome and Utica, so the commissioners' decision added fifteen miles of canal that could be easily excavated and require no locks or other substantial engineering. The middle section now would include the largest town before the valley's first steep descent, where a series of locks would be required. Multiple locks were a challenge the commissioners and their surveyor-engineers were not prepared to undertake just yet. There was no reaction to the commissioners' decision in Albany, where the legislature had gone out of session. In Rome, few citizens realized that the decision would help make their town a canal byway and Utica a canal city. After the groundbreaking, it would be all downhill for Rome.

Though he had been by his own candid admission "little more than a nominal commissioner," Joseph Ellicott continued as a commissioner with the rest of his colleagues under the 1817 law. While Ellicott politely thanked Clinton at the end of April for the "honor that I had not anticipated," both men knew that the "little part" Ellicott took in the commissioners' routine business was much less relevant than his continued involvement in the overall business. As the de facto representative of the Holland Company, Ellicott needed the canal commission, and the commission still needed him.

When the canal law was passed in mid-April, it was not expected that nearly three months would pass before a groundbreaking. On May 7 commissioners Holley and Young had met at Rome with surveyors Wright and Geddes to plan a final resurvey of the first segment of the line leading west from Rome: fifteen miles arcing along Wood Creek down to Oneida Creek above its entry into Oneida Lake. It had seemed a simple task involving level, much-studied, and familiar if at times swampy terrain. But the survey took nearly seven weeks, thanks largely to the anxieties of commissioner Young, a respected lawyer and earnest and honest politician devoid of surveying knowledge.

"The whole project hangs upon an attenuated thread which will break and cause our destruction, if we do not exercise the utmost care, caution and vigilance," Young worried to Clinton. Placement of the first stake marking the highest level of the canal on the middle section was to Young a decision of fearsome import: "A mistake in the summit level would bring irrevocable damnation in this world."

This detail from an 1823 map of Western New York by David H. Vance, enlarged to the east by J. Ogden Dey in 1824 and 1825, shows how the canal avoided the maddening windings of the upper Mohawk River and especially Wood Creek, and passed just enough south of Rome to reduce its historic role as an interior navigation center. (*The Lionel Pincus and Princess Firyal Map Division, The New York Public Library, Astor, Lenox and Tilden Foundations*)

Finally, on May 17, "[a]fter many plans and repeated alterations," as survey chief Wright caustically wrote in his official field book, Young agreed to a summit level where Wright and Geddes had decided it should be: five feet lower than originally planned. Instead of a short summit level through Rome with locks on either end, similar to the old Western Inland Lock Navigation Company canal and locks that joined Wood Creek and the Mohawk, Wright and Geddes had realized since their surveys of the previous year that they could locate the canal at a lower elevation a mile south of the village and get a seventy-mile summit level, all the way from Frankfort, nine miles east of Utica, to Salina, "superior in length to any summit level in the world." Thus, the eastern sixty of the middle section's ninety-six miles could be built with no locks, reducing engineering concerns, planning, time, and expense during construction, and maintenance costs and transit time once the canal was opened. In their annual report several months later, the commissioners wrote only that "[a]fter a minute and laborious examination, this alteration was adopted," without noting Young's anxiety about the change and their surveyors' exasperation. Neither commissioners nor any Romans, including Wright himself, noted that the canal's gain of a long level was also Rome's loss: the removal of the canal from the center of town to its low-lying outskirts would be a blow to its prospects.

With the summit set and staked, Wright and Geddes were happy to continue their survey work without Young. He headed off to New York City for the next commissioners' meeting. This meeting focused on the creation of a staff of engineers from a handful of country surveyors.

Two men would not make the transition. After a quarter century of adventurous surveying on the New York frontier, Charles Brodhead opted to spend 1817 on a commission that set off Whitestown from Utica. Brodhead subsequently settled in Utica, taking up a largely reclusive, bachelor existence until his death thirty-five years later, a forgotten surveyor who never turned engineer. After his initial survey for the Champlain canal, the obscure Lewis Garin likewise dropped canalling. The Champlain construction would be taken over in the fall of 1817 by Geddes, marking the onset of a less prominent role than Wright's in the Erie project.

It is part of Erie lore that the canal was engineered entirely by upstate surveyors who trained themselves to be engineers. This is not entirely true. In May 1817 De Witt Clinton and his commission were still not entirely convinced that more seasoned men were not needed. Englishman William Weston had taken himself out of consideration. So Clinton looked south.

Isaac Briggs had traveled a long, rough road before Clinton interviewed him in New York City for an engineering position on the Erie canal. The oldest son of a Pennsylvania Quaker farmer, miller, and carpenter, Briggs had earned bachelor's and master's degrees at the College of Philadelphia (now the University of Pennsylvania) before heading to Georgia in 1787 to seek his fortune as a land speculator. He had started laying out the first six thousand of his eventual eleven thousand acres when he accomplished a bit of engineering history: a month after Georgia ratified the federal Constitution in January 1788, Briggs and a partner were awarded a state patent for a steamboat, the first steamboat patent in the country. This was three years before John Fitch famously won the first federal steamboat patent. Fitch and his boats were not unfamiliar to Briggs: in 1786, his father had helped fellow Bucks Countian Fitch with engine castings for his experimental boat. The boat that Briggs experimented with on the Savannah River at Augusta worked but, like Fitch's, not in any practical way. The patent proved the only one issued by Georgia.

By the early 1790s Briggs had abandoned Georgia for reasons unknown and relocated to Washington, where he served with the brothers Ellicott—Joseph and Andrew—in the surveying department of the new national city. He was also involved with a family nail factory in Georgetown (then part of Maryland), which featured a nail-making machine patented by the Briggses in 1791; the technology would revolutionize the building industry but be perfected by others. In 1793 Isaac Briggs obtained a measure of Southern comfort by marrying Hannah Brooke of Brookeville, Maryland, and starting a family with her in the Quaker community at nearby Sandy Springs along the Patuxent River, one valley removed from the Ellicott homestead on the Patapsco River. Over the next decade Briggs pursued surveying work and other business, published an influential but short-lived Georgetown semiweekly newspaper, and put out several annual almanacs for locations from Pennsylvania to Georgia, all with little apparent profit. At the same time, he forged deepening relationships with the Washington elite, especially Thomas Jefferson.

One of Jefferson's plans as president was to establish a national prime meridian at Washington that would be used as a basis for the maps of Lewis and Clark and other western explorers and trump England's campaign to establish its Greenwich meridian as the world's longitudinal reference point. In early 1804 Jefferson named Briggs to make the observations. Briggs started the work that spring, but left the placement of permanent stone markers to another surveyor in order to take up a greater assignment from Jefferson: surveyor-general for the Mississippi Territory. The Mississippi Territory then comprised all of the country south of Tennessee. Coming on the cusp of the Louisiana Purchase, this assignment to conduct surveys, build roads, and make other improvements was a part of the southern territorial expansion of Jeffersonian America, and a significant opportunity for Briggs.

"He is a Quaker, a sound republican, and of a pure and unspotted character," Jefferson wrote to the territory's governor. "In point of science, in astronomy, geometry and mathematics he stands in a line with Mr. [Andrew] Ellicott, and *second to no man* in the United States." Over the next two decades Jefferson's advocacy of Briggs would dwindle in proportion to Briggs's professional success.

The Mississippi work went badly. The highlight of Briggs's four-year tenure was the small part he played in the unmasking of the greatest threat to American expansion: he was a courier of ciphered dispatches to Jefferson that helped foil Aaron Burr's strange plot to make a personal empire of the southwest. Otherwise, Briggs's sojourn in the primitive, fever-plagued, and rumor-ravaged lower Mississippi valley was a professional and personal disaster. His youngest brother died there from yellow fever. Briggs himself sickened from malaria, which nearly killed and permanently weakened him. His wife and children refused to forsake genteel Maryland for rude New Orleans. By the time he quit and returned home in 1808, his finances, family life, and social and political connections had started a long, downward spiral. The *Congressional Record* is scattered with Briggs's petitions over many years for relief from debts incurred in the Mississippi Territory. Briggs's marital correspondence portrays a distant husband and a domestic wife lamenting inadequate togetherness and money.

Though he was still close to Jefferson and successor Madison socially and in scientific interests (together they attempted to establish a national agriculture society), Briggs's business failures began to pile up after his return home. With two brothers-in-law (also married to Brooke sisters), Briggs in 1809 laid out Triadelphia, a factory town on the Patuxent with a cotton mill as its centerpiece. Though later successful as an industrial center under different proprietors (and now submerged beneath the Triadelphia Reservoir), the venture struggled through the war and beyond. In early 1814 Briggs lamented his "broken fortune" to President Madison. That summer, when the British had set Washington afire and its people and the president aflight, the nation's gold, along with Madison's cabinet, took refuge at Briggs's home, without pecuniary benefit to the host. By early May 1817 lean postwar years had reduced Briggs, then fifty-four years old, to desperation: "all my expectations of advantageous business . . . have been disappointed in succession," he wrote to Jefferson, "and almost every door of hope . . . closed in anguish."

Briggs's apparent plight was unknown to De Witt Clinton when he sent word through intermediaries to Briggs, then managing a struggling cotton works near Wilmington, Delaware, that New York was considering his services as an engineer. On the afternoon of May 8, "when almost every hope had fled, the information of this prospect in New York, broke suddenly and unexpectedly upon me like a light from Heaven."

Whether Briggs was as reduced as he made himself out to be or was trying to gain sympathy and fast action from his "dear Friend" Jefferson is unclear. Apologizing for his intrusion on the great man's retirement, Briggs unabashedly beseeched Jefferson to send a note to Clinton in New York City by May 15, when the commissioners were to meet: "[I]t is supposed a line from thee would have more weight" than testimonials from Briggs's lesser friends.

Briggs rushed from Wilmington to New York by horse and boat and awaited Jefferson's response. As a solicitation for a character reference, Briggs's letter to Jefferson failed quite completely: Jefferson didn't receive it until May 17. Between the lines of his eventual reply containing measured praise for Briggs's "qualifications, industry & integrity [and] high talents as a Mathematician" is a whiff of relief that Jefferson had avoided any agency in Briggs's prospective new employment.

Briggs got the job anyway. After meeting with Clinton in the city, he was hired at a rate of $5 a day plus expenses, the same arrangements made with Wright and Geddes. Clinton and the other commissioners considered their "eminent mathematician" the equal of their provincial surveyors. Briggs's assignment for 1817 was to lay out the fifteen-mile extension of the middle section from Rome to Utica.

From the moment he was hired, Briggs pursued a broader Southern interest. During his visit to the city, Briggs lodged at the home of former canal commissioner Thomas Eddy, who had rescued his fellow Quaker and native Pennsylvanian from a stay at the City Hotel, where dinner was a dollar and Briggs's "finances would not long bear it." To Eddy,

Briggs suggested the idea of hiring his brother-in-law, Virginian Thomas Moore, to take charge of the entire Erie project.

Where Briggs was damaged goods but passed for an accomplished and connected American professional, his "bosom friend" Moore was accomplished and untainted. Their lives were closely intertwined.

One of the Brooke-wed Triadelphia founders, Moore is preserved in popular history as the inventor of the refrigerator, a word he coined in 1803. This was not the electric appliance of modern domestic convenience, but Moore's patented, portable wooden box within a box, insulated with rabbit fur, charcoal, and tin. Moore delivered refrigerated butter from his Brookeville dairy farm to many customers in Georgetown and Washington, his friend president Jefferson among them.

Fresh from his icebox success, Moore was named by Jefferson to the first commission for the Cumberland Road; he left the long-delayed project before the start of construction. Over the next fifteen years Moore distinguished himself on numerous southern projects, including the first surveys for the Chesapeake and Ohio Canal. "[T]here are very few men in our country who so well combine good theory with successful practice," wrote a friend in a professional testimonial; "He is moreover a man of the greatest integrity and of the utmost concern—and possesses an exceedingly amiable and conciliatory disposition."

Eddy knew of Moore by reputation but wanted the opinion of Jefferson, whom Eddy also did not know personally. So, within hours of his hiring, Briggs wrote to Jefferson, introducing Eddy and suggesting that Moore was up for the opportunity of a lifetime: "I am induced to believe the Commissioners would be liberal in their offer; and I also believe his correctness and economy to be such in the application of public money, that more would be saved by giving *him* a salary of 10,000 dollars a year, than employing one less qualified for nothing."

Briggs's letter came to Jefferson enclosed in Eddy's. The commissioners, Eddy wrote, "have not yet appointed an engineer, and it is difficult to select a person for so important and responsible a situation." To "direct the manner in which the various parts of the work should be executed" required combined "talents, industry, and intelligence . . . rarely to be found in an individual." Eddy hoped Jefferson might recommend Moore as such a person.

Jefferson answered neither Eddy nor Briggs. Perhaps the Virginian discounted Eddy as a former commissioner or unduly influenced by the suspect Briggs, or both. More likely Jefferson calculated that better than a good Virginia engineer building New York's canal was a good Virginia engineer building Virginia roads and canals; in 1818, with Jefferson's backing, Moore would be named principal engineer of Virginia, the second leader of the country's first state board of public works. In office or retirement, Jefferson always put Virginia's interests ahead of New York's. Together Moore and Briggs might have earned southern credit for New York's canal and, as a foreigner such as William Weston might have, diminished the engineering destinies of Wright, White, Geddes, and other homespun heroes of the Empire State.

Briggs did manage smaller measures of outside influence on the canal. In 1818 Moore's son would serve as a surveyor in Briggs's crew. For the 1817 season Briggs took on Valentine Gill, a fresh "exile of Erin [and] a regular bred Engineer, versed in all its various branches." On his route of emigration through Halifax that spring, Gill had written to James Madison seeking help in securing an engineering position. President Madison replied without enthusiasm a month later, stating that he had brought Gill to the attention of the governor of Virginia but no positions were immediately available there. Given Briggs's contemporaneous hiring in New York, his continuing friendship with Madison, and Gill's lack of other contacts, it seems likely that Gill found his way to Briggs via Madison. For 1817 Gill was hired onto Erie merely as a draftsman. Two seasons later he would be one of a half dozen full engineers, earning the top daily rate of $5 plus expenses, but always with an eye on southern opportunities: his son Edward ultimately became a prominent canal and railroad engineer in Virginia, before and during the Confederacy.

New York did not get leading Virginia engineer Moore, but brother-in-law Briggs arrived upstate to national notices: "Practical mathematics and mechanics are, certainly, this gentleman's *fort*," reported Niles' *Register*, "and our confidence has been increased as to the final and *complete* accomplishment of the great work in which he is engaged, by his employment therein." None of New York's country surveyors yet merited even so much as public mention, let alone acclaim. None knew much about anything outside of upstate New York; certainly neither Wright nor Geddes could speak about the state of national manufactures, as Briggs did to a Utica audience shortly after his arrival.

Briggs brought a considerable sophistication to the woods and swamps. His personal library included, in French, Francois Andreossy's 1799 history of the Languedoc Canal and the 1810 memoirs of bridge and road engineer Pierre-Charles Lesage. His diary boasted Horace, in Briggs's own translation from the Latin:

> *More lasting than Brass, I've accomplish'd a monument,*
> *And higher than Regal pride fashion'd the Pyramids;*
> *Not showers corrosive, not violent winter winds,*
> *Not numberless ages, nor time ever fugitive*
> *Can sap, or destroy this immortal memorial.*

Briggs invoked Horace on August 17, slogging through the bogs of the upper Mohawk Valley. Perhaps he was inspired by whisperings from Rome: ground finally had been broken there six weeks earlier, but acting commissioners Young and Holley were very unhappy with Benjamin Wright.

"Mr. Wright is absent on his private business," Young complained to Clinton on August 11. Young and Holley were eager to dispatch James Geddes north to oversee the Champlain canal work but were compelled to keep him at Rome to check Wright's work. Test levels conducted by each man in the relatively short distance between Rome and Oneida Lake differed by nearly a foot. Young insisted that Geddes and Wright determine who had made the mistake: "I predict that Geddes will be found to be right and Wright wrong." The outcome is unknown, but the favorite was clear: "Geddes rises daily in our estimation; he is a man of the most persevering and laborious industry, and his head is stored with the raw materials of science which only need to be manufactured and methodized."

Clinton could not discount Young's concerns about Wright as personal or political; two days earlier, Holley had sent a similar critique to his good friend Clinton. Wright, it seems, had been everywhere but the canal line. He was north along the Black River as agent for a land developer, or at home in Rome avoiding Erie field work in unhealthy terrain. "We feel very much dissatisfied with the conduct of Mr. Wright, and think the combined effect upon him of transferring the route of the canal to the swamp [south of Rome] and his private business, has been to detach him injuriously and improperly from his duty as Engineer." Holley recognized Wright's abilities but questioned his commitment: "His superintendance [sic] of the party, led by White in his absense [sic], his experience in running the line formerly, together with his knowledge of the country and the accuracy and perspicuity of his returns, are so valuable, that we have not considered it prudent to break with him, tho' his negligence must eventuate in his dismissal, if it be not speedily discontinued."

It is incredible to think that Benjamin Wright was nearly fired from the job that would earn him the sobriquet "Father of American Civil Engineering." It would not have been the first time; exactly half his life earlier, as a twenty-three-year old surveyor, he had been dismissed by French land developers for failing to complete a road from Utica to their property along the Black River.

Wright's failings might have given Briggs an opening, but Holley and Young were disappointed with him as well: "Mr. Briggs is nearly stationary," Young complained to Clinton. Holley had come to believe that Briggs could not make much progress from Rome to Utica without help. Wright was absent, so Geddes, who had completed his assignment farther west, was being rushed to Briggs's stalled crew before heading north to the Champlain.

Thus, in the heat of the inaugural summer, it was entirely unclear who would emerge as the true chief of the Erie project. Briggs, Wright, and Geddes were employed at the same pay rate, but the first two had not earned the confidence of their employers, and Geddes was needed elsewhere.

Without a reliable Erie chief, the commissioners eased the pressure at the top by adding several subordinate or assistant engineers to the staff. Notable among these was David Stanhope Bates. Like Nathan Roberts, hired the previous year, Bates came to canalling at the ripe old age of forty.

Bates was born near Morristown, New Jersey, on a farm established by his Welsh grandparents. He was given a thorough education from ecclesiastic tutors but spurned the ministry—his father's wish—for the merchantry—his elder brother's store in Parsippany. Bates flourished as a New Jersey merchant until 1810, when he accepted an offer to survey and sell a tract in the half-million-acre Scriba Patent between New York's Oswego and Salmon rivers. With his wife and young children, Bates moved to a tiny settlement named Constantia (originally Rotterdam) on Oneida Lake. When De Witt Clinton passed through that summer on the first commissioners' tour, he found Constantia "a decayed settlement . . . containing eight or ten houses, and marks of a premature growth." Local fortunes presently rose with the success of an ironworks mining rich local ore deposits; businesswise Bates was hired as superintendent while continuing to accept attractive surveying assignments. For good measure, he studied law in the evenings and became an attorney, eventually earning a county court appointment and his lifelong title as Judge Bates. Surveying remained his favorite occupation. When Bates applied in the spring of 1817 to his frequent survey partner for a job on the Erie project, Benjamin Wright was happy to have him hired as an assistant engineer, at a very modest $3 a day without expenses. It was the start of a great career in New York and later as the principal engineer of Ohio, where three Bates sons would have their own distinguished careers.

Universally regarded as an urbane gentleman of modest manner, David Bates cut a commanding figure, "agreeable rather than handsome," a "lively but gentle" expression, "cheerful, witty, and often brilliant" in conversation, "the cherished companion" of his associates. "He gave no orders," an Ohio canal official later recalled, "but made simple requests as favors to himself, and the result was, that the duties were performed with alacrity and pleasure." Once, an Ohio story goes, when he saw a contractor puddling earth too loosely against a stone wall, Bates apologized aloud to the nearby assistant engineer for forgetting to give proper instructions, though the assistant and contractor, thus gently chastened, knew that he had.

Bates joined Roberts and Canvass White as assistant engineers for the 1817 season. Having served Wright in 1816 as a target carrier, White was made an assistant at $3 a day plus expenses. At just twenty-six years old, White was a favorite among equals.

Among the least-paid hires in 1817 was a Rome farm boy named John Bloomfield Jervis. Like White, Jervis would be mentored by Benjamin Wright. Unlike White, Jervis had little education, worldliness, wit, and family prosperity, but he would eventually rival and surpass White in American engineering. White had come to engineering carrying a surveyor's target; Jervis arrived with a woodsman's axe.

The Jervis family had been established on New York's Long Island in the 1650s. When John was three years old, his father Timothy, a carpenter, sought better opportunities upstate, on what became a heavily mortgaged farm at Rome. Educated until age fifteen at local common schools alongside juvenile Hathaways and Wrights, Jervis "entertained the idea of obtaining an education of a higher order." But he was the eldest of by then seven Jervis children, and "my father was not able to help me, and in fact, he needed the service I could render him." This meant tending fields and a sawmill in summer, and hauling lumber in winter. Jervis briefly pursued Latin by arrangement with a local teacher, but study time was restricted to late nights before the fireplace: "The demands of the work I had to do absorbed so much of my time and thought that I felt compelled to give up the attempt." For the next seven years Jervis remained on his father's struggling homestead, "unsettled as to any definite vocation." It was, he wrote in later life, "a great error to bring up a boy without giving him the training of a regular vocation. But my home was pleasant, and my father . . . though he manifested anxiety in regard to my future . . . could not overcome the urgency of my usefulness to him." Jervis was deeply influenced as a teen by the Yale-educated Calvinist pastor of the local Congregational Church, but his deepest beliefs became hard work and honest habits, little influenced (unfortunately for his biographers and his wife) by humor or emotion. Sorting out the conflicts between experimental science and organized religion, Jervis "fell back to the idea of a personal God."

Jervis's chosen deity allowed the young man an energetic pursuit of profit. During one of his final winters on the family farm, Jervis engaged with a Rome merchant to transport a load of wheat to Albany for $11. The sledding was easy until Schenectady, where the snow thinned out and the hard work began. After buying oats for his horses and his own provisions and paying his expenses, the farm boy netted $4 for a week's labor. The journey "impressed upon me the importance of the canal" that was then exciting speculation across the state. His own thoughts then on the canal went no deeper than the marketing prospects for Jervis lumber, though he heard "many intelligent men [regard] it as a measure that would involve the state in inevitable pecuniary ruin."

It was a matter of chance that canal work began near Rome and the Wrights and the Jervises prayed at the same church. As with the locating of the summit level outside Rome, more differences of opinion delayed final location of the line through dense cedar swamp farther south and west. When Nathan Roberts finally set out to stake through the swamp in late fall 1817, his party was short two axemen to clear the way. Benjamin Wright asked Timothy Jervis to borrow two of his lumber workers. The senior Jervis, who had been contemplating a bid on a two-mile canal section through the swamp, asked his eldest son to take one of the positions so he "would be able to obtain useful information as to the character of the work." John Jervis, along with another "first-rate chopper" from the Jervis farm, "entered on this new field with good spirits, not doubting we could do anything required."

Jervis was twenty-one, slender, and weighed barely 125 pounds, but "[h]aving been brought up in a new country [was] very handy" with an axe. In his memoirs, eminent engineer Jervis lamented his father's failure to educate and select a vocation for his son, but it was axe knowledge acquired on the family farm that launched Jervis's career.

His future took shape on Roberts's crew. The brush was thick, the ground soft, keeping on a line an unfamiliar skill, and early snow made the going even more disagreeable, but Jervis "soon got the run of the work, and having myself a pretty good eye for a line, we worked our way in what appeared a satisfactory method." The arbiter of satisfaction was chief Roberts. Jervis found him "a man of austere manners who did not hesitate to speak plainly" and whom the survey party regarded "with a reverence that did allow familiarity."

After a few weeks of hacking brush, chopping trees, cutting stakes, and fashioning pegs to support the leveling instruments, Jervis's attention was drawn to their "profound mystery." With "great modesty, as they quite outranked me in the service," Jervis began to ask the young target-men for whom he drove pegs about the workings of their gear. Emboldened by "some approving words for my expertise as an axeman," Jervis asked to examine the target and its movements himself: "On reflection it appeared to me I could do that service if I could have a little practice."

Jervis did not feel free to direct any questions to Roberts, until the last day of the survey. By then the survey chief had commented occasionally about his dexterous axemen, indeed, "that he had never had a pair . . . so skillful and efficient as we were." They had won Roberts's favor as "men who were not afraid to work." Huddled in the swamp for the survey party's last supper together, Jervis saw his opportunity to approach Roberts. Casually, as a buffer against disappointment, the young man asked, "What will you give me to go with you next summer and carry one of those targets?" "Twelve dollars per month," the math-trained engineer promptly replied. Without thinking, Jervis as promptly assented. With that, John Jervis was enrolled in the new Erie School of Engineering.

One other important hire in 1817 was not a budding engineer. At a commissioners' meeting in Utica in mid-July, the commissioners hired Andrew Abramse Bartow as a land agent, at $4 a day without expenses. Bartow was a friend of De Witt Clinton, but this was no courtesy hire.

Bartow was a Westchester native, descended from a Cambridge-educated Anglican minister assigned in 1702 to southern New York. Among Bartow's notable American relatives was cousin Theodosia Bartow, Aaron Burr's adored first wife, whose early death from cancer set him adrift emotionally for the rest of his enigmatic life. In 1806 Bartow, his wife Mary Hunt—of New York's Hunt's Point—and their several children relocated to a large homestead in the Herkimer County town of Fairfield.

A civic leader from his arrival, Andrew was instrumental in Fairfield's selection in 1812 as the home of the College of Physicians and Surgeons of the Western District of New York (commonly known as Fairfield Medical College), the sixth medical school in the country and the first west of the Hudson. As a school trustee, Bartow often appeared in Albany before the state Board of Regents, of which Clinton was a longtime member. At one session, the story goes, a regent addressed the medical college's representative as "Dr. Bartow." The genial layman began to correct what he perceived as light humor but was interrupted by Clinton: "Go on, Doctor, the Board of Regents never joke." The room erupted, the story spread west, and "Doctor Bartow" as he came to be known earned his honorary degree. Clinton cherished Bartow, "a sprightly, pleasing gentleman, who possesses a great fund of information, which he [is] by no means parsimonious in imparting."

The amiable Doctor Bartow, who would serve the commissioners throughout the construction years, met with great success as a land agent in his first season. Bartow rode the entire line on horseback from Utica to the Seneca River, taking "particular pains to call on every resident land holder" he could find. He secured voluntary cessions from 90 percent of them. The following spring, the commissioners named Bartow their agent to make contracts for all the timber, sand, and lime required for construction along the middle section. It was in the procuring of the last item, essential to the making of waterproof cement, that Bartow would make a crucial discovery later in 1818.

While the commissioners built their staff in 1817, financing the canal remained an uncertainty. "Money is very scarce in this city," Clinton wrote anxiously from New York City in early May to Joseph Ellicott. If the anticipated first loan issue of $200,000 "should fail, it would have a very pernicious effect on all our future operations and I am not certain but that it would gratify the President of the Canal fund board," the despised lieutenant governor Tayler, who would have been happy to bury the incoming governor in his unfinished ditch. Clinton asked Ellicott to write to his influential boss, Paul Busti, in Philadelphia and "urge his favorable interference" with friendly bankers who might buy canal bonds.

Two weeks later Albany entrepreneur Josephus B. Stuart, a former army paymaster and recent chancellor to the U.S. consulate in London, informed the canal fund commissioners that certain banks in London had authorized him to offer a $1.5 million loan. Stuart gave no details of what perhaps was a speculative scheme. The resourceful William Bayard had found no such success securing a European loan in 1816 and, in any case, the 1817 canal law had shifted financing from large, open market loans to a conservative mix of taxes and scheduled borrowing.

The fund commissioners did not reply to Stuart, but when the first canal loan issue was offered in June 1817, the 6 percent, twenty-year bonds were fully and quickly subscribed. Over a third was taken by two London insurance men; the huge $40,000 investment by the director of the Royal Exchange Assurance Company wouldn't be exceeded by an American individual until four years and ten loan issues later. The record is not plain, but Busti, Stuart, and other men of money presumably influenced the market for the successful first loan. Though the country's economy was headed into recession, there would be little trouble subscribing future canal loans. "There is money in abundance to loan in our commercial emporium," Clinton wrote to an Ohio canal promoter just a year after the anxiety over the first loan.

The success of the first loan gave the commissioners confidence to move forward. In June the commissioners met at Utica to lay out the details for contracting the work. As usual, Clinton had written a personal invitation to Ellicott, and Ellicott had stayed out west. But also as usual, he was present in concept. His recommendation that a single acting commissioner, preferably Clinton, actively oversee the work had been ignored since he had offered it a year earlier. Now Myron Holley and Samuel Young were both designated acting commissioners, with $1,500 salaries plus expenses. Young was named the commission's secretary, and Holley, in a move that would haunt him, the commission's treasurer. Holley also emerged as the commission's principal writer. "Some of the most luminous reports and communications have proceeded from his pen," his friend Clinton wrote several years later. Though he remained the commission president, Clinton's main advocacy for the canal would be as governor. Longtime commissioner Stephen Van Rensselaer's role would remain largely ceremonial, even after succeeding Clinton as commission president in 1825. And commissioner Ellicott always saw the canal as a function of his duty to sell and settle Holland Company land.

Following from their earlier decision to have contractors build the canal, the commissioners now directed their protoengineers on how to divide the line into short sections for contracting. Where practicable, each section was to have a brook, ravine, or low ground at one end, so the contractor could drain off water without interfering with work on adjoining sections. In the preparation of each section's specifications, the surveyor-engineers were turned into geologists: with twelve-foot augers they were to make perforations into each section's ground so that "every alternation in its strata, its hardness or softness, its inclination to vegetable matter, clay, loam, sand, gravel or other substance, and also its porosity or impermeability to water, might be ascertained with the greatest possible accuracy." On the surface, all previous levels were to be reexamined and adjusted as necessary, permanent benchmarks fixed, and five rows of stakes placed: one marking the center of the canal line; two marking the forty-foot width of excavation; and two, sixty feet apart, marking the outer edge for grubbing of trees, brush, and rocks. In addition, "perspicuous" profiles and plans, numbered or alphabetized by section, were to be prepared showing each section's length, soil variations, quality and quantity of grubbing, and assorted other details. In this way, each of the eventually hundreds of sections became in effect a miniature, manageable canal.

Satisfied that the surveyor-engineers could prepare the first fifty sections in a month's time, the commissioners decided that ground could be broken at Rome on Independence Day, with acting commissioner Young presiding.

Ellicott may have been flattered by the adoption of his acting commissioner concept, but he remained as ever a company man. "Should this Herculean work ever be effected," he wrote in mid-June to Busti, "and the canal take the direction as explored under my instructions [by William Peacock], it would in its passage through the Holland Purchase intersect unsold land belonging for the great part to our Principals, and enhance the value of it." Indeed, "whether it is ever accomplished or otherwise," the project had already proved a "considerable auxiliary" in promoting sales and allowing Ellicott to raise prices on prime land by over a dollar and half per acre.

The bidding process for the first sections appears to have been more by word of mouth than by competitive bid. The record is blank on how the contracts were awarded. The first was taken on June 27 by John Richardson; by the groundbreaking ceremony a week later, forty-nine other contracts had been awarded for fifty-eight miles of the middle section.

The commissioners effectively passed on the construction burden to their contractors, who as a general rule were as inexperienced as they in making a canal. The incentives were great for the commissioners. Risk shifted from the state to private individuals but was limited by the small size of each contract; the failure of one contractor jeopardized the completion only of his short section. Cost shifted from the inefficient state, vulnerable to bureaucracy, patronage, and waste, to the limited economy of the small contractor. Several smaller southern canals had experimented to some degree with contracting, and contractors had built a substantial portion of the twenty-seven-mile Middlesex Canal, but New York's canals standardized the practice.

The dozens of men who took contracts during the first season were nearly all local farmers and frontier merchants who lived or owned land along the canal line. A scattering were men "recently arrived in this country" who brought some experience with canal work. One was a veteran of the Middlesex Canal, but he did not last long; by 1820 Timothy Hunt had given up several uncompleted sections to Rome's Jeremiah Brainard, who would become one of the most prominent and innovative Erie contractors.

Once the commissioners had committed to a system of independent contracting, they adopted a paternalistic relationship with their contractors. The sections were kept as short as forty rods and no longer than three miles, so that "men in moderate pecuniary circumstances" would be able to take them, after posting an adequate security. Though the multiplicity of contracts made more paperwork for the commissioners and engineers, this system was, to the commissioners, "more just and equitable" than having larger sections and fewer contractors, which would have "put it in the power of a few wealthy individuals to have monopolised the whole, and to have made sub-contracts, at reduced prices, with the laboring part of the community." A certain amount of subcontracting did develop over the years, but the canal builders largely remained the modest local farmers and small upstate merchants with a vested interest in the canal's successful completion.

Few contractors had the financial reserve to purchase tools, provisions, and animal teams, so the commissioners generally offered advances of up to $2,000 on the security of "some responsible individual" such as a prominent local citizen who accepted liability along with the contractor. If the contractor failed either to start work within a short time (usually two months) or complete it in the time and manner specified, the advance had to be repaid with interest. The particulars of each advance were handwritten on the back of each printed contract.

Under the standard contract language, a contractor was required to finish his whole job and have it inspected and accepted by the engineer assigned to his section before payment was made. In practice, though, contractors faithfully pursuing their work were given monthly payments of slightly less than the value of the work performed, with a final payment on the contract balance, less advances, made on completion of the job. If contractor deception was discovered, in-progress payments were suspended and strict compliance with the contract was enforced.

New York's canal contractors were often of the same social class and well known to the engineers who oversaw them and the commissioners who paid them, so the financial arrangements could be relatively casual. Although the fear of dishonest "jobbers" motivated close scrutiny, most of the first Erie contractors were, as the commissioners reported after the 1817 season, "men of property and respectability, whose reputations are intimately connected with a faithful performance of their contracts."

The combination of respectable contractors and safeguards against those who might stray allowed the commissioners to "safely anticipate" that their canal would be built "in the most substantial and durable manner." Although many post–Erie Canal projects suffered from contractor corruption and engineer inattention, New York's pioneer projects substantially met the commissioners' expectations.

By the end of July 1817 some five hundred men were at work on the contracted sections and all seemed well. Then the rains came. For the

De Witt Clinton (1769–1828), by John Wesley Jarvis, circa 1816, in his political and physical prime. A year later the guiding spirit of the canal to Lake Erie would be governor of New York; another year later, a riding accident would shatter Clinton's robust health, and ultimately shorten his life. *(Collection of the New-York Historical Society; accession no. 1940.958)*

Elkanah Watson (1758–1842), circa 1805–1810, creator in 1792 (with Philip Schuyler) of the much-maligned Western Inland Lock Navigation Company, and highly opinionated commentator on Erie progress. *(Collection of the New-York Historical Society; accession no. 1924.11)*

Gouverneur Morris (1752–1816), lesser Founding Father and early but misguided supporter of the Erie project, shown with his infamous wooden appendage. *(Emmet Collection, Miriam and Ira D. Wallach Division of Art, Prints and Photographs, The New York Public Library, Astor, Lenox and Tilden Foundations)*

Jesse Hawley (1773–1842), by Ezra Ames, circa 1825, the year his speech at Buffalo officially opened the Erie Canal, an idea he had launched eighteen years earlier with his "Hercules" essays written in debtors' prison. *(Collection of the New-York Historical Society; accession no. X.29)*

Myron Holley (1779–1841), by Ezra Ames, circa 1820, when the canal commissioner and commission treasurer was at the height of his substantial authority, four years before a small misappropriation of canal funds ruined him. *(Collection of the New-York Historical Society; accession no. 1892.4)*

Joseph Ellicott (1760–1826), circa 1820, when the legendary surveyor for the Holland Land Company and the tyrannical powerbroker of Western New York was still master of his prodigious faculties. He withheld support to Buffalo settlers, never fully embraced the canal, and ten months after it opened ended his gathering derangement by hanging himself. *(Reproduction by author)*

Peter Buell Porter (1773–1844), in War of 1812 uniform. The early but ambivalent canal commissioner relentlessly promoted Black Rock to be named western terminus of the Erie Canal: he won battles, but lost the war to Wilkeson's Buffalo. *(Courtesy of Buffalo and Erie County Historical Society)*

Samuel Wilkeson (1781–1848), the master builder of Buffalo's harbor, and vanquisher of rival Peter Porter and nemesis Joseph Ellicott. *(Courtesy of Buffalo and Erie County Historical Society)*

Utica, August 1822, watercolor attributed to Knickerbocker editor and summer traveler Johnston Verplanck. The passage of the canal directly through Utica was a boon to its prospects, just as the canal's passage south of Rome was a permanent setback for its prospects. *(Courtesy of the New York State Library)*

The canal and towpath bridge across the Cayuga Marsh at Montezuma, sketched on November 9, 1825, by Rev. John Henry Hopkins: peaceful scene then; a place of sickness and suffering by Erie builders earlier. *(Clements Library, University of Michigan)*

John B. Jervis (1795–1885), circa 1835, well on his way to a long and prominent American engineering career that started eighteen years earlier with an axe clearing trees from the path for the canal near Rome. *(Jervis Public Library)*

Isaac Briggs (1763–1825), undated, the only known depiction of the Jefferson protégé who briefly brought some southern engineering influence to New York's great project before broken dreams in Virginia, and death from despair. *(Courtesy of the Maryland Historical Society)*

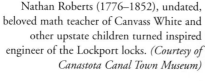

Nathan Roberts (1776–1852), undated, beloved math teacher of Canvass White and other upstate children turned inspired engineer of the Lockport locks. *(Courtesy of Canastota Canal Town Museum)*

William Peacock (1780–1877), circa 1820, Jesse Hawley friend, "Hercules" confidant, and Joseph Ellicott's dutiful nephew and canal surveyor. *(Reproduction by author)*

Benjamin Wright (1770–1842), undated, who overcame youthful surveying failures to become Erie chief engineer; his project guidance and management skills earned him (in 1969) the title "Father of American Civil Engineering." *(The Granger Collection, New York)*

James Geddes (1763–1838), undated, the lesser-celebrated other "chief engineer" of the Erie and Champlain canals, whose earliest surveys proved that building a canal to Lake Erie was possible. *(Reproduction by author)*

Canvass White (1790–1834), circa 1820–1830, when the young and promising engineer was rising fast from his first work on the Erie Canal to other major projects around the country; delicate health led to his early death. *(Munson-Williams-Proctor Arts Institute, Museum of Art, Utica NY, 58.104)*

Navigation on the Mohawk River in 1807, as depicted in a contemporary book by traveler Christian Schultz. Note the bateau being poled in the foreground and the crew of the larger Durham boat struggling by various methods through a Western Inland Lock Navigation Company wing-dam. *(Clements Library, University of Michigan)*

Serene canal boat travel along the Mohawk River, circa November 10, 1825, as sketched by Rev. John Henry Hopkins, rector of Pittsburgh's Trinity Church. *(Clements Library, University of Michigan)*

Entrance of the Erie Canal into the Hudson River at Albany, 1823, from Colden's *Memoir*. Note the Masonic arches over lock number one, where the completion of the canal's eastern section was celebrated. *(Reproduction by author)*

The side-cut from the Erie Canal to the Hudson opposite Troy, circa 1830. The controversial decision to crisscross the lower Mohawk and run the canal to Albany close to the western bank of the Hudson allowed for a short side cut that served Troy's long-term commercial interests. *(Collection of the New-York Historical Society; negative no. 46562A)*

The "Lower Aqueduct" carrying the canal across the Mohawk at Fonda's Ferry (now Crescent) in 1826, drawn by German traveler A. Duttenhofer. A wooden trunk on twenty-six stone piers, it was the longest bridge on the canal and, with the "Upper Aqueduct" twelve miles upriver, a crisscross that engineers John Randel and John Jervis deemed unnecessary. *(Rare Books Division, The New York Public Library, Astor, Lenox and Tilden Foundations)*

Canal lock and arched, navigable feeder over the Mohawk at Little Falls, sketched circa November 11, 1825, by Rev. John Henry Hopkins. The depiction by the canal traveler is considerably less romantic but more realistic than later popular images by professional painters. *(Clements Library, University of Michigan)*

Utica, August 1822, watercolor attributed to Knickerbocker editor and summer traveler Johnston Verplanck. The passage of the canal directly through Utica was a boon to its prospects, just as the canal's passage south of Rome was a permanent setback for its prospects. *(Courtesy of the New York State Library)*

The canal and towpath bridge across the Cayuga Marsh at Montezuma, sketched on November 9, 1825, by Rev. John Henry Hopkins: peaceful scene then; a place of sickness and suffering by Erie builders earlier. *(Clements Library, University of Michigan)*

The canal aqueduct over the Genesee River at Rochester in 1826, as drawn by German traveler A. Duttenhofer. Note the sharp entry turn and narrow width that, along with the inferior sandstone construction, required the aqueduct's replacement just ten years later. *(Rare Books Division, The New York Public Library, Astor, Lenox and Tilden Foundations)*

Lockport in 1825, drawn and lithographed by George Catlin, from Colden's *Memoir*. City is replacing forest at the brow of the sixty-foot ridge that Nathan Roberts conquered with his double set of five locks. *(Reproduction by author)*

Excavation of the Lockport Deep Cut, circa 1825, drawn and lithographed by George Catlin, from Colden's *Memoir*. Even after the state took over the excavation from earnest but overmatched local contractors, the Deep Cut would not have been completed by late 1825 without Orange Dibble's innovative cranes to remove debris from the cut; unfortunately for Lockport, there was no plan for removing the mountain chain of debris from the town. *(Reproduction by author)*

The finished Deep Cut, 1825, drawn and lithographed by George Catlin, from Colden's *Memoir*. The cut was just wide enough for passing boats, and the towpath was just wide enough for passing horses (later mules), with a low timber sill for a bit of security. *(Reproduction by author)*

Frontier innovation was essential to Erie construction. Tree stumps were pulled by these oversized contraptions built with forest supplies; smaller growth was cut by a newly designed plow and scraper; muck was more effectively carted by a new wheelbarrow with a rounded basin; and painstaking experiments resulted in the discovery of hydraulic cement for making canal masonry watertight. *(American Heritage Picture Collection)*

Black Rock in 1825, redrawn by a later artist from an original sketch by George Catlin, showing the relatively large anchorage on the mainland side of Squaw Island and the slender pier leading south toward Lake Erie that gave hopes of local advantage over Buffalo's much smaller harbor. *(Courtesy of Buffalo and Erie County Historical Society)*

Buffalo harbor in 1825, drawn and lithographed by George Catlin, from Colden's *Memoir*. Projecting into Lake Erie on the right side is the breakwater that made a harbor of a storm-ridden inlet with a nasty sandbar. *(Reproduction by author)*

De Witt Clinton wedding the waters of Lake Erie with the Atlantic Ocean at the mouth of New York Harbor, on the afternoon of November 4, 1825 (with a robed Samuel Latham Mitchill waiting his turn to spout), from Colden's *Memoir. (The Granger Collection, New York)*

The small wooden keg—sixteen inches tall and twelve inches across—that traveled on the *Seneca Chief* from Buffalo filled with Lake Erie water for Clinton to pour off into the Atlantic. *(Collection of the New-York Historical Society; accession no. X.48)*

Neptune and Pan sharing their bounties, engraved by Asher Durand, from Colden's *Memoir*. The image appeared on silk badges worn during New York canal celebrations festivities; a modified design appeared on the face of the commemorative medals presented early in 1826 to various dignitaries, including President John Quincy Adams and the four surviving ex-presidents. *(Reproduction by author)*

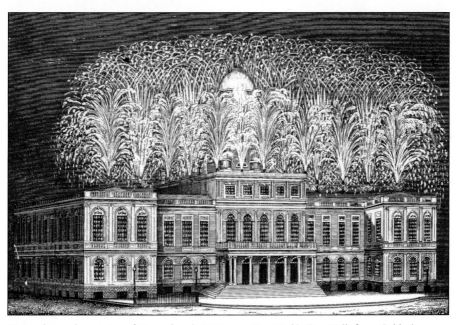

Fireworks on the evening of November 4, 1825, over New York's City Hall, from Colden's *Memoir*. Eight years earlier every vote by the city's state representatives in Albany on the enabling legislation for the Erie Canal was a nay. *(The Granger Collection, New York)*

De Witt Clinton, by George Catlin, circa 1825, looking triumphant but with the weight of sedentary years upon him. He would be dead at age 58, in less than three years, denied much time to contemplate the impact of the Erie Canal on his state and nation. *(Collection of the New-York Historical Society; accession no. 1946.163)*

next two months, "repeated inundations . . . surpassed in extent and duration all former example." In early October the swollen headwaters of the Mohawk River reversed direction, flowing west through Rome into Wood Creek, breaching the ancient carrying place and submerging canal work old and new. The flooding, greater "than was ever before witnessed in any season by the oldest inhabitants," effectively discharged the waters of the upper Mohawk into the St. Lawrence, "converting the northern and eastern part of this state, and indeed, all the country east of the Hudson and south of the St. Lawrence, into an island."

Looking on the bright side, the commissioners discerned divine purpose in the floods, "as if to indicate at the commencement, by the height, impetuosity and durability of the greatest floods, the exact dimensions and strengths of the works necessary to discharge or resist them." The record drought of 1816 had permitted essential and extensive surveys and revealed the least supplies of water available along prospective canal routes. The record flooding of 1817 showed the canal builders how substantial their works would have to be. The commissioners, "with minds accustomed to view in every occurrence a particular dispensation of a benign and superintending Providence," were inclined to believe that Heaven was indeed signaling approval.

While the flooding indicated safe design parameters for future locks, embankments, and other hydraulic structures that the commissioners and engineers were otherwise largely guessing at, the downside was that many of the first-year contractors saw their profits burst by flood damage and delays. The rains of 1817 were in large part responsible for many in the first group of contractors failing to complete their jobs. In fact, as the legislature ordered the commissioners to detail after the 1818 season, on the first thirteen sections from the Rome area west, ten original contractors would abandon their work. In most of these cases the contractor had accomplished a fair portion of his contract and, after settling his financial obligations to the commissioners, the job was taken up by a new contractor at the same or a slightly higher price. One of the failed original contractors was a distillery owner in Lee (near Rome) named Moses Hall. He had contracted for a half-mile portion of section three but, after taking a $400 advance, did no work at all. The commissioners threatened a lawsuit

until Hall's guarantor—"a man whose responsibility is unquestionable"—
gave assurances that the advance plus interest would be returned
promptly. In the meantime, a partnership of two other Oneida County
men took over the work at the same price, and by the end of 1818 completed all of the grubbing and clearing and half of the excavation.

The same partners took over for a number of the failed contractors,
most notably Rome's own Joshua Hathaway, who had turned the first
ceremonial furrow. After over $11,000 worth of grueling labor on his
mile and a quarter section in the swamps just south of town, Hathaway
gave up. To excavate up to ten feet below the surface of the swamp, his
crew had built dams and drainage channels to dry the section, only to be
inundated by mud during the 1817 floods. After that they unexpectedly
encountered quicksand and an impenetrable clay. What geologists now
know to be a dense, glacier-compressed till of clay, sand, gravel, and
crushed boulders, the Erie excavators of 1817 dubbed hardpan, and the
name has stuck. The deep excavation that Hathaway had contracted for
at thirteen cents per cubic yard was completed by his successor at twenty-
five cents.

"[A]mong our first contractors," the commissioners were compelled
to admit, "there were a few, who had not all the qualifications necessary
to ensure the fulfillment of their engagements." But most were "worthy
and respectable men," the commissioners stressed, "the best men . . . that
could be selected out of the whole community." The commissioners estimated that the "extraordinary wetness of the season" had increased contractors' costs by up to 30 percent, but they were wary of assessing blame
that might give a particular section "a bad name, and [make] it less easy
to let it out again on reasonable terms." Instead, when entering into second contracts, the commissioners often as not chose "to give something
more, to induce the contractor to take upon himself the risk of these difficulties." Under this policy, only one contractor who signed on in 1818
later joined the shortening list of delinquents.

Joshua Hathaway's fellow Independence Day performer, John
Richardson, had a better contracting experience. Despite the excavation
of section one being "almost incessantly interrupted or incommoded by
repeated inundations," Richardson's was the only section completed (but

for some finish work) by season's end. By the end of 1820, Richardson would take all or part of five more sections, plus a low dam to water the canal from Oriskany Creek between Rome and Utica. These contracts, worth a total of nearly $40,000, would put Richardson among the top contractors on the Erie line.

Among the few early Erie contractors who were not local farmers or frontier merchants with limited engineering knowledge was Simon Newton Dexter. Raised in Providence and Boston, Dexter was the son of the first American manufacturer of cotton goods and a nephew of John Adams's Treasury secretary, the predecessor of Jefferson's Gallatin. Dexter moved his textile business to the mid-Hudson Valley in 1810 and upstate five years later to Whitesboro, where he flourished for the next half-century. Dexter sized up canal opportunities quickly. In the first four seasons of construction, alone or with partners he was involved in nearly $60,000 worth of contracts for various sections, structures, and supplies; his $38,000 in individual contracts put him among the leaders, with John Richardson. In 1820 Dexter would organize the first canal packet boat company; twenty years later he would be named a canal commissioner.

Dexter was an active canal maker in 1817, and so were his workers. The labor highlight of the 1817 season took place on a section he shared with two partners from Rome. In one extraordinary burst of energy, a team of three anonymous Irish laborers reportedly excavated a fifty-foot length of canal in five and a half days. Their daily pay for digging 250 cubic yards of earth, packing the canal banks, and clearing a towpath amounted to $1.88 each, "very liberal wages" and an inspiration to all workers and contractors, in the opinion of the commissioners. This was at a time when unskilled laborers back in Ireland earned about ten cents a day.

The event was unusual on many counts. Though legendary gangs of Irish laborers were destined for grueling work on the line in coming years, the early laborers, like the contractors, were predominantly local. Even after the 1818 season, the commissioners made a point of reporting that "three-fourths of all the labourers were born among us." Dexter's Irish trio were also unusual in that they were paid according to the amount of work they did. The piece rate was very uncommon. An incentive for industrious workers, it was resented by most as inviting abuse from contractors and was shied away from by contractors as difficult to budget. Erie contractors and laborers preferred set wages, by the day or especially by the month. A month's employment at the prevailing day rate of fifty cents might bring greater earnings than the monthly rate of eight to twelve dollars (for twenty-five days of work), but the day wage included neither room and board nor the promise of a full month's employment. Though the commissioners marveled at the $10 earned in a spectacular week by Dexter's crew, few others offered to do the same or took the bait.

The popular image of the Erie as an Irish-built canal was fostered by otherwise reliable people. "Wild Irish bog trotters from West Ireland" were rampant around Rome from the first days of construction, in the reminiscence of Oliver Payson Hubbard, retired professor of chemistry, mineralogy, and geology at Dartmouth. They "were set to work knee deep in the wet muck; they could wear no clothing but a flannel shirt and slouch cap. . . . It was a weird sight to see . . . hundreds of these wild Irish men at work. Saturday nights in their board shanties, 'fighting drunk', and contractors had to go in and club them right and left to quiet them." Hubbard recalled seeing a Rome schoolteacher "screaming 'Murder!' and running . . . to get out of the way of a half dozen of those fellows, each with a paving stone or shillelagh in hand."

Hubbard wrote this in his late eighties, when he might have forgotten that in 1817 he was a schoolboy of eight, only recently arrived in Rome with his family from Connecticut. The "wild Irish" would certainly find their place on the canal, but not for several years, and mostly far west of Rome.

From late summer into the fall of 1817, the *Dublin Journal* promoted Irish emigration with optimistic items about opportunity in America. Escapees from economic collapse in Ireland began flooding into New York City. Unskilled laborers not finding work there quickly fanned out into their new country, but not yet in droves north to canal country. In August the final sentence of an item in an Irish immigrant paper in New York City, *The Exile,* advised its newest readers that the canal "will afford steady and permanent employment, as laborers will have work winter as well as summer." The bulk of the item, though, urged readers to "proceed immediately" to central Pennsylvania, where a glass factory, as well as "farmers, gentlemen, and manufacturers," were in need of "sober and industrious" laborers. The paper provided travel directions—west to Pennsylvania, not north to upstate New York.

By October 1817 a thousand mostly local men were working on the fifty-eight contracted miles of the Erie canal. By the end of the construction season in December, unconnected portions totaling fifteen miles had been completed.

As geological and other lapses in the preparatory surveys became evident when some contractors ran into trouble on their sections, the commissioners late in the first season developed "considerable solicitude" about the long level that Wright and Geddes had come up with for the middle section. To quell their anxiety before too much work was done, the commissioners gave Geddes an exercise just prior to his shift to the Champlain canal. "[A]s a test to the accuracy of the work," Geddes was sent with his leveling instruments on a circuitous hundred-mile route from Rome via Oneida and Onondaga lakes to Salina, over twice the distance of the canal line between Rome and Salina. Arriving at Salina the long way around, Geddes found that the difference between his test level and the level already established was less than an inch and a half. "This result, so satisfactory" to the palpably relieved commissioners, "exhibits in the engineers a degree of care, skill and precision, in the delicate process of leveling, which has perhaps never been exceeded." Not that the commissioners had a broad frame of reference about delicate engineering; after one construction season, New York's canal makers had yet to build any of the substantial structures that would make Clinton and especially Holley and Young the commissioners of an actual canal and their surveyors actual engineers.

The flooding in 1817 made canal work more difficult than expected, but many of the contractors were settlers used to adversity. They responded by beginning to develop the clever and incredible labor-saving and profit-increasing tools featured along the line in future years. The short inaugural season produced the first breakthrough in excavation: the fitting of a cutting blade on wrought iron plows to sever small roots. Twice as efficient in dry ground as the traditional spade and wheelbarrow, the "plow and scraper" featured a heavier but thinner iron plow than was commonly used, with a sharpened steel edge. "Two yoke of oxen will draw this utensil through any roots not exceeding two inches in diameter," the commissioners reported. "By moving it, at short intervals, through the surface of any ground to be excavated, the small roots and fibres are so cut up as to be easily picked and harrowed out of the way of the shovel and scraper." A mile of canal could be excavated in one season by a team of oxen or horses and three men, with the added benefit that their repeated heavy passages compacted the earth that would form the canal's banks. The plow and scraper only worked on dry ground, though, of which there was precious little in the sections begun in the flood summer of 1817. In soft ground, only a spade and wheelbarrow would avail; in the swamps west of Rome and at Montezuma on the western end of the middle section, even tools gave way to mucking by hand.

The first construction season closed quickly with ice and snow in early December. When the frozen ground prevented more digging, the commissioners offered contractors advances of up to $1,000 to buy beef, pork, flour, and other provisions at seasonally low prices. Over frozen swamps, contractors' sleighs hauled the stores to where they would be needed in spring.

The year ended with vindication of the conservative fiscal plan required by George Tibbits. After the initial $200,000 loan seeded the canal fund, it accumulated another $72,000 in auction duties, $16,500 in steamboat passenger taxes, and just under $3,000 in salt duties (for which collection hadn't begun until August). After paying out to the canal commissioners the proceeds of the fully subscribed loan and $6,000 in interest to bondholders, the canal fund ended its first year over $85,000 in the black.

As sections took shape in upstate New York, the canal quickly evolved from a visionary project to one that could actually be seen, in physical and cartographic reality. The first state map to show the Erie and Champlain canals as their lines had been surveyed was completed late in 1817 and published the following year. Remarkable for its detail and clarity, "The State of New York with part of the adjacent states" was said at the time "to exceed all other maps hitherto published in America" in style and accuracy; it remains one of the most beautiful maps ever made of the state. The map was engraved and published posthumously. Its creator, thirty-three-year-old John Eddy, died of uncertain causes on the morning of December 22, 1817, at his father's house in New York City. The deaf geographer, already the author of acclaimed maps of New York City and the western part of the state, had spent the last four years of his life laboring over his masterpiece. He completed it in the months before his death and seven years after the statewide tour with his father and the other original commissioners that had opened De Witt Clinton's mind to the possibility of an Erie canal.

CHAPTER 9

Securing the Middle

*The truth is, opposition to the Canal is dwindling away. The mis-
creants in N.Y. who have opposed it from vile motives are properly
appreciated—and the opposition of the South will cease because it is
understood that we can do without national aid.*
—De Witt Clinton, March 1818

[N]o man can calculate the effects to be produced by the Erie canal.
—*Niles' Register*, November 1819

Back on his father's farm for the 1818 winter, John Jervis began to wonder what he had agreed to. Twelve dollars a month was not much on
which to launch a career. "It was natural the question should arise, could
I ever become an engineer?" In his brief axe work, he had "only seen a
very small edge of the great field." With little education, none in science,
and only some cursory examination of a target, "the mystery of the level,
the taking of sights, its adjustment, and the computations of the observations were all dark to me." He considered that Nathan Roberts's offer
might have been a joke, unexpectedly accepted. After several weeks' uncertainty, Jervis called on Benjamin Wright at his house in Rome "and requested him to inform me if they certainly accepted my position."
Wright promptly replied, "If you say you will go, I say you shall go."

Jervis "had no fancy for appearing more ignorant than those engaged
in the same field," and so began educating himself for the job ahead. "I

had voluntarily put on the harness, and had faith to believe that what others had learned, I could learn." On evenings and the occasional days when weather prevented outdoor work, he studied surveying books, purchased on Roberts's recommendation.

While Jervis spent the winter of 1818 in provincial Rome pondering his future as a fifty-cents-a-day targetman, Canvass White was in England studying its canals and spreading the word about New York's. Having participated in Erie surveys for two seasons, White was now a veteran, with an old mentor in Wright and a new fan in governor and canal commission president Clinton, who had urged White to take his trip (at his own expense). Alone among New York's surveyors and imminent engineers, White had been to England before, as a prisoner of war and stranded seaman five years earlier.

During an exhausting six-month, two-thousand-mile tour, White closely observed dozens of British canals. He took particular note of Thomas Telford's masterpiece, the thousand-foot Pontcysyllte Aqueduct, rising on cast iron arches a hundred feet above the River Dee in North Wales. Completed in 1805 after ten years' work, Pontcysyllte remains in operation and in excellent condition.

White made detailed drawings of what he saw in England, purchased sophisticated new leveling instruments on New York's account, promoted emigration to experienced canal contractors and skilled workers, and brought back a canal boat model that would inform the design of the first Erie canal boat.

White met many engineering authorities in England, none more remarkable than John Isaac Hawkins, an ingenious Londoner with an eminent American past. Hawkins had spent most of his first thirty years in and around Philadelphia. In 1800 he designed and built the first upright piano in America. In 1802 he patented a physiognotrace that helped make silhouette profiles the ubiquitous wall art of early nineteenth-century American homes. In 1803 he patented an improved pantograph that he dubbed the polygraph, a multiple-penned device that produced exceptionally true copies of documents as they were written. Thomas Jefferson got a Hawkins polygraph early in 1804, calling it "the finest invention of the present age," and wrote with one for the rest of his life.

Succeeded by new wonders of mechanical copying ability, the polygraph survives as the graphic lie-detecting machine of modern criminology. Though Hawkins partnered with Jefferson friend Charles Willson Peale to market his inventions, patent infringers outstripped the lawsuits, especially after Hawkins returned in 1803 to England, where he continued his inventive firsts: a mechanical pencil (1822), trifocals (1827), and a gold pen nib (1834), which Russia's first Tsar Nicholas ordered for his court.

When White visited with the prolific polymath in 1817, Hawkins was a prominent civil engineer with a considerable knowledge of the waterproof cement required for hydraulic works. New York's canal commissioners had not thought much yet about the mortar that would be needed to make their locks, aqueducts, culverts, and other masonry structures waterproof. The issue had been neatly avoided during 1817 with the long level on the middle section, which required no substantial hydraulics. By late in the 1818 season construction would be extending into the varied levels of the westernmost portion of the middle section, where locks would have to be built. More experienced than anyone involved with New York's canal, Hawkins knew what was in store for them.

Hawkins explained to White the necessary components of a good waterproof cement and sent the young man off with specimens of the minerals required. Hawkins assumed that when New York needed it, cement perfected in England would be exported by him at substantial profit.

Back in New York, new governor Clinton opened his first legislature in late January 1818. "Notwithstanding the unfavorable season, the inexperience of the contractors, and the late commencement of operations," the progress on New York's canals in the first season had far exceeded expectations. Triumphantly, Clinton detailed a broad vision for New York's future:

> The enhancement of the profits of agriculture; the excitement of manufacturing industry; the activity of internal trade; the benefits of lucrative traffic; the interchange of valuable commodities; the commerce of fertile, remote and wide-spread regions; and the approximation of the most

distant parts of the union, by the facility and rapidity of communication that will result from the completion of these stupendous works, will spread the blessings of plenty and opulence to an immeasurable extent.

Clinton launched an activist agenda unprecedented in the annual legislative messages of previous governors. He argued for government's leading role in promoting and supporting education, commercial agriculture, and internal improvement; roads and canals would join prosperous and productive farmers with educated and industrious townsmen into "a free, high-minded, enlightened and magnanimous people."

For this to happen, it was necessary that the legislature authorize the eastern and western sections of the Erie canal. This was the subtext of Clinton's speech and, four days later, the overt message of the annual report from his canal commission: "To join the east to the west; to unite the forty-fifth degree of latitude on Lake Champlain with the farthest verge of Lake Superior; to connect the whole with the ocean, and to bestow the blessings of an easy intercommunication upon the millions of human beings who are destined to flourish along these extended lines, are within the resources of this state." The completion of the canals was, in language suggesting Clinton's influence on a report ostensibly written by Myron Holley, a rare opportunity for "the limited powers of man" to rise above "all the ordinary attainments of human imbecility" and "emulate the bounty of Heaven itself, which showers its benedictions upon whole states and kingdoms."

The insinuation of imbecility in their own ordinary workings was not lost on Clinton's many enemies in the 1818 legislature, which took up canal funding with intermittent enthusiasm over the next three months. The commissioners' report was "a luminous and very satisfactory statement," Western District senator Jediah Prendergast wrote to Joseph Ellicott in mid-February 1818, but he feared the legislature would fail to "make the necessary appropriations to the speedy completion of the Canal." Ellicott, who typically had participated neither in drafting nor signing his fellow commissioners' report, doubted Prendergast's information and wrote confidently to Clinton in early March that it would be "extraordinary" for the legislature to abandon the great object.

But by the end of March it was clear that there would be no additional construction authority in 1818. "An apparent disposition," observed John Pintard, "to paralyze every measure recommended by Governor Clinton wh[ich] might render his administration popular" motivated his influential opponents. Erastus Root, the Delaware County Republican, was back in the assembly after leading congressional opposition to New York's canal plans. He moved to suspend any more borrowing for the canal, but mustered few votes outside of fellow intractable anti-Clintonians. Their antagonisms, though, had their effect: borrowing authority in 1818 was limited to the same $400,000 level approved in 1817, effectively preventing the start of construction on the eastern and western sections.

Meanwhile, Clinton had quietly adopted a patient approach. In a letter to Ellicott marked "Private," the head of the state's government and canal revealed his satisfaction with continuing with surveys of the prospective eastern and western sections in 1818 and not demanding further construction authorization until the 1819 legislature: "The truth is, opposition to the Canal is dwindling away. The miscreants in N.Y. who have opposed it from vile motives are properly appreciated—and the opposition of the South will cease because it is understood that we can do without national aid." Here was the statesman grasping his state's inevitable rise, internal opposition silenced by success, national antagonists diminished to geographic jealousies. "My object is to cultivate a spirit of good will & benevolence among the people—to unite our energies in favor of great & extensive improvements and to this end to discourage those factious combinations which are formed with a view to office and which are cherished by cupidity, intolerance & persecution." Clinton was always a better populist than politician.

If Clinton was certain of eventual success against canal opponents, he knew that it would be more difficult to accomplish in the west without the continued allegiance of Joseph Ellicott. Yet that was suddenly in doubt.

In early March 1818 Clinton had dutifully requested Ellicott's advice on settling the line of the western section. "The State looks to you for an example of active and useful patriotism," the governor flattered his mercurial ally, "and I am sure there will be no disappointment." Having not received a reply two weeks later, Clinton wrote again that the commissioners would be meeting in Albany in mid-April, with Ellicott's presence "indispensable" in regard to decisions to be made on locating the western line and raising the $1,500 salaries of acting commissioners Young and Holley, for whom the canals had become full-time occupations. "Do not neglect attending," Clinton implored. A week later, he wrote again that Ellicott's attendance "will be peculiarly important."

Peculiar was the news that topped Ellicott's late and lengthy reply, not written until early April. Ellicott would not be attending the April meeting because he had suffered "a severe contusion" on his right leg in a sleighing accident. The "unfortunate casualty" had kept him confined to his bedroom for the past three weeks, making travel to Albany impossible. Travel east and participation in canal commission meetings had always been improbable for Ellicott, but now, claiming that it would be unfair to burden the other commissioners with his duties, Ellicott offered his resignation.

Ellicott's apparently real physical infirmity was a prelude to his significant and fatal mental illness. After two decades, Ellicott was still the dominant personality in Western New York, but his agonizing decline had begun. Ahead lay a political break with Clinton—a critical loss for both longtime allies—and then his precipitous removal from the Holland Company's employ and territory.

For the moment, though, after floating the idea of his canal commission resignation, Ellicott expounded at length his thoughts on commissioner salaries and the western section route. Holley and Young ought to be given salaries between $2,000 and $3,000 for "their undivided labors" (by comparison, Ellicott was earning $1,500 plus a percentage of sales with the Holland Company), and each given well-compensated clerks to keep accounts. All moneys should be paid through the accountants and at no place other than commission offices. From his own experience with the Holland Company's extensive concerns, Ellicott advised that "the management of accounts is one that requires as much or more attention than any other part." The other commissioners—Clinton and Van Rensselaer—presently adopted these recommendations, raising

Holley and Young's salaries from $1,500 to $2,500, plus expenses. Grateful for the raise, Holley would pay slightly less attention to account management than recommended by Ellicott and suffer the consequences in six years' time.

As to the western line, Ellicott surprised his fellow commissioners by backing off the questionably watered southern route through company lands surveyed by his deputy Peacock in 1816. Ellicott now acknowledged that the "inexhaustible supply of water" available via the northern route of "Engineer Geddis" (discourteously misspelled as always) far outweighed that route's greater length and cost. Mercurial though he was, Ellicott had come to the understanding that the interests of the Holland Company were better served by a successful canal through Western New York than by a failed canal on Holland Company lands. Again, the other commissioners would follow Ellicott's guidance.

Ellicott's resignation did not occur immediately. Having conceded the northern route, Ellicott recognized that it increased the chances of archrival Peter Porter's Black Rock emerging as the canal terminus over the Holland Company's Buffalo. Geddes's northern route passed Black Rock on the Niagara River before reaching Buffalo, with its poor natural harbor exposed to Lake Erie storms. Ellicott watched closely as the legislature of 1818, acting on a petition by Buffalo's leading citizens, passed an act in April authorizing the governor to appoint a surveyor to draw up a plan for "a safe and commodious harbor" at Buffalo. In May Governor Clinton asked for Ellicott's recommendation. On June 18 Clinton appointed Ellicott's predictable choice: his "so well qualified and so meritorious" nephew, William Peacock. The following week, Ellicott resigned as canal commissioner.

Clinton let Ellicott go, calculating that there was some advantage to be had. With the legislature out of session, he quickly named an ardent supporter, Western District Republican senator Ephraim Hart, as an interim replacement for Ellicott. A Connecticut-born Utica merchant and bank director, Hart was "shrewd, self-reliant and diligent, original, outspoken and witty," according to a gracious local historian; as a legislator, he had an "utter want of political tact . . . acted without system, and sometimes apparently without any rational motive," observed astute state political historian and fellow Clintonian senator, Jabez Hammond, who nevertheless considered Hart "a very correct business man" and an "exceedingly judicious" appointment. Clinton designated Hart the commission's third acting commissioner, with full salary, even though he was just an interim appointment, and paired Hart with Holley on the important Erie Canal, shunting the anti-Clintonian Samuel Young to the lesser Champlain. A few months later Clinton was feeling pretty good about the situation. "My regret for your resignation has not ceased," he wrote to Ellicott, "but is diminished by the consideration of the useful services of your successor." In another three months, when the new legislature voted on a permanent replacement for Ellicott, Clinton would discover his miscalculation.

By the time Ellicott quit the canal commission, the second Erie season was well underway. In early April, "with my target on my shoulder," John Jervis set out with Nathan Roberts's party of twelve on a mud-logged, three-day hike from Rome to Geddesburg, the village founded by salt pioneer James Geddes near the future site of Syracuse. From there they would establish thirty-six miles of canal line west to the intersection of the meandering Seneca River and the eastern edge of the vast, malarial Montezuma salt marshes. This was the final, grueling survey before that westernmost portion of the middle section would be put out for contract. "My neighbors at home laughed at my venture, and predicted I would soon return home to sleep." Jervis disappointed those predictions,

The going was not easy. In late April the crew was driven to their tents by a blizzard. In June they retreated to their tents along the boggy Seneca River to escape choking swarms of mosquitoes. When the weather was mild, the chief was not. The crew was talented—its younger members included two future Erie chief engineers in Jervis and Alfred Barrett—but faced Roberts's frequent rebukes for surveying errors.

Nevertheless, Jervis was "very naturally impressed" with his leader's "profound sense of responsibility" in establishing a correct level. Jervis noted that Roberts labored alongside his crew, walked the same long miles between camp and work site, and took for himself no more than the half-hour dinner allotted to the lowest axeman. While other young engineering aspirants in the party considered axe work "an infringement on their dignity" and did it poorly, Jervis embraced Roberts's occasional orders to cut stakes and clear brush, and gained favor with the chief. Though only Roberts worked the levels, he allowed others to practice when he was busy on calculations and plans. With "a very plain set of drawing instruments" brought for just such opportunities, Jervis spent rainy days plotting lines and profiles, making "such a map as my limited skill allowed me . . . of no business use except for my own improvement."

On July 10 the crew reached Montezuma, the swampy settlement that marked the western terminus of the middle section. By Jervis's estimate, in exactly three months they had walked some eighty miles to lay thirty-six miles of canal line. Reassigned for the rest of 1818 to a different crew, Jervis took with him "the discipline I had had under Mr. Roberts [and] the necessity of great care in observations and computations."

While Roberts's crew located the westernmost portion of the middle section, Isaac Briggs was hard at work surveying forty miles of the prospective eastern section line from Utica toward the Hudson, "including all the difficult places" through Little Falls. In 1817 Briggs had failed to have his brother-in-law Thomas Moore hired as the chief engineer of the Erie project. For the 1818 season, Briggs added Moore's son Asa to his surveying party, along with future Virginia engineer Valentine Gill. The elder Moore had needed some convincing to send his "very backward" son north: "My greatest fear," he confided to Briggs in May, "is that he will not get through enough to be perfectly satisfactory to the Commissioners. His general morals are good and I hope will not be deteriated [sic] by the new associations." The Virginian apparently mistrusted the corruptions of New York. To a professional associate, the father wrote more proudly: "I have a son who is about 21 years of age who is a good mathematician and a fine pensman, possessed of a mind very much alive to this kind of work. He is now engaged with the principal engineer in laying out the Grand Canal in the State of New York, and will probably continue there for the remainder of this season. This I believe is the best school that this country at present affords for an education calculated to be useful in works of this nature."

At the start of the 1818 season, it was still not clear whether the commissioners' dissatisfaction of the prior year with Wright might mature into the elevation of Briggs to leadership of New York's great canal. Moore considered Briggs at least *a* if not *the* "principal engineer." Asa Moore may have been the advance guard in a renewed Southern thrust into a Yorker project that the commissioners were still not absolutely certain their homegrown surveyor-engineers could handle.

But two months after his son joined Briggs in New York, Thomas Moore was offered the job of Principal Engineer of Virginia (at an enormous $3,500 salary, more than double the pay of Briggs, Wright, and Geddes). Briggs and Moore *fils* would stay the season in New York, but their futures were told: assignments awaited them in Virginia.

Briggs was excited by the prospect of a return to the Southern fold after the 1818 season in New York, but it would mark his doom. Starting in 1819, Moore would employ Briggs as assistant engineer on numerous Virginia surveys, including the latest round for the endlessly plotted Potomac canal. In late September 1822 Moore contracted "a severe illness" during a "laborious survey and examination" of the Potomac and died eleven days later. Briggs took over Moore's duties and expected to be named his official successor. Seven months later, however, the Virginia Board of Public Works, with Jefferson's quiet counsel, disregarded Briggs as well as Erie engineer and former Briggs assistant Valentine Gill, and named Napoleonic military engineer and West Point professor Claudius Crozet. Crozet, who survives in every student's life for introducing blackboard and chalk to the American classroom, would guide Virginia's transportation progress for two decades. Crushed, Briggs would retreat home to Maryland and descend into "a long and painful illness." Broken in health, finances, and spirit, Briggs died in January1825, nine months before the completion of the canal that might have been his salvation.

Moore's elevation in Virginia, which portended Briggs's departure from New York, might have put the commissioners in a quandary about the engineering leadership of their canal. But the opening months of the 1818 season brought renewed confidence in Benjamin Wright. He had begun to apply himself more closely to Erie fieldwork. In May Holley reported to Clinton that Wright was fully engaged in locating the canal line and making maps in the western portion of the middle section, enabling Holley to prepare contracts. The possibility of Wright's dismissal receded. Controversies awaited, but thanks in part to Virginia and to his own improved behavior, Wright was now back on track toward becoming the "father of American civil engineering."

As the commissioners gained confidence in their engineering staff during 1818, they also gained confidence in the canal's financial condition. The first canal loan in 1817, amid economic uncertainty, had proved uniquely successful because two London investors subscribed a third of the issue. By the spring of 1818, Clinton's anxiety about the local loan market was easing, an attitude that was justified in July with the offering of the next $200,000 issue. This time two New York merchants took nearly $60,000. Of nearly seventy other New York subscribers, over fifty invested less than $2,000 apiece and most of those less than $1,000.

The investors in canal stock in 1818 were primarily young rising merchants, supporting a venture as novel and promising as their own investable income. Small investors would dominate the canal loan subscription lists for the next two years, when the successful completion of the middle section and the beginning of the eastern and western sections made confident canal investors of the richest New Yorkers. In 1818 prominent men still preferred to invest their wealth securely in the stock of the new Bank of the United States rather than risk it on a state issue of as yet uncertain viability. They also knew when to wait for a bargain. The national depression that began in 1819 helped drive discounts into future canal stock issues, and large investors loaded up then. In 1818 the eager small investor paid a 4.5 percent premium, an added boon to the fledgling canal fund.

Merchant strivers were not alone in their early exuberance for the canal in 1818. Veteran New York canal promoter Elkanah Watson was sixty years old when he set out in June from Albany to Detroit, his final long journey in four decades of travels. It was fitting that, after reaching Manlius by land on June 7, the founder of the unprosperous Western Inland Lock Navigation Company should happen to take passage on the first boat to navigate the state's hopeful project.

With "lads and lasses, old and young," Watson accepted an impromptu invitation for an eight-mile test run of a boat from Manlius to a point just east of the settlement not yet called Syracuse. These were the westernmost miles of the middle section's long summit level. Before setting out on their Sunday cruise, the passengers were chased below decks by a spectacular thunder and lightning storm. At the threshold of travel on a man-made river, Watson reckoned "there is nothing else so calculated to make poor, proud, insignificant, pigmy man feel his nothingness and impotency" as the power of the heavens. The weather quickly passed and "gallant swains handed up their lasses, and spread the deck with chairs and benches, which were filled by a happy, joyous crowd, full of life and hilarity." Then it was Watson, with typical self-importance, to the rescue:

I had observed, some distance in advance, a bridge, that seemed unusually low, and watched our rapid approach to it with some anxiety, although relieved from apprehension by the feeling, that the officers of the boat knew and would discharge their duty in watching the safety of the passengers. My alarm and agitation increased to the utmost intensity, when I perceived that we were only two or three rods from the bridge, that no notice was taken of the danger, and that inevitable destruction was impending over the whole happy and unsuspicious mass. I cried out in the highest pitch of my voice, "Down! down—off the deck!" Fortunately, the boat had a considerable space between the cabin and the gunwale, and into these gangways the greatest proportion precipitated themselves, while the rest tumbled into promiscuous heaps, in the narrow spaces at the bow and stern. In another instant, the chairs and benches were crushed into atoms with a tremendous crash, the fragments flying in every direction. To the astonishment of us all, upon regaining our feet, after the passage of the bridge, we found that not a person had been injured. It turned out, that the captain was engaged in administering his bar, and that the helmsman was an ignorant novice.

Thus passed the first recorded occurrence of the soon to be legendary, "Low bridge! Everybody down!" which was to sound for decades from Albany to Buffalo and still does in American canal folklore.

A week or so later Watson was in Seneca Falls, visiting with his old friend Wilhelmus Mynderse, the mill pioneer to whom failing grain merchant Jesse Hawley had poured out his Erie canal ideas in 1805. Mynderse informed Watson, who had long eschewed canalling for agricultural promotion, that although the Western Inland Company's "valuable improvements" had reduced transportation costs considerably, the state's publicly funded grand canal promised "proportionably greater advantages."

Watson moved off overland toward Detroit, bypassing the boggy regions where Nathan Roberts's survey crew was completing its work. As the spring 1817 surveys had brought about the long level between Utica and Salina and the elimination of locks at Rome, Roberts's 1818 survey led to two substantial alterations just west of Salina. Original plans called for a mile and a half embankment across a swampy plain after two locks of ten-foot drops ended the long level at Salina. Now Roberts recommended, and the commissioners soon approved, scrapping the embankment and lowering the line across the Salina plain with six-foot locks at either end. The commissioners also agreed with Roberts to avoid several miles of excavation through a marl meadow near the village of Camillus by shifting the line farther south and establishing a lower, twelve-mile level to the outlet of Skaneateles Lake, with eleven-foot locks at either end.

There were good reasons for these changes. The lowered level through the Salina plain would avoid a costly embankment, facilitate the digging of a level side canal to the ever-increasing salt works a mile off the main line, and, in the commissioners' parlance, "promote the convenience of all those people, who, from the fertile country on both sides of the canal, shall hereafter have occasion to communicate therewith, on the Salina plains [which t]here is little doubt . . . will soon become the scene of extensive dealings." In other words, there would be no embankment dividing what was rapidly to emerge as the capital city of salt, Syracuse. The Camillus level, meanwhile, released the commissioners from an excavation that they "very much feared . . . would have been discouraging to the public spirit, by which this great enterprize is supported." That is, the commissioners were unsure their novice engineers and contractors were ready to undertake it. The marl meadow was a closed swamp fed by a brook and numerous springs; it would have required draining at its eastern and western extremities and then laborious excavation from the ends toward the center. Instead of the normal process of excavation through dry land "by stationing numerous parties of labourers upon it, at short distances from each other," here only small crews would have been able to cart away barrows of muck at lengthening distances through an excavation too narrow for the usual assistance of cattle or horses. By the commissioners' reckoning the excavation could easily have cost more than the budgeted $75,000 and delayed the completion of the middle section by a year or more.

The downside of the Camillus and Salina changes was a near doubling in the number of locks that would have to be built. Between the two locks that would drop the long level just east of Salina and three dropping the line twenty-five feet more at Montezuma were now added four locks that raised and lowered the line a total of thirty-four feet. None of this masonry work could be built successfully without hydraulic cement, of which there was none in America.

Hydraulic cement—a mortar that hardens underwater to seal masonry joints—is essential to any structure in or involving water. The basic ingredients of modern cement were established twenty-five hundred years ago when Greek builders mixed lime, sand, and water. Romans perfected a lime cement with fine volcanic ash from Pozzuoli near Naples and built with it throughout Europe until the end of their empire. Cement was a dead art for centuries, until John Smeaton experimented with a clayey limestone for the mortar of his celebrated Eddystone Lighthouse in the English Channel, completed in 1759. In the ensuing decades, various cements were named for the locations where limestone with the right mineral properties was found, often proximate to an English canal project. In 1824 Yorkshire mason Joseph Aspdin burned and ground a mixture of limestone and clay and came up with an artificial hydraulic cement resembling the yellowy gray color of the stone quarried at Portland. Aspdin named and patented his cement; subsequently improved with the addition of other minerals, Portland cement is used all over the modern world.

No one had come up with a good American cement when the time came to assemble the locks and other masonry structures of New York's canals. Two decades earlier, the builders of the many locks of the Middlesex Canal had been unaware of Smeaton's Eddystone cement formulas, which weren't published until the 1790s in London. The Middlesex builders did learn that a volcanic ash was available in the West Indies and arranged for the shipment of forty tons in 1796. Experiments with limestone, sand, and the mineral-rich ash yielded a Roman-type cement that worked well enough on the short canal.

Two decades later, New York had plenty of limestone but no knowledge of how to make waterproof cement from it. The calcareous remains of Paleozoic sea creatures, compacted hundreds of feet thick for countless millennia after land replaced ocean, make up a wide band of varied limestones from Buffalo to Albany and down the Hudson Valley. Little of it has the qualities for a waterproof mortar. Pure limestone, burned and pulverized, yields common or quick lime; hydraulic lime requires stone composed of anywhere from a fifth to a third of clay. When combined with sand and water, common lime makes an excellent cement for dry structures; only hydraulic lime, combined in precise ratios with sand and water, makes a cement that is waterproof. Though Canvass White had been tutored in London about hydraulic cement and presumably had access to the writings of the late John Smeaton, New York's canal commissioners in mid-1818 had made no arrangements for either the expensive import or local development of a proper hydraulic cement, The commissioners "appeared to think," Benjamin Wright testified six years later to an assembly committee, "that common quick lime would do for the work."

The commissioners largely avoided the cement issue well into the 1818 season, because construction was on the long level between Utica and Salina, which required only simple digging with no locks and little other hydraulic masonry like aqueduct bridges or culverts. The situation became urgent when it became clear from Roberts's survey that the westernmost portion of the middle section would best be built with nine locks.

As soon as Roberts's survey party returned from the field to Rome, "great numbers of wealthy and respectable citizens sought contracts," even before the commissioners had drawn up specifications for each section's letting. The avid competition between the upper echelons of the local population was "highly gratifying" to the commissioners: "A very few of the contractors are foreigners, who have recently arrived in this country; but far the greatest part of them are native farmers, mechanics, merchants and professional men, residing in the vicinity of the line." By mid-July, all but a few of the new sections had been contracted. Within a few weeks the new contractors had assembled their workers, provisions, tools, and animal teams, and the line became "a scene of the most animated and laborious exertions." Over the remaining months of the 1818 construction season as many as three thousand men, and half as many horses and cattle, were at work on the line. In late September Clinton wrote to Ellicott that the middle section "will in all human probability be completed next year."

"[T]he whole was taken up," the commissioners discreetly noted in their January 1819 report to the legislature, "except a few short places necessarily left, where structures of wood and stone were to be erected." Those "few short places" included the places where locks had to be built; without cement to build them, they could not be put out to contract in 1818. But just when the commissioners might have been charged with negligence about the cement, they caught a break.

In their report the commissioners remarked briefly that excavation had been difficult in some places during the 1818 season because of unexpected "indurated clay, and stone, of various descriptions." Some of this was apparently "a kind of meagre lime-stone." Almost as an aside, the commissioners indicated that they "expect to make a very important use" of this otherwise troublesome stone during the 1819 season: "[B]y a small number of experiments, in which, after being thoroughly burnt and slaked, or ground, and mixed with equal portions with sand, it appears to form a cement that uniformly hardens under water"; that is, hydraulic cement. The discovery was fresh and its full significance not yet known, and the commissioners offered few details, including who made the discovery and how. They never would provide that information.

In fact, the first account of the discovery of the cement that made completion of the Erie Canal possible was not published for another thirty-one years, in *Onondaga; or Reminiscences of Earlier and Later Times, being a series of historical sketches relative to Onondaga, with notes on the several towns in the county and Oswego*. An informal local history in two volumes, it was written by Joshua V. H. Clark, a prosperous farmer with literary aspirations. The hero of Clark's cement tale is Canvass White.

According to Clark, White had returned from his tour of English canals to his engineering duties in upstate New York, where he undertook the search for the right limestone for hydraulic cement. White, the story goes, soon became aware that a supplier of quick lime in the Madison County village of Sullivan had delivered some that unexpectedly kept its shape when wet. White called in "a scientific gentleman from Herkimer County . . . to make experiments, to prove what this new substance should be." This expert "came on, took some of the rough stone, and in the trip hammer shop of John B. Yates, at Chittenango, burned a parcel, pulverized it in a mortar, and in Elisha Carey's bar-room . . . in the presence of Messrs. Wright, White, and several others, mixed it with sand, rolled a ball of it, and placed it in a bucket of water for the night. In the morning it had set, was solid enough to roll across the floor." The expert dramatically "pronounced cement, not inferior to the Roman of Puteoli, or the Dutch Tarras of the Rhine." Subsequently, writes Clark, White himself "[a]t considerable expense, and by repeated experiments . . . found this to be an excellent substitute for the Roman cement, and he sought for and obtained a patent right of the United States for this discovery."

A half-century later, Clark's folksy account—neither documented nor corroborated—was bulk quoted in what is now the gospel text for canal historians, Noble E. Whitford's two-volume *History of the Canal System of the State of New York,* a state publication issued in 1906. For a century since then, Erie historians—scholarly and otherwise—who write about the canal's hydraulic cement invariably cite Whitford or other accounts based, wittingly or not, on Clark's original tale.

There is no obvious reason to doubt it. White had learned about hydraulic cement in England. The 1820 patent for "water lime cement" was in his name, and he defended it vigorously in courts. He subsequently became a prominent manufacturer of hydraulic cement and a nationally renowned engineer before his premature death in 1834, fifteen years before Clark told his story. Also dead by then were Wright, Clinton, and nearly every other Erie principal who knew that the only thing that Clark got right was that White got the patent.

Clark probably did not know that the man who knew the most— the one who supposedly rolled a ball of cement along the floor of a

Chittenango tavern—was still alive, but had gone blind in 1836, about the time his oldest son, the treasurer of the Commercial Bank of Albany, notoriously disappeared with most of the $87,000 in its vault. Already elderly, the father had thereafter adopted a low public profile, and had left upstate with his wife for their native Westchester in 1850, almost certainly unaware of Clark's new book. All that Clark apparently knew about this "scientific gentleman from Herkimer County" was to identify him by misspelled last name and false honorific: "Dr. Barto." The scientific gentleman was well known to his contemporaries as "Doctor" Andrew Bartow, the canal's diligent procurement agent for lime and other materials and the man who really made possible the successful completion of the Erie Canal.

"It is with extreme diffidence as well as with indescribable anxiety" that Bartow penned a statement to the commissioners in late 1818 detailing his claim "as the first discoverer [of] the important and usefull cement—the water lime." This obscure manuscript differs substantially from the legend that has come down through the generations as fact.

"Sometime about the first of August last," Bartow wrote, he and Benjamin Wright were searching at quarries in Onondaga County—not Madison County—for suitable stone for locks and lime for their cement. At Nicholas Mickle's furnace outside the village of Onondaga Hill, "Mr. Wright remarked that some lime laying on the floor resembled the Welch lime in colour." The two men made "considerable enquiry respecting it," and examined the stone that had been burned and ground to make it. Bartow took some of the powder away to mix with varying amounts of sand and water, to no avail: "[E]ither from the length of time in which it had been burnt, or my ignorance in compounding it, my first experiment failed."

With Wright's encouragement, and unwilling "to abandon a subject which I conceived of so much importance to the safety of the canal," Bartow returned to the furnace with an English mason in his employ. The mason remarked that the material resembled Barrow lime, a prized hydraulic lime from stone quarried at Barrow-upon-Soar in Leicestershire. This time, Bartow and the mason took samples of the stone in their pockets as well as more of the lime powder. They burned and pulverized the stone themselves, but "again we failed in our experiments."

Bartow, "not yet discouraged," went back to the furnace again, this time with a wagon, and loaded up "a sufficient quantity of stone . . . to make a full and more satisfactory trial" back home at Fairfield in Herkimer County. There Bartow, with a local assistant, burned and ground sample after sample of the stone. "[A]lthough baffled at first, we ultimately succeeded in reducing it to lime, and formed a cement which I have the confidence to think fully answers my most sanguine expectations." Subsequent experiments by James Hadley, a young chemist at the medical college that Bartow had helped establish, confirmed the result. Much less dramatically than the barroom demonstration conjured by Clark, Bartow submitted his samples to the chief engineer: "I . . . formed several small cakes, which was immediately put in water and left with Mr. Wright. The simplest mixtures set the hardest, to wit: ⅓ lime and ⅔ sand, was in Eight days very hard, and ½ lime and ½ sand, made also a very hard cement."

Bartow was sensitive to the personal and broader implications: "I . . . can truly say that independent of the gratification of being the first to demonstrate the plenty and existence of this useful cement, *and the probable benefit to myself,* nothing affords me so much solid pleasure, as rendering a benefit to the canal" (*emphasis added*).

Of the many and obvious differences between Clark's tale and Bartow's account, none is more glaring than the absence of Canvass White. Modest, plain spoken, but firmly principled, Bartow made a point at the beginning of his statement "to acknowledge my obligations to those gentlemen, and particularly Mr. Wright, who have rendered me their assistance in bringing my experiments to the present results." Bartow named many names, none of them Canvass White. It is possible even that when Bartow wrote, immediately after his first successful experiments but before his protégé Hadley's were complete, White was not even yet aware of them. "It was supposed Canvass White made the experiments which showed the hydraulic quality of the cement," recalled John Jervis years later, but it was Bartow who "took great interest in it when it was generally regarded with doubt, and insisted it would be a success . . . and discussed the matter freely with the young engineers. . . . Doct. Bartow often showed specimens of the cement; he seemed always to have them in his pockets."

The commissioners made a point of acknowledging no individual discoverer. In their January 1819 report, they noted the recent experiments but named no one. A year later the cement had proven "a discovery of the greatest importance." It was used during the 1819 season for practically all masonry work on the canal, including the newly contracted locks that would complete the middle section. "This material has been discovered in the progress of *our* exertions," the commissioners asserted in their annual report of February 18, 1820, "and it will doubtless hereafter be considered as an article of prime necessity, throughout our country, for all hydraulic masonry" (*emphasis added*). The cement "sets much quicker, and becomes much stronger in the air, than common lime mortar; and under water, where common mortar will not set at all, it begins to set immediately, and in a few weeks acquires great hardness and tenacity." But it was the commissioners' discovery: "*We* failed repeatedly in burning, pulverizing and mixing it; but many trials have now shown *us* the way to succeed in these operations" (*emphasis added*).

The commissioners had good reason to invoke the royal "we." Seventeen days before their report, Canvass White had been granted his potentially lucrative patent for "water lime cement."

If Andrew Bartow was the true discoverer of hydraulic cement in America, how is it that Canvass White got the patent? That answer is found in letters between the two men, and the recollections of two Bartow daughters who saved them. In 1880 Mary and Elizabeth Bartow broke a long silence. They told family friend and Herkimer lawyer Samuel Earl that it was their father who made his cement experiments known to White, not White who requested them of Bartow. When Bartow's experiments proved successful, the two men made an agreement: White paid Bartow a substantial $2,000 for the privilege of obtaining a patent in his own name, with Bartow retaining a 25 percent silent interest in future royalties. The daughters, aging spinsters, are the only source for the origins of the deal, but the Bartow–White letters make clear Bartow's "fourth part of the patent." If White had made the discovery, there would have been no reason to share the proceeds with Bartow.

Bartow had good reason to make a deal. He was aware of "the probable benefit to myself" from his discovery but was also certainly aware that patents were notoriously difficult to defend in those days, especially one involving a discovery by a state employee arguably in the course of his duties. White was young and perhaps more willing to assume all the risk, trouble, and expense, while Bartow was happy for a $2,000 windfall. Possibly there was some deeper calculation between the partners. Bartow was specifically employed as the commissioners' agent to find lime for the canal; White, who had done cement research in England on a trip at his own expense, was employed in the engineering department, with no specific duties involving lime or cement. Arguably, White had a better chance of securing a patent than Bartow, and the two men decided that $2,000 plus 25 percent was a fair price for Bartow's sale of his discovery and White's assumption of the risk.

Once White and Bartow became silent cement partners, they found nothing but frustration. "This has so far been a bad business for me," White complained to Bartow in April 1823. For three years the commissioners had refused to offer compensation for cement produced by suppliers who hadn't paid the four cents per bushel royalty, leaving White $1,600 in debt. "These men may combine," an exasperated White advised Bartow, "and make a good deal of trouble."

Bartow was equally exasperated with his partner's "ill success attending the introduction of our water-cement into common use." In an attempt to compete with other suppliers, White had set up a plant in Chittenango—this is the likely origin of Clark's Chittenango reference—but the purchaser of a large order had claimed the cement was of poor quality and refused to pay. "The reverses experienced in your attempts," Bartow wrote to White, "appear to be owing to the want of your personal skill and attention, in the selection and calcination of the lime in grinding, and compounding it for use." At least as far as Bartow was concerned, White was not the great cement mixer of enduring legend. The partners considered selling out their patent interests to each other or third parties or pursuing their interests separately by region, but these discussions came to nothing.

In the end they remained partners in the patent, with White's assurance to Bartow that "you shall have your portion of any remuneration that may be obtained from the State." By late 1823 that seemed their best hope.

After obtaining the patent in 1820, White had sued Timothy Brown, a cement supplier from Madison County (this may be the origin of Clark's assertion of a Madison County discovery). "In a compromise so far as my interest goes, I am willing to be liberal," Bartow assured his partner; "but if by the refusal of the Commissioners to do us justice, we are driven to prosecute, I ask the utmost farthing which can be recovered." Once they were successful in the courts, Bartow reasoned, the state legislature could choose to indemnify the losers. A federal district court subsequently awarded White $1,700, but Brown hadn't paid up by September 1823, when White hoped to get the case to the U.S. Supreme Court: "That decision will be law; and if it should be favorable, we shall stand a chance to be remunerated by collecting a percentage on all that has been manufactured."

Brown, meanwhile, took his case to the state legislature, which was more interested in canal economics than federal patent rights. An 1824 assembly report on the petition of Brown and other cement manufacturers determined that the canal commissioners had "appropriate[d] the discovery of this water lime cement to their own fame." Rightly or wrongly, the committee concluded, "the manner in which they announced the discovery, was well calculated to lull contractors into a belief, that the discovery was the common property of the canal commissioners, who carefully avoided recognizing" White or any other person. The 1824 session ended with no action being taken.

During the 1825 session another assembly committee recommended that the state purchase the patent rights for $10,000. It was "just and equitable" that Brown be indemnified against the outstanding judgment, advisable that further prosecutions be prevented, and "highly important to secure to the people of this state the free use" of proper cement for its canals. The committee reported White's willingness to take the deal, but the session ended that spring without further action. With the Erie Canal just months from completion, it seems that White—and Bartow—had tired of the fight.

Over half a million bushels of cement were used to complete the Erie Canal. If royalties had been paid on every bushel, White would have earned $15,000, Bartow $5,000. As it happened, nearly all of the cement was produced without any royalties paid by some two dozen suppliers. If all were sued successfully, they would have been liable under federal law for triple damages.

By 1825 White and Bartow had no illusions about profiting from their patent. Each had moved on. White was already a nationally prominent engineer. He had left the Erie project before its completion to become chief engineer of Pennsylvania's Union Canal, and he was advising New York City on its water supply. Under his younger brother Hugh's management, the Chittenango cement plant was prospering. Instead of fighting cement suppliers in court, the Whites were beating them in the marketplace. The Whites later opened another plant at Cohoes on the Hudson north of Albany. After Canvass's death in 1834, Hugh White followed the band of hydraulic limestone down the Hudson Valley to Ulster County, where he opened a cement works near Rosendale. "White's Cement" was shipped down Rondout Creek to the Hudson and off to construction projects throughout the northeast, including the Croton Aqueduct, which began supplying New York City's first clean drinking water in 1842. Hugh White later sold out his interest to the Rosendale Cement Company, providers of the mortar for the Brooklyn Bridge, the pedestal of the Statue of Liberty, and the Panama Canal.

Rosendale would not have become the center of the American cement industry without Andrew Bartow. In December 1825 Bartow was a contractor for the Delaware and Hudson Canal Company, attempting to link the Hudson by canal and rail with coal mines in eastern Pennsylvania. Company president Maurice Wurts of Philadelphia asked Bartow to conduct experiments on limestone found near the line of the planned canal. "You will readily perceive the necessity of our having this matter attended to immediately," wrote Wurts, desperate to know before substantial construction began whether he could avoid purchasing and expensively transporting cement from upstate New York. Bartow ran his familiar tests there in Ulster County and found that its native limestone made a very superior cement. The Delaware and Hudson Canal would be the first of the many works built with Rosendale cement. Bartow made no claim for discovering this limestone, but his proof of its hydraulic properties was his second great contribution to American engineering.

Hydraulic cement was the most important discovery in all the years of Erie construction, but there were other major innovations during the 1818 season. With upwards of three thousand men and dozens of contractors along the line, it was natural that inventions would arise to save labor, time, and money.

The grandest innovation was a tree feller, a large machine operable by a single, agile person. First he would climb up the target tree to attach one end of a long chain or cable. Back on the ground, he wound the other end of the cable onto a roller set in a wood and iron frame "immovably fastened on the ground" at roughly twice the distance from the height of the tree. He then worked a crank that operated an endless screw turning a wheel at one end of the roller. The tree would gradually yield its ground, eventually brought down by its own weight, its roots torn from the earth. Cadwallader D. Colden, grandson of the canal-minded colonial official, glimpsed the divine in the machine: "[T]o see a forest tree, which had withstood the elements till it attained maturity, torn up by its roots, and bending itself to the earth, in obedience to the command of man, is a spectacle that must awaken feelings of gratitude to that Being, who has bestowed on his creatures so much power and wisdom." Colden was unaware that European creatures had long possessed such power and wisdom. A quarter-century earlier, French land development engineer Desjardins had been astounded at the failure of the Western Inland Company contractor to employ "the simplest labor saving power" at Wood Creek: "[I]f [he] would use a windlass, or only a cable and pulleys fastened to the trees along the bank, he would do thrice the amount of work in half the time." A generation later, the technology finally transferred to America. The Erie tree feller was an ingenious new thing to Colden and generations of prideful Americans.

For trees brought down the old-fashioned way, by axe and saw, the residual stumps and roots submitted to a Bunyanesque stump puller. Two wood-spoked supporting wheels, sixteen feet in diameter, were slipped over the ends of an axle fashioned from a tree trunk roughly thirty feet long and twenty inches thick. Fixed near the midpoint of the axle was a fourteen-foot, broad-rimmed wheel with spokes passing through the axle; a rope was dead-ended through the rim, wrapped several times around it, and led to a team of two to four oxen or horses. Next to the central wheel, a chain was attached through the axle, wrapped several times around it, and attached to the stump positioned directly below. With the outer wheels braced, the team pulled, turning the smaller wheel, winding the chain onto the axle, and pulling the stump neatly from the ground, the roots snapping cleanly from the powerful force exerted by the central wheel over the slender axle. The large wheels were then unbraced, the excised stump wheeled away from the line, and the contraption wheeled into place over the next stump. At some $250 to fashion one, the stump puller was an expensive machine, but it was efficient; as many as forty stumps could be pulled in a day.

These innovations were "unremittingly employed" during the 1818 season and beyond; the appreciative commissioners noted "our citizens west of Utica . . . every day multiplying these evidences of their industry."

Of the thousands of men on the line in 1818, the overwhelming majority were both industrious and citizens. Immigrant Irish laborers had not yet arrived in significant numbers. The first notable foreign workers were Welsh, joining a cluster of their countrymen already settled in Utica. One new arrival in the summer of 1818 was William Thomas, a carpenter who found canal work just west of town. He was earning $13 a month and getting "my food, drink, and washing as well," including a daily half pint of whiskey. But William Thomas was not a happy canaller.

Upbeat letters from Utica by two Welsh townsmen had induced Thomas to leave Wales that spring. He arrived to find the letters "a lot of lies." One of the men had abandoned his wife; the other was sick and in rags. "The land is a desolate wilderness," Thomas wrote to his parents that August, with unbearable heat and no seasonal fairs or markets as back home. The young carpenter feared a four-month winter, "freezing those people who are on the roads without clothing." Despite reports of opportunity in America, "[i]f it were not for the canal, many of the Welsh would be without work. . . . The carpenter who is out of work, works on the canal." The long winter promised no canal work around Utica, where clothing and housing—$6 a month "and wooden houses at that"—were expensive: "I beg all of my old neighbors not to think of coming here . . .

to love their district and stay there. I am thinking of coming home myself this spring if I have support from the Lord." He closed ruefully, "the country is just what my father said it was before I left."

Thomas was not alone in his despair. "This country is not what we had heard about it in any way," wrote new Utican Hugh Jones to his parents in early September; "Be happy in your own country and do not be surprised to find me back in Wales." The crops were poor, the weather extreme, the sabbath an expected day of work, and land "dangerous for anyone with money to buy . . . because it is difficult to know who has the right to sell" it. Worse were the employers of Utica, who "live like gentlemen but . . . have not the money to pay wages after they have been earned." Seasonal work with canal contractors was an exception. "I do not know what many would do were it not for the canal."

The situation was not as desperate as the young men made it seem. David Richard, an older neighbor in Wales and now in Utica, reported back home in December that his own son had found farm work "with some great gentleman" of Utica, while he and doubting Thomas were working together "on the arches under the canal," a reference possibly to the aqueduct over the Sadaqueda Creek at Whitestown just west of Utica. Richard offered details of the local economy: shoes at $2 a pair, wooded land at $20 an acre, horses at $100, a sheep or a bushel of wheat at $1.50. Utica in 1818 was still a very young market. "The wages of shopkeepers are not very good and much the same as laborers." December had come, and common digging in the hardening earth was ending, but canal work like carpentry and masonry continued, with an increase in wages: up to $1 a day or $14 a month with food, washing, and whiskey, reported Richard, or $23 dollars without. Either way, the pay was nearly triple what a worker could expect back in Wales, when work was available. At least for some immigrant Welshmen at Utica in 1818, the canal was a promising venture.

By mid-summer 1818 New York's major canal was attracting favorable notices out of state. "ASTONISHING AND GRATIFYING FACT" ran the headline in the Cleveland *Register* of August 18, reporting (overoptimistically) to its very interested readers that a quarter of the canal would be finished after just two construction seasons. In its next issue, the paper published a letter sent to De Witt Clinton earlier in the year by Alexander Kinghorne, a Scottish engineer who had studied canal plans and commissioner reports that had found their way to St. Boswell on the River Tweed. "I have every reason for believing that the surveys have been made with due attention, and that the choice of ground had been well considered," Kinghorne assured Clinton. The Cleveland editor was pleased to report the opinion of this "competent judge in Europe" (who soon left Scotland to run an Australian convict farm). The success of New York's canal to Lake Erie was central to Cleveland's future. The *Register*'s aggressive coverage of Erie construction was intended to induce Ohio to build a canal linking the Ohio River with the lake at Cleveland.

By fall, the Charleston *Times* (along the Ohio River valley in what is now West Virginia) expressed widespread opinion:

> We know not which to admire most, the active and enterprising spirit or the boundless and inexhaustible resources which are every where developing themselves in the state of New York. She is, without doubt, the foremost in the great American republic, and stands crowned among her rival sisters with the tiara of a Queen. . . . History presents no parallel to so stupendous and magnificent an undertaking. What were the Roman roads, what are all the internal improvements of the whole continent of Europe, for the last century, contrasted with this sublime spectacle exhibited by a single state in the new world?

The *Times* editor happily quoted the recent lament of the editor of the Montreal *Herald*: "When this Canal is completed . . . and our eyes are opened to the injuries we will severely feel from its operatics, it will be but a slender consolation, for us to think, a great part of it was made by our industrious peasantry, who passed through Canada, and went to be employed in the States, because there were no canals or public improvements by which they could obtain a living here." It is not at all clear that many canal workers passed through Canada in 1818, but it is true that New York had launched a great canal project before Canada had.

The notices were just as good at home. "It must be a pleasing reflection to the people of New York," observed the Clintonian Rochester *Telegraph* of July 21 (its third issue), "that . . . they have commenced, and will finish a work, that astonishes and interests the most enlightened characters of Europe." The canals were readily meeting "the most sanguine expectations of those who were friendly to their commencement," opined devoted Clintonian Solomon Southwick in his Albany *Register.* "The heretofore incredulous, who have visited them, have become converts to their practicability and exult in the prospect of seeing a work of such magnitude accomplished by the energies of a single state."

The year 1818 had proved a watershed for John Jervis. After serving in Nathan Roberts's party that established the line to the Seneca River, Jervis was reassigned as the single targetman in a smaller party headed by David Bates, staking out a fairly level seventeen-mile stretch of line from Canastota to just east of the hamlet soon named Syracuse. Although Bates was a surveyor of good reputation and "a man of very pleasant manner," Jervis found him little educated in the use of leveling instruments or the calculations required to conduct levels. To the young targetman's surprise, Bates "was ready to learn, even from me." Bates immediately allowed Jervis free use of the equipment, and quickly Jervis's levels and calculations were used as a check on Bates's own observations.

Shortly into the work, the party came upon a stretch of sloping ground that raised a question between the two men about the placement of a stake marking the outer edge of the canal bottom. Bates thought it should be set at the standard fourteen feet off center; Jervis's calculations suggested slightly less to take into account the downward slope of the ground. "We pondered over the question for a while, and then left for dinner."

While they were eating Canvass White showed up, conducting his general supervision of the line. Jervis and Bates posed the issue to White, and after dinner the three men walked back in the long summer evening to the place of contention. "Taking a seat on a log," the canal's principal assistant engineer, "appeared to us as making an examination of the question." Whether White was or not, the other two never discovered, because after sitting for an hour, White got up and "left without giving us his opinion." Jervis and Bates concluded that White intended for them to reach an answer on their own, which, after Jervis drew sketches to convince Bates, they did as evening came on. Such, Jervis reflected years later, was canal "science as held at that day."

Officially he was still a targetman earning less money than a contractor's carpenter, but Jervis was leaping forward under Bates's accommodating leadership. When the party's work was done in December, Jervis did not return to his father's farm for the off-season. Instead, the twenty-three-year-old took up winter quarters in a settlement near Onondaga Hollow, assigned to weigh stone for next year's locks. Weight was the basis for payments to masonry suppliers; with the fresh discovery of hydraulic lime, locks would be a major construction activity in 1819.

The summer of 1818 was a time of rising excitement about the progress of the canal, but it was also a period of foreboding for its great promoter. Early in July Governor Clinton, with his children and an ailing wife, sailed by sloop from Albany for a family vacation in the (then) restorative salt airs of Staten Island. Since her marriage twenty-two years earlier, forty-two-year-old Maria Clinton had borne ten children, of whom seven survived. During the previous year's delivery of a daughter, Maria had sickened and had not recovered. After some hopeful days during the vacation, she deteriorated amid a noxious plague of mosquitoes. The Clintons removed to an inn north of the city in Westchester, which presently suffered a worse mosquito plague. What ailed Maria was unclear to visiting doctor David Hosack and attentive friend and former city health official John Pintard. The end approached. With her husband at her bedside, just before ten in the evening on July 30, 1818, Maria "retired to another and a better world with characteristic fortitude," Clinton wrote in his diary, "leaving an immedicabile vulnus in my heart, which will be felt with the continuance of life." Days later Clinton suffered what proved his truly incurable wound: a fall from his horse, which hobbled the robust governor into the sedentary lifestyle that killed him ten years later.

Clinton's personal troubles notwithstanding, his canal's second year of construction was a resounding financial success. Total revenues for the canal fund topped out at over half a million dollars in 1818. The duties on auctions ($146,000) and salt ($49,000) nearly covered the year's single $200,000 bond issue. Some $9,000 in premiums on the fully sub-scribed bonds, plus nearly $19,000 in steamboat passenger taxes and the $85,000 surplus from 1817, kept the fund well in the black against the nearly $467,000 paid out to the canal commissioners for construction and some $16,000 in interest on what was now a total of $400,000 in loans. After two seasons, George Tibbits's canal-building fund, immu-nized by diversification from the fluctuating health of financial markets, was proving as robust as he had believed it would be.

By the end of 1818 over forty-six miles of the middle section had been completed, though none in any extended segment; without proper cement, the masonry for locks and numerous stream crossings that would link completed sections had not been started. Under James Ged-des's efficient management, meanwhile, nearly twenty of the Champlain canal's twenty-five miles were done, though the same lack of cement to start building its many locks also meant there was no continuous stretch of completed canal.

The nine locks and other masonry of the Erie middle section were the focus of construction activity in the 1819 season. Masons employed by the commissioners to oversee and work with lock contractors were skep-tical at first of the newly discovered hydraulic cement. "[F]or some time they were loth to use it, from an opinion which they uniformly enter-tained of its being of no value." Most of the masons were British and par-tial to the limes of their home districts, but they soon accepted the yellowish grey mortar that would "thoroughly cement any work of brick or stone, in which it is set under water."

John Jervis also faced new experiences in 1819. After weighing stone all winter, he looked homeward on April 1 to see what assignment awaited him for the new season. Joined by Alfred Barrett and another former Roberts party compatriot, Jervis tramped thirty-six miles to Rome along a mud and snow clogged road in fourteen hours, "pretty well fatigued, but hardly . . . the worse for it the next day." In his mem-oirs, Jervis noted that "not much of this sort of service is undertaken at the present day by young engineers."

At Rome, chief Wright informed Jervis that Bates was being moved up to general duties for the 1819 season and that Jervis would be taking over Bates's division as an assistant engineer. Jervis supposed that his "most cordial" relations with Bates had prompted his recommendation, but Jervis's obvious skills, attitude, and energy had been noted since the first swing of his axe. The $12-dollar a month targetman was now a $1.25-a-day engineer, with a $.50 daily allowance for expenses.

John Jervis's first year as a resident engineer was relatively easy. His segment, from Canastota in Madison County to the verges of Syracuse in Onondaga, was the easier portion of the line that he had staked as targetman in Roberts's party the previous year. It was dry and level land that required no locks or substantial masonry that might challenge or extend his expertise. Still, diligent oversight was required for the construction of waste weirs that spilled off excess canal water, culverts that allowed small streams to pass under the canal bed, and the wood aqueducts that carried the canal over larger streams.

The wood aqueducts were a reminder that New York's great canal was being built by frontier craftsmen, not civil engineers. The aqueducts were simple but effective boxlike structures of timber-framed heavy planking resting on stone piers. The designer of these aqueduct bridges of Madison County and beyond was Asa Waterman Cady, a flourishing Chittenango farmer and relentless inventor. In 1809 he had patented a steam-driven soil excavator and a threshing and shelling machine. After he and a brother had won nine contracts to build wood aqueducts along the Erie middle section, chief engineer Wright approved the design for crossing nearly all of the canal's substantial creeks and brooks. Sixty years later, acknowledged John Jervis, whose own carpenter father was a lesser craftsman, "it stands as a well-designed plan for this kind of structure."

The great technological advance of 1819 was a humble work of wood and local ingenuity, "a new and much improved" wheelbarrow, particularly suited to the swampy ground at the western end of the middle section. It was the product of off-season tinkering by Rome merchant Jeremiah Brainard, who had good reason to innovate. Already at work on a variety of canal sections and related construction, Brainard was emerging as the largest single canal contractor, with over $60,000 worth of business by the end of 1820. The Connecticut native had received his first patent, for a turnpike gate, back in 1810; the last of his numerous canal-related patents, for cocks used in weighing canal boats, came nearly three decades later. His wheelbarrow patent was approved on August 26, 1819. Until Brainard set his mind to it, the wheelbarrows used along New York's canal line and for countless prior generations were rectangular basins with vertical sides, inefficiently loaded, clumsily unloaded, and generally cumbersome. Brainard rounded out the basin by molding a piece of ash into a semicircle, "from which the muck slid out instantly." "Brainard's barrow," as it came to be called, was lighter, more durable, and the same $5 price as a traditional wheelbarrow. By the end of 1819 Brainard was turning out enough of his wheelbarrows to offer them for sale all along the Erie line. Erie contractor John Richardson certified publicly that he had personally used Brainard's barrows and found them "far superior to any thing of the kind used on the Erie Canal." The canal commissioners, at the same time that they refused to acknowledge the discoverer of the canal's hydraulic cement, were happy to praise Brainard and his barrow, in their annual report and in an advertising testimonial: "Its advantages consist chiefly in its being more durable, easier to unload and lighter. We recommend it to general adoption."

A better wheelbarrow was nowhere more useful than in the thirty-five miles of canal line from Salina to Montezuma along the sluggish Seneca River. Where the Roberts survey team in the spring and early summer of 1818 had endured but survived the "region of the rankest vegetable luxuriance," a thousand workers mucking out a canal during the summer of 1819 did not. There are no records to indicate how many, if any, died, but nearly all succumbed at one time or another to "extensive and distressing sickness." Scattered nearby homesteads serving as impromptu field hospitals "presented a most discouraging spectacle." The lone physician at Corinth (presently Syracuse) worked himself to exhaustion amid "scenes of suffering and distress . . . beyond conception."

No one, of course, had any idea that the violent fevers, bone-rattling chills, aching joints, vomiting, and convulsions were the work of parasites transmitted by the swarms of female anopheles mosquitoes feasting on the warm-blooded swamp invaders. The malaria was thought to be caused by just that, bad air—*mal aria*—rising from the fetid swamps. Among such attempted cures as bleedings, feverwort, snakeroot, green pigweed, and Seneca Oil (soon better known as petroleum), "Jesuit's bark" seemed to work best. The bark of the South American cinchona tree, which had cured a malarial Jesuit missionary in Peru two centuries earlier, had recently found its way in medicinal doses to upstate New York, where the bark's antimalarial active ingredient, quinine, saved the lives of hundreds of canal diggers. For dealing with the mosquitoes, the local remedy was "Montezuma necklaces": smoldering leaves in pots hung around workers' necks. The fiery charms tended to clog lungs better than they prevented exposed flesh from constant insect assault. "[A]lthough great exertions were made to supply the place of such laborers as became diseased," work was suspended for weeks at a time on certain sections and proceeded fitfully on others.

Worse than the mosquitoes were the frustrations of the work itself: mucking out short sections inside wood planking sunk through the mud down to hard clay to keep the section relatively dry. Invariably a developing mud berm collapsed, filling a nearly dried excavation and sending workers back into waist-deep muck to start again. Real progress was made only after the "sickly season" tapered off in late October, when the first frost began killing mosquitoes and firming up the bogs, which had been drying gradually since late summer.

While laborers with shovels suffered on the canal line, laborers with domestic jobs in New York City did their part for the canal less directly, through the efforts of Thomas Eddy. Eddy had not been involved officially with the canal since 1816, but since then he had been seeking the establishment of a unique bank that would incidentally help ensure the canal's financial success.

Conceived as the country's first savings bank in 1816 by Eddy with John Pintard, De Witt Clinton, and an array of public-spirited citizens, the Bank for Savings in the City of New-York had at heart the best interests of its desired depositors: to encourage "provident habits" among the laboring classes, who otherwise invested their hard-earned cash in easy dissipations. Chief founder Eddy was no romantic: "[T]ired of assisting [the poor] in their distress," he wrote to Clinton in 1817, "it appears to me more wise, to fix on every possible plan to *prevent* their poverty and misery by means of employment and establishing saving

Banks and to do all in our power to discourage the use of spirituous liquors, which is in fact *the true source of all the Evils attending the poor.*" Modeled after similar English institutions, Eddy's project was thwarted by anti-bank sentiment in the legislature (and America generally), until an incorporation bill sponsored by the newly formed Society for the Prevention of Pauperism passed the legislature during the 1819 session. By design, its charter restricted the bank to investing in U.S. and New York State securities and guaranteed depositors a minimum 5 percent return. The several bank employees received competitive salaries but the directors nothing, leaving most of the profits to the city's cooks, laborers, porters, boot cleaners, boatmen, washerwomen, maids, and other working poor who became bank depositors.

Many did. On Saturday evening, July 3, 1819, the bank opened its doors. In three hours it had eighty accounts, with deposits totaling $2,807. After further deposits on Monday, the bank did what it was chartered to do: on July 7 it purchased $4,256 worth of the new 6 percent State Canal Long Loan bonds. By the end of the year the bank had deposits of over $150,000, of which more than $40,000 was invested in canal stock. By 1821 the bank held over half a million dollars in canal stock, comprising nearly 30 percent of all outstanding canal loans and a portion of each of the by then dozen issues.

While the bank's decision to invest heavily in the canals proved wise for depositors, it was a risk that few of the bank's rich trustees chose to take for several more years. Eddy himself never bought any canal stock, but his bank's avid support of the project in its early years helped secure its financial success and prove the canal a viable investment opportunity for the larger and wealthier investors of the early 1820s. The bank, which flourished into the 1960s and was finally liquidated (after a series of reorganizations) in 1991, was the single largest canal investor by 1833, when it sold its portfolio of a million dollars in canal stock.

Construction during the 1819 season proceeded on the strength of the canal fund. Another $400,000 in promptly subscribed loans were supplemented by over half that in auction, steam passenger, and salt tax revenues, plus loan premiums and the prior year's surplus. Nearly $588,000 was paid out to the canal commissioners for construction in

1819, with nearly $40,000 in loan interest pushing the fund slightly into the red for the first time. After three seasons, nearly all of the middle section had been completed at an average cost of less than $11,800 per mile. This was just 10 percent over the original estimate, a remarkable accomplishment considering the size and novelty of the work. A total of only $61,000 had been paid out in loan interest, thanks to the substantial contributions of the various taxes and duties that had kept borrowing to a relative minimum.

By early fall, it was clear: "[B]efore the close of the season, salt will undoubtedly be carried from Salina to Utica by means of the canal." The middle section was not entirely complete, especially in the varied levels of the westernmost portion, but after three construction seasons, it was time for some public celebration of the "Great Canal."

The groundbreaking outside Rome in 1817 had lacked both substantial ceremony and significant attendees, including the governor himself, and went remarkably underreported. By contrast, Clinton placed himself at the center of festivities on Saturday, October 23, 1819, the first of increasingly larger and well-orchestrated celebrations of progress on what was not yet an Erie canal. The chosen venue was the fifteen level miles between Rome and Utica.

The preparations had begun two days earlier, on Thursday afternoon, when workers dug away earthen bars holding back the feeder waters of Oriskany Creek, roughly midway between Rome and Utica. "The first admission of water into a canal is always attended with much solicitude," observed the *Utica Patriot*: "It is the ultimate test of the accuracy of the levels, and affords most important inferences, as to the solidity and fidelity, with which the banks have been constructed, and the sufficiency of the feeders." Workers were stationed on Oriskany Hill "to arrest, as quick as possible, the progress of any evil that might arise" as water flowed into the Rome-Utica section.

At first, all seemed well. "I beheld a sight that could not but exhilarate and elevate the mind," reported a gentleman correspondent to an Albany paper, who was perched on a bridge above the canal outside Utica; "The waters were rushing in from the westward, and coming down their untried channel towards the sea. Their course, owing to the absorption of the new banks of the canal, and the distance they had to run from where the stream entered it, was much slower than I had anticipated; they continued gradually to steal along from bridge to bridge, and at first only spreading over the bed of the canal, imperceptibly rose and washed its sides with a gentle wave." It was dark before "this new internal river rolled its first waves" into Utica, where the awed gentleman and his townsmen retired to dream of the canal age.

But while Uticans slumbered, others experienced certain realities of the new age. Some time after nightfall, the new canal breached near Oriskany. A recently patched construction drain in the canal wall had failed, and the new internal river, by then rolling at a depth of two and a half feet, quickly began emptying into the darkened countryside. The breach—the first of what would turn out to be many on newly opened sections—stranded the first official boat on the canal, fittingly carrying a load of Romans.

Earlier on Thursday, New York's pioneer canal boat had felt the first water under its keel. Designed from the model brought from England by Canvass White, built at Rome by Jeremiah Brainard and two other canal contractors, and named in honor of Benjamin Wright, the *Chief Engineer* was sixty-one feet long and seven and a half feet wide, with fourteen-foot-long cabins at either end and a flat deck amidships. These were the standard dimensions for the first generation of canal boats that prevailed throughout the 1820s; they could carry a thousand bushels of wheat, thirty tons of freight, or a hundred passengers. But only if the canal had water.

The *Chief Engineer* drew only a foot of water, and as soon as the canal had filled sufficiently, a single horse tethered to an eighty-foot rope had taken the boat's tow from outside Rome. For the maiden voyage, the load was thirty Romans and a military band. J. Burr Brainard, a young relative of Jeremiah, scribbled his impressions in verse:

> *We sailed from Rome, though sails we had none,*
> *We had the bugle the fife and the hollow bass drum.*
> *The loon she might hollow we feared not her note,*
> *While we played Yankee Doodle on the floating boat.*

It is not completely clear why the *Chief Engineer* was still en route to Utica after nightfall, but the fun was suddenly ended when

we came smack on dry land . . .
Stop, stop the shrill fife: just muffle the drum:
In distress blow the bugle, let us echo along;
Let a black flag be hoisted to express our sad fear
That we can not proceed with the Chief Engineer.

Word of the trouble quickly reached engineers and contractors. The creek feeder was reclosed and, working through the night and the morning, they managed to repair the canal wall. By noon on Friday, water was again flowing into the canal, and the *Chief Engineer* resumed its voyage to Utica.

Apparently the natural surface of the ground where the canal had breached was two feet below the canal bottom, adding substantially to the pressure exerted by the two and a half feet of water. "But this pressure would have produced no injury," scolded the Utica paper, "if due care had been taken in raising the bottom of the canal, and breaking in the sides of the drains, and puddling the earth required in closing it."

When the Roman boaters finally brought the *Chief Engineer* into Utica later on Friday, they were long past their welcome but in plenty of time to understand that they were just the delivery men. The real celebrations were scheduled for Saturday.

Just after nine on Saturday morning, Clinton led commissioners Van Rensselaer, Holley, and Young, namesake engineer Wright, and dozens of other celebrants aboard the *Chief Engineer* for a round trip to Rome and back. Church bells rang, throngs cheered, drums rolled, and the boat set out. "From bridge to bridge, from village to village, the procession was saluted with cannon, and every bell, whose sound could reach the canal, swung as with instinctive life, as it passed by." Clinton was in his glory: "The Governor sat upon deck, contemplating the interesting and joyous scene." A large white flag with embroidered canal scenes waved over his head. Pulled by its single horse, and attended by hundreds of spectators walking along the canal banks, the boat stopped at Whitesboro to pick up

Canvass White and others. An artillery salute sent the boat on its way toward Rome, where "an elegant dinner had been provided." Unfortunately for Roman pride, the feast was uneaten, because the governor and his elite party had a full banquet awaiting them back in Utica. Some "suitable refreshments" were brought to the turning point at a bridge outside Rome, a fresh horse was hitched, and after what one passenger unkindly termed "a delay of 48 minutes" in Rome, the *Chief Engineer* departed.

"The experience of this day's excursion," the Utica village president addressed the commissioners upon their return, "must do away all doubt, if any remain, of the practicability of constructing this 'stupendous artificial river of the West.'" "We shall employ the means confided to us by the state," Clinton triumphantly replied, "and in the course of five years we anticipate the completion of an easy navigation between the great lakes of the west and the Atlantic ocean." As often happened with significant canal events in New York, sixty-one-year-old Elkanah Watson was on hand: "It was impossible for stupidity itself not to have been electrified on this joyous occasion, and to stretch their opaque minds from Erie to the ocean."

As a practical matter, the *Chief Engineer* on its round-trip from Utica had averaged four miles per hour under tow, "in a safe and comfortable manner." The speed was equal to that of a stage in bad weather on a bad road, and the transport was much less jarring and fifty times more efficient: one hundred boat passengers by the power of one horse versus one stage horse for every two passengers.

Clinton was at the center of the 1819 celebrations, but the unsung hero of the Erie accomplishments to date was his friend Myron Holley. Since taking on the role of acting commissioner in 1817, Holley had thrown himself increasingly into the job: "To no man is the state so much indebted for useful exertions as to Mr. Holley." The public was not generally aware that over the course of three seasons, the canal line had become Myron Holley's home. "His whole time has been devoted to the work from its commencement. He has not spared the labour either of body or mind. Every thing personal has been neglected. Private interest, social enjoyments, for which he possesses a keen relish, even domestic comforts have been renounced, in the performance of his duty." Holley had effectively abandoned a devoted and beloved wife and their ten (of an eventual twelve) children in

Canandaigua, but their loss had been the canal's gain, as the *Utica Patriot* attested: "His fine, interesting and conciliatory manners, in avoiding difficulties, in hushing murmurs, and in causing universal encouragement and animation, have silently effected what probably could have been effected in no other way." Holley's overarching dedication would deepen further over the next five years, nearly to the completion of the canal, when rising murmurs and difficulties would unavoidably ruin him.

In the meantime, the 1819 celebrations continued. Clinton went back to his duties as governor, leaving Holley in command of the *Chief Engineer* for a tour along the entire sixty-mile level to Salina. Crowds thronged the boat at every village along newly-filled sections; farmers and their workers ran from every field. "The spirit which manifested itself on our first attempt in navigating the canal, between Utica and Rome," Holley reported to Clinton, "seems to spread without losing any thing of its animation or joy." *Niles' Register* published the letter for its national audience and concluded that "no man can calculate the effects to be produced by the Erie canal."

At the end of November Clinton and his rival, Van Buren, joined the celebrations for the opening of navigation on the Northern or Champlain Canal with similar pomp and ceremony, transiting the canal in a boat provided by the navy. (The Champlain was not fully and officially completed until 1823.) Finally, on a suddenly wintry December 10, Holley led an attempted navigation of the completed westernmost portion of the Erie middle section, "in defiance of the inclemency of the season." Holley set out with seventy passengers from Montezuma toward Salina in an open boat fitted with a temporary cabin. They quickly ran into trouble: an inch of fresh ice. A pair of horses strained for three hours to make six miles to Mentz, where two more horses were added for the ten-mile haul to Jordan, arriving in bitter-cold darkness. In the morning, hopes of reaching another twenty miles to Salina were blocked by more ice, and the day was spent working the boat back through broken ice to Montezuma.

No one realized at the time that the frustrated navigation of early December 1819 was a foretaste of the canal's operational limits. "By the continual passage of boats in winter," wrote De Witt Clinton (as Hibernicus) the following spring, "the canal can be prevented from freezing;

and when frozen, a vessel may open its way by placing stampers for breaking ice at its head." "Stampers," alas, did not prevail.

As late as the spring of 1825 it was still the commissioners' "intention to keep the water in the canal during winter," but that December the completed canal was closed and drained, and it would be every winter afterward. Draining prevented ice from damaging canal walls and structures; closing, announced a week or so in advance, prevented loaded barges from being trapped for the winter. In its earliest years, the Erie's official closing date would be around December 14. By the end of the century it would be two weeks earlier; likewise, the average opening date would gradually slide from April 10 to April 21. It was all an effect of a global cooling that, despite the effects predicted even then from rampant deforestation, brought decreasing average temperatures into the 1880s. If Erie opponents and supporters had known before the canal was built that it would be open on average only 240 days a year in the 1820s, and just 212 days by the 1880s, one wonders if it would have been built at all.

Holley's chilling experience notwithstanding, the near completion of the ninety-six-mile middle section meant that commercial travel was ahead. In February 1820, canal contractors Simon Newton Dexter and Comfort Tyler organized the Erie Canal Navigation Company, the first canal boat business. Dexter, the textile manufacturer recently established at Whitesboro, was the company's treasurer. Tyler was the president and the sort of pioneer whose life seemed destined for fulfillment by the Erie Canal.

A Connecticut native and Colonial Army enlistee at fourteen, Tyler had moved before his twentieth birthday to the lower Mohawk Valley, where he established himself at Caughnawaga as a schoolteacher and surveyor. In 1785 he signed on with a survey party led by De Witt Clinton's father James, passing up the Mohawk Valley to establish the boundary between New York and Pennsylvania. The route by bateaux up the Mohawk, portage to Otsego Lake, and down the Susquehanna River exposed Tyler to the rigors and rewards of frontier boating. A chance involvement the following year with an association of would-be purchasers of native land in Western New York led Tyler as far as Canandaigua. The scheme quickly fell apart—only the state could buy Indian territory—but the young surveyor had arrived in the region of his destiny. In 1788 Tyler and another pioneer established the first permanent settlement in what became Onondaga County, fifty miles west of any white inhabitant. In local lore, Tyler felled the first tree. Dependent on the natives for the initial survival of his family (a wife and young daughter), Tyler quickly earned their favor and a name: To-whan-ta-qua, or one who is double, meaning both a gentleman and a laboring man.

Soon after the Tylers' arrival in Onondaga country, the natives provided them with a pound of salt and offered to show Tyler where they got it. Early one morning a guide canoed out of Onondaga Lake with Tyler and a fifteen-gallon iron kettle aboard, through marshes and along slender creeks to a "bluff of hard land . . . where he fastened his canoe, pointed to a hole apparently artificial, and said there was the salt." Over the next nine hours, Tyler boiled down a supply of salt. For the rest of the year and into the next, he returned regularly on his own, producing enough salt for his family's sustenance and each time stashing in nearby bushes the kettles, chains, poles, and wooden crotches that constituted the first salt works at the future village of Salina. Thus was born the New York salt industry. Other salt pioneers arrived each year, including Pennsylvanian James Geddes, who paddled up the Susquehanna with his boiling pots five years after Tyler's arrival.

As settlers poured into the region, Tyler rose as one of their leaders, a developer of the county's first roads, bridges, and schools. In 1798 he was elected to the state assembly, where he made the acquaintance of Aaron Burr. The salt pioneer subsequently became a willing participant in Burr's notorious conspiracy of 1805 to make an empire of the American southwest. Like Burr, Tyler eventually was acquitted of treason but was ruined as a public man. In 1811 he moved his family to the sloughs of Montezuma, where he began to rebuild his personal and financial fortunes with a salt manufacturing company. The company improved local prospects and its own by building bridges over the Seneca and Clyde rivers and a three-mile turnpike through the Montezuma marshes. When the Erie Canal beckoned, Tyler, well aware of its likely benefits, contracted for three of the middle section's westernmost portions. In 1820 he took the natural next step of partnering with Simon Dexter to form the first canal boat company.

The company meant business. Among the influential subscribers of its hefty $100 shares were original canal promoter and Syracuse founder

Joshua Forman and canal commissioner Myron Holley, a useful fellow traveler at a time when "conflict of interest" was not in the dictionary. After establishing the company in early February, Tyler oversaw the building of the *Montezuma*, an elegant barge ten years ahead of its time. At seventy-six feet long and fourteen feet wide, the *Montezuma* was the *Titanic* of its times; boats that size didn't become standard on the canal until the 1830s. The *Montezuma* had over twice the freight capacity of the *Chief Engineer*, which Tyler acquired to make a two-boat fleet for the start of canal travel in 1820.

The *Montezuma* made a splash on its maiden voyage. It arrived at two in the afternoon on Thursday, April 20, at the village that just two months earlier had been named Syracuse, where a hundred "ladies and gentlemen" boarded for the short run on the side cut to Salina. "The banks of the canal," reported the Onondaga *Register*, were "thronged by persons . . . witnessing, for the first time . . . a boat floating upon its waters." (They apparently had missed the *Chief Engineer* in October.) Cheers greeted the boat at Salina, a procession of passengers and spectators accompanied by a band marched to a local inn, and 150 passengers piled on for the return to Syracuse. "This practical illustration of [the canal's] benefits has been witnessed sooner than the most sanguine friends of the measure could have expected; and cannot fail . . . to incline the doubtful to its vigorous prosecution, and free it opponents from their fears and subdue their hostility." Soon enough the darker monopolistic intentions of Tyler's Erie Canal Navigation Company—"only One Line anywhere on the Canal"—would arouse a different sort of hostility.

An assortment of rafts and small boats had been launching into sections of the canal as soon as the ice began breaking up in March, but official navigation didn't begin until May, when toll rates for the 1820 season were announced. The first tolls weren't collected until July 1, though. Numerous breaches, weak canal walls, and settling embankments caused low water levels and required repairs before the commissioners felt "justified in asking toll." In the meantime they instituted symbolic ordering of canal travel: painted mile boards to make captains and passengers aware of the distances traveled and the charges incurred.

From the simple record of a rate sheet emerge the materials of life at the birth of the canal age, at rates ranging from five mills to two cents per ton or standard measure per mile: salt, gypsum, flour, meal, salted provisions, pot and pearl ash; timber, boards, plank, siding, lath, "and other sawed stuff"; shingles; brick, sand, lime; iron ore; stone; fence rails and posts; fuel wood; pipe and hogshead staves; and general merchandise. As an incentive to salt manufacturers whose duties were considerably augmenting the canal fund, any fuel used in the manufacture of salt would pass the canal's locks for free. Boats transporting commercial goods were to be tolled at a mill per mile per ton of capacity, passenger boats at five cents per mile.

Comfort Tyler's canal boats could well afford the toll. The *Montezuma* and others after it cost roughly $1,000 to build, $500 to furnish, and nearly $100 a month in pay for a six-man crew of captain, helmsman, bowman, cook, cabin boy, and driver, plus up to $80 for each horse and the continuing expense of its feed. On the other hand, the fare for the thirty-four-hour run between Utica and Montezuma (with an overnight layover in Canastota) in the company's first season was $4 including bed and board, with a three cents a mile rate for way passengers. With two round-trips and four hundred passengers a week, Tyler's boats cleared a 25 percent profit. Company investors received an $86 dividend on their $100 shares in 1822. The following season, the company had nine boats plying open sections of the canal.

In the early summer of 1820 New Yorkers were instructed by the newspaper accounts of Hibernicus (aka Clinton) that "cheaper and more commodious traveling [sic] cannot be found." The Hibernicus letters— canal boosterism that was printed and reprinted in papers across the state—reflected Clinton's experiences during May and June voyages on the *Chief Engineer* from Utica to Montezuma, and back to Utica on the *Montezuma*. Travelers, liberated from the interior's notoriously rutted roads, could now go by boat "without a jolt, or the least fatigue, and employ the whole time in reading, writing, rational conversation, amusement, or viewing the most interesting part of the globe."

Needless to say, people who were not the governor and canal commission president had different opinions. Right at the dawn of Erie travel, opinion was not universally favorable. In late June English traveler John Howison boarded a boat ten miles east of Montezuma at Weedsport, one of many inland "ports" founded along the canal. "I found its accommodations of a much meaner description than I expected." A gentleman of independent means, he had spent the past two years touring Ontario and was headed from Western New York to Manhattan to observe Fourth of July festivities. "The country through which the canal extends is far from being beautiful or interesting. Nothing but woods are to be seen, except in a few places, where cultivation has recently been commenced, and where incipient villages raise their unassuming heads." On the passage to Utica, the sophisticated traveler gained the unique wisdom of the boat captain, in a conversation about Clinton, whom Howison considered a leading American statesman. "Well, he's considerable of a statesman," the captain allowed, "though all don't think so now; but in a country like ours, the governors are continually changing, and the people alter their opinions, and are led about like a pig by the nose." As the boat glided east, the captain expounded on lawyers—"a damned deal too many"—and again on Clinton, who was rumored liable to suppress American democracy if given too much time in office. "Ah, sir," the captain told his astonished passenger, "the people of the United States will believe any thing; and if one takes the proper way, it is as easy to lead them as it is to lead ringed ox."

The canal may not have been uniformly pleasurable to travel, but its commercial benefits were immediately clear. At Utica in May, Clinton (as Hibernicus) saw "a raft of 440 tons of lumber." He learned that the raft had been floated for twenty miles in ten hours behind four horses at a total cost of $50: "The conveyance of this timber by land would have cost at least 1600 dollars."

By late spring 1820 Utica had taken on the air of a thriving port. In a two-week period from late May to early June, the "Canal List" in the Utica *Patriot* counted nearly fifty arrivals and departures of boats bearing passengers, flour, stone, pork, salt, and assorted other cargo. After sampling regional fish and fruits, Clinton predicted that soon "the epicures of the south will be treated with new and untried dishes of the highest flavor," preserved in ice and transported along the canal.

Little occasion for celebration was left to Rome. On July 1 village merchant John Westcott had the dubious privilege of paying the first toll on the canal, for a raft's worth of timber. Exactly $5,244.34 in canal tolls would be collected by the close of navigation in December. The take was

This detail from the Vance-Dey map shows the canal passing directly through the new village of Syracuse, with the established town named for local salt pioneer and Erie engineer James Geddes to the west, and the sidecut canal leading north to Salina on Onondaga Lake. (*The Lionel Pincus and Princess Firyal Map Division, The New York Public Library, Astor, Lenox and Tilden Foundations*)

offset somewhat by $900 in annual salaries for five state-appointed toll collectors at Utica, Rome, Canastota, Syracuse, and Bucksville, just east of Montezuma. The top salaried toll collector, at $250, was Syracuse founder and canal pioneer Joshua Forman.

Three days after the first toll collection at Rome, and exactly three years after the Independence Day groundbreaking there, the official celebration of the completion of the middle section was held, at Syracuse. It was the first time the nation's birthday was commemorated there. Syracuse then consisted of two taverns; a mill; a store; a schoolhouse that doubled as a meetinghouse; and the homes of half a dozen settlers, including developer Forman, who had been in residence for a year. Most of the buildings were built on stilts "to raise them out of the mud and slush." Newspaper editor William Leete Stone, making a canal boat passage with Forman, disembarked at desolate Syracuse and remarked to his friend, "It would make an owl weep to fly over it." "Never mind," Forman replied, "you will live to see it a city yet." Both men were right.

Rome was genteel by comparison, but celebrating the middle section's completion at Syracuse symbolized how the canal already was shifting the state's focus into the primitive but soon civilized west. Joshua Forman was determined to make a city of his newly purchased marshland. The canal would raise Syracuse's fortunes. Forman would raise Syracuse itself; over the next several years, he orchestrated the state-funded draining of Onondaga Lake, which lowered its level and turned swamp into real estate.

Unlike the small gathering that had assembled three years earlier outside Rome, many thousands participated in the festivities at Syracuse, where "a most brilliant day dawned upon a land heretofore a swamp and bog." Beside a spreading pine in a cleared grove on high ground outside the village, speeches and the Declaration of Independence were read, before the main event: seventy-three banner-festooned boats of all shapes and sizes floating in a procession along the side canal to the Salina salt works. The newest addition to Comfort Tyler's fleet, the *Oneida Chief,* bore Governor Clinton, the other canal commissioners, and dozens of the most prominent officials and private citizens of the state. "Such a spectacle, in point of novelty and grandeur, had at that time never been witnessed in the interior."

Elkanah Watson, the tainted saint of New York canalling, as usual marked this latest milestone for the canal that would cross the state. "I have dreaded its progress,—judging from the old canals,—that the real cost would exceed the estimate threefold. I am now satisfied of my great error." The Erie and Champlain canals would be "the most powerful and certain source" of state revenue; the rising western states "must become tributary" to the Empire State; and New York City, "[o]ur grand emporium . . . will of necessity command the greatest extent of inland commerce, of any given point on this globe." When Erie was complete, "England, or the European continent, will sink into a miniature scale."

It remained, though, for the complex forces of politics, local interest, and primitive technology to unite in completing the vision. New York had completed the middle section of its great canal with relative ease. The eastern and western extremities would present much greater controversies and challenges.

CHAPTER 10

Eastward Ho!

How we shall get a line from Schenectady to the Hudson I am most anxious to know.

—Henry Seymour to De Witt Clinton, October 1820

Governor Clinton opened the 1819 legislature on January 5 triumphantly recounting the canal progress and picturing greater glories ahead. By the end of the coming season, he proclaimed, the middle section would be complete; it would begin generating toll revenues the following season. Construction costs had remained within estimates; the flourishing canal fund obviated the need for taxes. Clinton had been willing a year earlier to wait on seeking approval for the eastern and western sections of the canal. Now "there cannot exist a doubt of the feasibility of the work or of the ability of the state." Goods that cost $100 to ship by land from Buffalo to Albany and just $25 by water to Montreal would, Clinton asserted, cost less than $10 by canal to Albany if the legislature authorized "the completion of the whole work as soon as possible." This was more than a state issue. When the canal to Lake Erie was complete and the Ohio River was also linked by a canal with Lake Erie, or the Illinois River with Lake Michigan, "[t]he most distant parts of the confederacy will then be in a state of approximation, and the distinctions of Eastern and Western, of Southern and Northern interests will be entirely prostrated." Clinton and others could not imagine then how New

York's canal would help prostrate the economic interests of the Southern confederacy within a generation. Indeed, he believed that failing to complete the nation-binding canal was the greatest threat to unity: "A dismemberment of the republic into separate confederacies, would necessarily produce the jealous circumspection and hostile preparations of bordering states: large standing armies would be immediately raised; unceasing and vindictive wars would follow, and a military despotism would reign triumphant on the ruins of civil liberty." Thinking both nationally and locally, Clinton advised that "all local prejudices and geographical distinctions should be discarded" in the interests of union and commerce.

Later in January the annual report of Clinton's canal commission detailed the remarkable progress outlined in his legislative address and asked for the authority and funding to complete the canal. In 1818 anti-Clintonian forces had stalled further construction; they would find that course more difficult in 1819. Public sentiment heavily favored completion. Even the anti-Clintonian New York *American* conceded, "An unanimity appears to exist in the support of this project."

Clinton was poised to ride the canal to political supremacy, but as the legislature settled down to its business the governor stumbled, committing one of his typical political indiscretions. Always adept at discounting delicate alliances after they had provided political capital, Clinton in late January indicated that he would not support the reelection (by the legislature) of venerable Federalist Rufus King to the U.S. Senate. Clinton's position on King arose from personal, not political, differences, but Federalists whose support had boosted Clinton into office quickly began forging allegiances with the strengthening Van Buren wing of the state Republican party, devoted to if not always successful at diminishing anything Clinton.

The first of many and greater political consequences from this Clinton–Federalist rupture was the battle in the legislature to name a permanent replacement for Joseph Ellicott on the canal commission. Clinton's 1818 recess appointee, Ephraim Hart, was like his mentor an indiscreet politician, and was personally disliked by influential Federalist legislators. They now considered supporting Western District senator Henry Seymour, the candidate of Burenite "Bucktail" Republicans.*

Seymour, who had been floated for a canal commission seat back in 1816, was Hart's antithesis: an effective, gentlemanly politician and ardent anti-Clintonian. Supporters warned Hart and especially Clinton to lobby, but they demurred, relying on a 3–2 majority of Clintonians and Federalists over Bucktails and other anti-Clintonians and remaining insensitive to shifting sentiments. At the end of March Seymour was elected over Hart by a one-vote margin.

The subtext was clearer for Clinton than he wished to acknowledge. "He is the political *Ishmael* of our times," wrote "An Old Federalist" in the *Evening Post*, "a sort of *political pirate* sailing under his own black flag, and not entitled to use that of either party." Clinton might have commanded navies, but he would have to settle for canal boats.

When he had appointed Hart the previous August, Clinton had designated him an acting commissioner, forming a majority with Clintonian Myron Holley over Bucktail Samuel Young. Now Seymour formed an anti-Clintonian majority with Young, and they initiated Bucktail influence and patronage over certain canal operations, Young on the Champlain and Seymour on the Erie. Though he remained the canal's public face and the commission's president, Clinton had lost control of the commission as a political instrument. Embarrassments loomed for Holley and Clinton. Unwitting as yet, Clinton would find Bucktail canal politics "until the day of his death used to annoy and to prostrate him." The lost skirmish over a canal commission seat gave off a whiff of decay in Clinton's long but tenuous control of New York politics and an early scent of Van Buren's Albany Regency, the voracious machine that would power state politics for the next generation and help get Van Buren into the White House, a lifetime goal that eluded Clinton.

---

*Originally a pejorative term for early Tammany clubmen of New York City who sported deertail hats, and then directed by Clintonians at the politicized Tammany, the Bucktail tag was adopted by Van Buren Republicans to distinguish themselves from Clintonian Republicans statewide. In the financial Panic of 1837 Seymour, then the president of the Farmers' Loan and Trust Company, a corporate ancestor of today's Citibank, lay down on his bed with a shotgun and used his foot to shoot himself through the heart.

Clinton was leaving blood on his tracks, but the canal was safe. "The opposition to internal navigation is entirely paralyzed," he gloated in late January. "The Canal improvements will be prosecuted with vigor, and the Legislature will pass favorable laws on the subject this Session." But it would require Van Buren's acquiescence.

In early March the assembly, still controlled by the unsteady coalition of Clintonians and Federalists, voted by a wide margin in favor of a bill empowering the commissioners to move forward with the canal. Bucktails and other anti-Clintonians led by Erastus Root voted as one against. The next day the opposition rallied to narrowly defeat a proposal to double annual borrowing for canal construction to $800,000. This effectively mooted the construction authority approved the previous day.

Anti-Clintonians then compelled the assembly to demand a public accounting by the commissioners of all the contractors who had abandoned or failed to complete their contracts. This put the commissioners in a quandary. Stalling would make it seem as if there was something to hide and bring legislative debate to a halt. Complying might embarrass otherwise "worthy and respectable men" and diminish legislators' willingness to approve more construction. Guided wisely by Clinton on this issue, the commissioners chose aggressive compliance, delivering all the details within forty-eight hours in perfect political style. "[T]he reluctance which the Commissioners might feel against making a communication, which might inflict additional pain upon the unfortunate, and which may have a tendency to destroy that competition for future contracts on the canal, which is a most important requisite to its economical construction, is entirely surmounted by the consideration, that the representatives of the people are at all times entitled to received such information as they may require from the public functionaries." Only Clinton among the commissioners could have written with such delicious condescension and perfect effect.

Canal groundbreaker Joshua Hathaway and other "delinquents" were humiliated by the public disclosure, but the accounting revealed that nearly all of the failures had occurred in the first season and that the contracting system had been working smoothly since then. A week after the accounting, Seymour won Ellicott's spot on the canal commission over Clinton nominee Hart. The day after that the assembly agreed to increase annual borrowing to an adequate $600,000 and sent the bill to the senate.

The senate had a large anti-Clintonian majority, but separate motions to prevent the start of either the western or eastern sections were narrowly defeated. The quiet voices of reason were Van Buren and canal commissioners and fellow senators Seymour and Young. They understood that a Bucktail senate killing of the popular canal would politically invigorate the governor.

Van Buren's task of reining in other anti-Clintonians for political purposes was made less difficult by Clinton himself, the uneasiest of heads to wear a political crown. Early in the legislative session Clinton had rejected the Republican caucus choice for assembly speaker in favor of a Republican with Federalist leanings. On the strength of Clinton's authority as governor, his puppet Obadiah German gained the office, but Clinton lost another measure of party respect. At the same time, the governor was using his control of the Council of Appointment (composed of himself and four friendly senators named by the Clintonian-Federalist assembly majority) to purge Bucktails from thousands of appointive state and local offices. Van Buren himself would eventually be turned out as attorney general, an office he had held for three years. "I confess myself among those who were deceived by Mr. Clinton," a disillusioned Utica Republican wrote to Van Buren after abandoning the governor, "not as to his talents . . . but in his whole course as a politician. It is all too evident that he has acted a direct hostility to the Republican party." In a few months, Clinton had managed to alienate both Federalists and Republicans.

During the course of the legislative session, Van Buren quietly worked out a new strategy: show support for the popular canal and discredit the politically vulnerable Clinton. "Tell the people that Mr. Clinton was not the real projector of it," *National Advocate* publisher Mordecai Noah reportedly ordered a subordinate, explaining, "Every thing [sic] is fair in politics." Like other anti-Clintonian papers, Noah's Tammany mouthpiece retained its opposition to Clinton, but dutifully became an apostle of the canal it had long decried as a tax-inducing project that would bankrupt the state.

Confident that he could support the canal without benefiting Clinton, Van Buren guided the canal construction bill through the senate with the $600,000 annual borrowing authority approved by the assembly. On April 7 the act that effectively authorized the completion of the Erie Canal became law. Clinton claimed victory, but increasingly his standing would be measured not by political constituencies but rather by public milestones in the progress of the canal.

Two weeks after winning the canal vote, Clinton celebrated by marrying Catherine Jones, a socially adept and politically sophisticated granddaughter of Philip Livingston. Maria Clinton, dead less than nine months, had provided Clinton with a family; Catherine would accompany him along the peaks and valleys of his remaining years.

Although legislative approval of the canal was a political game, the selection of contractors and engineering staff appears not to have been, regardless of frequent allegations and accusations. During the construction years at least, "no notice was taken" of any contractor's politics, as far as John Jervis could tell (or would admit). Jervis, only mildly political himself, knew of no effort to influence chief Wright in his selection of assistants: "Whatever may have been the views of men in high official station, it was not regarded proper to interfere with the economical conduct of business on the canal." In his seven years of dealings with canal commissioners and engineering superiors, Jervis received "no intimation . . . to look to the right and or the left for any motive but the strict interest of the canal."

On the other hand, politics and personality did influence commissioner relations. In late 1819 Clinton and Samuel Young traded accusations, that Young had secret interests in contracts he was awarding for locks on the Champlain Canal, and that Clinton habitually claimed all the credit for the commission's accomplishments. In bitter and unrestrained letters to each other, Clinton called Young a "blackguard" and a "dastardly accuser"; Young accused Clinton of "malicious slander." At a not too remote time, these might have been dueling words. Instead, the two men got their satisfaction by not speaking to each other for their remaining years together on the canal commission.

Clinton, of course, was used to having enemies in his midst—he thrived on it—and his conflict with Young did not prevent the commission and their engineers from laying out the eastern and western section work. The great challenge of the eastern section was to create canal navigation where an often narrow, steep valley had made river navigation impossible in places and arduous throughout.

During the 1818 season Isaac Briggs had conducted detailed surveys that located the upper forty miles of the eastern section line, from Utica down the Mohawk Valley beyond Herkimer. It was Briggs's "decided opinion" that though the eastern section included some of "the greatest difficulties" in the entire project, the portion that he had examined could be built for some 16 percent less than the commissioners' earlier estimate of roughly $17,000 per mile. Further surveys consumed the 1819 season, until the commissioners decided in October to bid out the twenty-six miles from Utica through Little Falls. By December the eight easy miles from Utica to Frankfort—the eastern end of the long level out to Salina—had been contracted "at reasonable prices, by good men."

The prices were "reasonable" not so much because, as Briggs suggested, the commissioners had originally overestimated costs, but because an economic panic was taking hold of the country. The Panic of 1819, precipitated in the spring by a credit collapse (among myriad causes), would blossom presently into the nation's first depression. In the next two seasons, Erie contract prices would drop from budgeted estimates by up to 40 percent.

"[T]he distresses of the community have continued to increase," Clinton noted in the first line of his speech opening the 1820 legislature. Pushing forward toward "a vast system of internal trade" was the answer to economic distress. Short-term financial pain notwithstanding, it was as good a time as any for a massive public works funded increasingly by loans at falling interest rates and built by local citizens at increasingly diminishing prices.

In his speech, the governor warned that "persons . . . in furtherance of selfish designs will strive to destroy the great fabric of internal improvements by withdrawing or dispersing the fund appropriated for its support." As the 1820 legislative season intensified, "insidious enmity" indeed rose up: a proposal that the eastern section be completed before any construction began on the west. An assembly resolution demanded that the commissioners justify their intentions to the standing canal committee. The resolution's sponsor was none other than canal fund creator George Tibbits, one of many anti-Clinton Federalists turned anti-Clinton Bucktail. In a series of pseudonymous articles in his hometown Troy newspaper, Tibbits decried "the impolitic proceedings" of the Clinton-led canal commission. Pursuing construction on two fronts in a panic economy would stress the fund's health, Tibbits argued; focusing on the eastern section alone would more quickly generate toll revenues to help defray future western section construction costs.

The west, of course, was where support for the canal and its champion was strongest. The east was where Bucktails flourished and feared that a canal all the way through to Erie would tip commercial prosperity to the west. In his speech Clinton had warned of the danger of working exclusively on the eastern section: the greater population of the east could be politically manipulated to demand that western construction be abandoned altogether. The Great Western Canal, as Erie was often called then, would amount to little more than an improvement of the traditional river route to Lake Ontario.

The east–west issue split the canal commission. Bucktail commissioners Young and Seymour, effectively siding with eastern interests, refused to sign the official commission response to the canal committee. Over the signatures of only Clinton, Holley, and Van Rensselaer, the commission argued that too much had been committed already to the western section—surveys, contracts, and land grants—to forsake the inevitable benefits to all New Yorkers. "[T]his state can never enjoy a tenth part of the advantages of the Erie canal, till the tide of inland commerce, of which it is to be the channel, is permitted to flow, without a mile of portage, from the great lakes to the Atlantic." The committee, fortuitously stacked with Clintonians and presented with a majority report of the commissioners and no minority opinion, reported to the assembly that they were unwilling to "interfere, in any way, to counteract or control the plans of the commissioners, who have hitherto managed the business with success." The western and eastern sections would proceed as already authorized.

The skirmishing was not over. Procanal Bucktails used the few remaining weeks of the 1820 session to distinguish themselves from anti-

Clintonians who remained opposed to the canal, like Erastus Root. Root led an effort to start collection of the tax on lands within twenty-five miles of the canal; authorized after much debate under the 1817 law, the provision had been suspended the following year. Root's motion was defeated; the tax deemed so essential in 1817 to passage of the first canal authorization law would never be imposed. Senator and commissioner Young pushed through a law allocating a quarter of all canal spending to completion of the navigable but unfinished Champlain Canal, with remaining available funds to be spent equally on the eastern and western sections of Erie. A provision in the law, though, gave the commissioners broad discretion in changing the allocations, effectively mooting the fiscal constraint. Another provision designated the first $25,000 from state land sales to accrue to the canal fund for improvement of Oswego River navigation. This was a token to those who would have stopped the "Erie canal" at the Seneca River and channeled trade the old way to Lake Ontario.

While all of this horse-trading was generally good for the canal, none of it accrued substantially to Clinton's political interest. At the end of April, two weeks after the close of the 1820 legislative session, Clinton faced a tight contest for reelection as governor, against Bucktail Republican Daniel Tompkins. Clintonian legislative candidates anticipated short coattails.

It was Tompkins who had quit as governor in 1816 to serve as Monroe's irrelevant vice president, paving Clinton's way to the statehouse. And it was Tompkins who had spoken unguardedly and unwisely against the canal-enabling legislation in 1817, prompting James Kent's deciding vote in the Council of Revision. Now Tompkins had been enlisted by Van Buren to displace Clinton.

The effort failed, but only barely. On the strength of majorities in counties along the canal line, Clinton sent the hapless Tompkins back to his superfluous federal job by a margin of just fifteen hundred of over ninety-three thousand votes. That was the good news for Clinton. With evident but ultimately unpunished illegal electioneering by Monroe operatives, Bucktails gained a wide majority in the assembly to go with their retained advantage in the senate. Clinton suddenly found himself at the head of a government of which he would have no legislative control.

He tried to spin his personal victory as a Bucktail defeat but Van Buren, whetting his knives, gloated, "We have scotched the snake not killed it. One more campaign & all will be well."

As the 1820 political season gave way to the canal-building season, the Western Inland Lock Navigation Company finally met its fate. The company had controlled and marginally improved Mohawk River navigation for nearly three decades. Now the state was extending canal navigation alongside the company's old domain. Negotiations with the company had sputtered along since 1811, when the original canal commissioners rejected a buyout demand of $190,000 as excessive. Among the provisions of the 1817 law authorizing the start of the Erie and Champlain canals was the appointment of state appraisers to set a new value on the company's works and rights. With construction through the company's territory underway, that value was rapidly diminishing. Negotiations intensified throughout the summer of 1820 before the company's directors, including longtime treasurer Thomas Eddy, accepted just $91,616. That was sixty-five cents on the dollar for the 1,680 outstanding shares held by the company's long-suffering investors. Few complained.

River navigation continued after the buyout. The state took over operations at the company's Little Falls locks late in the 1820 navigation season, collecting some $450 in tolls from the array of Durham boats, bateaux, scows, rafts, and assorted traffic that worked the river. As portions of the canal were completed, temporary channels would link canal and river to maintain continuous navigation. Crews poling boats upriver found relief at completed canal segments where horses took their tow. Gradually, as the native canoe had ceded supremacy of the river to bateaux, and bateaux to Durham boats, barges would come to command the artificial waterway. The vessels of older generations would find their way to other rivers or oblivion, slowly rotting into the banks and backwaters of the Mohawk.

The demise of the Western Inland Company prompted co-founder Elkanah Watson to publish his account of its history and achievements, with himself as the pioneer of the state's inland navigation. Public credit seeking had started the previous December when original company investor Robert Troup (under a pseudonym) noted in a Geneva newspaper that the success of the Erie middle section had "excited a laudable curiosity to know who was the projector of the canal policy" of New York. As far as Troup was concerned Watson was the man, an infuriating assertion to De Witt Clinton who, as pamphleteer Tacitus in 1820, lauded his own role. Clinton had been introduced to the idea of an Erie canal by Jonas Platt and Thomas Eddy, though once on board he had seized the object more completely than anyone else. Watson was certainly the first person (with the late Philip Schuyler) to actually make some improvements to east–west navigation, but he openly admitted in 1820 that he never had in mind the essential extension of navigation directly to Lake Erie; in fact, Watson credited the Hercules essays as the original arguments for the Erie Canal and even outed Jesse Hawley as their author after seventeen years. Hawley had written the seminal newspaper essays but, having published under a pseudonym while jailed as a bankrupt grain merchant, he was in no hurry to acknowledge his identity; when he finally did, five years after Watson published his name, Hawley refrained from grandiose claims. Joshua Forman, on the other hand, had written the first canal legislation and let few forget it, but he thereafter was involved in the canal mostly indirectly as founder and promoter of Syracuse. Many of his surviving contemporaries hailed the vision of the late Gouverneur Morris, but he died without making any practical contribution. In truth, there was no single "projector" of New York's "canal policy."

The beginning of work on the eastern section opened new possibilities for John Jervis. He had spent 1819 as the resident engineer for a portion of the middle section. On his way home for the winter he passed through Constantia on Oneida Lake, where Erie engineer Stephen Bates had started as a New York surveyor ten years earlier and where Jervis's maternal uncle John Bloomfield made his home. In his uncle's considerable library, Jervis found the *Edinburgh Encyclopedia*, with authoritative articles on bridges, canals, and waterworks. The young and undereducated engineer took the volumes to Rome, where he crammed until spring. His study was unrewarded at the opening of the 1820 season; rather than getting a desired assignment on the eastern section construction, he was returned as resident engineer to a stretch of the completed middle section. "I felt that some special favor had been extended to those who, from social position, had been preferred." He characteristically didn't complain, and he performed his duties overseeing the repair of weak earth embankments and other maintenance "so well that my chief would not like to spare me." In October his perseverance paid off, with an assignment from chief Wright to an engineering party working on the eastern section below Little Falls that had just been put under contract. In the spring of 1821 Jervis was given charge of a seventeen-mile division from Anthony's Nose down to Amsterdam, seventeen miles above Schenectady. The division featured four locks and the important crossing of Schoharie Creek, the main feeder of water to the lowest fifty miles of the canal. Jervis would retain this division until its completion at the end of the 1822 season. His experiences as one in the handful of resident engineers are a microcosm of how the eastern section got built.

"I entered on my new field with a determination that no effort of mine would be wanting to give satisfaction, and at the same time improve my knowledge of engineering." Most of Jervis's engineering knowledge about locks and stream crossings came from the pages of his uncle's encyclopedia. Fortunately the eastern section had been readied for contracting by Canvass White, allowing Jervis the initial luxury of simply overseeing the contractors' implementation of White's specifications.

Jervis himself was regularly overseen. Wright, White, and eastern section acting commissioner Seymour (often accompanied by his eleven-year-old son and future governor, Horatio) made monthly inspection tours of the line, in an open wagon when roads were passable and on hikes of up to five miles at a stretch when they (often) were not. White, now a full engineer at the same $1,500 salary as Wright and Geddes, visited the line most often, showing support for the resident engineers and keeping contractors on schedule.

At first Jervis rarely offered his own opinions during the inspections. In time he gathered the confidence to make suggestions, especially about facilitating the safe passage of flood-prone streams beneath the several aqueducts that carried his section of canal hard by the south bank of the Mohawk. Soon enough, his designs for dams and guard gates to channel potentially damaging streams most efficiently around aqueduct piers were routinely adopted.

After the 1821 season White raised Jervis's daily salary from the $1.25 he had received for three seasons to $3.00, plus board and expenses. Like other resident engineers and their assistants, Jervis lodged and took three meals a day at private houses along the line. "In some cases, the fare was indifferent, but in the most part it was comfortable and met the wants of men engaged in vigorous work."

Jervis spent little of his earnings. "Being economical in my habits, [my] pecuniary affairs [were soon] in a growing condition." Jervis had two financial goals. One was to follow the advice of White—"a man of much experience in affairs [and] educated in the best society of Oneida County"—that a man needed only a respectable income, savings of $20,000 invested at 6 percent, and a comfortable house. Jervis's primary goal—"seriously at heart"—was paying off the mortgage on his father's farm. In a few years he was able to clear the mortgage and "other debts that pressed" his overmatched father, and then he began saving for himself.

Erie engineers naturally developed relationships with the contractors they oversaw, bonded as fellow pioneers of canal craft. Often the contractor was a local farmer, and the engineer no older than the farmer's sons and often a farmer's son himself. Such was the case with engineer John Jervis and contractor "Jamie" Archbald, two farmers' sons in their twenties.

Two miles above Schoharie Creek, on Jervis's division, was the 170-acre farm of James and Mary Ann Archbald, Jamie's parents. They had emigrated with their four children in 1807 from Little Cumbrae Isle, in the Firth of Clyde. James Archbald had been a successful farmer in Scotland. Along the Mohawk River, planting wheat, rye, corn, barley, peas, oats, and potatoes, he had found mixed fortune, much as John Jervis's father had after moving his family upstate from Long Island. Jervis was an oldest son, as was Jamie Archbald, who took the contract for the short, level canal segment that passed two hundred yards from the family farm. Like the senior Jervis, the senior Archbald never took a canal contract. Like John Jervis, who was two years his junior, Jamie was opting for the emerging field of canals over the slender mercy of farm fields, work more of the head than the hands. The two young men became lifelong friends.

Like many who took Erie contracts as the Panic of 1819 matured into depression, Jamie Archbald would make no money on his section. But he became the first of John Jervis's many engineering protégés. When he left the Erie project just before its completion to become Benjamin Wright's principal assistant for the Delaware and Hudson Canal, Jervis hired Archbald as a rodman. He was "eminently upright in purpose," with "an excellent engineering mind and great practical sagacity." Jervis soon succeeded Wright as a D&H chief, and on Jervis's recommendation Archbald soon succeeded Jervis. Archbald became a prominent canal and railroad engineer and executive, especially in Pennsylvania, where the borough and town of Archbald remain.

Jamie Archbald earned his fame and fortune after his Erie work, but some of his fellow Erie contractors sought more immediate profit. The settling of contractors' accounts upon completion of their jobs was one of the most challenging aspects of Erie engineering (and contract engineering ever since). During chief Wright's inspection tours all along the line, informal discussions with contractors did not always become formal written contract variations. From this fog, the sharper contractors made claims for extra work that were difficult to reject. This did not happen in Jervis's division. He made it a habit to listen closely when variations were discussed and to take accurate notes, earning Wright's gratitude: "In any case of dispute on his division, [Jervis] pulls out his papers, and that helps matters very much." When the accounting was completed on Jervis's division in late 1822, commissioner Seymour estimated that the young engineer had saved the state $30,000 on questionable claims. "The whole is in a nut shell," Jervis later advised young men starting out, "a steady, resolute, discreet, and upright purpose is the basis of all worth, for any profession."

Jervis glossed over it in his memoirs, but construction in his division did not go perfectly. In fact, his seventeen miles and the next seventeen down to Schenectady leaked so badly during test fillings in 1822 that both divisions had to be drained and the canal banks entirely relined

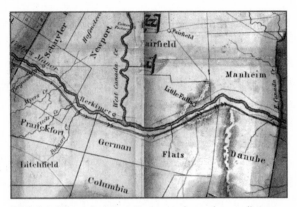

This detail from the Vance-Dey map shows the canal's passage through the section of the Mohawk River valley first settled by German refugees in the early 1700s. The arched, navigable feeder across the river to Little Falls is not shown, but the hash marks [>] along the canal line indicate the many locks required to lead the canal through the descending valley. (*The Lionel Pincus and Princess Firyal Map Division, The New York Public Library, Astor, Lenox and Tilden Foundations*)

with clay. The reworking was ascribed to the difficult and novel conditions, not to the resident engineers' inattention or inexperience.

The challenges of the eastern line as a whole began right up at Frankfort, where the long level stretching from Salina ended. The line dropped nearly a hundred feet in the thirteen miles from Frankfort to Little Falls, requiring twelve locks. The entire middle section had required only nine locks. In all, the 110-mile eastern section would require more than fifty locks to negotiate over 425 feet of descent through the Mohawk valley. Just ten miles downriver from Frankfort at German Flats, where the canal dropped seventeen feet through two locks, an embankment repeatedly collapsed, draining the canal and stopping traffic until effective repairs were made. "Occurrences of this kind are unpleasant to those travelling [sic] on the Canal," scolded a newspaper correspondent, "and should be more carefully guarded against."

The width of the valley was more troublesome in places than its height. Locks were expensive and time-consuming to build but, with ample stone and hydraulic cement, lock construction quickly became routine. For the most part, the canal line had room to pass at a comfortable margin between the south bank of the river and side hills. In many places, however, the valley was so narrow that the side hills came down to the edge of the river. In these places the canal had to be laid partly or even wholly in the riverbed itself, requiring overbuilt embankments and canal walls to withstand the flooding that plagued the river.

As if by divine intervention, a flood was delivered in mid-November 1821 to test the engineers' designs. The heavy rains were responsible for at least two boatmen's deaths on the river but played the partially completed canal above Schenectady to a draw. On the canal's north side along the Mohawk, the river nowhere rose above the canal's walls, but waters running in torrents off the hills on the south side damaged mostly uncompleted walls, culverts, and other structures. Had those works been complete prior to the flooding, damage would have been less severe. Only one subsequent flood (in the spring of 1833) would do enough damage to partially interrupt navigation.

The November 1821 flood largely proved what the commissioners called the "correctness" of the canal line only *above* Schenectady, because at the time of the flood no work had been done at or below Schenectady. The flood figured significantly in resolving two ongoing controversies: the route of the canal at Schenectady and for the final run down to Albany.

The working plan for passing Schenectady was to carry the canal in the strip of land between the southern bank of the river and the tongue of land just above it. On this slightly higher ground was the residential portion of the town, with the intersection of the well-traveled Albany road and others leading west. Down by the river was the Binne Kill, with the boatyards, wharves, and storehouses that had serviced Mohawk River navigation for generations. Two years before the flood a fire had swept through the Binne Kill waterfront, devastating mercantile Schenectady. With the coming of canal navigation, Binne Kill would not be rising from the ashes.

Preparatory excavations for the canal in the broad river plain just west of town and a certain amount of work along the strip below it had already been done when the flood of 1821 damaged upriver sections wedged between side hills and the river. The flood, combined with the earlier fire, served the interests of certain Schenectadians, included one Resolved Givens, proprietor of the popular Givens Hotel in the center of town.

Givens was a relative newcomer, having acquired the Schenectady Coffee House and put his name on the old roadhouse seven years earlier. But he and others recognized that the canal portended dramatic change for Schenectady. The eastern terminus of Mohawk navigation for generations thanks to impassable Cohoes Falls downriver, Schenectady would soon be turned into a backwater, watching from above as canal boats passed by the burned out commercial riverfront. Givens's idea was to shift the canal's path up from the riverside to the middle of town.

For some time, Givens and friends had been lobbying commissioners and engineers to elevate the canal. Conveniently, a number of commissioners and engineers were gathered at the Givens Hotel when the flood hit, transforming their host's arguments from persistent to persuasive. The engineers now realized that if they built the canal as planned beside the river at Schenectady, expensive additional banking would be needed to protect it. To shift it as Givens insisted would also be expensive but would remove any possibility of flood damage. "Mr. Gevins [sic] was a sagacious man," observed John Jervis, who had come to know him well, "and one that could keep his own counsel." The decision was made to reroute the canal through Schenectady.

The day after his arguments prevailed, Givens ran into Joseph C. Yates midway along the Albany road. Yates was a Schenectady native, its first mayor, and soon Clinton's successor as governor. He believed the relocation of the canal line past Givens's front door was a bit self-interested. He harangued Givens as "an uneasy Yankee [who] could not be kept still." Givens "took the rebuke very quietly, knowing the matter was settled."

Still, the passage of the canal "through the very heart of this town" would not be enough to raise Schenectady's prospects. "Canal when completed will in all probability be a final stroke to the increase of this city," noted a prescient traveler in September 1822: "Will never be equal to what it 'once was' . . . although its inhabitants pretend to imagine that 'trade is increasing.'" Already the number of inhabitants was decreasing. In 1815 Schenectady had over 7,100 residents; it was the twenty-second largest city in the country and third largest in the state, just behind Albany. By 1830 Schenectady would dwindle to sixty-fourth in the nation and ninth in the state; only forty-two hundred people called Schenectady home. Even Rome, also stripped of its historic role as a river navigation terminus, would grow slightly and pass Schenectady. The population of every other existing canal-bordering city or town would at least double, while new canal cities would be born and quickly outstrip Schenectady.

The canal did not kill Schenectady instantly. Twenty-eight locks would be needed in the twenty-eight canal miles between Schenectady and Albany, making for a full day's transit that induced some shippers and travelers to retain a preference for a few hours on the sixteen-mile Albany–Schenectady road and canal loading and unloading at Schenectady. But better technology made for fewer and larger locks a generation later, confirming Schenectady's fate.

Givens got a canal in front of his hotel, but it did not come easy. To alter the route through town instead of down by the river, a six-foot lock just to the west was eliminated, but the intervening canal banks had to be raised along a section of trough that would have to hold water to a ten-foot depth. The ground was supposed to be impermeable, but test fillings during the 1822 season proved it "to be full of holes like pipe stems, made by the decay of aqueous roots." Courses of lumber sheet piling were laid along the inside of the canal banks, and sand was laid along the bottom, but low water levels weren't solved until a dam and feeder fifty miles upriver at Minden were added during the next season. Then an embankment in town collapsed, requiring extensive repairs and the further strengthening of all canal walls in and around Schenectady. It all proved to be an extraordinary amount of effort for not much advantage.

The rerouting through Schenectady was a minor affair compared with the bitter controversy that developed at the same time over the route between Schenectady and Albany: follow the river valley in some manner along its most precipitous, circuitous miles or take a more direct course between the two cities. This controversy presaged the greater battle over the western terminus of the canal. More immediately, it made lifelong enemies of two important men: Erie chief engineer Wright and a surveyor-engineer named John Randel.

Wright preferred the river route. Randel promoted the direct route, and he knew a thing or two about route making. Randel had mapped the Albany–Schenectady road as a young state surveyor back in 1805, and he had just spent a dozen years surveying and mapping the island of Manhattan for the creation of its famous grid, the rectilinear streets and avenues of the future metropolis. Every traveler in the modern city follows the footsteps of John Randel. In 1821 Randel thought he knew better than Wright the canal path best taken into Albany.

Wright and Randel could not have been more different in character and conduct. That Wright came to consider Randel a "complete *hypocritical, lying nincompoop* (and I might say scoundrel if it was a Gentlemanly word)" is as much a reflection on the accuser as the accused.

For guiding the great Erie project toward successful completion, Wright is justly considered the "Father of American Civil Engineering." But he earned the honor from the American Society of Civil Engineers in 1969, not from his contemporaries. In life, father did not always know or do best. As a young man, Wright had been dismissed by an upstate land development company for failing to survey and lay an access road. During his Erie years and especially later, he had a tendency to avoid hazardous fieldwork and to please generous employers while denying credit to subordinate engineers. Even John Jervis, whom Wright mentored for many years (and to whom Wright confessed his ungentlemanly opinion of John Randel), was dismayed to discover that Wright had downplayed his contributions on a post-Erie railroad project. Wright was involved during the late 1820s in New York City's agonizing search for an adequate water supply, but all his efforts as a company president or city official and consultant were self-interested or misguided. When the country's leading engineers attempted to form the first professional society of engineers in 1839, with Wright "placed at the head" of the otherwise alphabetical list, a large majority including John Jervis voted against the society's proposed constitution; the present society, which conferred engineering paternity on Wright, was established in 1852, ten years after his death. Outside of mandatory progress reports on his many projects, the "Father of American Civil Engineering" left relatively few papers or other engineering scholarship.

John Randel was in many ways Wright's opposite but also no angel. Randel was independently wealthy; well connected by family in Albany and New York City; fully educated; devoted to grueling fieldwork; and as individualistic, idiosyncratic, and opinionated as Wright was managerial, accommodating, and political. Wright was a self-taught provincial, Randel a self-possessed sophisticate. On assignments before and especially after his Erie involvement, Randel had a habit of alienating, publicly attacking, and suing anyone who slighted him or his work. Wright would come to feel all of Randel's heat.

In 1821 Randel was in his late thirties and possibly the state's outstanding surveyor. After early survey and mapping work in and around his native Albany, he had been hired in early 1808 by the state commission charged with planning the physical development of New York City. Founded as a trading outpost nearly two centuries earlier, the city had Dutch streets that were notoriously haphazard, crooked, and narrow, and English and American streets laid on no unified plan. Rival Philadelphia had been established on an elegant plan, Washington and other American cities similarly since. By the early 1800s New York was beginning its rapid expansion from the southern tip of Manhattan. The randomness and disorder that reigned below the limits of substantial habitation at North (now Houston) Street was anathema to merchant-developers, who feared the entire island might be overspread by illogic.

Three considerable men were named in 1807 to make the city's future right: Simeon De Witt, the longtime state surveyor-general; John Rutherfurd, a New York lawyer and former U.S. senator then largely retired to a New Jersey farm; and Rutherford's half-brother, the inexorable Gouverneur Morris.

Three years before he was named to the state canal commission that he nearly ran (downhill) into oblivion, Morris took charge of the Manhattan "street grid commission." The result, pronounced in 1811, in this case exactly met Morris's vision. There would be none of "those supposed improvements by circles, ovals, and stars, which certainly embellish a plan, whatever may be their effect as to convenience and utility." No, Morris wrote, "a city is to be composed principally of the habitations of men, and . . . straight-sided and right-angled houses are the most cheap to build and the most convenient to live in." Thus, Manhattan was to be gridded over with rectilinear regularity: nearly two thousand identical blocks with rectangular lots defined by (initially) a dozen parallel avenues and 155 parallel streets.

The grid commissioners found a kindred spirit in Randel, whose appointment as surveyor and chief engineer came through his youthful service for De Witt as a state surveyor. The street grid, Randel later wrote, became "the pride and boast of the city," and he was glad to be its designer.

Randel had an extraordinary experience planning a future city from the twenty-five square miles of farms, homesteads, country estates, scattered villages, and open land that was the bulk of Manhattan in the early 1800s. It was no longer a wilderness by any means, but still a mostly rural place that looked much as nature had made it: rolling hills, long valleys, rocky ridges, meadows, forests, swamps, streams, and ponds, with fish, flora, and wildlife in abundance. Randel and his survey crew began ranging over Manhattan in May 1808. At a time when sophisticated surveying instruments were a rarity in America, Randel designed and built his own.

The original survey work took nearly three years, a Herculean task of varied labors. "I was arrested by the Sheriff, on numerous suits" by outraged squires "for trespass and damage committed by my workmen, in passing over grounds, cutting off branches of trees, &c." Randel would be bailed out by the grid commissioners or prominent friends and reimbursed for court expenses by the city government. Colorful accounts have Randel and his crew driven off by packs of dogs, bands of men, and on one occasion, "while drawing the line of an avenue directly through the kitchen of an estimable old woman," by a barrage of cabbages and artichokes. In less-cultivated districts, Randel found the terrain "impassable without the aid of an axe."

After completing the survey, Randel was hired by the city to implement the street grid plan. Over the next decade he marked imaginary intersections with over fifteen hundred white marble monuments, each engraved with the numbers of its future street and avenue, and its elevation; where the landscape was rocky or rugged, Randel used scores of iron bolts to secure the markers. At the same time, he produced dozens of small-scale topographical maps covering the entire survey area. These exquisitely detailed and accurate engravings are the atlas of what lies beneath the modern city. Randel's Manhattan labors, Simeon De Witt publicly attested, were performed "with an accuracy not exceeded, I am confident, by any work of the kind in America." Half a century later, when much of Manhattan had been built over as Randel planned it, it was said that "no error has ever been discovered in any part of the work." When John Randel suggested publicly in June 1821 that the plans for the eastern end of the Erie Canal were not straight enough, it was difficult to ignore him.

How Randel came to be involved in the canal's eastern affairs is unclear. Though Randel under a pseudonym would write ill of commissioner Clinton, Clinton and fellow commissioner Van Rensselaer would afterward attest that Randel was "an eminent mathematician, and a most skilful practical surveyor [and] a gentleman of excellent character, and worthy of public and private confidence." The canal commissioners had sought to engage Randel as an Erie engineer at the outset of the project, but he had declined for what mentor De Witt termed "reasons of a private nature." Possibly Randel simply felt he could not take on a major assignment before concluding his Manhattan work in the spring of 1821, when, after a long pause in outside work, he took on the layout of half a dozen rising Western New York villages, including Syracuse. In any case, Randel made his way to Albany in June 1821, "in accordance with the wishes of a respectable body of citizens" but with "no pecuniary aid," in order "to discover whether a practicable route for the canal could not be found shorter than that which follows the valley of the Mohawk" down to the Hudson.

Randel was entering an unsettled and unsettling field. "[H]ow we shall get a line from Schenectady to the Hudson I am most anxious to know," acting commissioner Seymour had confessed to Clinton at the end of the 1820 construction season. In its final thirty broadly winding miles, the Mohawk River drops more than two hundred feet, in torrents through steep and narrow ravines and over the broad seventy-five-foot falls that the natives had named for their broken canoes and that had defied navigation by European-descended peoples for two centuries. The Western Inland Company, which had created imperfect works in places along the upper Mohawk, very early had abandoned any efforts below Schenectady. The course of the canal down from Schenectady had never been determined. The commissioners and their engineers had postponed surveys and serious analysis for years. Back in their preconstruction report of early 1817, the commissioners had suggested that the canal might turn south out of the Mohawk Valley west of Cohoes Falls and cross overland to Albany, but they had made no pronouncements since.

Absent an actual survey, through the 1820 season the general presumption was that a way would be found somehow to continue the line along the south side of the Mohawk Valley, skirting the falls, all the way to the Hudson River valley. Finally, during the fall of 1820 Canvass White was assigned to make an examination. His findings appear to have been the dispiriting cause of commissioner Seymour's rising anxiety. They were not publicly acknowledged by the commissioners for a year and a half, creating a vacuum of transparency and a fertile opportunity for John Randel, who never shied from a challenge.

After several days of surveying ground that was already very familiar to the Albany native, Randel sent his findings to the commissioners on June 25 via Simeon De Witt, who advised that Randel's recommendations were "of such importance as highly to merit their deliberate attention." New York's surveyor-general of thirty-seven years favored "the adoption of the route he proposes in preference to the one contemplated along the valley of the Mohawk." Commissioner Van Rensselaer made the materials available to the *Albany Gazette & Daily Advertiser*, which published them on June 27; two days later, readers in New York City found everything reprinted on the front page of the *Evening Post*.

Randel's idea was for the canal to follow the south side of the Mohawk from Schenectady down to the river's southernmost point just east of Niskayuna and there, where the Mohawk begins a long arc north, leave the Mohawk Valley and run up a short stream valley leading south.

This little valley was separated by about three and a half miles of high ground from the valley of a creek draining southwest into the Hudson above Albany. Taking this route to Albany instead of following the Mohawk would save seven and a half miles of canal. The trick was linking the valleys. For this, Randel proposed a seventeen-foot-wide, arched, brick tunnel.

"Tunnelling [sic] is a novelty in our country," De Witt had noted with superb understatement in his cover letter. The United States had no navigable tunnels. Randel was proposing one roughly the same length as the world's longest, outside Paris, completed in 1810 after eight years of construction. England had the next half-dozen longest canal tunnels, including the 1.75-mile Blisworth tunnel on the Grand Junction Canal in Northamptonshire. Randel mentioned none of this, other than the construction costs of the sixteen-and-a-half-foot-wide Blisworth. He did not mention that the first effort to build Blisworth during the mid-1790s had ended with a collapse that killed fourteen workers, or that the successful effort had taken another nine years. Randel's tunnel would be expensive, he acknowledged, but compared with the higher construction, maintenance, and freight costs of the longer "river route" along the Mohawk, his direct or "tunnel route" offered long-term annual savings of nearly $115,000. Randel had generated his remarkable proposal in just a few days with little engineering detail, but he hoped the commissioners would give the concept "deliberate consideration before the line of the canal is unalterably fixed."

Randel's very public proposal startled New York's nascent canal establishment. In five construction seasons, no one had questioned or offered significant alternatives to any plans of the commissioners or engineers. Canal construction to date had been in the relatively remote interior of the state, and there were few people qualified to offer alternative plans. In the early summer of 1821, though, the canal was approaching through long-settled territory the seat of state government, where people like John Randel had knowledge and others had interest.

Merchants in Troy, six miles above Albany on the opposite shore of the Hudson, wanted the canal to closely follow the Mohawk past Cohoes Falls to within a few hundred yards of the Hudson before turning south to Albany. This would facilitate the shortest possible side-cut between the canal and the Hudson opposite Troy, effectively making Troy a canal terminus. Certain merchants in Albany disliked the so-called Cohoes or river route, preferring that the canal lead more directly from Schenectady to Albany, thereby lengthening or perhaps even making impractical a side-cut to the Hudson opposite rival Troy. Randel's route would make the side-cut to Troy as much as three miles long. It is unlikely that the fiercely independent Randel offered his direct route in service to any interest other than his own perception of good engineering. But on paper—in fact, as he traced it on a large-scale map provided by commissioner and Albany patroon Van Rensselaer, whose vast manor would give a right of way to the canal—Randel's route looked a lot better to Albany than Troy.

The commissioners did not know what to do. On Friday, July 13, they gathered in Albany, with the "principal object" of determining the route from Schenectady. When their meeting ended five days later, it was unclear what they had decided; they made no announcement, and no official record survives. The *Albany Gazette & Daily Advertiser* "understood" from its sources that the canal was to "embrace the valley of the Mohawk" all the way down past Cohoes, where it would join with the Champlain Canal and run south to Albany close by the Hudson, with a short side-cut to Troy. But the paper reported in the same item that Wright had been ordered to "re-view and re-examine Mr. Randel's route" and give his opinion "at some future meeting of the commissioners." Another Albany paper, the *New-York Statesman*, heard somewhat differently: "[W]e were informed by one of the commissioners, on the day of their adjournment, that they did not come to any *absolute* determination." Rather, they were merely "in favour" of the Cohoes route, and Wright was report to them in the fall "whether *any route* is preferable." Presumably the Clintonian paper's source was the commission president himself. "Both Albany and Troy will probably be accommodated," confided the *Statesman*; "we should regret to see any new jealousy spring up between these two rival cities, and the junction of the canal with the Hudson made a bone of contention."

Wright was not in Albany during the commissioners' five-day meeting. Randel subsequently discovered that they had received a letter from

Wright the day before their adjournment, indicating that he was willing to examine both the Cohoes and direct routes, but that there was a problem with the Cohoes route if it followed the *south* side of the Mohawk: in places where the canal of apparent necessity would have to be laid in the bed of the river, Wright warned that the bed was too unstable to support canal structures with any permanence.

This was news, as there had never been any question about the stability of the Mohawk riverbed. As Randel later heard it, the commissioners were astonished, one of them saying that he knew building in the river "would be expensive, but did not know that there was any danger of its permanence." The next day, as Randel came to understand, the commissioners ordered Wright to explore the direct route and expand the Cohoes route examinations to include the *north* side of the Mohawk as well. This apparently was what was meant by "*any route*" preferable to the south side.

Shifting the canal to the north side of the river for a certain distance between Schenectady and Albany would mean several things: crossing and recrossing the flood-prone Mohawk in some manner, probably increased distance and cost, and taking the canal out of Albany County for a run in Saratoga County. In Saratoga were orchards, brickworks, and lumber operations with friends in Albany.

Randel smelled a rat. Until his proposal for a cheaper and shorter direct route, there had not been "one word heard about crossing the river, nor did any serious difficulty present itself on the south side." Contracts on the south side had already been prepared and some assigned. Suddenly these were suspended, engineers were dispatched across the river, "and in a few days it was reported that the north side afforded every advantage and facility for a canal."

Randel was not privy to whatever Canvass White's discoveries might have been in the fall of 1820. The commissioners' annual report in the spring of 1821 didn't mention them or any trouble with the route along the south side of the Mohawk; indeed, the commissioners had written that "the canal can be constructed, along this route, at an expense much within the original estimates." Now, just as Randel was dramatically proposing veering the canal away from the Mohawk and more directly to Albany, Wright was dramatically proposing taking it in the opposite direction.

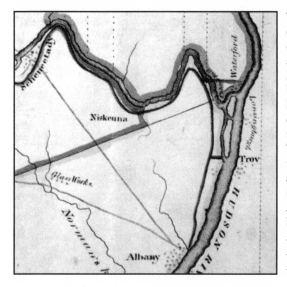

This detail from the 1821 commission map shows how the canal was to continue its long run along the south side of the Mohawk nearly to the Hudson, before John Randel got involved. Randel's "direct route" would have drawn the canal away from the twisting lower Mohawk—and Troy—by following the valleys of the unnamed streams leading southeast from Niskeuna (Niskayuna) and northwest from Albany with a tunnel or deep cut in between. (*The Lionel Pincus and Princess Firyal Map Division, The New York Public Library, Astor, Lenox and Tilden Foundations*)

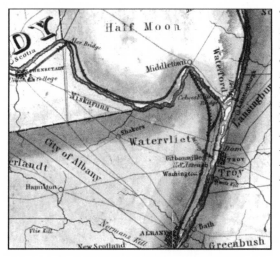

This detail from the Vance-Dey map shows what happened: the Mohawk crisscross that took the canal across the river and back, making for a most indirect route to Albany and a very convenient route for a short sidecut to the Hudson opposite Troy. (*The Lionel Pincus and Princess Firyal Map Division, The New York Public Library, Astor, Lenox and Tilden Foundations*)

Randel soon discovered the seriousness with which Wright intended to pursue the direct route. They met, for perhaps the first time, on August 14 just east of Schenectady. While walking south in a party with other engineers for about a mile, Wright admitted that he had "never examined this route." He would not examine it any further. Rain the next day and the day after prevented surveying. Wright, with White and Geddes, took the opportunity to slip away from Schenectady to the north side of the river, where they conducted examinations for the rest of the week without Randel.

Further informal efforts by Randel to engage Wright were unavailing. In October the commissioners authorized Randel to seek answers from Wright about his ongoing Schenectady–Albany investigations. After weeks of delay, Wright informed Randel that he had "no leisure to bestow upon this subject." The commissioners did not insist. By December, newspapers in Albany and New York reported that "a new route for the Canal . . . which will compel them to cross the Mohawk River, twice, is contemplated—and that a survey is now making, under the actual direction of the Commissioners."

Randel was outraged. Having apparently lost the ear of the commissioners, Randel found a soapbox in the pages of the Burenite *Albany Argus*. Eleven days into 1822, under the byline "A Friend to the Canal," he launched a four-month series of essays decrying the "devious and almost impracticable direction" the canal apparently was to take across "a broad unbridled and impetuous stream." Whereas earlier important canal decisions had been "publicly exhibited," the eastern end "has been managed as a close concern, withdrawn with retiring diffidence from the public eye, involving in equal mystery the beauties and deformities—the simplicity and complexity of the incomprehensible design." The chief culprit was commission president Clinton: "[T]he firmness of the president, well known to be true to his political points as long as he is convinced they are advantageous to himself, has been staggered in his favorite project of exhausting the treasures of the state." Subsequent essays offered historical details of river flooding and the risks to the success of the entire project from "an incomprehensible trip across the Mohawk!"

In January Randel also issued an anonymous pamphlet detailing "the impropriety and ruinous consequences" of crossing the river twice. Here, the chief villain was Wright, who apparently had "come to view the ground [of Randel's direct route] with his mind already made up [that the canal] ought to follow the Mohawk for the accommodation of Troy. . . . I understand the location of the canal line has been left wholly to the decision of Judge Wright . . . it will in the end prove the tomb of his reputation." The Albany Chamber of Commerce attempted unsuccessfully to purchase the copyright of this provocative pamphlet "for the purpose of suppressing it."

In early March the commissioners finally sought to explain themselves publicly, with unusual length and defensiveness in their annual report. "The termination of the eastern section," they wrote, "has been with the canal commissioners, as with the public, a subject of much solicitude." Wright and White, they dubiously claimed, had "repeatedly traversed . . . every valley or ravine which afforded the probability of a passage from the valley of the Mohawk. All these examinations have however proved fruitless." Whether by tunneling or deep cutting, the direct route was "altogether impracticable." Even if, as "some persons have lately considered practicable," the canal were to diverge from the Mohawk way up at Schoharie and avoid tunneling or a deep cut by maintaining a long, high level passing south of Schenectady toward Albany, feeder water would be available only at Schoharie and prove "scanty" farther east. In any case, as canal construction was already underway down to Schenectady, and the line had accordingly dropped in elevation to that point, "the great expense and delay" of changing course had convinced the commissioners that the Mohawk had to be followed.

The commissioners now revealed White's examinations of a year and a half earlier, the fall of 1820, when he supposedly discovered that if the canal were to remain along the south shore of the Mohawk below Schenectady it would have to be laid partially in the bed of the river with substantial banking "capable of resisting the force of its most impetuous floods." Reexaminations by White in the spring of 1821 had reached the same conclusion. The commissioners said nothing about Wright's supposed concern, expressed in his letter at their July 1821 meeting, that the bed of the river was too unstable to support canal walls of any size. Instead, they reported, it was White, frustrated by the south side that spring, who looked across the river where "the country of the north bank appeared to him to present a more practicable route." Crossing the river, White supposedly had found that from a point four miles below Schenectady a line could be carried for twelve miles on the north side down to a point four miles above Cohoes. "[H]e became fully satisfied that is would be better to cross and re-cross the river . . . than to encounter the difficulties on the south bank." This, in the commissioners' calendar, was before Randel's first public suggestion in late June of taking the canal on a direct route from Schenectady to Albany. At some unspecified time thereafter, "the two nearest acting commissioners"—that is, Bucktails Seymour of the Erie eastern section and Young of the Champlain—ordered chiefs Wright and Geddes to survey on both sides of the river with White. The engineers reported unanimously in favor of the crossing plan, the acting commissioners concurred, and the full board then unanimously approved it.

The twelve-mile northern route with its two crossings, the commissioners surprisingly reported, would actually be one and a half miles shorter and 28 percent less expensive than staying on the south side with its greater windings, excavations, and embankments. Again, there was no mention of Wright's supposed contention that the southern route, regardless of whether it was longer and costlier, was impracticable because of the unstable riverbed. If staying on the south side had somehow been shorter and cheaper, would the commissioners have resorted to the unstable riverbed as the reason for crossing to the north? In a curious bit of additional justification for crossing the river, the commissioners suggested that the length of canal "thrown on the north side of the ravine of the Mohawk" would have the added benefit of being "exposed to the rays of the sun, by which the ice will be dissolved, and the navigation opened some days earlier in the spring." As an incredulous Randel would shortly note, what of the other hundred miles of canal happily run on the southern side of the Mohawk? The specious ice-melting contention likely as not sprang from gentleman-scientist Clinton, who two years earlier had suggested that boats might be equipped with ice "stampers" to allow the canal to remain open in winter.

Again namelessly referencing a point made by Randel in his anonymous public writings as "apprehensions . . . entertained by some" that the upper of the two contemplated crossings would be insufficiently elevated above the river, the commissioners claimed they could reexamine their plan after the spring floods and somehow find "an additional elevation of several feet" to keep the river out of the canal. They did not explain how finding elevation would be possible.

As to the construction of the crossings, the commissioners resorted to expedience. The bridges would have masonry abutments and piers "laid in water lime, and clamped with iron," but the aqueduct troughs carried across the capricious river would be wood, of disquieting impermanence for such essential duty. "The wood will decay in about fifteen years," the commissioners acknowledged, but "the old trunk may always be replaced by a new one, during the winter, while the navigation is obstructed by ice." At some unspecified time, "indestructible trunks of cast iron may be made, composed of large plates, with flanges connected by nuts and screws, in the same manner as many of the modern aqueducts in England are constructed." But not, for now, New York's.

With that, the commissioners ended their eastern explication. Nowhere did they make plain that the crisscross would take the canal into Saratoga, or as Randel had mockingly put it, "crossing the river, in order to pay the county of Saratoga a compliment; and . . . recrossing again to convince the public how easy and practicable a matter it was."

Regardless of issues that might have borne closer scrutiny, the crisscross—pointedly accepted by Bucktail acting commissioners Seymour and Young—turned the Bucktail *Albany Argus* away from its commission-bashing "Friend": "[N]otwithstanding the great respectability of the author of these numbers, it appears to us that the measures which are reprobated by them, are justified by the circumstances." The paper continued to run new contributions from its old Friend but starting making space for sharp rebuttals by "A Friend to the Commissioners," who may in fact have been one of them.

Randel responded to the commissioners' report and the loss of editorial favor with a new book-length pamphlet. For the first time he put his name on this writing. With some care, he countered many of the commissioners' assertions and offered details of a modified direct route of which the commissioners were already informally aware. In his *Description of a Direct Route for the Erie Canal at its Eastern Termination*, Randel charted mile-by-mile specifications and cost estimates for excavation and construction. This route—diverging from the Mohawk up at Schoharie Creek and crossing the high ground between Schenectady and Albany with a deep cutting instead of a tunnel—would be over 19 miles shorter and $630,000 less expensive than the river-crossing route. More than his pseudonymous writings, this Randel pamphlet survives as the closest thing to an indictment of chief engineer Wright's and commission president Clinton's Mohawk crisscross. Which is not to say, as we now say, it gained traction.

By the time Randel's *Description* appeared in early April, the 1822 construction season had begun and the legislative season was wrapping up. No one, even from among that "respectable body of citizens" who had spurred Randel's involvement, appeared interested, at least publicly, in allegations of wasted money and undue influence. Randel's claim that the canal was going to be longer, more expensive, and riskier than it needed to be would await future judgment.

Randel, neither a politician nor a brooder, went off west with his commissions to lay out Syracuse and other towns. Wright, however, a former assemblyman and increasingly political engineer, could not let go. Two years later they found themselves side by side on the Chesapeake and Delaware Canal, Wright as chief engineer, Randel as main contractor for the private company attempting that short but important link between the two deep Atlantic bays. Wright outrageously and unjustifiably accused Randel of failing to perform his duties, and Randel was summarily fired. Prominent company board members protested Wright's allegations and resigned over Randel's firing. Economist and company shareholder Mathew Carey led Randel's many public supporters, accusing Wright in particular of "shocking oppression and injustice." Randel sued Wright and the company. "This J.R. is so full of his lies and schemes of trouble," Wright grumbled to John Jervis, "that I have a new scene before me and as much correspondence as a Minister of Foreign Affairs of any nation." The case against Wright was dismissed, but in protracted litigation that reached the U.S. Supreme Court, Randel won from the company a historic judgment of $226,885, over a tenth of the value of the entire project. Randel ultimately collected every dollar, for many years hampering the C&D's profitability. He used his winnings to build Randalia, a spectacular estate on thousands of acres overlooking the Maryland end of the canal that had been completed by others on the route he had suggested.

More quickly, two canal aqueducts rose over the Mohawk. The "Upper Aqueduct," at a place then known as Alexander's Mills (now the hamlet of Rexford) four miles below Schenectady, featured sixteen unarched stone piers carrying the canal in its wooden trough 748 feet across the river. The "Lower Aqueduct," at Fonda's Ferry (now Crescent) four miles above Cohoes, rested on twenty-six stone piers. At 1,188 feet between abutments, it was the longest bridge of any type on the entire canal. Both of these "stupendous aqueducts," as the commissioners boasted in 1824, were completed without incident. "And although it was feared by some, that they would not be able to resist the impetus of the ice and current, in the breaking up of the river, by winter freshets," the aqueducts had by then survived two winters (one during construction, one after completion) "without exhibiting the least appearance of injury or damage." Emboldened, the commissioners now claimed "these works will probably be as permanent as any works of similar nature on the canal."

Indeed, the aqueducts were not swept away, even during the historic floods of May 1833 in the eastern United States, when many people in the Mohawk and upper Hudson valleys drowned and substantial damage was done to other Erie sections and structures. Risk, waste, and needlessness had been Randel's arguments against the aqueducts. For a dozen years, his arguments found little support or justification. Then John Jervis weighed in.

In 1835 Jervis was among the country's leading canal and railroad engineers and among the surveyors for the pending first enlargement of the Erie Canal; he would shortly be named chief engineer of its eastern division. "It had appeared to me that errors had been made in the original work which it was important to correct." The biggest error had been the crisscross. "Aqueducts with wooden trunks are to be avoided in all cases where the line can be maintained without too great additional expense, or the sacrifice of the convenient accommodation of trade and navigation." Unlike White and Wright in 1821, Jervis in 1835 found no trouble with the south side. "I had a line continued on the south side of the river, with a view to judge the propriety of dispensing with the aqueducts. The surveys and estimates induced me to recommend the abandonment of the canal on the north side, and of course the two aqueducts, and to adopt the line on the south side of the river." What opinion the young pupil of White and Wright had of their crisscross in 1821 is unknown.

And yet the north held. The canal commissioners, by then a bureaucratic dozen, split six to six on Jervis's recommendation, and it was rejected. Jervis, who had argued that changing "the route to the opposite side would not wholly destroy [private] interest [on the north side] but . . . create a closer competition from the people on the new route," accepted the commission's decision. Canal historian Noble Whitford has written that "the desire to gain needed political support [for the proposed enlargement] and to please the people of Saratoga by not removing the canal from their county played a large part in influencing the decision." It was, in the end, hard to retract the original "compliment" to Saratoga that Randel had originally discerned.

As for the much-maligned wood trunk aqueducts, they would never exchange their wood for more durable iron. Both survived intact until they were replaced in 1842 by more substantial and elegant arched masonry aqueducts designed by Jervis, who that year completed the iconic Croton Aqueduct, the modern water supply for New York City that Wright had failed to deliver. Jervis's Erie aqueducts served without problem until the early 1900s, when the second and final Erie enlargement made a broad canal of the locked and tamed Mohawk River itself.

The Mohawk double-cross was a small piece in the constant political gamesmanship statewide. The April 1820 elections had barely returned Clinton as governor and had given the 1821 legislature to the Bucktails, prompting Martin Van Buren to liken Clinton to a scotched snake facing imminent political death. If it was indeed to come, the maneuverings got off to an early start, with the brief special legislative session in November 1820, called primarily to choose electors for the December presidential election.

In his opening speech to a legislature controlled by enemies, Clinton was pleased to note that thirty miles and twelve locks on the eastern section were under contract, and that work had proceeded with unexpected speed: excavations of rock at Little Falls had been completed in less than eighty days, not the anticipated two years. "[T]he prices of money, of labor and of commodities are uncommonly low," Clinton observed, warning his political detractors that public opinion unified in support of the canal would crush "chimerical apprehensions . . . selfish views . . . jarring interests, and . . . local competitions."

The legislature that Van Buren and his emerging Albany Regency now dominated no longer had any intention of threatening the canal, but the canal could be used to threaten Clinton. During the November special session, the senate started work on what became a major bill. The financial component was a proposal to authorize the borrowing of $1 million in both 1821 and 1822, on top of the annual $600,000 approved in 1819. The money was necessary to continue the substantial construction in the east and the west. The deepening national depression made for a good time to issue debt; rates in the broad U.S. loan market were dropping, from just under 6 percent in 1817 to 4.5 percent in 1821, and another quarter point over the next two years. The senate used the several days of the special session to approve the financing provision easily, by a final 23–6 vote. The only nays were senators from New York City and surrounding areas, all opposed to Clinton and the canal.

During the main session in early 1821, the assembly added two volatile proposals: that a seventh canal commissioner be appointed by the legislature, and that every commissioner be removable by a majority vote of both houses. With the Bucktails holding wide majorities, a new Bucktail commissioner would tilt the commission—then split between Bucktails and Clintonians—immediately into a Bucktail majority, while the three Clintonian commissioners would be under the threat of removal.

One man wise to the Bucktail game was Jesse Hawley. Disguised as "Hercules" nearly fourteen years earlier, he had written the newspaper essays that launched the canal idea. Then a bankrupt grain merchant serving a twenty-month term in debtors' prison, he had since rebounded, with a bump or two. Upon his release in 1809, Hawley became a county deputy sheriff and jailer for the same Canandaigua lockup that had held him. Three years later he was the assistant postmaster and, at age forty-one, married.

Betsy Ralston Tiffany was a young widow recently arrived in Canandaigua from New Hampshire with her sisters and their husbands. A month after Jesse and Betsy's May wedding, the War of 1812 began, causing mayhem in Western New York for the next two and a half years. In 1813 the couple relocated to the new settlement of Rochesterville, where Hawley thrived. After repairing his fiscal health with wise land investments, Hawley was appointed customs collector for Rochester's port in 1818, a lucrative federal position he held for the next twelve years. In the spring of 1820 he had been one of very few Clintonians elected to a first term in the state assembly. Wife Betsy and her family were unimpressed with Hawley's resurrection. Persuaded by her parents, for reasons unknown, to sue for divorce, she quit her marital home "in a temper . . . thus condemning her unhappy husband, under existing laws, to a life of restless celibacy."

Hawley, a freshman assemblyman but well-seasoned in adversity, understood that the Bucktails' commissioner removal provision was an attempt to outrage Clintonians into opposing the entire bill, with its $2 million borrowing authority. Clintonians would then be tagged as opponents of canal funding.

For once the governor listened to his political allies. In two days Hawley and other Clintonians rammed the measure without amendment through the assembly, senate, and still-Clintonian Council of Revision.

Clinton would suffer from the subsequent appointment to the commission of Bucktail and future governor William C. Bouck, but what came to be called "the Two Million Bill" brought Clinton long-and short-term gains. It was now absolutely certain that the great canal could be completed and that then-governor and still-commissioner Clinton would be permanently associated with it. "Ever since the canal was begun," wrote a gratified Myron Holley, "the dearest hopes of its friends have been precarious . . . until passage of the great appropriations law." "Our Canals," Clinton wrote to John Pintard, "are now safely anchored in the affections of the people beyond the power of faction and the reach of ordinary fatalities. When this great work is finished there will be no limits to our financial prosperity." And Clintonians earned the public perception, especially in the rapidly populating west, that they were the heroes of the Two Million Bill. "If Bucktailism does not receive its death blow at the approaching election," Clinton vowed to Pintard, "I will renounce all pretensions to political sagacity." In the voting two weeks later for the next legislature, Clintonians won a senate majority and narrowed the Bucktail advantage in the assembly. Neither death nor renunciation occurred, but for a year at least, Holley, Clinton, and Van Rensselaer were safe from demise as canal commissioners. If neither a political sage nor a sapskull, Clinton seemed to be recovered at least from his recent scotching.

Van Buren, though, was not through with Clinton. Later in 1821 the Bucktails called for and then controlled a state constitutional convention. Among the primary targets were the councils of appointment and revision, aristocratic and unpopular relics of the state's 1777 constitution. Clinton, the leader of what was never a well-organized political movement, was increasingly dependent on the undemocratic councils but aware of their creakiness and incompatibility with his populist appeal. At first he opposed the calling of a convention, but he ultimately stood aside as the state gained more representative government. The Council of Revision was replaced with a gubernatorial veto and legislative override, the Council of Appointment with elections by the legislature for state offices and by popular elections for most of the thousands of local offices.

Not all the reforms of the new state constitution were so pure. Van Buren pushed through one aimed directly at Clinton: the reduction of the governor's term from three to two years. Seven months after canal funding and political victories, Clinton could look ahead to just thirteen more months as the incumbent governor, three years or more before the completion of his canal.

Regardless of Clinton's fate, the Two Million Bill of 1821 guaranteed the continuation of canal building and inspired unprecedented investment in the project. While New York City politicians continued to vote in Albany against the canal, merchant New Yorkers started to load up on canal bonds. With the completion of the middle section, the Lorillards of first leather, then tobacco fame quietly began buying canal issues. Retired Manhattan sailmaker Stephen Allen was typical of the wealthy merchants broadening the canal investor lists; he was the city's Republican mayor, supposed to oppose Clintonian things but more concerned with a diversified portfolio than divisive politics. Investors outside of New York also flocked to the new stock issues, led by the $45,000 stake of South Carolina's Langdon Cheves, president of the second Bank of the United States and, ironically due to his bank's credit policies, partly responsible for the 1819 panic that made canal construction more economically feasible. At the same time, the city's major brokerage houses finally became active in canal bond trading. The country's richest man, John Jacob Astor, waited until 1822 to make his move but did so in a hurry, ending the year with a $213,000 stake. Astor's high-profile acquisitions helped trigger a massive influx of foreign capital, especially English but also from investors in a dozen countries, including China. By the end of 1824 the legislature had authorized and the canal fund commissioners had sold a final total of nearly $7.5 million in canal bonds. Excepting $1 million worth of stock not identifiable by owners' residence, Americans held nearly $4 million, and foreigners just under $2.5 million. Even before it was completed, the Erie Canal had become a local, national, and international financial event.

The start of the Erie investment mania came at the bottom of the five-year national depression brought on by the Panic of 1819. "There has been . . . an immense revolution of fortunes in every part of the Union," observed secretary of war and failed national improver John C. Calhoun, "enormous numbers of persons utterly ruined; multitudes in deep distress." While wise and wealthy investors were buying canal stock, farmers were going broke. From 1817 to the end of 1820, the price of wheat fell from $2.72 to 68 cents a bushel, potash nearly in half from $200 a bushel. There was an upside, however. "The want of money, in the country," wrote the commissioners in their 1821 report to the legislature, "and the growing reputation of the undertakings, have greatly increased the number of responsible competitors for contracts," with a resulting reduction in contract prices. Excavation work, which had gone for as much as twenty-five cents per cubic yard on the early portions of the middle section, was let for as little as four cents in 1821, and it was eagerly taken up. Many pioneer farmers survived the depression as canal contractors and held on for the reward of an easy and cheap path to market via the completed canal.

By the time of the November 1821 flood, some five thousand workers were on the eastern line from Utica down to Schenectady. Now they were not only the sons and hands of farmers and local merchants, but also increasingly the fresh Irish immigrants who had found no work in New York City but enough on the canal.

In 1821 twenty Irishmen were working Jamie Archbald's canal section and boarding on the Archbald farm. Matriarch Mary Archbald, from a long line of Presbyterian Scots, initially disdained the "wild Irish" but soon enough reshaped her early prejudices and grew close to them. The Archbalds' Irish were invited to a family wedding and caused no trouble. When one of the workers was beaten nearly to death by a gang of "free-born Yankees as they are pleased to style themselves," and then sentenced harshly and unfairly for starting the disturbance, Mary Archbald wrote to Governor Clinton. After Clinton's promised investigation, the man was released.

The eastern section down to Little Falls was completed by early November 1821. Employing a sense of ceremony learned in the progress of the middle section construction, the commissioners sent the *Chief Engineer* on a much-publicized inaugural run from Utica with a steersman who as a boy had ferried Washington along the Hudson during the Revolution.

The canal had two main functions: to transport goods and people. When the 1822 season opened, a third of the canal—120 miles from Little Falls to Syracuse—was fully navigable. The promises of fantastically reduced shipping costs were quickly being met. In June, wheat flour was shipping on the canal at a dollar a ton, a tenth of the former cost by wagon. A hundred thousand barrels of flour were reported waiting along the line because of a lack of boats. A boom in canal boat building was just getting underway. An elaborate barge wasn't necessary; a well-strapped timber raft capable of carrying four hundred barrels of flour could be fashioned for as many dollars.

Passengers were flocking to the canal as well. "Numerous emigrants from the hardy and industrious northern and eastern hive," reported *Niles' Register*, "are to be seen transporting themselves and their families, at little or no expense, to settle the lands bordering on the canal." At four cents a mile including room and board on a boat that made a hundred miles a day without stopping, canal travel could be as rapid as stage travel, "much less expensive, no risk of life or limb, and no fatigue or dust attending."

Niles' was wrong about the risk. A week before the paper's euphoric report in late June, curiosity got the better of a Mrs. Harvey of Camillus. She was aboard the *Commerce of Camillus*, a freight boat, returning with an infant child from a visit with her father in Whitesboro. The young mother was alarmed when the boat's bow struck the guard lock at Oriskany. "[S]he looked out of the cabin window; her head was caught between the boat and lock, and crushed in the most shocking manner."

Little Falls became the treat of the eastern section as soon as the canal opened there. It was one of five places on the eastern section where creek or Mohawk River water fed the canal. The Little Falls feeder was also navigable; a spectacular stone aqueduct, still abuilding in 1822, linked the canal on the south side of the river with the village on the north side. A central arch of seventy feet, flanked by fifty-foot arches, spanned the river just above the fourth of the five locks that negotiated the mile-long gorge. "Taken as a whole, the scenery of this Pass, this gorge of the Mohawk, in works of nature and art, is unrivaled," advised the first canal travel guide, published two years later. "[G]rand, imposing, and highly picturesque: 'all hands upon deck,' especially from the Ladies' Cabin: we are approaching the Little Falls. What a tremendous, awe-inspiring scene!"

American and European landscape painters portraying the romantic harmony of nature and art(ifice) quickly became enamored of Little Falls, but not all canal travelers were so inspired. On Independence Day 1822, the heat in the ladies' cabin of the *Oneida Chief* was "intense and suffocating" for its twenty passengers, including a young Philadelphia Quaker keeping a diary of her summer tour into Canada. She had embarked at Little Falls, but found it "rather a rapid than what we should call a fall." In the twenty-two miles to Utica, she was obliged to duck beneath eighty-four bridges and pass along three seemingly fragile aqueducts "formed not of stonework and arched, but of wood and supported on timber props." A canal commissioner who happened to be on board offered her the small assurance "that they would last at the very least 12 or 14 years." On the long level west, "[n]ot a breath of air [was] felt . . . the waters [were] green, turbid, and stagnant . . . [and at] sunset we were attacked by swarms of mosquitoes of gigantic size, the sons of the forest, which rendered our situation doubly disagreeable." She "bid a final adieu to the canal" at Syracuse "with heartfelt rejoicing," and vowed never to set foot again in a canal boat.

A better time was had by another anonymous tourist, escaping a yellow fever epidemic in New York City that killed nearly four hundred people during the summer of 1822. At the four score bridges between Little Falls and Utica, he stood in the boat's bow, "obliged to make to each of them a 'circumbendius' of the body, in other words an obeisance, as if we wished to pay salute to each of these said bridges. Excellent school for politeness." If (as the Philadelphia filly had discovered) "a 'quaker stiffness' was persisted in, you risked having your head taken off." The journalist—recently identified as young and dissipated Knickerbocker editor Johnston Verplanck—was genuinely impressed with the lofty "romantic" hills around Little Falls, and the "elegant Aqueduct" joining the town to the canal: "It is in a great state of forwardness, cut stone arches well turned, and when finished will be a superb structure, and partake of the 'magnificent'." Verplanck was less impressed with a fellow passenger who complained that the canal had split his farm, was giving unfair advantage to western farmers, and had provoked the suicide of a neighboring farmer: "The wreck of matter and the crush of Worlds." Addled by drink, Verplanck would be dead himself in a few years.

The unfinished canal could be an annoyance or an amusement for some, but cathartic for others, such as an itinerant, thirty-something portraitist seeking a place with enough wealth and power to support art. Having found mixed success in New Hampshire, South Carolina, and his native Massachusetts, he rejected Boston, Philadelphia, and Baltimore before choosing Manhattan. "New York does not yet feel the influx of wealth from the Western canal," he wrote to his wife, "but in a year or two she will feel it, and it will be advantageous to me to be previously identified among her citizens as a painter." Soon an easily identified painter and legendary inventor, Samuel F. B. Morse had quickly decoded what the canal had wrought for New York.

As Morse opted for the canal-made city, the state opted out of Clinton and Clintonians. In November 1822 Clinton stayed on the sidelines for the state elections (shifted from April under the new state constitution). The Clintonian candidate for governor, Albany newspaper editor Solomon Southwick, put up only token resistance to Schenectady's Joseph Yates. The longtime Federalist turned Bucktail Republican won 98 percent of the vote. Bucktails also regained control of the senate and enlarged their assembly majority. When the legislature convened in January, ex-governor Clinton was at risk of removal from the canal commission and any official connection with the ongoing project that defined and was defined by him.

Rumblings were heard throughout the 1823 session in both houses of the legislature and in the Bucktail press for the removal of commissioners Clinton, Holley, and Van Rensselaer, but nothing happened. Van Buren, in Washington as a freshman senator, kept his Albany forces on a short leash, wary of a popular backlash. Indeed, the canal was becoming known fondly as "Clinton's big ditch." A Van Buren ally in the state senate refrained from introducing a removal bill, conceding that "it would appear as a pitiful exertion of power" to suddenly oust the man who, in thirteen years on the canal commission, had brought the great work so far. "The Canal Commissioners have escaped the sword of destruction," Clinton wrote to a friend after the session ended in April, "I made no advance or effort to retain my place . . . but as it now stands, I shall endeavor to close the great operation as soon as possible."

Ex-governor and still-commissioner Clinton was in demand on the lecture circuit. In July he gave the annual address to the Phi Beta Kappa Society of Schenectady's Union College. It was an amply reported reminder that Clinton was not just a politician and canal maker but also a fair intellect. "Whatever may be our thoughts, our words, our writings, or our actions, let them all be subservient to the promotion of science and the prosperity of our country. Pleasure is a shadow, wealth is vanity, and power a pageant; but knowledge is ecstatic in enjoyment, perennial in fame, unlimited in space, and infinite in duration." Governor Yates was incapable of such phrasemaking.

Heavy spring snowstorms had made for a late start to the 1823 construction season, but it was soon clear that the eastern section could be completed by early fall. Canal commission president Clinton decided that a major celebration was in order. With no elective office to distract or otherwise exalt him, Clinton directed the arrangements, well aware that a ceremonial platform offered public dividends for future political gain.

For the first time in over six years of canal construction milestones, the celebration would not be in a provincial place but at Albany, the seat of government in the nation's increasingly dominant state. Clinton decided on October 8, a Wednesday.

Church bells and cannon signaled the dawn of a "fine autumnal morning," setting thousands of people in motion. Eight miles north of Albany, where the Champlain Canal joined the Erie, a "new and superb packet boat" aptly named for the occasion was readied. On board the *De Witt Clinton* were its namesake, his fellow commissioners, and their engineers. Committees from Albany and New York City that had implemented the day's arrangements, featuring John Pintard among numerous Clinton friends, arrived by carriage from Albany for breakfast aboard, before horses took the tow for a triumphal float to the capital. At the basin of the side-cut to Troy, the *Clinton* met up with the veteran *Chief Engineer*, carrying the West Point military band; the new *Henry Seymour* loaded with canal contractors; and the *Governor Yates,* bearing "200 ladies and gentlemen." Another mile south, the fleet was completed by the *Chancellor Kent*, also "crowded with a fashionable party of ladies and gentlemen." The *Chief Engineer* led the procession toward Albany. The "line of Canal boats, with colours flying, bands of music, and crowded with people, were seen coming from the north, and seemed to glide over the level grounds, which hid the waters of the Canal for some distance, as if they were moved by enchantment."

Then came a bit of reality. At Watervliet, a mile and a half north of Albany, the flotilla stopped in its towpath. In Albany, it was unclear why. The delay lengthened to nearly an hour, raising "many feelings of anxiety among the thousands of impatient spectators, who were gazing intently for the signal of approach." The masses learned later that stones had tumbled into the canal, blocking the eleven-foot gates of Lock No. 2, one of the deepest on the canal. Workers scrambled to dredge the rubble. By noon, "the doubts and fears of the multitude were dissipated by the appearance of the squadron." Some 50,000 people—triple the population of Albany—rejoiced: "The banks of the canal, the bridges, and the roads, were thronged with carriages and citizens, and the whole presented a mass moving onward to the rich music of the band, with flags displayed, and with every indication of joy."

The only practical effect of the delay seems to have been an opportunity, whether by serendipity or design, for a rearrangement of the squadron. When the boats approached the top of Lock No. 1, the leader of the pack was the *De Witt Clinton*, with its namesake in the bows as the boat claimed the lock and center stage for the official ceremony.

The boats were met at the lock by a large procession of marchers, who had anxiously halted their own progress through town while the boats were delayed. The head pedestrian, denied passage even on the boat bearing his name, was governor Yates, accompanied by his lieutenant and fellow Clinton antagonist Erastus Root. They had been joined mid-march by a retinue of crimson-robed Masons, the featured performers of the day.

Masonic officers and priests, accompanied by their own band and armed with wands and swords, bore the paraphernalia of their rituals—a Bible, compass and square, silver cups filled corn, wine, and oil, and an engraved copper plate. The Masons' solemn duty this day was to bless Lock No. 1, adorned for the occasion by a massive wooden arch covered in evergreens. Clinton, who happened to be the country's leading Mason—the General Grand High Priest of the General Grand Chapter of the United States—had carefully arranged the lock consecration with Albany painter Ezra Ames, Grand High Priest of the state Grand Royal Arch chapter.

In formation with prayers and chanting, Masons circled the lock once, before the highest officers set the copper plate—engraved with the names of Clinton and his fellow canal commissioners—in its place on the lock and laid the capstone over it. Grand High Priest Ames poured the holy corn, wine, and oil on the lock masonry, while praying aloud for the blessings of the Creator of the Universe. Masonic officers circled the lock three more times, in synchronicity with nine cannon firings and musical flourishes. The sanctifying Masons, resplendent in their "new, rich, and beautiful" robes, were (at least to Clintonian editor William Stone) awesome: "Indeed, if the appearance of the Jewish high priest, when he went out in his sacred robes, to meet Alexander of Macedon, was equally imposing, we do not marvel at the awe with which the conqueror was for the moment inspired."

Early nineteenth-century cornerstones were often laid with some Masonic ceremony, but extensive reportage and word of mouth about the extraordinary Albany festivities may have provoked the impressionable son of an unproductive farmer two hundred miles west in the budding canal town of Palmyra. Proclaiming his Mormon visions three years later, young and restless Joseph Smith alleged that his first visit from the robed angel Moroni directing him to buried tablets had come on the night of September 21, 1823, a convenient couple of weeks prior to the majestic, mysterious, and curiously similar Masonic doings at Albany.

The Masonic ritual completed, Dr. Samuel Latham Mitchill took over. He was the leading man of science in New York City, which, given Gotham's commercial preoccupations, was akin to being a minister in Dodge. The crowd remained obeisant as Mitchill delivered an extended epithalamium overflowing with polysyllables and featuring "carefully incased" bottles of water procured by a commodore and a merchant captain from the Atlantic and Indian oceans: "I am authorized to say, that the venerable sovereign of the deep is proud of the contemplated connection between the circumfluent oceans and the land encircled seas, and that he foresees many of the incalculable benefits which will ensue from the intercourse." Long before certain moderns developed such skills, the good Doctor Mitchill apparently had channeled "Neptune [who] having understood that projects were on the point of completion, by means of which his dominions would be very much enlarged, and rendered more useful and convenient," and had "directed the collection of these samples of his saline element." One wonders if all the men who conceived, designed, and built a very real canal kept straight faces. At long last Mitchill uncorked his waters, sprinkled some on the capstone, and poured some more into the lock itself, and then, as if the lock could abide no more, "the lock gates were opened, and the *De Witt Clinton* majestically sunk upon the bosom of the Hudson," accompanied by the "deafening peals of applause by the multitude, and the still louder roar of artillery."

No participant in this wonderful scene of Masonic, technical, and intellectual conception could have imagined that exactly nine months later Lock No. 1 would collapse in a very "public disaster." It seems that the ground was unstable along both sides of the lock. Early in the morning of July 8, 1824, "deep fissures" caused the masonry walls to sag and then cave in. The lock drained, stranding dozens of boats on the bottom: "a melancholy spectacle." By evening workers had thrown a temporary dam across the basin, but there would be no connection with the Hudson for months. Cargoes would have to be loaded and unloaded above Lock 2. It would be an unexpected boon to local cartmen, laborers, and especially wits. "I told our folks," said one, "that such a sandy foundation would not bear up so great a weight." "Aye," observed another, "by the holy Saint Patrick it's a judgment for turning out that Mr. Clinton!" By then, Clinton was having greater issues than a collapsed lock. In any case, the lock's second coming that fall occasioned no celebration, Masonic or otherwise.

For the time being, all was well. After parading on the Hudson under the tow of steamboats, the canal boats docked at the city wharf, and the leaders of state government and canalling marched up to a pavilion in front of the Capitol for toasts and more speeches. Albany's Bucktail mayor held forth long enough to make even a Mitchill blush, before ceding to Clinton, always most at home at a podium with relatively few but well-chosen words. "For the many errors we have committed we have no other apology than the purity of our motives," offered the humble patron of the mostly-built canal. "Futurity will disclose the benefits that it will produce, and experience will pronounce an unerring decision."

Clinton's friend William James, a rigid Scots Irish Presbyterian and prosperous Albany merchant, delivered the final and longest speech, praising a work "surpass[ing] any national improvement that has been attempted in any country." True or not, James declared that Americans owed a debt to Heaven: "Nothing, but the torpid stupidity of atheism, can prevent the reflecting mind from perceiving the special care and interposition of Providence in protecting and advancing our national honor and greatness." (No wonder, perhaps, that his young son Henry, who had just suffered disfiguring injuries in a barn fire of his own accidental doing, eventually turned from religious orthodoxy to Swedenborgianism, and grandsons William and Henry created American psychology and horrible fictional beasts.)

The speechifying concluded with a *feu de joie* from the gathered troops, after which the crowds dispersed while a sumptuous dinner was laid for the day's 150 most important and mostly Clintonian gentlemen, among them original canal promoters Thomas Eddy, Jonas Platt, and John Pintard. Dozens of toasts ensued, interspersed with music from the West Point band, including the premier of *"De Witt Clinton's Grand Canal March,"* written for the occasion by Richard Willis. After dining, the gentlemen rejoined the hoi polloi on the capital's hill for a *feu d'artifice* illuminating the evening sky. Alas, reported Clintonian editor Stone, "the fire-works, . . . , though they cost enough, were but poorly got up." Probably a Bucktail arrangement. The only other reported disappointment of the day was that of a gunner, whose hand was blown to bits by the premature discharge of one among the day's hundreds of artillery rounds.

A few days later the thrill was gone for Clinton. Invoking Cicero, the politician without office wrote drearily to a friend: "The laudari a laudato viro is more pleasing to me than the huzzas of thousands or the pageantry of public celebrations." Hard to believe, considering that New York's uneasy Caesar had organized the celebrations that saluted him as much as the canal.

* * *

If his political future looked bleak—out of elective office and remaining on the canal commission only at the pleasure of political enemies—Clinton could take some comfort from the canal's progress, and some pleasure from the *laudari a laudato viro* of Thomas Jefferson, Clinton's aging and defeated Southern adversary in the struggle to reach west. "[Y]our great canal," Jefferson had written to Clinton a few months earlier, suggests a question both curious and difficult, as to the comparative capability of nations to execute great enterprises. It is not from greater surplus of produce, after supplying their own wants, for in this N.Y. is not beyond some other states. Is it from other sources of industry additional to her produce? This may be; or is it a moral superiority? a sounder calculating mind, as to the most profitable employment of surplus, by improvement of capital, instead of useless consumption? I should lean to this latter hypothesis, were I disposed to puzzle myself with such investigations. But at the age of 80 it would be an idle labor, which I leave to the generation which is to see and feel its effects.

The full effects of the Erie Canal would not be felt until the canal in fact reached Lake Erie. By the fall of 1823, the middle and eastern sections were complete, but a battle over how to complete the western section was already in full force. Clinton was wounded politically but, twenty-six years Jefferson's junior, had plenty of active labor left.

Back in 1808, Jefferson had mocked New York's canal as "a fine project [that] might be executed a century hence." The commissioners, extraordinarily relieved to have overcome the "formidable and appalling obstructions" that characterized the easternmost portion of the eastern section, now could contradict Jefferson's prophesy, with self-congratulation for having had the wisdom and good fortune to get around it:

> [The] commissioners and their engineers do not hesitate to admit that had this section been commenced originally while their information on the subject of constructing canals was merely theoretical it is probable that the attempt to complete it would either have been entirely abortive, or so imperfectly executed as to have defeated, and perhaps postponed, for a century, the accomplishment of the great work of internal improvement, which is already so nearly perfected.

CHAPTER 11

How the West Was Won

[T]here is such a thing in politics as killing a man too dead.
—Martin Van Buren, 1824,
on the removal of canal commissioner De Witt Clinton

New York's Great Western Canal, as it was called early on, would not become the Erie Canal until its western section joined the completed eastern and middle sections with Lake Erie. The middle section was mostly level; the eastern section followed the course of a steep but long-settled river valley. The western section offered one long level but would have to traverse 150 miles of mostly unbroken, forbidding, and ill-watered territory.

The western section began in malarial swamp on the indifferent western shore of the sluggish Seneca River and ended where two struggling settlements battled to be named the canal's western terminus. Their pioneers pinned their outsized dreams on Albany politicians and novice engineers, many with as much interest as expertise. The eastern and western sections were both begun in 1819. The east, even with the complexities of the tumbling lower Mohawk River valley, was completed in four years. The west would take half again longer, with extraordinary engineering challenges, political upheavals, and bitter frontier rivalries.

A great embankment would have to carry the canal high above the Irondequoit Valley. An arched stone aqueduct would have to span and withstand the raging Genesee River. A stupendous lock set would have to notch a staircase of water into the densely forested glacial ridge where Lockport would be conceived. A subterranean waterway would have to be blasted through miles of solid limestone to make a deep cut leading west from the ridge. Settlers of neighboring frontier villages would struggle against storms, ice, floods, and each other to fashion a harbor good enough to win the western terminus. These were among the engineering challenges of the western work. At times, the ongoing political and social dynamics would by comparison seem tame.

☆ ☆ ☆

In the spring of 1819 the legislature approved the start of work on the western and eastern sections. Surveys to locate the western line took up much of the season, which ended with the first contracts between the Seneca and Genesee rivers. The western section met the middle section in a swamp. In earlier years, the earnest sons of stern Yankee farmers had mucked out the canal east of the Seneca River. It was done with duty and devotion and without complaint. It was their land, and they meant to improve it. Starting in 1820, however, the marshes were worked to a loud and mournful tune:

> We are cutting the Ditch through the mire;
> Through the mire right up to our necks, dammit!
> We are cutting the Ditch through the mire
> And the mud is our principal hire;
> In our pants, down our boots, down our necks, by God,
> In our pants, down our boots, down our necks!

The "Song of the Canal" was not written in upstate New York. Otherwise known as the "Canal Digger's Lament," it had long been heard along English canals dug by Irish labor. Irish diggers brought the tune with them, adapting the lyrics to the locale:

> We are cutting the Ditch through the gravel,
> Through the gravel across the state, dammit!

We are cutting the Ditch through the gravel,
So the people and freight they can travel,
Can travel across the State, by God,
Can travel across the State!

Fresh Irish immigrants also adapted their hopeful "Paddy of the Canal" to the canal country of Western New York:

When I came to this wonderful empire,
It filled me with the greatest surprise
To see such a great undertaking,
On the like I've never opened my eyes.
To see a full thousand brave fellows
At work among mountains so tall
To dig through the valleys so level.
Through rocks for to cut a canal.

I learned for to be very handy,
To use both the shovel and spade;
For I learned the art of canalling,
And I think it's a wonderful trade.

Our provision it was very plenty.
To complain we'd no reason at all,
I had money in every pocket,
While working upon the canal.

Not all singers finished the song. As in 1819 at the end of the work on the middle section, swamp laborers sickened and untold numbers didn't survive. In early August 1821 a vicious "sickness began to manifest itself" on the western side of the Seneca River. Over the next two months "no efforts could keep up the necessary number of workmen." The ranks thinned from seven hundred to two hundred. Malarial mosquitoes did not discriminate: "[A]ll the principal contractors, with many of the sub-contractors and hands, became diseased."

Winter froze the swamps and killed the mosquitoes, but progress at the start of the 1822 season was slowed by quicksand and heavy rains. Early that spring, contractor Alfred Hovey and a partner were still seeking five hundred laborers at a rate of $12 to $13 a month, with assurances the work would be complete by mid-July, before the marshes became dangerous. "When these marshes are drained," declared the 1824 travelers' guide to the nearly finished canal, "here will be the garden of the State." For many years, however, this remained the state's mosquito coast.

Though opened for navigation in 1822, the unlocked eastern end of the western section quickly proved needful of additional engineering. In the fall of 1823 quicksand and low water in the Seneca River that fed the segment made it impassable by fully loaded boats, requiring offloading to flat-bottomed lighters. Only after the 1824 season was "the evil" of "frequently detained" boats permanently remedied with deeper excavation and a new lock.

After passing through eleven miles of swamp west from the Seneca River, the canal line began to rise out of the slime at Clyde, a new hamlet at the site of an old French trading outpost. The line made its way thirty miles beside meandering Mud Creek, stepping up in ten locks. In these drier elevations, work proceeded rapidly. Nobody was more amazed at the progress than Webb Harwood, the first permanent settler of what became Palmyra.

Harwood was just twenty-two when he arrived in 1789 from Massachusetts, a revolutionary war veteran, husband, and expectant father. He and his wife started a family and farm along Mud Creek. Over the decades, both prospered.

"It seemed to me like building castles in the air, and I did not dream of the practability of such a thing," Harwood wrote to a friend in late 1821, "but to my great astonishment [the canal] is nearly completed for 20 miles" west of his homestead. "I have had the pleasure of seeing a boat pass my door with 300 souls aboard, drawn by 2 horses, for their pleasure." The Harwoods were invited aboard one afternoon, cruising for ten miles before returning home late in the evening. These were possibly the most leisure hours ever spent by the pioneer couple turned wide-eyed elders: "[M]y wife observed that to see vessels and boats sailing on large waters was no paradox, but to see a large boat floating through where but a few days before the plow was going and where large timber was growing and swamps almost impassable for either man or beast, that was worthy of all our attention and very entertaining."

Founded in a wilderness, the Harwood farm was now situated in a work zone. Nearby were two canal-bearing aqueducts crisscrossing Mud Creek; five soon-completed locks raising the canal to meet the embankment through the Irondequoit Valley; and, a few miles farther west, more locks that established the sixty-five mile "Genesee Level" to what would become Lockport. "[N]othing seems to impede the progress," Harwood reported with wonder. The canal work fronting the Harwood farm was among a total of fifty miles of the western section completed by the end of 1821, and none to soon: "We now just begin to rejoice in a retired life again—for 18 months our house has been thronged with from 20 to 60 men & some of the roughest creatures, our life has been very uncomfortable, but two days ago they went away."

Just after the turn of the new year, the rapid progress on the eastern portions of the western section, combined with the near completion of the eastern section and the earlier completion of the middle, prompted a notable boast. "The internal concerns of New York," wrote the New York *Spectator*, "extensive as it is in territory, and with new resources unfolding themselves to public view, appear like those of a mighty and flourishing empire" From this early reference matured the common perception of New York as the Empire State.

Webb Harwood was the rare local farmer who did not take a canal contract. New Palmyran Seymour Scovell made up for it, to a degree that infuriated at least one other local. At the depths of the depression in late 1820, the only way for many debt-ridden Western New York farmers to make money was "by getting a job on the canal," observed "Phocion" in the Bucktail *Rochester Gazette*. But "noisy Clintonian" Scovell had cornered the market, allegedly with "jobs on the Canal to the enormous amount of nearly seventy thousand dollars, when there were more than five hundred mechanics, unable to obtain a job to the amount of a single dollar." Scovell had obtained these contracts, Phocion alleged, by pledging his workers to pamphleteer for De Witt Clinton, seeking re-election as governor, and Myron Holley, seeking election to the assembly (both successfully).

In fact, although thirty-five-year-old Scovell certainly had been making connections since his arrival from Vermont—he would be named the canal toll collector for Palmyra in 1822—he held contracts in 1820 for only three sections worth less than $10,000.

Regardless of his veracity and politics, Phocion's broader point was sound: "The Canal should be let out in small jobs, to relieve the necessities of as many as possible. In this way the honest labouring man would be fairly rewarded for his services and would be placed beyond the reach of the merciless grasp of the mammoth speculators and it would be the means of saving hundreds of Farmers, who are more or less indebted, from bankruptcy and ruin." Canal contracting did remain largely a local affair, but successful contractors did seek and secure more contracts. The commissioners and their engineers were happy to have proven expertise on the line.

☆　☆　☆

When the commissioners won approval from the legislature in April 1819 to begin building the 160-mile western section, they knew where it would start—at the Seneca River—and where it had to go—to Lake Erie—but they were entirely uncertain about how it should get there. The first thirty-five miles to Palmyra would indisputably follow the valley of Mud Creek. The remaining miles from Palmyra to the lake were open to substantial debate.

Back in 1816, when the canal was still only a possibility, the commissioners had rejected a southerly route proposed by Holland Company man William Peacock that was convenient to company land but inconvenient to water sources. In December 1818 a group of Genesee County pioneers asked commission president and then-governor Clinton "to procure an *accurate survey and level*" of an even more southerly route. Early in the 1819 season the commissioners assigned Valentine Gill to survey the suggested route from Palmyra to Lake Erie, attempting to improve on James Geddes's preferred northerly route.

Since starting his Erie service as a draftsman for Isaac Briggs two seasons earlier, the veteran Irish engineer had risen to be one of a half-dozen Erie engineers earning the top daily rate of $5 plus expenses. Gill promptly surveyed a course that crossed the Genesee River twelve miles south of what was still called Rochesterville and continued on to a junction with Lake Erie south of Buffalo. This route was squarely through Holland Company land and was avidly encouraged by influential Batavians. But while Peacock's rejected 1816 route aroused concerns about water supply, with its summit level seventy-four feet about Lake Erie, Gill's was another twenty feet higher than that. Gill claimed that local streams would be enough.

The commissioners submitted Gill's extreme southern course to his fellow engineers. Canvass White surveyed the route himself later in 1819 and reported to chief Wright, who advised rejecting it. The commissioners did so and returned to Geddes's original northerly route. Joseph Ellicott would not get a canal through his Holland Company land. Still, the northern route was not without issues.

The stretch of canal west of Webb Harwood's farm ended at the descent to the Irondequoit Valley. Here, eleven Decembers earlier, James Geddes had shouted "Eureka!" across the snow-capped ridges. Now, having picked Geddes's northern route, the commissioners were undecided just how to turn his discovery into action.

Geddes originally envisioned an embankment of earth and stone to cross the main portion of the valley and link with natural ridges. In early1820 the commissioners opted instead for a quarter-mile, sixty-foot-high wooden aqueduct: "Economy induced us to make the substitute." Examinations of the ground suggested also that the soil had too much gravel and sand to support a heavy embankment. Soon enough, however, there was reason to think twice about high wooden structures.

A year earlier, a remarkable bridge had been completed over the Genesee River at an aspiring new settlement downstream from Rochesterville. With its roadway passing two hundred feet above the river, Carthage Bridge was the highest wooden arch bridge ever built. Alas, the contractor hired by the settlers to build them a modern wonder was incompletely schooled in ancient engineering. The under-built crown of the arch quickly sprung. That summer, Scottish tourist and future American feminist Fanny Wright discovered the fatal flaw during an impulsive venture onto the framework, making her way back to land in breathless expectation of being crushed at any moment. The following May, just fifteen months after it opened, the bridge collapsed in a "horrible confusion" of shattered pine, wrenched iron bolts, and wrecked civic ambition. Without its bridge, this Carthage fell and faded without a trace.

The notorious failure of the bridge induced the canal commissioners to rethink their wooden Irondequoit crossing. Before any work had been done, they abandoned wood for "permanent works" of earth and stone. The official reason was "fear that winds might have an unfavorable effect" on a long, high wooden aqueduct. Also, the prospective contractor for the original embankment had chopped his rate for earth fill from twenty-five cents per cubic yard to fourteen cents.

The issue of uncertain ground remained, though. Engineer David Bates, the Erie veteran initially given overall charge of the western section, created careful specifications. To provide secure support for the culvert crossing Irondequoit Creek and the great embankment in which the culvert was to be set, Bates planned to sink down to bedrock over nine hundred log piles, each a foot wide and up to twenty feet long; the tops of the piles would be overlaid with timber mats. The heavy masonry culvert would span the creek with a 26-foot arch set in a 245-foot-long section; the culvert would be set at right angles in the longer of two gravel, sand, and earth-filled embankments, one over 1,300 feet long, the other 230 feet. Much as James Geddes had first imagined back in 1808, the artificial embanking would fill the spaces between three natural ridges, for a total valley-crossing span of nearly a mile. The two embankments were to be built up into pyramiding mounds seventy feet high to meet the height of the natural ridges. Finally, along the narrow top, piles would be sunk into the embankments to support a wooden canal trough.

"So far as I understand your plan," chief engineer Wright wrote anxiously to Bates, "it appears to be correct. I pray you to see that the piles are well and faithfully driven. It is all important to the safety of the whole work that there should be no settling nor any precariousness, as you know that would destroy all instantly."

The culvert was finished during the 1821 season but early the following season the contractor suffered an unspecified severe illness, and the embanking proceeded slowly. As it gained height, the embanking also lost breadth, making it progressively "impossible to employ as many teams and hands upon it, as had before been used." In addition, as the commissioners enlightened those less experienced than they in such things, "a mass of fresh earth, raised gradually by human labor, to an elevation of more than seventy feet, will at all times settle very much as you approach the top."

By June 1822 the work was complete enough for test fillings of the canal trough to help settle the embankment. "This operation is to prevent sudden breaking," chief Wright advised Bates. "[I]t may and probably will settle so as to make some large cracks, but they would be of such a character as to give timely notice of the discharge of water before any great injury could arise."

In October the contractor pronounced the Great Embankment finished. The commissioners weren't so sure. The canal was otherwise complete to its four-foot depth between Rochester—a ville no longer—and the Seneca River (and east all the way to Little Falls), but only two feet of water was let into the embankment section for the rest of the year. For many weeks the commissioners feared collapse and flood. The trough was drained nightly, then left empty for the winter.

At the opening of the 1823 season, there was still "much anxiety." It was decided to line the embankment trough with two feet of clay. The contractor hired for this work was Jireh Rowley, a War of 1812 captain then commanding a large family along Irondequoit Creek a few miles from the embankment.

Captain Rowley took no uncertain command of this job. On one of De Witt Clinton's frequent visits, the anxious commission president and his party "got in the way of the laborers and their teams." Rowley "pretty sharply ordered them to get out of the way." The once and future governor was not one to take such things personally: "Instead of being offended at the brusque manner of the Captain, [Clinton] had the good sense to remark to his friends that he should go home with his mind at rest concerning the job, as Capt. Rowley evidently meant business."

The whole business was nearly complete by the end of the 1823 season. The embankment trough, now filled to a three-foot depth, "leaked much less . . . than it did at the commencement; and although an alarm was circulated of its being in danger," a postseason inspection yielded "a firm conviction that the alarm was groundless." The section was filled to the standard four-foot depth for the 1824 season, but commissioners and engineers were still "watching it unceasingly." Finally, in 1825, convinced by "evidence of increasing strength and solidity," the entire Great Embankment was officially declared "perfectly safe."

By then the sight of canal boats transiting the valley above its treetops had inspired confidence and awe. No one was more gratified than James Geddes. As the embankment rose from the valley, the country surveyor turned canal engineer dared to invoke the icon of British civil engineering: "How would the great Brindley, with all his characteristic anxiety to avoid lockage, have felt in such a case: all his cares at an end about water to lock up from the Genesee river, finding no locking up required. Boats to pass over these arid plains, and along the very tops of these high ridges."

The line returned to earth at the little village of Pittsford, and the going got easier. "The country being level, and the soil easily worked, they made rapid progress in the excavation," reported the English traveler John Howison while watching a dozen laborers digging outside Pittsford in June 1820. Increasingly typical of Erie labor, the men were neither locals nor well paid, boarded by the contractor but earning only fifty cents a day, "a wage which shows how much the price of labour has declined." In the deepening economic depression spawned by the Panic of 1819, canal employers weren't getting rich, either: "Many of the first contractors realized a great deal of money by the business; but there is now so much competition in the purchase of the sections, that the persons desirous of obtaining them are obliged to offer at the lowest rates possible." Nevertheless, the completion of the ten-mile run to Rochester was duly observed on July 4, 1822: "The Erie Canal—Great! Stupendous! Magnificent!"

The Genesee River presented the next great challenge. David Bates's design for crossing the unpredictable river at Rochester was an 802-foot long stone aqueduct, with nine fifty-foot span arches over the river on stone piers and smaller arches in the abutments at either end, "the great-

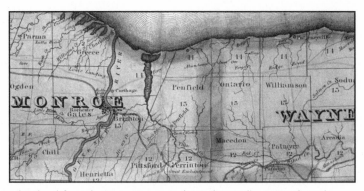

This detail from the Vance-Dey map shows the canal's passage through Rochester, with the Great Embankment to the east, and the continuation of the canal to the west by Geddes's "northern route." (*The Lionel Pincus and Princess Firyal Map Division, The New York Public Library, Astor, Lenox and Tilden Foundations*)

est mass of mason work" in any Erie or Champlain structure. Bates and chief Wright wanted the bridge built entirely of durable limestone, but the commissioners opted for piers and arch work of cheaper Red Medina sandstone quarried at nearby Carthage; only the coping would be of hard stone, a grey limestone from Cayuga County.

The contract was awarded in June 1821 to William Brittin, "an ingenious and enterprising man" in the eyes of the commissioners. The villagers, whose numbers had already doubled from the 1,502 recorded in the 1820 census, were dubious about one aspect of Brittin's enterprise. A master carpenter, Brittin had built the state's new prison in Auburn several years earlier and then served as its first warden. He was bringing with him to Rochester to cut stone for the aqueduct some of his former charges. This was unwelcome news in some editorial corners: "Who can contemplate without horror, one hundred and fifty convicts, in the constant view of the children and youth of this populous settlement, pouring the sound of curses and profanity into the ears of all who may be attracted by the novelty of the scene to visit the encampment?"

In the event, Brittin employed no more than thirty convicts, all of them Irish, serving terms on minor convictions, but pardoned by governor Clinton provided they worked at prevailing canal wages for the duration of their sentences. Any man who tried to escape faced resentencing for his full term. Brittin housed his convicts with other workers on an island in the river. Nevertheless, as many locals feared, a quarter of the convicts took their liberty and weren't recaptured.

There were problems with the early work as well as the workforce. By the end of the 1821 season, the stone slab foundation for the first pier, iron bolted to the smooth bedrock of the swift river, had been built up two feet. It was quickly swept away. Only the bolts, "bent down, with the course of the stream," remained. "[I]t served to impress us," acknowledged the commissioners, "with juster views of the prodigious violence and power" of the Genesee. Brittin was not afforded a second chance; in December, a sudden fatal illness swept him away.

Spring 1822 brought Erie veteran Alfred Hovey to start the work anew, promising to finish in one season. It would take him two. Annoyed by the requirement to use soft sandstone instead of hard limestone, an "extremely anxious" chief Wright advised engineer Bates in June "to have every attention paid to the construction [and] see that no bad material or ill workmanship is permitted. . . . It is a great work, and any defect in it would ruin yourself as well as me."

Under Wright's orders, squares of river bedrock were blasted out in the exact dimensions of each pier. The bottom course of two-and-a-half-foot thick stone was attached to the bedrock by larger bolts than Brittin had used. Each succeeding course of stone was joined by iron bars and hydraulic cement and secured by bolts, "to prevent any stone from being started." By the end of the 1822 season Hovey's crews had completed the bridge up to the top of its arches, fourteen feet above the river; stone for the parapet walls, canal trough, and coping had been quarried and cut. By the following September the longest stone bridge in America and one of the longest in the world was complete. "It is a structure of admirable solidity and beauty," the commissioners boasted, "and is composed of the most durable materials." This, it was presently discovered, was manifestly untrue.

But first the obligatory celebrations. On October 6, 1823, decorated canal boats cruised the aqueduct, newly filled by a river feeder. The village band entertained with the Masonic theme song, "The Temple's Completed." Among the celebrants was William Morgan, a shadowy journeyman mason from Virginia who had worked on the aqueduct since the previous year. Three years later, his threatened exposé of Masonic secrets would win him a kidnapping and disappearance at the hands of a mob, a notorious event that spawned the anti-Masonic political movement and ruined Freemasonry as a powerful force in American society and politics.

After public speeches, the leading citizens (Morgan not among them) and canal officials repaired to a private banquet, where septuagenarian village founder Nathaniel Rochester declared the aqueduct "the most stupendous and strongest work in America." "May its nine splendid arches be as permanent as the rock upon which they are founded," proclaimed another hopeful toast maker. Jesse Hawley, by then a respectable Rochesterian, more cautiously toasted canals generally: "the modern monuments of national glory." Three weeks later, the first canal boat loaded with Rochester-milled flour transited the aqueduct headed east. Wheat, which had been selling for as little as twenty-five cents a bushel during the worst of the national depression, had risen in recent months to over a dollar, and the cost of transporting it to Albany was now dropping from $100 a ton by wagon to a fraction of that by boat. Local millers were daily grinding 25,000 bushels of Genesee wheat into Rochester flour; some 40,000 barrels were shipped east by year's end. The Flour City on the Genesee was born.

By 1824 Rochester's aqueduct was hailed as "the grandest single feature of the Canal." The grandeur was short lived. The canal trough in the aqueduct was only seventeen feet wide, less than half the normal width of the canal, preventing two-way traffic. A sharp left turn from the west onto the aqueduct further slowed the passage. Traffic jams and fistfights among boat crews over who should proceed first quickly became common.

Almost as quickly, the aqueduct itself began to fall apart. Its Medina sandstone was too weak and porous for heavy hydraulic duty. Water leaking from the canal trough hastened the decay of the aqueduct's arches and piers. Just ten years after its completion, the aqueduct was "in a state of rapid dilapidation." To forestall collapse, it was reinforced temporarily with wood timbers, to no avail. "This structure is now . . . nearly in ruins in consequence of the disintegration of the stone," concluded a state report in 1836, as planning began for a larger and more substantial bridge, this time properly built of limestone.

While Rochester's wonderful and wonderfully flawed aqueduct was abuilding, work proceeded with greater ease west of Rochester along the "Genesee Level": sixty-five miles of canal without locks. The first twenty miles were put out to contract in July 1821. Longtime Clintonian commissioner Holley, now forced to share active oversight of the western section with newly appointed Bucktail commissioner William Bouck, had extraordinary luxury in selecting contractors: twelve hundred written proposals were made for the sections in those twenty miles. Contracts were made for as little as four cents per cubic yard of excavation.

The line leading west from Rochester may not have been lucrative for laborers and contractors, but there was opportunity for speculators. The commissioners originally intended that Rochester would serve as the temporary western terminus of the canal, from the fall of 1823 until the completion of the long level to what would become Lockport. Hiel Brockway had a different idea, and influential friends.

Brockway was another of Connecticut's Yankees who found their fortunes in Western New York. He, his wife Phebe (a descendant of Pilgrim John Alden), and the first several of their eventual thirteen children had arrived in Ontario County in the early 1800s, where Brockway established himself as a builder and speculator. When digging began for the Erie Canal in 1817 at Rome, Brockway quickly bought up undeveloped land twenty miles west of what was not yet Rochester. The tract soon went by the name Brockway, and then, as the canal approached, Brockport. The shrewd speculator then joined forces with the developer of an adjoining tract to lobby the canal commissioners to shift the temporary terminus from Rochester to Brockport. It was not inconvenient that among the adjoining developer's silent land partners were two canal commissioners: his cousin Henry Seymour and Myron Holley. Needless to say, a favorable decision was rendered. For one year, the Great Western Canal began in Albany, capital of the Empire State, and ended 287 miles west at Brockport, population a few dozen.

Giddy from increased land sales, Hiel Brockway raised his glass at the end of the 1823 season and toasted: "The United States—cutting canals while Europe is cutting heads" (though continental slaughter had long met its Waterloo). As if to justify their concession to Brockway, the commissioners made a point of noting in their annual report the following February that $141.13 in tolls was collected between Rochester and Brockport before the end of the 1823 season. Tolls in 1823 on the western section were over $21,000, and they were over $125,000 for the rest of the canal; the Brockport terminus was considerably more of a benefit to its namesake than to the state.

The 1824 canal travelers' guide sniffed at Brockway and his "port," correctly gauging its long-term prospects: "When the Canal is completed, this place will be much more like a *way* than a *port*." But Hiel Brockway had a long last laugh. After contracting for a canal bridge and two short sections, he turned Brockport into a boatbuilding center and organized his hundred-foot cedar packets into the Red Bird Line, which flourished on the canal into the 1850s.

The atlas of the Erie Canal is filled with pretensions—Palmyra, Syracuse, Rome, Utica, Troy—and conceits—Rochester, Brockport—but Lockport had none of that. It earned its name with hard labor. The Peacock and Gill routes west of the Genesee would have avoided the "mountain ridge" by running south before turning west. The Geddes northern route was lower and suitably watered but required scaling the ridge that modern geology calls the Niagara Escarpment. At the western end of the escarpment, the Niagara River tumbles a combined height of 325 feet down three falls. Eighty miles east, the Genesee River drops 210 feet down three lesser falls. But just seventeen miles east of Niagara, the ridge sags to only sixty feet. That is where commissioners and engineers decided to build locks and create Lockport.

Although Hiel Brockway guessed early and right where the canal would pass, others guessed wrong. Back in 1816, before any portion of the canal had been approved, a group of Ontario County Quakers led by the extended Comstock family established an unnamed settlement in dense woods and rattlesnake bogs along the ridge near Eighteen Mile Creek, thirty rugged miles northeast of Buffalo. By 1819 it seemed a good bet that the canal would be ascending the ridge at one of two places near the scattering of log cabins and cleared fields. The handful of frontiersmen began jockeying for position. Twenty-five-year-old Zeno Comstock, proprietor of the first sawmill on the creek, owned two hundred acres at one location but, on a hunch, bought up land at the other spot after selling his first plot to his uncle, Jared Comstock. A year later, the engineers decided on the spot that Zeno had sold. "Mortified at the result," Zeno "pulled up stakes and went West." Meanwhile, uncles Jared and Darius became major Erie contractors; they and other Comstocks became partners in nearly $200,000 worth of canal work through 1825. By then, their isolated settlement of rough-hewn log cabins had become the canal-made city of Lockport.

The question perplexing commissioners and engineers was how to make the canal go up a nearly vertical ridge. Each of the engineers put his mind to work on the problem. The winning concept came from former country schoolteacher Nathan Roberts. Since 1819 Roberts had been in charge of locating the canal line and designing locks from the Seneca River to Rochester. "Without consulting any one; with but little aid from published works on the subject of engineering," Roberts envisioned twin sets of five twelve-foot locks, side by side, one after the other in a tight staircase up the steep ridge, one set for boats headed west, the other for boats headed east. It would be "a more elaborate scheme of locks than had ever been constructed in America." In a long engineering career, Roberts would regard the Lockport set as his "proudest triumph."

Contracts were let in the spring of 1821. Though Roberts was soon put in charge of the line from Lockport to Lake Erie, including his locks, Stephen Bates remained in overall charge of the entire western section and under the close eye of chief Wright regarding the locks: "I hope you will watch the stone-cutters, and check at once any deviation from the right workmanship. I feel alarmed about the water-lime, lest they should not calculate upon the importance of this material. . . . This part of the work I beg you will attend to personally, as every thing depends upon it."

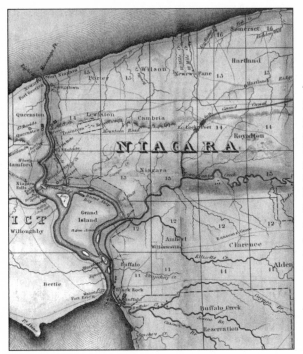

This detail from the Vance-Dey map shows the canal's passage through the ridge at what had become Lockport, into the canalized lower Tonawanta Creek, and down through Black Rock to Buffalo. (*The Lionel Pincus and Princess Firyal Map Division, The New York Public Library, Astor, Lenox and Tilden Foundations*)

When work began early in 1821 at Lockport, it numbered a handful of resident families. By the following January, there were over three hundred families, with more arriving daily. Another year later, Lockport was home to fifteen hundred permanent residents, twenty-four mechanic shops, twelve stores, eight public houses, eight doctors, five law offices, four schools, one newspaper, and one house of public worship (with another under construction). Among the many newcomers was Jesse Hawley.

Now a prominent citizen of Rochester, Hawley had been quick to capitalize on the impending birth of Lockport. With his brother-in-law William Bond, Hawley began buying up land along the ridge in 1820. Hawley was the Rochester port collector, a successful speculator, and a newly elected Clintonian assemblyman. Presumably he had obtained solid advice on his latest investment. When Erie County was created from Niagara County territory in the spring of 1821, assemblyman Hawley, old anti-Clintonian Erastus Root, and soon to be deceased Rochester aqueduct contractor William Brittin were named as a commission to locate a new Niagara County seat. The following year, Root's preferred Lewiston lost out to Hawley's Lockport, and brother-in-law Bond gave up two of his acres to site official county buildings. As happened with his wife, Hawley's relations with Bond would soon sour, but for the time being the two chose the Lockport site wisely.

Nathan Roberts laid the first stone for the locks in a small ceremony on July 8, 1823. By the end of the year the lock contractors had made "reasonable exertions" in advancing the work. Nearly all of the fifty thousand feet of facing stone had been cut and half of it delivered to the site, and the laying of the two lowest locks had begun. The commissioners were "confident, that all mason work will be done next season." It was not. "The Ravine, through which the Canal rises the Mountain Ridge, is a singular and interesting curiosity," canal guide writer Horatio Spafford observed during the summer of 1824: "Here is the *Back Bone* of the Erie Canal, which will hardly be completed, I am afraid, by the close of 1825." The fear was nearly realized. The Lockport locks, "a work of the first magnitude on the line, and one of the greatest of the kind in the world," would be the last work completed on the entire canal, barely in time for its formal opening in October 1825.

The locks were one aspect of the activity around Lockport that transformed it in two years from "a perfect wilderness" into the "shire town of Niagara county." Extending southwest from the brow of the ridge toward the lower Tonawanta Creek would be the Deep Cut: three miles through solid limestone, then another four in a mix of rock and wet earth, at an average depth of twenty-six feet below the landscape. The cut would have vertical walls and a width of just twenty-seven feet, with a towpath carved out on one side and boat-sized bays to let traffic pass: a subterranean rectangular prism leading the canal from deep in the rock at the edge of the ridge southwest to ground level. The Deep Cut work was let out in four sections to what the commissioners "regarded as men of business and good contractors." The section requiring the deepest rock excavation— over thirty-one feet—went to Lockport pioneer Darius Comstock.

The work started slowly in 1821. The ground was still heavily timbered, unsettled wilderness with extensive bogs. "It was not therefore, without great difficulty at first, that the contractors erected their houses for shelter, opened roads for the delivery of their provisions and tools, and collected their hands." By fall, all grubbing and clearing along the route had been completed and blasting had begun. The rock "flies like hailstones," visiting Palmyran Webb Harwood reported to a friend, "the most formidable thing I ever saw . . . if you were to see it, you would say the one-half was not told you." The work crews "stop not for winter, no weather detains them, nor stands before them."

But at year's end, only 15,000 cubic yards of rock had been blasted out and carried off or set aside for the lock works down the ridge. Over 300,000 cubic yards of rock remained to be blasted. The contractors "went on with resolution" through the winter, but doubts rose about whether the work could be completed at the agreed upon prices by the agreed time, September 1823. Meeting at Buffalo in the spring, the commissioners concluded, "it was perfectly apparent that the work . . . would soon fail entirely if a new course was not adopted."

The new course was for the state to take over the excavation. This made of the Deep Cut a public works, which the commissioners had rejected for the whole canal back in 1817. No fault was found with any of the contractors, but the work was clearly beyond their frontier resources. To all appearances willingly, the contractors became wage earners overseeing their crews, also now paid by the state. The entire deep cutting was put under the direct control of the engineers. Early in July 1822 the state advertised for a thousand laborers "to be employed on excavating earth, blasting and quarrying" and be paid $12 a month plus "good accommodations for subsistence."

The hail of stones of the previous year became a full out battlefield of flying rock in 1822. Workers drilled holes by hand in the flinty rock with drill bits of varying quality. The holes were filled with newly patented DuPont blasting powder and packed with brown paper. A worker lit the paper, shouted a warning, and ran. Everyone within earshot ducked and covered. The timing of the crude fuse and the extent of the explosion varied considerably, and the casualties grew among workers and unwary villagers. Residents rapidly clearing a town from the oak and black walnut forest protected their new homes by leaning tree trunks all around as a blockade against blasted stone. Local lore has it that one of Lockport's young new lawyers was knocked from the chair in his Main Street office by a twenty-pound stone that landed on his front porch and bounded inside like a disenchanted client.

Lockport limestone occasionally flew without benefit of black powder. With few local farms from which to draw a labor force, most of the canal workers who came to Lockport were fresh Irish immigrants recruited off the docks in New York City. To some degree, they justified the widespread prejudice of transplanted Yankees. "[A]fter getting fairly into their cups" on Christmas Eve 1822, Irish laborers "engaged in an unprofitable contest to see which could do the other the most harm." Pitched battle degenerated into riot. "Stones flew thick as blackberries, and bludgeons were brandishing in every direction." When the Irish, by some accounts running short on whiskey, attacked a tavern, townsmen emerged to engage them. Two were seriously injured, and one died from his injuries a few weeks later. After Lockport's first murder trial the following fall, thirteen people, mostly Irish, were sent to jail; twenty others escaped prosecution by fleeing to Canada.

Riots and violent strikes among Irish laborers became common on later American canals and railroads, but only one other reported incident troubled the Erie work: a dustup in Lockport on July 12, 1824, between hundreds of northern and southern Irish on the anniversary of the Battle of the Boyne. "Orangemen," pledged by secret oath to the Protestant English king, provoked violent confrontations with Catholics in Lockport, in Paterson, New Jersey, and in what was still the village of Greenwich on Manhattan. It was the first time that such ancient Irish antipathy had found vicious expression in America, and it alarmed the lawful. In Greenwich, a club-wielding Orange gang "cried out for croppies [Irish Republicans]—they halloed, come out papists—they cried out for king William, king George, &c. and brandished their weapons, and terror and dismay followed them wherever they went." No one died, but among the bloodied was a pregnant woman beaten "to insensibility." Criminal prosecutions arising from the Manhattan violence aroused passionate argument by the top lawyers in the city, which had been stunned by the dramatic breakdown of urban order. In Lockport the local militia succeeded in putting down the combat before any significant destruction or casualties. The worst damage was to Irish reputation.

Still, although the events of 1822 and 1824 reconfirmed anti-Irish prejudice, Lockport's laborers were largely law-abiding. When the canal was done, hundreds of Irish remained to help populate the growing city.

The greater part of Irish reputation was not for brawling but for hard and willing labor. Gangs of Irish laborers were employed on the Deep Cut leading west from Lockport, but even with the state takeover, the work moved slowly and costs rose. By the end of 1823, when the cut was originally supposed to have been finished, nearly half the rock was still in the ground. It was of "a worse description" than anticipated: "It consists of a mixture of flint and lime; in irregular layers, dipping in different directions, which is found hard to drill, and after it is drilled and charged, no ingenuity or skill in blasting, is at all times sufficient to prove much effect by the explosion." Meanwhile, water from adjoining wetlands would flow into ongoing excavations, requiring constant draining. Provisions, supplies, and laborers were proving expensive to transport to the primitive region, remote from markets and accessible only by bad roads. The commissioners now expected to complete the Deep Cut no earlier than May 1825. By the end of the 1824 season, the cost of the Lockport locks and Deep Cut was approaching half a million dollars, with substantial work remaining.

There was some good news. The frontier ingenuity that had spawned tree fellers, stump pullers, root-scraping plows, and a better wheelbarrow early in the Erie construction materialized again at the Deep Cut. As the cut took shape, engineers and builders became perplexed about how to remove excavated material. The deeper and longer the cut got, the more impractical and expensive became the removal of material by small wheelbarrows, no matter how improved their design. The solution to the problem came from one Orange Dibble.

In 1811 Dibble had been among the first settlers of Evans, a Holland Company village on Lake Erie south of Buffalo. Ten years later he was one of the four original contractors for the Deep Cut. Dibble was a creative thinker and handy craftsman. He designed an immense wood-framed crane with a horse-operated boom that swung over the cut with a large bucket raised and lowered by rope and pulley. Rock rubble and earth could be removed from the excavation as quickly as they accumulated. Dibble's cranes were assembled at seventy-foot intervals along the deepest segments of the cut. Looming over the barely broken landscape, the line of cranes became an iconic image of the industrial future surmounting the American wilderness.

As often happens, no one devised the means for disposing of the new technology's waste. Long after the completion of the canal, Lockport looked west at a range of rubble mountains. As for Orange Dibble, he moved on to become a major contractor on numerous American engineering projects and, for a time, handled Buffalo's mail as its postmaster.

By September 1824 the forty miles of level canal between Brockport and the boat basin below the ridge at Lockport were filled with water, ending Brockport's *annus mirabilis* as the canal's western terminus. It had no locks, but the run required nearly one culvert per mile to cross small streams, large embankments at four substantial creeks including a sixty-foot stone aqueduct spanning Oak Orchard Creek, and a feeder there supplying the run at its midway point. The initial filling of the section "gave a flattering test of the solidity and permanency of the works." The first canal boat reaching the basin was the *Roberts*, named for the engineer still laboring then to complete the locks that would allow the canal to extend farther west.

The work had not been without suffering. That August, "sickness prevailed in almost every house" west of Rochester. "[H]eaven knows," reported a Canadian settler passing through, "we found sufficient sickness to have broken down the stoutest spirits; and yet . . . we never heard a complaint." Workers at Oak Orchard were happily earning $13 a month. Inferior land was selling for $8 an acre when the best Canadian land went for $1: "Such are the effects of spirited exertions for the internal improvement of a country!"

While the Lockport locks and Deep Cut started transforming wilderness into city, construction of the canal's final miles to Lake Erie moved forward. From the Deep Cut, the line would track south to the lower Tonawanta Creek for a twelve-mile run in the creek itself, the only section of canalized natural waterway on the entire canal. From there what would happen was anybody's guess.

By 1823 intense power struggles were underway at the geographic extremities of the mostly complete canal. At Albany, the ascendant Bucktails were plotting against the canal's great champion but were unprepared for the popular reaction. At Black Rock and Buffalo, its pioneers were deep in protracted gamesmanship to have their respective settlements designated as the canal's western terminus.

The seeds of the Black Rock versus Buffalo debate were planted early in the century, when Peter Porter and Augustus Porter founded their Niagara Falls portage monopoly on lands secured from the state three miles down the Niagara River. They placed their settlement where a large, flat ledge of black Onondaga limestone lay along the shore, forming a natural wharf and a lee from the river current. At the same time, the Holland Land Company established its Lake Erie beachhead at the outlet of Buffalo Creek. The Dutch company called the place New Amsterdam but, as with the earlier settlement at the mouth of the Hudson, the name didn't stick. The settlers preferred Buffalo.

The neighboring and rival settlements grew slowly. Both were burned and devastated by the British on the next to last day of 1813, but they began rebuilding as soon as hostilities ended. In 1810 Buffalo had fifteen hundred residents; emptied during the war, it had recovered to a thousand by the end of 1814 and topped two thousand by 1820. Black Rock experienced similar growth, loss, and recovery, reaching roughly fifteen hundred in 1820.

As a canal terminus, each place had its advantages and disadvantages. Black Rock had a small natural harbor protected from Lake Erie's frequent storms, but sailing ships could not make out for the lake against the river's strong current and the prevailing westerlies without harnessing the "horn breeze," an upriver tow by a large team of oxen. Black Rock also was exposed to future British threat across the mile-wide river. Buffalo was on the lake but had no natural harbor. A sandbar, formed and reformed by lake storms and creek floods, required large ships to anchor off, transferring their cargoes by lighter in settled weather.

From the founding of Buffalo, Joseph Ellicott had considered the construction of a pier or breakwater necessary to create a proper anchorage. Meanwhile, at the behest of influential congressman Peter Porter, Washington in 1811 designated Black Rock the region's official American port of entry from April to December. Buffalo was made the official port only for the brutal winter months, when little business was entering.

Until the Erie Canal decided their fates, it was unclear which village would predominate. In 1813 (before war ravaged the New York frontier), the first state gazetteer deemed Black Rock "a better site for a great trading Town than that of Buffalo," while Ellicott at the same time self-interestedly proclaimed Buffalo the future "grand Imperium of the Western World."

For Porter, the early alliance of Ellicott and De Witt Clinton, compounded by the resolve of Buffalo settler Samuel Wilkeson, would prove difficult to counter. The 1816 western route survey by Ellicott's nephew William Peacock not surprisingly posited Buffalo as the canal terminus, and that summer visiting commissioner Clinton was charmed by Buffalo's prospects. Earlier that year, Wilkeson and other Buffalo pioneers, frustrated with the Holland Company's refusal to spend its own money, began pressing the legislature for funds to improve Buffalo's harbor. In their January 1818 annual report, the commissioners wrote about the canal's prospective "western termination at Buffalo." But the game was just getting started.

The first significant action came in April 1818 when the legislature, prompted by a memorial from the citizens of Buffalo, authorized Governor Clinton to appoint a commissioner to survey and make a plan for a harbor there. Clinton asked for a recommendation from fellow canal commissioner Ellicott. Ellicott naturally recommended Peacock. After the state gave Peacock the assignment, Ellicott resigned from the canal commission to focus on his company duties, confident that the state would organize what the company was unwilling to fund.

While company man Peacock attended to his work for the state during the summer of 1818, the Porters sought to stem the tide by walking on water, literally. Conceived three years earlier for "the mortification & disappointment of the Buffalonians" and financed by a consortium of top New York City and Albany investors, the 120-foot, 340-ton, 200-passenger steamboat *Walk-in-the-Water* was built at Black Rock and launched there in August. It was the first steamboat on the upper Great Lakes. It was immediately put into service on weekly round trips to Detroit (population 1,110), with scheduled stops at every important lake port but one. The sight of the boat steaming past Buffalo, combined with the Porters' well-developed commercial operations at Black Rock and the three fewer miles of canal to be built if it terminated there, put Buffalo back on the defensive. "There are . . . so many intrigues going on by the knowing ones," Ellicott wrote to his boss, Paul Busti, in Philadelphia the day after the *Walk-in-the-Water*'s first voyage, "that it is difficult for those of us not in the Cabinet to know the truth."

Not surprisingly, Peacock's report in January 1819—questionably reviewed by then ex-commissioner Ellicott before it was forwarded to Clinton—envisioned no problems building a Buffalo harbor. Peacock recommended the construction of a $12,000, thousand-foot stone pier extending into the lake that would give safe anchorage to large vessels and, over time, work to dissipate the sandbar: "Buffalo from its local situation is apparently the key which opens to the People of the State of New York a most stupendous path of navigation and of commerce extending the distance of more than 2000 miles." The prior submission of a state report to a private citizen suggests how deeply Ellicott was entrenched as the gatekeeper of the west.

The pioneers of Buffalo were still largely unprosperous settlers on expensive company land, whereas the Porters of Black Rock were rich merchants with national influence. "The Buffalo harbor will not I am fearful meet with many supporters," new senator David Evans wrote from Albany to uncle Ellicott in February. Politics further complicated Buffalo's interests: Samuel Wilkeson and most of his comrades were Clintonians, while Ellicott's Big Family was on the verge of its break with Clinton and a political alliance with the Bucktails, with whom Peter Porter had long maintained cordial relations.

On the same day in April 1819 that it approved construction of the eastern and western sections of the canal, the legislature gave Buffalo's settlers more and less than what they wanted. An incorporation of nine Buffalo citizens would be loaned $12,000 to build the harbor on their own. The loan was to be repaid in ten years unless the state ultimately chose Buffalo as the canal terminus, in which case the loan would be canceled. The kicker was that the incorporators were to personally secure the loan for twice its value. A month after this mixed legislative blessing for Buffalo, the Panic of 1819 diminished the ability or willingness of all but two of the potential harbor company incorporators to go forward. Ellicott characteristically refused to pledge any Holland Company money. The Buffalo harbor project faltered.

Into this thickening stew stepped David Thomas. A devout Quaker raised along the Schuylkill River twenty-five miles above Philadelphia, Thomas, with his wife and the first of their several children, had settled a hundred-acre farm on Cayuga Lake in 1805. As did many industrious frontiersmen whose farms generated little income, Thomas turned to surveying, by which he obtained a measure of prosperity. He also nurtured a deep interest in natural history, botany, and mathematics; the story goes that he had studied so hard as a youth that his health had failed. Not exclusively bookish, he also wrote poetry on wilderness themes, from the majesty of mountain ranges to the suffering of a wounded lake duck. Self-taught in medicine, Thomas concocted a natural remedy for an 1812 fever that proved fatal throughout Cayuga country but not among the many neighbors who became his patients. In 1816 Thomas made a horseback journey through the nation's western interior, taking close notes on the natural history, topography, geology, agriculture, nascent industry, and commerce of the Wabash and Ohio river valleys. Passing through Buffalo in May 1816, he wrote, "At this place, a ship navigation commences of more than one thousand miles in length. The term of 'INLAND SEAS' may be used here with much propriety; and from its general excellence, the soil that surrounds them, must one day support a vast population. Give their commerce an outlet to the ocean, and these shores will rival in prosperity those of the Mediterranean."

Two months later, on the commissioners' tour of 1816, De Witt Clinton had his lakefront vision at Buffalo. Though they visited Buffalo independently that year, Thomas and Clinton had been acquainted since 1810, when Thomas hosted the first commissioners' tour as it passed through Cayuga County. "[H]e is a poet and great botanist, and careless in his dress," Clinton noted with typical candor in his journal; "He corresponds with Dr. [Benjamin Smith] Barton" of Philadelphia, the author of the first American botany book. Clinton and Thomas subsequently became correspondents themselves on scientific subjects. When Thomas's book about his 1816 western travels was published early in

1819, the governor bought a dozen copies and remarked to a fellow commissioner, "The man who wrote that book will make an excellent canal engineer." By summer Thomas was on his way to such a new career: Clinton appointed him at the top rate of $5 a day to investigate the question of the western terminus. In this role, Thomas became as much a Buffalo hero as its own Samuel Wilkeson, but the final resolution did not happen quickly.

Thomas's sudden insertion into the top rank of Erie engineers was not wholly welcome among the increasingly professional engineering staff. Chief Wright would closely monitor Thomas on report writing ("giving Items and the expense of each may lead to difficulty and error if made public"), management ("there must be a congeniality of minds in comparative description to communicate between persons understandingly"), and especially design: "*always regard form and conform to natural obstacles so as to have persons of judgment see after the Canal is formed why curves and sinuosities were made*—this constitutes and exhibits the skill of the Engineer and is always beautiful." The poet, naturalist, and Clinton compeer would have to prove himself a capable engineer, and an engineer capable of independent judgment.

Thomas's first stop as an engineer was Black Rock, where the anti-Clintonian Porters and their partners in the newly formed Black Rock Harbor Company presented their own harbor improvement plans: a thirteen-hundred-foot dam from the banks of the Niagara River out to Squaw Island midstream, an embankment along the low mile-long island, and a five-hundred-foot pier extending south to Bird Island where the river met Lake Erie. The dam would raise the level of the river to that of the lake so it could supply water to the canal as far as Lockport. Thomas listened and then moved on to Buffalo.

Thomas reviewed the details of Peacock's long-pier plan and endorsed it, with modifications. He recommended an additional 1,150-foot leg, set at a slightly different angle to the shore, and log cribs filled with stone and gravel, instead of solid stone. The cheaper construction would bring the total cost in well below the state-authorized $12,000 loan.

In his October 1819 report, presented to the legislature the following February, Thomas officially threw his support to Buffalo. Though larger and safer from gales than the Buffalo harbor, the Black Rock harbor would be of uncertain but substantial expense to build. Its channel would be too narrow for sailing vessels working upwind. The location would still be highly susceptible to damage by current-driven ice in winter and to easy capture from the opposite shore in war. And, Thomas pointedly noted, any upset to a Black Rock harbor terminal would threaten use of the entire canal. Thomas's report encouraged Samuel Wilkeson.

Wilkeson had been raised and minimally schooled on a Pittsburgh-area farm; his father was a Scots-Irish immigrant and Revolutionary War veteran. By 1809, when he was twenty-eight, Wilkeson was a former Ohio farmer and a pioneer Chautauqua County boat builder and lake and river trader, especially in Onondaga salt, at what became Westfield on Lake Erie. After building boats for a stranded American army during the War of 1812 and participating in the unsuccessful defense of Buffalo, he moved to the burned settlement at the end of the war with his wife and their several children and opened a general store, the first of many successful business ventures in Buffalo.

Wilkeson immediately emerged as the leader of a community beset with drifters, discharged soldiers, and other frontier dregs. In the spring of 1815 his fellow settlers compelled him to become justice of the peace. The position was reluctantly taken but diligently pursued. "His methods may sometimes have been extra-judicial, for he knew little of the law, but he was a terror to evildoers. Punishment for misdeeds was swift and sure, and in a short time he had made Buffalo again a law-abiding community." Tall and stern (with an extraordinary likeness to Andrew Jackson), eloquent, and eventually literate well beyond his formal education, the merchant-builder became a county judge, state senator, and in 1836 Buffalo's still best-regarded mayor. "This man was a king among men," wrote his namesake youngest son forty years after his father's death. "Men obeyed him without loss of self-respect. . . . He moved masses of men and did not excite jealousy. . . . His knowledge was prodigious. His imagination was extraordinarily rich. His humor was fine. Through all his life men considered it a privilege to hear him talk. The graphic art with words was his." Wilkeson began earning his epitaph—*Urbem Condidit*—building a harbor to bring the canal to Buffalo.

Wilkeson had not been among the original nine would-be financiers of Buffalo's harbor in the spring of 1819. At the time, he had been preoccupied; his wife Jane was sick. She was the daughter of his father's closest friend—a fellow Scots-Irish immigrant and revolutionary veteran—and the mother of their six children, including Wilkeson's two-year-old namesake. Since their marriage seventeen years earlier when she was eighteen and he twenty, they had experienced together the pioneer life as far west as Ohio, enlarging their family throughout before settling and thriving in Buffalo. In April 1819 she died, and for a period he mourned.

Finally, toward the end of 1819, Wilkeson joined with the two remaining backers—Charles Townsend and Oliver Forward—to revive the harbor project. By the following May, a year into the deepening national depression, Wilkeson, Townsend, and Forward had pledged personal property for twice the loan value as required and were making preparations to build Buffalo's harbor.

Meanwhile, though Thomas's report appeared to be convincing, the commissioners hesitated, Clinton included. In early 1820 they reported that a final decision on Buffalo or Black Rock was "premature." Surveys to date were not "affording all the information which is desirable" in determining how and to where the canal should run from Tonawanta Creek.

Regardless, Wilkeson pressed forward. A contractor was hired to oversee the Buffalo harbor work. His name is lost to posterity, but his expertise was evidently deficient. He was quickly dismissed and Wilkeson—no engineer but a veteran of building things that had to survive in water—resolutely took over direction of the work himself.

For the next six months Buffalo settlers worked from dawn to dusk in all weather. By the time winter closed in, they had completed a pier of stone-filled timber cribs reaching 850 feet from the mouth of Buffalo Creek. The following spring, Wilkeson ingeniously built a temporary dam across the creek and waited as the creek backed up with spring rains and melting snow. When the dam was intentionally burst, the flood raced out of the creek and washed away the sandbar, creating a channel twelve feet deep inside the pier. Over the remaining warm months of 1821, the pier was extended twelve hundred feet.

As he moved boldly forward at lakeside, Wilkeson made a bold move on Ellicott, who had remained aggressively unwilling to commit any company resources to the harbor effort. Now the acknowledged leader of Buffalo, Wilkeson led the successful effort to have the "ungentlemanly, morose, inaccessible, inhospitable and abusive" agent removed from the company he had served for two decades.

Five days after Ellicott's reluctant resignation from the Holland Company, Buffalo and Black Rock both suffered a blow to their aspirations. In the predawn of November 1, 1821, a violent storm wrecked the three-year-old *Walk-in-the-Water*, on the shore just south of Buffalo's incomplete harbor. It was a graphic demonstration of how unlikely it was that any man-made harbor could protect ships from the worst Lake Erie weather.

Undaunted, the Buffalo forces sent a memorial a few weeks later to the incoming legislature asking that Buffalo be declared the canal terminus and that construction of the canal from the Tonawanta Creek to Buffalo begin. At the same time, the canal commissioners ordered their top engineers to investigate and report on the terminus dilemma. Presently seen separately in the disputed region were James Geddes and Nathan Roberts, both rumored to be advocates of Black Rock. "All well and in high spirits at Black Rock," wrote Porter partner James Barton early in January 1822.

Wilkeson, meanwhile, had been hard at work in Albany. By the time of a crucial February meeting of the commissioners to work out their upcoming annual report, Wilkeson had met more than a dozen times with Clinton. Whether their discussions among themselves and with others had any untoward influence is unknown, but on February 12 principal engineers Wright, White, and Thomas, and assistant engineer Roberts gave their unanimous opinion to the commissioners that "the canal ought to terminate in Buffalo creek." Only principal engineer Geddes came out for Black Rock. He argued that at only thirty acres of anchorage, the Buffalo harbor would be less than a quarter the size of Black Rock's and never be safe from "the stress of weather." Two weeks later, the commissioners sided with the engineering majority and reported to the legislature in favor of Buffalo.

As if on cue, a late winter storm blew up on the lake in mid-March. Two hundred fifty feet of Wilkeson's pier collapsed into the unfinished harbor. The sandbar, so ingeniously flooded away a year earlier, reformed at a harbor-blocking two-and–a-half-foot depth. Wilkeson quit Albany and hurried home. The Porters remained at Albany, lobbying without challenge for the first time since the commissioners' report.

As the legislative session dwindled down in early April, the commissioners suddenly advised the assembly that now they were unanimous in their uncertainty. Termination of the canal at Buffalo would provide ample lake water to the western end of the canal, but the newly obstructed harbor proved that the location was "not free from doubt and difficulty." Geddes, meanwhile, had offered a modified plan for a Black Rock harbor. The commissioners now acknowledged it "would undoubtedly afford a large, commodious, and elegant basin." Still, they hedged, "the permanency of the works" was unknown. The commissioners therefore suggested that if the legislature authorized or encouraged harbor work at both places, the commissioners would convene out there later in the spring to make "the necessary examinations, and a final decision on the question."

Accordingly, on April 17, the final day of the 1822 session, the legislature by nearly unanimous votes evened the score. The commissioners were given discretion to contract for a Black Rock harbor on the Geddes plan to be completed by the end of 1823, while the Buffalonians were given the same amount of time to reopen their harbor entrance to an eight-foot depth.

By the time the commissioners met at a Buffalo tavern in June 1822, the citizens of Buffalo had heroically employed their limited resources and labor over three months to clear the obstructed harbor. Wilkeson and Porter presented their respective plans and arguments to the commissioners, and engineers Wright, Thomas, and White. Black Rock supporters Geddes and Roberts were elsewhere, the former in Ohio consulting on nascent canal efforts there, the latter consumed with work at Lockport.

Despite their earlier promise of a final decision, the best the commissioners could come up with was another temporary arrangement. If

Black Rock was successful "in a fair experiment" to build a pier of at least ten rods that survived the 1823 winter, the commissioners pledged to contract with Black Rock for a complete harbor. At the same time, the commissioners raised Buffalo's hopes with an order that contracting should begin for two miles of canal line from the southern end of the proposed Black Rock harbor to Little Buffalo Creek, which flowed into the main creek that emptied at Buffalo. Neither Buffalo nor Black Rock could claim victory as the anointed canal terminus. The commissioners admittedly had "postpone[d] the ultimate decision of the harbor question" for at least another year.

Whatever private or political interest was operating on the commissioners and engineers, it was clear that in 1822 they were truly uncertain, or at least lacked a consensus, about the correct choice, especially with the related work at Lockport only getting underway slowly. It was at their Buffalo meeting in June that the commissioners took over the stalled Deep Cut excavation from its overmatched contractors. The commissioners as a group were in no hurry to make an engineering (or political) mistake at the lake.

The failure to settle matters in 1822 sparked a yearlong war of attrition between Buffalo and Black Rock. Peter Porter oversaw the successful beginnings of Black Rock's pier, while the rival villages vilified each other by newspaper, pamphlet, broadside, and not so private correspondence. Even the engineers and commissioners were drawn in. David Thomas wrote publicly of the "disregard of truth, distortion of facts, and malicious aspersions" of the Black Rockers, who were "on the wrong and weaker side." Geddes and Roberts, both of whom had openly resented the sudden elevation of Thomas to engineer, became devoted Black Rock partisans to counter his alliance with Buffalo, whose greatest proponent was Thomas mentor Clinton. A Buffalo pamphlet published over the winter called the Black Rock harbor project "wild and unattainable," and accused Niagara portage monopolist Porter of subversively pursuing his traditional opposition to the canal reaching either Buffalo or Black Rock. In Black Rock's first newspaper, which he just had established, Porter complained of "the machinations of a cold-blooded conspiracy, entered into by some half a dozen men in Buffalo, to destroy my character and consideration in the community." The Black Rock *Beacon* ran affidavits of captains whose ships had grounded on Buffalo's notorious sandbar during the winter. In January 1823 Wilkeson delayed a Porter lobbying trip to Albany by sending a delegation of Buffalonians to Black Rock to verify Porter's claims about the sufficiency of his experimental pier.

The commissioners gathered again on the western front in late June 1823. By then, much had changed politically. Clinton was no longer governor, and the Bucktails controlled all of Albany, with visions of purging the canal commission of Clinton, Holley, and Van Rensselaer. Meeting at Black Rock, the commission's Bucktail majority proclaimed the harbor work there "reasonably safe and permanent" and voted to make a contract with Porter to complete his harbor on the Geddes plan. Clinton's was the only dissent; Van Rensselaer abstained. Holley actually went with the Bucktail majority, apparently either from political pressure or a conviction beyond his allegiances of Black Rock's superior possibilities.

"[T]he extraordinary and unexpected decision of the canal board [is] a decision, that I cannot account for in any reasonable way," exclaimed Buffalo harbor planner William Peacock. Clinton comprehended the longer view. He was convinced that Buffalo's harbor was the likeliest to succeed in the end. Now, as he saw it, instead of constant attention on Buffalo's troublesome sandbar, the pressure would be on Black Rock to build a harbor safe from the Niagara's currents and ice. When and if Black Rock's harbor failed, the public would blame the Bucktail commissioners who authorized it and pressured all but Clinton to support it.

The editor of the more moderate of Buffalo's two weeklies was ready to concede defeat: "As the die is cast, it is of little use to us to quarrel with the commissioners or our neighbors at Black Rock." Black Rock's paper appeared humble in victory: "The cause of the quarrel having ceased, the feelings we have enlisted in it, are at an end, and we trust that neither the 'rod' nor the pen may again interpose, to interrupt our confidential anticipations of harmony and good fellowship." Then, the knife: "If there were ever a people who had reason to be satisfied with themselves, it is the people of Black Rock."

To appearances, Black Rock had won. Time would prove the victory Pyrrhic and Clinton prescient. One conciliatory editor excepted, Buffalo never accepted the June 1823 results as final. Legislative and other tactics ensued for several more years, with ambiguous results.

In the meantime, if Buffalo could not have the official canal terminus harbor, it could have the canal. In June 1822 the commissioners had authorized the continuation of the canal through Black Rock to Buffalo. That guaranteed Buffalo at least a share of the eventual glory.

The first contractors for the several canal miles between the villages made little progress in the first year. The effort began anew on August 9, 1823, with the festive digging of the first dirt in Buffalo, on two short sections contracted by Major John G. Camp, a Buffalo pioneer.

"All were invited to come into the village from the surrounding country to take part in helping the great work," recalled William Hatch, then the nineteen-year-old son of a new Buffalo settler. Hatch had yoked a team of family oxen to the largest plow he could find and stood by while, beneath the national flag planted at the site, clergymen offered prayers and a half dozen early Buffalonians turned ceremonial shovels. Then, to accompanying cannon fire and marching music, "the word was given to 'go lang Buck,' and with our big plow and strong team we turned up the black mold and sod" along the staked canal line.

Diggers following the plow gained energy from "the only refreshment furnished" by Major Camp: "simply pure whiskey that was provided bountifully and in true western style," that is, in barrels "with part of the head cut out and a tin dipper lying by and all were expected to help themselves." The placing of whiskey barrels had been adopted elsewhere along the line as an incentive to hired laborers, often priming them for illicit evenings. At Buffalo it was no more than frontier etiquette. "Those were not the days of strict temperance in Western New York, nor was total abstinence so necessary as in these later years," Hatch observed near the end of his long life. "All of our house and barn raisings, logging and husking bees, in fact all rejoicing and festal assemblies were accompanied with a good supply of ardent drink."

The Buffalo *Patriot* reported only that "the citizens partook of a beverage furnished by the contractor." Urbane eastern papers, however, later

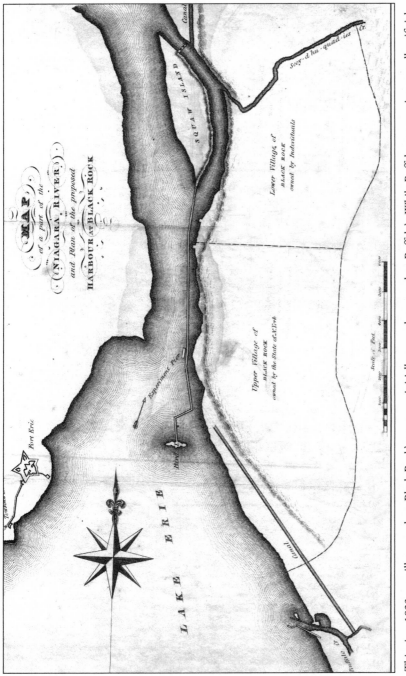

This circa 1823 map illustrates how Black Rock's prospects initially seemed greater than Buffalo's. While Buffalo was creating a small artificial harbor with a breakwater zigzagging out into tempestuous Lake Erie, Black Rock was fashioning nearly two miles of artificial harbor, from the dam where the canal entered the Niagara River near the northern tip of Squaw Island, all the way out to Bird Island on the lake. Soon enough, the canal line would be continued directly to Buffalo and storm-driven ice would wreck Black Rock's piers and dreams. (*Historical Collections of the Great Lakes, Bowling Green State University*)

snorted that the frontier celebration had been "a wild orgie." Eastern editors were unaware that Major Camp was a sober Episcopalian and the first sheriff of Erie County.

Camp did sin that day, but it was not in providing whiskey; it was in failing to provide proper wheelbarrows. Instead, there were eight-by-two-foot boards nailed between pairs of long poles. Camp fancied them "hand-barrows," but "we who used them that day called them soul carts, it being such hard work to use them." Nevertheless, Hatch and his supposed fellow orgiasts set to the work with spirit: "On these the earth and sods were piled and then with one man at each end and between the poles they were carried out beyond the stakes. All took a hand in carrying earth . . . from the honored judge down to the schoolboy urchin."

The active canal work between Buffalo and Black Rock soon made it apparent to some observers that Black Rock had won a harbor but Buffalo had won the canal. "Buffalo Creek . . . furnishes a very commodious harbor for its shipping," observed a visiting schoolteacher in the spring of 1824. "The Erie Canal will terminate here and receive a principal feeder from the mouth of this creek." Officially, however, both places were building harbors, and neither was yet assured of commercial dominance over the other.

In one sense, the Black Rock versus Buffalo controversy was no more than "a neighbourhood quarrel," as David Thomas tried to dismiss it. But it was also a battle in the war for political control of the state that rivaled Virginia for control of the nation. New York Republicans gathered under Martin Van Buren's Bucktail flag wanted all trace of Clinton and his followers eliminated from New York politics. Van Buren, ambitiously engaged as a U.S. senator in a realignment of national politics that eventually would lead him to the presidency, had come to understand that his ascent to the White House as the first president from the Empire State would be facilitated by Clinton's creation of the Erie Canal. Sensitive that any attack on Clinton might destroy the popular support that Van Buren needed in New York, he had dissuaded his followers from throwing former governor Clinton off the canal commission in 1823.

By early 1824, however, Clinton had notions of challenging for the presidency in a crowded field. A dozen years earlier he had nearly succeeded in toppling incumbent Madison. Now Clinton stood at the head of New York's new People's Party, an amalgam of state and national interests that looked both to influence the presidential race and loosen the Bucktail grasp on Albany. The Black Rock–Buffalo battle was a microcosm of near-term New York politics. The Bucktails and Black Rock won on paper, but Clinton and Buffalo soon claimed the true victory.

In the meantime, regardless of the outcome out west, certain Albany Bucktails were eager for Clinton's head in 1824. They tested their aim on a softer target, Myron Holley. He had voted for Black Rock with the canal commission's Bucktail majority in 1823, a decision by the longtime acting commissioner with which political ally Clinton took no issue. If it was also calculated to win some favor with the Bucktails, it failed. As treasurer of the canal commission and acting commissioner of the western section, Holley had long been a target of anti-Clintonians, but his admirable record in securing contracts at low prices and drafting the commissioners' articulate annual reports shielded him from trouble. Then came the legislative session of 1824, a season filled with portent at the state and national levels.

Partly in connection with the unresolved western terminus issue, but mostly as a fishing expedition for rumored financial improprieties, the Bucktail-controlled assembly in February 1824 demanded an accounting from each of the four acting commissioners of all their expenditures. At the end of March, Bucktails Bouck, Seymour, and Young provided paperwork clearing their accounts. Holley could not.

Since 1816, originally as commission treasurer and for many years as the only acting commissioner on the Erie canal, Holley had disbursed over $2.5 million. That was half a million more than Seymour and more than Bouck and Young combined. But in early 1824 he could not account for just under $30,000, roughly 1 percent of the money that had passed through his hands over eight years.

It was a small but real impropriety. Reporting to the assembly on March 30, Holley unfortunately took an aggressive approach. Since his appointment as treasurer and subsequently as acting commissioner, he had devoted himself exclusively to his official duties, "under all vicissitudes and apprehensions, with constant, persevering, and lively zeal." He had been "withdrawn from the education" of his children, "had relinquished the enjoyments of domestic life—had encountered, without flinching, all the dangers of sickness, in seasons and situations, eminently unhealthy, whenever and wherever" his duties had required. This all was true—similar words had been written publicly about him five years earlier at the opening of the first canal section between Rome and Utica—but it was also true that Holley had used the $30,000 to buy land for himself at Brockport and other places under his administration along the western section line.

As an acting commissioner, Holley earned a substantial $2,500 salary. Now he argued that the state should compensate him for his unpaid services as commission treasurer, in an amount equal to what he saw as justifiable real estate speculation with public money. This argument met a chilly reception in a hostile assembly gearing up for an embarrassing investigation. On April 8 Holley resigned.

His closest allies were horrified at Holley's revelations and self-righteous attitude. Even Clinton, scrupulous to an impecunious fault with public money over his long career, found his friend's conduct "very reprehensible." "If my conduct . . . was reprehensible," Holley later wrote to his wife, "it is difficult to distinguish it from Seymour's." If this was true, Seymour did a better job of covering his tracks, although his tracks had no Bucktails dogging them.

In 1825 Holley would repay the state with real and personal property, reducing his large family to near poverty, an indication that he hardly had been enriched by his malfeasance. Three years later, a more sympathetic legislature would restore the property to him, which Holley alone interpreted as exoneration. Ruined in regular society, he soon devoted himself to heartfelt causes: first anti-Masonry, then antislavery, for both of which he became an influential editor and local and national political organizer. The abolitionist Liberty Party, of which he was a founder, erected a monument at his modest grave in Rochester, where he died impoverished in 1841.

Holley's quick resignation from the canal commission emboldened certain Albany Bucktails. Six days after Holley went down with barely a fight, Clinton's enemies lifted daggers for him in the final fifteen minutes of the legislative session. At a quarter to noon on April 12, Rochester lawyer John Bowman stood up in the senate chamber and introduced a brief resolution just handed to him by a colleague who moments earlier had received the go-ahead from an ally crossing the hall from the assembly chamber. Devised, it was later revealed, the night before by lieutenant governor and Clinton-hater Erastus Root, without the approval of the wiser but Washington-based Van Buren, it was a resolution calling for Clinton's removal as canal commissioner.

Without any discussion or debate about why or whether Clinton should be removed, the motion passed quickly by a 21–3 vote. Eight senators had already left the chamber. In the rush of final senate business, many of those who voted yes didn't fully understand what they were voting on and the broader implications.

With the clock ticking toward the noon adjournment, the resolution was run into the assembly chamber, where it "was received with unmingled astonishment" by the majority of members, who knew nothing about it: "A sort of panic seemed to prevail, and men looked at each other with fixed and unutterable amazement."

Some assemblymen had already left the chamber; remaining members had been clearing their desks and putting on overcoats. In the bustle, two minor members exclaimed briefly against the resolution, to little effect. Then, as "others stood hesitating and abashed," one of the youngest assemblymen became sensible to what was happening. Thirty-three-year-old Henry Cunningham of Montgomery County "was not an educated man, but was a man of genius, warm hearted and naturally eloquent." He "with difficulty obtained the floor" and, standing overcoat in arm on the floor of the chamber, delivered a ten-minute lecture, a "torrent of eloquent denunciation against the authors of this deed."

I hope there is yet a redeeming spirit in this house—that we will not be guilty of so great an outrage . . . The senate, it appears, have been actuated by some cruel and malignant passion unaccounted for, and have made a rush upon this house and taken us on surprise. The resolution may pass, but if it does, my word for it, we are disgraced in the judgment and good sense of an injured but intelligent community. Whatever the fate of this resolution may be, let it be remembered that Mr. Clinton has acquired a

reputation not to be destroyed by the pitiful malice of a few leading partizans of the day. When the contemptible party strifes of the present day
shall have passed by, when the political bargainers and jugglers, who now
hang round this capitol for subsistence, shall be overwhelmed and forgotten . . . the pen of the future historian . . . will do him justice, and erect
to his memory a proud monument of fame as imperishable as the splendid works which owe their origin to his genius and perseverance.

Righteously indignant, Cunningham asserted that Clinton's "doings
as a canal commissioner are unimpeached, and unimpeachable, and
such as have even elicited the plaudits and admiration of his political
enemies. This . . . is the official character of the man whom we now seek
to destroy."

No Bucktail wasted time offering contrary evidence. The resolution
was put promptly to a vote. The assemblymen remaining voted 64–34 to
remove Clinton, put on their overcoats, and fled into the noonday sun.

In fact, the removal motion, as Cunningham and some others had realized, had been designed only to seem like an effort to remove Clinton.
It was not supposed to pass. The deeper design had been to affect the fall
presidential election.

While Van Buren and his closest Albany cronies favored Georgia's
William Crawford, the more popular early favorite in New York was
John Adams of Massachusetts. State presidential electors were still named
by the legislature; supporters of Adams or Andrew Jackson or Henry
Clay, gathered into the new People's Party with which Clinton was now
associated, were promoting a bill to have electors named by popular vote.
Clinton, lobbying hard for this reform, quietly imagined it raising him to
the top of the presidential contenders list.

Only after it unexpectedly passed the assembly was the motion to remove Clinton from the canal commission recognized in the national
press as "one of the deepest finesses ever played by politicians," "a mere
political *ruse de guerre*, to operate on the presidential election!" Clintonian editor William Stone, with informants and his own watchful eyes on
the legislative chambers, was among the few who fully understood what
the renegade Bucktails were doing: "Availing themselves of the supposed

unpopularity of Mr. Clinton at that moment, they hoped at once to extinguish all clamour upon the subject of the electoral law, and ruin the cause of Mr. Adams, by identifying the friends of this measure and this candidate, with what they were pleased to consider the broken fortunes of the illustrious individual then suffering the pains of political banishment." The expected majority of legislators who would vote *against* the unjustifiable removal motion, sponsored in the senate by known Crawford backer Bowman, could then be tagged as supporters of Clinton, electoral change, and Adams, allowing Crawford to find his way to the presidency thanks to New York.

The flaws in the plot were two. The majority of legislators still in Albany during the eleventh hour were only too willing to dump Clinton without cause. And the vast majority of the public was only too willing afterward to raise him on their shoulders.

Cunningham's impassioned speech was printed four days later in a Clintonian Albany newspaper, but the verdict on the legislature's action was already in. Nobody cared about the politics, only about the injustice to the sponsor of New York's great canal. As soon as word came down the Hudson from Albany, New York City's leading editors competed for words to express their unanimous disgust. "The envenomed malignity," wrote the *Evening Post* a day before the printing of Cunningham's reproach

> which displayed itself on this occasion, the ungrateful return for 14 years of mental and bodily exertion on the part of Mr. Clinton, to ensure success to a measure which will redound to the credit of the state and the honor of the country, and for which no pecuniary compensation has ever been sought for, or accepted, must cause the cheek of every honorable man who calls himself an inhabitant of New York, to glow with a blush of shame and indignation.

"We cannot believe this most unjust measure will meet with the approbation of the respectable citizens of this great state," the *Daily Advertiser* chimed in the same day. "To Mr. Clinton's policy they are indebted, for all the advantages which this gigantic work promises to them and their posterity, to all future generations. We shall be too much disappointed if they, as a body, do not express in a most decided manner, their resentment for a measure which not merely disgraces those by whom it was adopted, but degrades and discredits the character of the state."

The disgust extended far beyond the Clintonian press. The New-York *American* called it "a littler act of little minds, a more pitiful and contemptible exhibition of impotent malice, was never recorded in any legislative annals." The Boston *Commercial Gazette* described it as "Political Lunacy . . . as gross and foolish an abuse of power as was ever recorded. . . . [Clinton] is at this late hour of his life insulted by a band of unprincipled demagogues."

From Washington, Van Buren himself was outraged at the foolish scheming of his provincial lieutenants, especially Saratoga judge and former senator Roger Skinner, the former dispenser of Bucktail patronage from the final Council of Appointment who was eventually exposed as the manager of the misbegotten plot: "I hope, Judge, you are now satisfied that there is such a thing in politics as *killing a man too dead*." Within months Skinner himself was dead, in Van Buren's arms, literally mortified by his colossal political blunder.

"[A] glorious exit—equal in renown to that of Aristides," an old friend privately counseled Clinton a week after the removal: "Those fellows can not beat the lustre of your deeds—it humbles them in the dust. I rather should prefer the most outrageous removal above a vote of thanks of a similar gang." "Never was there a meaner act," wrote Clinton, who nonetheless thrilled to the unprecedented public outrage that quickly matured into his political resurrection.

Massive rallies for the martyred canal hero, spontaneous and otherwise, sprang up in New York City, Albany, and elsewhere around the state. Bucktails, back under the direct oversight of Van Buren, whose broader Crawford plans were disintegrating, had no good public explanation for why an unpopular politician but heroic canal commission president and former governor should have been turned out of his canal office in a nefarious manner without cause.

In September the People's Party named Clinton for governor. Two months later he defeated the Bucktail candidate, canal commissioner

Samuel Young, by nearly 17,000 out of 190,000 votes. Candidates aligned with Clinton won six of eight open senate races and claimed a two-thirds majority in the assembly.

In the November national election, Crawford polled the fewest popular votes among the quartet of nominally Republican candidates; he carried only Virginia and Georgia. Adams won New England and two-thirds of New York's electoral votes; he eventually was named president by the House on the deciding vote of New York's Stephen Van Rensselaer, the lone surviving Clinton ally on the canal commission and his successor as its president. New York had broken the Virginia Dynasty and had a nearly complete canal that would break Virginia commercially as well. Clinton was out of the canal commission but back in control of New York as it prepared for the opening of its great canal.

"I am elected governor by the greatest majority that was ever given in this state in a contested election," Clinton puffed to New Yorker John Jacob Astor after the results were in, and began imagining himself a presidential contender in 1828. After the Bucktail blunder of 1824 receded and the broader trend in New York politics toward Van Buren's dominance reasserted itself, Clinton would trim his sails.

For the time being, Clinton could crow legitimately to Astor, the richest American, about their city's resurgent economy. A record three thousand new houses had been put up in 1824: "This extraordinary prosperity is principally imputable to the great canals."

The national economy was only just stirring from its long depression, with long-term interest rates hitting a record low of 4.25 percent in 1824. At the same time, $1.5 million worth of 5 percent New York canal bonds were sold in 1824 at premiums well over 10 percent, not the last time that New York's economy would lead the nation out of dire straights.

Canal debt now totaled $7.5 million, but annual toll receipts in 1824 of $325,000 for the first time nearly equaled annual debt service. Just a decade later, total toll revenue would cover the entire cost of the canal. With completion of the canal expected in 1825, thanks to his blundering political enemies Clinton was miraculously positioned as governor to lead the celebrations of the great work that he had overseen for fifteen years.

Less well situated was Clinton's former western ally, Joseph Ellicott. He had been forced to resign from the Holland Company in 1821 after rising protests by predominantly Clintonian settlers against his tyrannical behavior. For three years Ellicott had remained at Batavia in deteriorating mental health. A long, cogent, and well-reasoned letter to the remaining four canal commissioners in the summer of 1824 warning of likely disappointment with Black Rock's harbor suggested that Ellicott was still master of his faculties. By November, however, he had suffered a physical breakdown. Thomas Eddy and other friends advised his travel to New York City for the attention of specialists.

Escorted by a doctor, friends, and relatives, Ellicott left the territory of his fame by chartered canal boat at Albion, bound for Albany and a Hudson River steamer. "Passing down the canal," observed a companion, "he would give his attendants minute and interesting details of its history, the part he had taken in it; and converse upon general topics, in the absence of all indications of impaired intellect. But changing the theme to himself his mind would wander and conjure up fearful apprehensions of present and approaching disease, and their speedy and fatal termination."

A recuperative sea voyage or a visit to "the scenes of his youth" in Maryland had been considered, but immediately after arriving in the city, it was decided to take Ellicott directly to the Bloomingdale Asylum, recently founded and administered by Eddy in upper Manhattan.

Sanatory treatment of what was diagnosed as "inveterate hypocondria, acting upon a very extraordinary mind" did not avail. Some of the patient's scribblings later surfaced:

> It is a strange medley; as perfect an indication perhaps as could be given of his peculiar malady. In a few lines he would seem to be writing to a friend; then in direct connection occurs soliloquies, the subjects, the pathology and prognosis of disease, and its remedies. Occasionally, his sentences are well connected, and his ideas well expressed; generally it is so, until he begins to talk of himself and his own infirmities; then he becomes wild and incoherent; dwells upon his afflictions, imagines that his digestive organs are all out of tune—his whole system undermined by disease and the injudicious use of medicine.

Over the next year a half Ellicott made several suicide attempts. Finally, ten months after the official opening of the canal that Ellicott had been instrumental in creating, he would escape from further torment by the length of his looped handkerchief.

As Ellicott spiraled toward his fate, the final pieces of the canal in his former territory came together. By the end of 1824 the canalized Tonawanta Creek was complete. During the spring of 1825 the nine miles of canal between the Tonawanta and Black Rock were finished. National reports hailed this segment winding along the Niagara River as "remarkably beautiful, having been laid out with great taste and judgment, and faithfully executed."

On the evening of June 4 the gates at Black Rock's harbor were opened and Niagara River water flowed toward the Tonawanta. Peter Porter led a local celebration dubbed "Termination of the Grand Canal." A few months earlier, Rochester's *Monroe Republican* had declared, "Black Rock is destined by nature to take precedence of Buffalo at no distant day." Two months later Buffalo's cherished canal link to Black Rock was filled with Erie water; eventually Erie water would supply the canal all the way to Rochester. In the meantime, the Black Rock–Buffalo rivalry continued.

Hours before Black Rock's canal gates opened, a Lake Erie steamer deposited at Buffalo Marie-Joseph Paul Yves Roch Gilbert du Motier, commonly known to grateful Americans as Lafayette. The Revolutionary War hero was in the midst of a triumphal yearlong American tour. Nine months earlier, at one of his numerous New York City appearances, "The Nation's Guest" (so dubbed by his promoters) had been seated at a huge banquet table hollowed out and lined with lead to display an astonishing sixty-foot-long replica of the Erie Canal: "[A]n extremely limpid water filled the canal, which was bordered with green sod, imitating meadows, in the midst of which were models of houses, trees and animals. Bridges beautifully crossing the stream, and masses of rock under which the canal passed, and forests through which it wound along, all combined to complete this unique masterpiece of topography."

The sixty-seven-year-old Marquis was supposed to have landed at Buffalo at noon but, reported his secretary Levasseur without knowing that this often happened, "violent and contrary wind" prevented the boat from entering the harbor until mid-afternoon. Safely ashore, the Nation's Guest was promptly contested for by competing delegations. Buffalo's Eagle Tavern barely earned its "Lafayette Slept Here" plaque before he was put in a carriage at six the next morning for breakfast with the Porters at Black Rock, "a small but handsome port which rivals that of Buffalo in bustle."

The canal from Black Rock east had been filling overnight in preparation for Lafayette but, alas, not sufficiently for boat travel. So his entourage traveled overland toward Lockport, where a canal boat awaited in the basin below the uncompleted locks.

As Lafayette emerged from the forest, a troop of Lockport citizens on horseback rode out to meet him. They proceeded into town "saluted by an extraordinary kind of artillery" alongside the nearly finished Deep Cut: "Hundreds of small blasts, charged with powder by the workmen engaged in quarrying the bed of the rock to form the canal, exploded almost at the same moment, and hurled fragments of rock into the air, which fell amidst the acclamations of the crowd."

Lockport filled the Frenchmen "with astonishment and admiration." The sounds of hatchet and hammer were everywhere. Trees were being felled and converted on the spot into houses. Yet "luxury already appears in the light wagons drawn by splendid horses." On the large public square, "which exists as yet only in project, an immense hotel already opens its doors to new settlers, who have not any other habitation." Lafayette's secretary had never "seen the activity and industry of man conquering nature so completely as in this growing village."

The canal's effect on America was manifest: "[I]n the midst of these encroachments of civilization on savage nature, there is going on, with a rapidity that appears miraculous, that gigantic work, that grand canal, which, in tightening the bonds of the American Union, spreads comfort and abundance in the wilds through which it passes." As Lafayette had helped create the nation, he now beheld the creation that helped make it great. His tour glided east along the canal to similar receptions, wonder, and validation at Rochester, Syracuse, and on to Albany

Three weeks after Lafayette graced Lockport, its locks were complete. The celebration on the morning of June 24 featured obligatory Masonic content. All of Lockport crowded around garbed Masons ringing the locks. Reverend Francis Cuming, Rochester's first pastor, delivered his blessing: "The mountains have been levelled; the vallies have been filled; rivers and gulfs have been formed over them, by the exertions of art, a channel in which the waters of the distant Hudson, the waters of the still more distant Atlantic, will unite with the waters of the remote west, and constitute a river." Reverend Cuming acknowledged the contributions of everyone, from commissioners and engineers down to the lowest of his fellow Masons: "Let us remember also that those who have served only as entered apprentices, especially those who here have stretched the line and handled other implements of their art, richly deserved to be passed and raised, to higher degrees, and to be received and acknowledged as Most Excellent Masters." The reverend did not remember the twelve hundred Irish who had labored at Lockport, of whom hundreds were on hand. The ceremony closed with engineer Roberts placing the capstone in the uppermost of his locks.

Mason Grand Master Cuming's sin of Irish omission went unpunished that day, but his future clouded the following year. "The enemies of our order—may they find a grave six feet deep, six feet long, and six feet due east and west," he reportedly shouted at a Masonic banquet from which revelers dispersed to murder heretical Mason William Morgan. Implicated in Morgan's notorious disappearance and probable drowning, Cuming resigned from his Rochester pulpit and disappeared himself into the Michigan Territory.

Four months after Nathan Roberts capped his locks, the first boat to transit them rose like magic up the mountain of water, an experience "calculated to bewilder the senses" of inaugural passenger Ira Blossom: "Unmoved as I usually am by surrounding objects, I am willing to confess that I was more astonished than I ever was by anything I had ever before witnessed." A decade later Ellicott's successor as Holland Company agent was bewildered again: a mob of neglected settlers laid siege to the company office in Batavia, trapping Blossom inside until he met their demands.

Lockport's locks were quickly renowned around the country and Europe, a perennial subject for painters and writers. Southern poet and children's editor Caroline Gilman, a best seller in her day, beheld Lockport in 1836: "Here the great Erie Canal has defied nature, and used it like a toy; lock rises upon lock, and miles are cut in the solid stone."

Eight Independence Days after missing the Erie Canal groundbreaking at Rome, De Witt Clinton hoisted a shovel and, to the cheers of a large crowd, thrust into fresh earth. A fellow governor followed, and chief engineer David Bates came after them. The other governor was host Jeremiah Morrow of Ohio. The ceremony was on July 4, 1825, at Newark, Ohio, midway between Cleveland on Lake Erie and Portsmouth on the Ohio River. This was the groundbreaking for the Ohio & Erie Canal, the long-contemplated project that, with the Empire State's great canal, would join the Hudson with the Mississippi, New York City with New Orleans.

On Clinton's recommendation, James Geddes had begun surveys for Ohio's canal in 1822, and Bates had continued them before being named chief engineer early in 1825. Likewise, the borrowed services of Wright, White, Roberts, Jervis, and other Erie-made engineers were increasingly in demand by states and new incorporations suddenly clamoring for great canals of their own.

Clinton's visit to Ohio was brief. After touring the staked route of its canal, he hurried home to plan the incredible celebration that would officially inaugurate the nation's canal mania and confirm his own place in history.

CHAPTER 12

Ten Days That Shook New York

[A] massive demonstration of the Enlightenment faith in progress which animated the first century of the Republic.

—John Seelye, "Rational Exultation: The Erie
Canal Celebration of 1825" (1985)

Of all the celebrants at the western end of the extravagant Erie Canal opening festivities, few could have felt more gratification than Jesse Hawley. His had been a very long haul. His newspaper essays of 1807 and 1808 were the first published arguments proposing the great canal. He had written them under cover of a pseudonym while serving time in debtors' prison as a broken pioneer grain merchant of Western New York. Since then he had found unhappiness in family and marital relations but considerable, if regional, success in business and political affairs.

As Hercules, Hawley's essays had sparked the imaginations of influential men and were carried by the first commissioners on their initial exploration of the frontier territory he proposed to cross with a canal. Unlike Founding Father and frustrated canaller Gouverneur Morris, who died clinging to a vision of Lake Erie spilling across the state into the Hudson in a massive inclined plane, Hawley had retreated from that impractical high ground and embraced a traditional canal of locks and levels. Eighteen years after Hawley's essays, the Great Western Canal, or Erie Canal as it quickly became universally known, had been completed along a course and at a cost remarkably similar to what he had first suggested.

In October 1825 Hawley was no longer the effusive maniac conjuring a ship canal a hundred feet wide and ten feet deep atop a towering linear mound, but the prescient projector of the route taken and the money needed. Only three months earlier, he had finally acknowledged publicly, in a Rochester newspaper, that he had been Hercules, his essays "written when all my private prospects were blighted." Finally he had "by laborious industry, attained from bankruptcy to a comfortable moderate competency" that enabled revelation. Now, Jesse Hawley was the chairman of Rochester's official delegation to the canal celebration.

Although Black Rock and Buffalo were in full competition for primacy at the western end of the canal, the celebration in a state governed by DeWitt Clinton would begin at Buffalo. At nine-thirty in the morning, after a parade as large as Buffalo itself, Clinton, Hawley, and others boarded the brand new *Seneca Chief*, Buffalo-built of local red cedar. The boat was waiting at the head of the canal to lead a flotilla on a triumphant parade east to Albany and then down the Hudson to New York City. As a sign of his rising regional stature and acknowledgment of his Herculean past, Hawley had been selected to deliver the sendoff speech from the deck of the *Seneca Chief*.

Hawley spoke with wisdom and brevity that would prove rare for speechmakers in villages, towns, and cities over the next ten days. The canal, Hawley addressed the crowd, had opened "the grand epoch of uniting the waters of the great Inland Mediterraneans of North America, with those of the commercial Atlantic." As neatly as Hercules had laid out the idea, Hawley memorably encapsulated its execution: "An epoch that will be recorded in the tablets of history, as among the greatest events of our Nation—for having in 8 years—with 8 million of Dollars—made the longest Canal—in the least time—with the least experience—for the least money—and of the greatest public utility of any other in the world."

After another speech (by Buffalo harbor sponsor Oliver Forward) came the first salvo in the most remarkable exercise of the entire ten-day celebration: the Grand Salute, a thousand-mile artillery telegraph from Lake Erie to the Atlantic Ocean and back. "The firing of heavy cannon along the line of the Erie Canal," mused Clinton while plans were forming, "may afford a good opportunity for some interesting experiments on the phenomena of sound by the use of accurate chronometers at suitable places." The science experiment went undone, but the cannon fire itself would send a resounding message: the sonic representation of the water communication accomplished by the canal.

The artillery pieces had been rounded up from forts and arsenals around the state; some were veteran big guns that had cost less to fabricate than to transport to Lake Erie battles. Rescued from the dustbins of recent history or appointments with the smelter, they were pressed into a final bit of service. The pieces were placed ten to fifteen miles apart, depending on caliber, from Buffalo to Albany to Sandy Hook, where New York City's vast harbor meets the Atlantic. The biggest gun, a thirty-two pounder, was placed at Buffalo, aimed appropriately at the tempestuous lake that Buffalo had subdued with its hard-won harbor.

At 10:00 a.m., the Buffalo gunners fired the big cannon. At the speed of sound, gunners at Tonawanta heard the report from Buffalo and fired their cannon "which belching forth its thunder tones sent the joyful news on the wings of the wind toward the seaboard, where, flying from gun to gun, it arrived in one hour and twenty minutes." Just before one in the afternoon, the Buffalo gun fired again. As it "died away over the waters of the lake," the final blast in the return sequence concluded "this novel first attempt" at communicating between the interior of the United States and the gateway to the Atlantic world.

For Manhattanites, the novel telegraph was more than a passing phenomenon. In a seventeen-minute span starting at 11:17, cannon fired sequentially at Fort Washington on upper Manhattan, Fort Gansevoort at the foot of Christopher Street in what was still the village of Greenwich, the Battery at the southern tip of Manhattan, Governor's Island in the upper harbor, Fort Lafayette at the Narrows, Fort Richmond on the lower harbor, Sandy Hook jutting out into the ocean, and back again on the northward return. The telegraphic communication rang in New Yorkers' ears, and in the mind of recent newcomer Samuel F. B. Morse. Eighteen months later the painter attended electricity lectures that led him away from his studio and toward the invention of the electromagnetic telegraph and the alphabetic communications code that bears his name.

As a practical matter, the first gun had signaled the departure of the boat flotilla from Buffalo, at the canal speed limit of four miles per hour. The *Seneca Chief*, "drawn by four grey horses, fancifully caparisoned," led the procession. Among the passengers were Hawley; lieutenant governor James Tallmadge; canal commission president Stephen Van Rensselaer and his brother Jacob; Benjamin Wright; James Geddes and other engineers; surveyor-general Simeon De Witt; the official representatives of major canal towns (including Buffalo delegation head Samuel Wilkeson); a committee from New York City; editor William Stone, who wrote a narrative of the journey; and two De Witt Clintons, the governor commanding the deck and his full-length portrait ruling the well-appointed cabin.

The allegorical painting featured Clinton in Roman toga posed before a canal lock. The hero is flanked on the left by Hercules—a nod to the essayist—resting after canal labors, and on the right by an uncertain Neptune in a seashell chariot attended by Naiades. Having thrown open the lock, Clinton invites Neptune "to pass through and take possession of the watery regions which the Canal has attached to his former dominions." The god is seen recoiling, "as if confounded by the fact disclosed at the opening of the lock." The Naiades also hesitate, "as if half afraid they were about to invade forbidden regions."

The creator of this scene was, as briefly noted in the lavish official *Memoir* of the celebration festivities, "a Mr. Catlin, miniature-portrait painter." The four-hundred-page *Memoir: Prepared at the Request of a Committee of the Common Council of the City of New York and Presented to the Mayor . . . at the Celebration of the Completion of the New York Canals* was the first American book to use lithography. It featured nearly four-dozen illustrations, by the already accomplished and acclaimed Asher Durand, Anthony Imbert, and Archibald Robertson, among others. George Catlin, who had just given up a frontier Pennsylvania law practice for brushes and paint, contributed several images for the *Memoir*, including drawings of Buffalo's harbor and Lockport's locks and Deep Cut. A year later the portraitist for the *Seneca Chief* would paint the real Seneca chief Red Jacket, before heading west to become the iconic portrayer of the North American Indian, "rescuing the looks and customs of the vanishing races of native man in America from that oblivion to which I plainly saw they were hastening before the approach and certain progress of civilization."

Native man had largely vanished from New York in advance of the civilizing canal that Catlin was hired to evoke in 1825, leaving only props for the last boat in the line out of Buffalo. Among a menagerie of eagles, fawns, a bear, fish, other birds and beasts, plus "creeping things" carried aboard *Noah's Ark* were "two Indian boys, in the dress of their nation." Which native nation was not specified. The concoction of former canal opponent Mordecai Noah, this *Ark* would miss the tide; it would fail to keep pace with the fleet and drop out at Rochester.

The *Seneca Chief* also paid tribute of sorts to its nominal heritage. It carried a canoe "made by the Aborigines inhabiting the shores of Lake Superior." Its emblematic cargo also included potash, flour, and butter from Lake Erie ports as distant as Detroit and Sandusky, white fish from the lake itself, and some special forest products procured in Buffalo by the heads of New York City's delegation: logs of bird's eye maple and red cedar for fashioning into boxes for commemorative medals and two wooden kegs—"beautifully painted in green with gilded hoops"—filled with Lake Erie water and ceremonial intent.

Another boat, bearing furs, flour, butter, apples, and a determined crew, set the early pace east. In inimitable fashion, Peter Porter had gotten a jump on all the Buffalo celebrants. Porter and the citizenry of Black Rock had ignored Buffalo's formal invitation to attend its ceremony. Instead, Porter led his village's own celebrations earlier in the morning, before boarding the *Niagara* and setting out east ahead of Clinton's fleet. The Clintonians caught up with Black Rock's craft at Lockport. Porter had given the early impression, at least to his partisans, of Black Rock's priority over Buffalo, but the *Niagara* fell into the rear from that point on. The main fleet, meanwhile, graced Black Rock for just a few minutes before moving on toward Lockport.

The boats made a great procession along the canal, with welcomes large and small: artillery rounds, bands, banquets, fireworks, and fulsome speeches. There was a sumptuous dinner in Lockport before Clinton's inland navy took their horse tows after nightfall, receiving "most enthusiastic huzzas" passing through Newport, Holley, and Brockport on the way to Rochester. In the morning on open canal west of Rochester, the procession received its most surprising and gratifying salutations of the entire journey.

Back on July 5, the day after De Witt Clinton lifted a shovel to break ground for the Ohio and Erie Canal, thirty-seven-year-old ship's carpenter Lars Larson, his pregnant twenty-one-year-old wife Martha, and fifty countrymen and women had set sail from Norway in a tiny gaff-rigged coastal fishing sloop, the fifty-four-foot, thirty-nine-ton *Restoration*, bound for New York. They were Norway's first Quakers, escaping Lutheran persecution. They were also the first Norwegian emigrants to the United States, where they had purchased land on Lake Ontario north of Holley.

After a harrowing voyage featuring a wine-drunk sojourn in Madeira and Martha's delivery of a daughter, the "Norse *Mayflower*" sailed up New York Harbor on the morning of October 9. The arrival of America's first Norwegian immigrants brought widespread newspaper coverage and the prompt seizure of their boat and jailing of the captain and crew by customs officials. Under recent American law, of which the Sloopers (as they came to be called) were ignorant, a boat of the *Restoration*'s tonnage could enter U.S. waters with only sixteen passengers. The Norwegians were more than three times over the limit.

While Larson and others remained in Manhattan to sort out their legal troubles, including a $3,150 fine that they had no means of paying, the majority of the Sloopers set out for their American acres, with cash, clothes, and Hudson steam and Erie canal boat tickets donated by New York's Quaker community. On the morning of October 27, between Rochester and Holley, the Sloopers' westbound boat met Clinton's entourage headed east.

Observing canal navigation rules, the eastbound boats stopped and dropped their towropes to the bottom to allow the westbound traffic past. Clinton hailed the passing boat. Its passengers responded loudly in Norwegian. It was a language neither Clinton nor any other aboard the American boats recognized. But the foreignness of it instantly impressed

Clinton with the transformative impact the canal would have on the state and the nation.

Larson, meanwhile, struggled to resolve the Sloopers' legal and monetary affairs. A federal court petition, pleading "utter ignorance" of American laws and language, found its way via influential Quakers to the White House, where John Adams issued a presidential pardon in mid-November, waiving all fines and threatened forfeitures. The local boat market proved sharper, bringing only $400 for the sloop, which had cost three times as much. In early December Larson finally took passage by steamer to Albany, where he found the canal already shut by ice. Legend has it that Lars Larson purchased a pair of skates and in Nordic style strode and glided 290 miles along the frozen canal to rejoin his people.

Regardless of the likelihood of this tale—the canal was drained in the winter of 1825 and every winter thereafter—the Norwegians generally and the Larsons in particular quickly prospered. He became a leading Rochester shipper and boat builder. Over the ensuing decades, he and Martha— "a woman of great intelligence and force of character"—provided food, lodging, money, and materials to thousands of Norwegian immigrants passing by the Erie Canal through Rochester to settle Illinois, Wisconsin, and points west, where Norse Americans still thrive.

Clinton's inspiring encounter with the newest Americans kept spirits warm despite a cold rain at Rochester. Theatrics marked the arrival at two in the afternoon. Undaunted by the weather, crowds lined the banks leading into town. Uniformed militia fired gun salutes. The canal boat *Young Lion of the West*—Rochester's new nickname—guarded the entrance to the Genesee Aqueduct. "Who comes there?" she hailed. "Your Brothers from the West, on the waters of the great Lakes," came the reply from the *Seneca Chief.* "By what means have they been diverted so far from their natural course?" "By the channel of the Grand Erie Canal." "By whose authority, and by whom, was a work of such magnitude accomplished?" "By the authority and by the enterprise of the patriotic People of the State of New York." With that, the fleet was allowed to pass over the Genesee River and into town, and the *Young Lion* passed its audition. In the hold it carried flour, butter, apples, brooms "of a superior quality," and cedar tubs and pails "of very elegant workmanship" by a Rochester crafter. On deck was "a collection of wolves, foxes, racoons [sic], and other living animals of the forest" by which the *Young Lion* supplanted *Noah's Ark* as the fleet's zoo.

The four-hour stop at Rochester featured prayers at the Presbyterian church, a banquet, a ball, and an illumination. The considerable reception attested to the canal's essential role in the village's rising prospects. "After a revolution of eight years we behold the work accomplished," reported the local paper; "its advantages we have already begun to enjoy and the prospect which it opens before us, is bright with anticipated blessings." The village, which didn't exist ten years earlier, had grown in the past five years from 1,500 citizens to 5,300; by the end of the century, the canal-made city of 162,000 would be over half again larger than Dutch-built Albany and second only to Buffalo along the canal line. In 1817 Rochester's first Genesee-powered mills had exported 26,000 barrels of wheat flour, mostly north to Canada. Ten years later, 200,000 barrels of Genesee flour were shipped, mostly east along the canal. By then Rochester counted ten flour mills, including the nation's largest. By the late 1830s twenty-four mills would ship half a million barrels a year from what was then called the Flour City, the country's fifteenth largest city and the largest producer of wheat flour in the world.

The passing fleet was heartily but briefly received on the morning of October 28 at Palmyra, Macedon (where breakfast was served beside a temporary canal-spanning arch proclaiming "Clinton and the Canal" and "Internal Improvements"), and Newark, before lingering during midafternoon at Lyons for a meal and considerable speech making. "From the Halls of the Capitol to lowest bar-room in the state, coarse epithets, and vulgar sarcasms were heaped upon the abbettors [sic] of this project," observed the local editor, crediting the perseverance of the "many steady and firm friends of the canal policy."

Fireworks heralded the nighttime approach to "handsomely illuminated" Clyde, with similar nocturnal displays at Buckville and Port Byron, where "thirty to forty ladies, arrayed in their sweetest smiles and most beautiful attire" graced a post-midnight ball and an illuminated balloon "rose majestically" to point the travelers' way east.

There was no joy in Weedsport, a few miles on. The familiar artillery rounds greeted the approaching flotilla, but shortly after the landing came word that one of the cannon had misfired and "two gunners were blown to atoms." Early morning refreshments at the village inn were abruptly concluded and wives, children, and townsfolk were left to their mourning as the boats slipped away.

Spirits recovered during the six-hour run to Syracuse, "the offspring of the canal," as village president Joshua Forman described it in his formidable welcoming speech:

> This . . . marks a new era in the history of man, the example of a nation whose whole physical power and intelligence are employed to advance the improvement, comfort, and happiness of the people. To what extent this course of improvement may be carried, it is impossible for any mere man to conjecture; but no reasonable man can doubt, that it will continue its progress, until our wide and fertile territory shall be filled with a more dense, intelligent, and happy people, than the sun shines upon in the wide circuit of the globe.

Forman, rich and powerful from wise land speculations, liked to talk, especially to a captive audience.

> It has long been a subject of fearful apprehension to the patriot of the Atlantic states, that the remote interior situation of our western territory (for want of proper stimuli to industry and free intercourse with the rest of the world) would be filled with a semi-barbarous population, uncongenial with their Atlantic neighbours; but the introduction of steamboats on our lakes, and running rivers and canals to connect waters which nature has disjoined . . . have broken down the old barriers of nature, and promise the wide spread regions of the west all the blessings of a seaboard district.

As the author of the 1808 state law that authorized James Geddes's "Eureka" survey, Forman considered himself "the first legislative projector of the greatest improvement of the age." He used his celebration speech to fire away at what he later termed "the over-zealous advocates of Governor Clinton [who] had been in the habit of attributing to him the originating as well as the execution of the canal project." Clinton's "early and decided support . . . turned the poising beam," Forman now put it: "Without his efforts . . . the canal project might still have been a splendid vision—gazed on by the benevolent patriot—but left, by cold calculators, to be realized by some future generation." Turning to the governor, Forman concluded "we will not withhold from you your due meed of praise." Forman's "important views," Clinton pointedly noted in response, were such as he "had expected from an individual who . . . had devoted much thought and reflection to the subject."

The wordplay at Syracuse eased the sorrows over Weedsport, but spirits were mixed at Rome. The artillery telegraph of October 26 had been the signal for Rome's mournful citizens to march south from town to the beat of muffled drums bearing a black barrel of water from the old Western Inland Lock Navigation Company canal. The barrel was emptied into the new Erie canal passing a mile south. When it arrived four mornings later, Clinton's entourage stopped for just an hour. For the old fortress town at the storied Great Carrying Place—the ancient divide and old canoe portage between the eastern and western waters of New York—the future had been told. Rome, the only place along the canal line to lose population over the eight construction years, quickly faded from the western terminus of Mohawk navigation into a canal byway on the long level between Syracuse and Utica.

Passing joyful crowds at the numerous villages and settlements of the upper Mohawk Valley, the fleet pushed on for Utica. Festivities in that canal-prospering city continued from Sunday afternoon well into Monday. A local minister was so moved by the Utica celebrations that he wrote and published a paean to "ruling *genius*" Clinton, a seven-stanza "Ode on the Completion of the Erie Canal" that concluded:

> *Our noble* guest *awakes delight;*
> *From port to port loud thunders greet*
> *His welcome barge; the joyful treat*
> *Sheds mimic day amid the night.*

Now all conspire in one grand cause,
And swell the notes of just applause.
Go, vassal waves, in pomp convey
Down through the state your charge *along!*
While future years revive this day,
And barges float let CLINTON'S name be sung!

The romantic Rev. Charles Giles later mailed his masterpiece to Clinton, whose secretary eventually responded, "Whatever doubts there may be about the merits of the subject, there certainly can be none about those of the poetry." The ink-stained cleric proudly printed the poem and reply (as an appendix to his humorless satire on intemperance), missing the subtlety of the reply.

As the leader of Utica's official delegation bound for New York City, canal pioneer Jonas Platt made a speech before boarding one of the boats. Also boarding at Utica was Charles Brodhead, the early canal surveyor turned bachelor recluse (but wise canal boat company investor).

From Utica, the fleet curtailed shore visits while working down the increasingly steep Mohawk Valley. On All Hallows' Eve, bonfires blazed above the boats as they slipped through the chasm at Little Falls. In darkness they passed old villages of Schoharie Country first settled by the Palatine Germans. Minden, Palatine Bridge, Stone Arabia, Canajoharie, and others were "deprived of the opportunity of giving utterance to their feelings," but the bright and crisp new day brought crowds to the canal banks at Fort Hunter, Florida, and other towns leading down to Schenectady. At Schenectady, the weather and reception perceptibly turned.

Despite boasting the former governor in Joseph Yates and a resolute booster in hotelier Resolved Givens, Schenectady's population in 1825 was a third less than it had been twenty years earlier and still dropping. Already Utica, Rochester, and Buffalo had surpassed the old Dutch town; others would do the same. The canal would curtail Mohawk River navigation and permanently end Schenectady's historic role as a commercial terminus.

Clinton's fleet appeared under grey skies at midafternoon on November 1, two hours ahead of schedule. Schenectady had prepared nothing.

Hastily mustered Union College students in military uniform fired off an impromptu rifle salute. At Givens's Hotel, Clinton and company were given a sullen meal: "There were no cheers, nor, on the contrary, any audible murmurs. On the whole it was a rather grave reception." Within an hour the unwelcome guests returned to their boats, accompanied by a drizzling rain and the Union militia boys: "[E]ach drew a blanket from his knapsack, and in a moment the graceful youths were metamorphosed in their apparel to the appearance of a band of Indians."

As if on cue, the dreary weather lifted overnight while the boats locked down toward Albany. By mid-morning on November 2 the "banks of the Canal were lined with people, and the roads were filled with horses and carriages, galloping and whirling towards the scene of the anticipated festivities." Flags stood out in the clearing northwest breeze as the boats descended Lock No. 1 and entered the canal basin to the accompaniment of a twenty-four-gun salute. Bands played as the canal boats picked up tows from sailing yawls and paraded along the riverfront. The lock's great collapse of a year earlier was a distant memory.

In due course, Clinton and the canallers were landed for ceremonies at the capitol and throughout the city. The evening featured the obligatory lighting displays and a banquet for six hundred notables. Among them was Martin Van Buren, who kept a relatively low profile, knowing that Clinton's sun was setting, however gloriously. Among the day's innumerable speeches was that of William James, who pontificated on "the glory of the nation, its territory, its institutions, its wealth, its liberty, and its spirit in local and general improvement." The Irish native was then the richest of Albany's new merchant elite, an early investor in steamboats and the canal. Future audiences would better enjoy grandsons William and Henry.

In the morning, all of Albany turned out to see the fleet off. It was a brilliantly sunny, breezy fall morning. Banners, streamers, and flags on buildings, docks, and river craft painted the canal and river city a richly colored festival. "Such an animating, bright, beauteous and glorious spectacle had never been seen" at Albany. Bands on steamboats maneuvering to take canal boats in tow filled thousands of ears with the sounds of music, with "large columns of steam rushing from the fleet, rising majestically upwards, and curling and rolling into a thousand fantastic and beautiful forms, until mingled and lost in surrounding vapors." There were no speeches, just awe: "At a given signal, the fleet was under way in a moment; and the Albanians, with long and reiterated cheers, took leave of such a spectacle as their eyes will never more behold." Alas, this was more truth than hyperbole.

Trading horses for horsepower, Clinton's fleet followed their steam tows south for the next twenty-four hours. Demonstrations at towns along the banks of the Hudson surpassed those along the canal. Artillery rounds from the shore were met by return salvos from the steamboats. Even the *Young Lion,* carrying a small cannon, joined in. Finding thick crowds on the high ground at Hudson and on the opposite shore at Athens, the steamboats stopped their clanging engines to drift down with the river "like a fleet from the dominion of the fairies." In the evening, Poughkeepsie and Newburgh were illuminated; the boats fired rockets. At West Point just past midnight, a twenty-four-gun artillery salute, rockets, and reverberations across the glaciated cliffs. "Indeed, after Alexander of Macedon had carried his arms into India," puffed editor William Stone aboard the *Seneca Chief,* "he did not descend the Indus with greater triumph, or make a prouder display." After West Point, Clinton and his fellow travelers bedded down for the final sleep of their journey. In the morning Clinton would enter his home city, the conqueror of all there who had discouraged, opposed, or rued the building of the Erie Canal.

The boats anchored off the village of Greenwich before dawn on November 4. The forecast was fine: "mild as May, & the waters calm and serene as the sky that smiled propitiously on us," observed John Pintard, one of the first New Yorkers to support and promote the canal project.

Originally the canal celebration had been conceived as a strictly Buffalo to Albany affair. Pintard and William Bayard, who a decade earlier had run the City Hotel meeting that revived the dormant canal project, took charge again. On the same early September day on which perpetual American tourist Lafayette finally sailed for France, Pintard and Bayard had held a meeting of New York City merchant and other civic leaders at the Chamber of Commerce. They resolved that the city ought to celebrate the canal that promised "benefits of immense importance" to the state and especially the city. Within weeks, plans were concluded to celebrate "in a manner suited to the character of our City."

That meant the most exhilarating civic event in the early history of the United States: jubilation on a scale with the canal itself, choreographed on land and water, succumbing at places to self-parody, but unsurpassed for the sheer totality of civic involvement. No ticker tape parade through today's "Canyon of Heroes" could match it. The Erie Canal celebration in New York City was Woodstock for the dawning of the "Age of Acquisition."

The city of 166,000 was roused from its beds before dawn on November 4 by church bells and cannon fire. By 9:00 the southern tip of Manhattan was "literally crammed with spectators" to watch the "Grand Aquatic Procession," a choreographed parade of fifty decorated ships, boats, and barges, viewed by tens of thousands of New Yorkers from riverside promenades, rooftops, piers, the ratlines of tall ships, and hundreds of small boats following the fleet. On its passage around the Battery, between the Hudson and East rivers, the procession paused for a speech (heard by few but read by many in the coming days) by Clinton from the bow of the *Seneca Chief.* "[T]here will be no limits to your lucrative extensions of trade and commerce," he told the citizens of New York City, whose elected state representatives had cast no vote in favor of the canal eight years earlier. "The valley of the Mississippi will soon pour its treasures into this great emporium through channels now formed and forming, and wherever wealth is to be acquired or enterprise can be attempted, the power and capacity of your city will be felt."

Then it was down the broad harbor to the sea in precise order of many ships and boats. The steam-towed barge *Lady Clinton* was second in line, adorned with evergreens, roses, and China asters and "crowded with the beauty and fashion of the City." Off Sandy Hook, the fleet circled up for the "Wedding of the Waters."

On a tranquil sea beneath a bright autumn sun on a windless early afternoon, Clinton spoke briefly: "This solemnity at this place on the first arrival of vessels from Lake Erie, is intended to indicate and commemorate the navigable communication, which has been accomplished between our Mediterranean Seas and the Atlantic Ocean . . . by the wisdom, public spirit, and energy of the people of the State of New York; and may the God of Heavens and Earth smile most propitiously on this work, and render it subservient to the best interests of the human race." Clinton then performed the iconic act of the day: raising up one of the two kegs of Lake Erie water brought from Buffalo and pouring its contents into the Atlantic. But not the entire contents; some was saved, bottled, boxed, and sent across the Atlantic to America's favorite tourist and last surviving Revolutionary War major-general, Lafayette. What became of the second keg is unclear.

Clinton kept things brief, but Samuel Latham Mitchill did not. Expanding on his overwrought baptism of the Albany lock two years earlier, the verbose professor brought with him on this day what he said were samples of *fifteen* rivers from four continents. These waters he now poured overboard, and began to lecture. "Man delights in types and symbols," he asserted and, before he was done many minutes later, had touched on Shakespeare, Jotham, Pilpay, Death, Janus, "the Soul of Man," "the Ruler of the Deep," "thou Monarch of the boundless Main," "the Roman fleets at Actium," "the Lord of the Seas," "the Lady of the Lakes," and more.

Mitchill's tortured water rite did not go unpunished; it was a "ludicrous exhibition" in one published opinion, a "piece of ridicule and absurdity" to the *Evening Post*. Mitchill's many friends and shipmates held their fire.

After the aquatic double wedding ceremony, Clinton concluded his ten-day voyaging with a final spectacle along Manhattan's Hudson River shore. The twenty-nine steamboats, towing several becalmed U.S. Navy sailing ships and three canal boats, formed into a rotating circle around two anchored British sloops of war. Cannon and flag salutes initiated the delicate maneuver, which concluded with military bands aboard the American ships playing "God Save the King" and British bands responding with "Yankee Doodle." A decade after warring with each other, Englishmen and their former subjects were able to celebrate together a great commercial triumph. The arrangement of American steamers encircling furled British windships suggested the global realignment to come.

People who had also seen the parade eleven years earlier on the Thames celebrating Napoleon's final defeat declared that New York's was now the grandest naval display ever. A veteran of revolutionary engagements in New York Harbor considered this "one of the most important days I ever saw since I was born." Seventy-four year-old mariner Christopher Prince, aboard one of the parading American tall ships, had seen many things since going to sea at age fourteen: "I cannot describe my feelings in what my eyes saw. Such a day and weather was seldom seen on the earth."

When the ships finally docked after 3:00 in the afternoon, the duties of Clinton and his several thousand fellow mariners were not yet concluded. They joined a citywide parade that had been underway for hours, "the largest of the kind ever witnessed in America."

The "Grand Procession" featured seven thousand marchers parading with rolling "Stages, Cars, and Models" through every major street of the Empire City. Three cannon shots at ten minutes before 11:00 had set the parade in motion, led by mounted trumpeters. Interspersed with marching bands, thirty companies of the city's professional societies paraded, a panorama of early nineteenth-century life: 550 hatters; 450 cordwainers; 420 shipwrights and caulkers; 313 tanners, curriers, and leather dressers; and so on down to 80 combmakers and 40 potters.

Over twelve hundred firemen from the city's famous (and often riotously infamous) volunteer fire companies marched beside their richly decorated engines. The engine of Company No. 41, raised on a stage drawn by four horsemen on blood bays, had been painted with an image of the Little Falls aqueduct and other canal scenes. It was a fitting "compliment paid to the individual whose name and fortunes have been identified with the success or failure of the canal." No. 41 was well known as the Clinton Fire Company, named for its founder and, in younger days, most active member.

For craftsmanship, the two hundred tinplate workers and coppersmiths outdid everyone. Their horse-drawn float featured a metal working model of the Lockport locks, complete with canal boats ascending and descending in water pumped from a tank beneath the ornate display.

The city's printers, three hundred strong, were the life of the parade. Their horse-drawn stage had two busy printing presses, overseen by the city's senior publisher, James Oram, seated between them in Benjamin Franklin's library chair. Four boys in *Herald* and *Mercury* costumes handed out thousands of freshly printed broadsides of the "Ode for the Canal Celebration," written for the occasion by Knickerbocker poet Samuel Woodworth:

> 'Tis done! 'tis done!–The mighty chain
> Which joins bright ERIE to the MAIN,
> For ages, shall perpetuate
> The glory of our native State.
>
> 'Tis done!–The monarch of the briny tide,
> Whose giant arm encircles earth,
> To virgin ERIE is allied,
> A bright-eyed nymph of mountain birth.
> To-day, the Sire of Ocean takes
> A sylvan maiden to his arms,
> The goddess of the crystal lakes,
> In all her native charms!
> She comes! attended by a sparkling train;
> The Naiads of the West her nuptials grace:
> She meets the sceptred father of the main,
> And in his heaving bosom hides her virgin face.

The Knickerbocker literati were nothing if not fools for romance.

By late afternoon the marchers, joined by the aquatic paraders, massed in the park in front of City Hall for speeches, music, and varied entertainments. In a place then expanding rapidly into the modern stewpot of urban tensions, the day passed remarkably peacefully. "We have witnessed (and we confess with wonder) that an immense population may pass a day in rejoicing and festivity, and exhibit a self-respect that forbade even the appearance of vice and depravity," Utica's Alexander Coventry wrote to mayor William Paulding, "without observing a single instance of inebriation, or hearing a sound that would shock the chastest ear." As a younger man, Coventry had been known to "resort to blows where he could not readily compass his ends in a more peaceful way." Now a respected obstetrician and member of the official Utica delegation, Coventry's New York rounds did not encompass all the city had to offer that day.

At four in the afternoon at Vauxhall Gardens, an open-air theater and park along suburban Bowery Road (now Astor Place), "Madame Johnson" prepared an encore of her historic performance eleven days earlier. A French widow with three young children and no reported forename, she had been the first woman to fly a hot air balloon in America, a national media event that had splashed down after an eight-mile flight in a Long Island salt marsh. This time there was a failure to launch, "owing to want of skill in the persons who undertook to inflate [the balloon] or to the badness of the materials." After ninety minutes, impatient and likely inebriated members of the paying crowd of five thousand "laid hold of the balloon," demanding satisfaction. The intrepid Madame J, elegantly attired, made her escape, but her drooping balloon "was literally torn to pieces." Feeling its oats, the mob then "committed some excesses" upon Garden furniture, fences, and shrubbery.

Somehow the amply reported riot failed to disturb the official line of the day: "[N]ot a solitary instance of riot or disorder of any kind was witnessed." Though Madame Johnson's sponsors might have found them handy, uniformed militia were not available (state law then prohibited the assembling of armed men within ten days of the November 7 state elections) but anyway were largely unnecessary, "gratifying proof . . . that the exhibition of bayonets is not essential to the preservation of order in New York."

In the evening New York became a city of light; dozens of public buildings, theaters, and hotels glowed with oil and gas illumination. The front of City Hall featured a transparency painted with views of the canal; the back of the building served as the launching area for an unprecedented fireworks display that sent "fiery serpents and dragons" into the sky, raining down "showers of stars" above the heads of ten thousand spectators crowded into or around the park. Entertainments, public and private, continued for days, until a final "Grand Canal Ball" on Monday, November 7, attended by two thousand of the city's elite. Gracing the table of the ladies' supper room was a model canal boat floating in a bowl of Lake Erie water: sculpted from maple sugar, the boat would dissolve as surely as the celebration itself.

Clinton had been the central figure of New York's Erie Canal celebration, from Buffalo to the final ball. Supporters had welcomed the opportunity to permanently conjoin Clinton with the canal in the public's imagination, and detractors mostly held their tongues. Except Elkanah Watson, who rarely let his opinions be unknown. Watson had been New York's first western dreamer three decades earlier. In 1819 he had thrilled to the filling of an early canal section. Now he despised the whole affair:

> Take it all in all it was undoubtedly the most splendid farce ever acted in any age or Country. To have celebrated on the completion of such a magnificent enterprize would have been peculiarly appropriate had it . . . been called forth by public sentiment to commemorate an event of such vital importance to the State—but when it is of public notoriety that the whole object was intended to produce a political result to agrandize [sic] a single individual to the exclusion of meritricus [sic] men, who conceived & projected the system many years before Clinton was known— & that he contrived & managed the celebration in all its branches, from Erie to Sandy Hook—& even the Splendid Canal ball to reflect a glow of glory around this person—these considerations deteriorate essentially from the real merits of the exhibition & place the whole scene with men of sense on the level of a *splendid farce.*

Fortunately for his public reputation, Watson made these opinions known only in a private letter to an old Albany friend.

★ ★ ★

In the days following the great celebration, the cedar and maple logs that had come to the city aboard the *Seneca Chief* were carted to the three buildings on Fulton Street that comprised the woodworking factory of Duncan Phyfe, the great craftsman of exquisite furniture for the young American nation. Over the ensuing weeks, Phyfe fashioned the cedar container for Lafayette's bottle of Erie water and oversaw the fabrication of hundreds of cedar and maple boxes for the commemorative medals to be presented by the city to many dignitaries. The medals, featuring Pan, Neptune, and canal locks and aqueducts in a design by the celebrated Asher Durand, were cast in various metals. Boxed pewter medals were sent in early 1826 to the celebration's invited guests, the committees from canal cities and villages, various educational and historical institutions, and many others. Boxed silver went to federal and state officials, military officers, and others. Gold medals were presented to the families of George Washington and Robert Fulton, Lafayette, the three surviving signers of the Declaration of Independence (Adams, Jefferson, and Charles Carroll), the four surviving ex-presidents (Adams, Jefferson, Madison, and Monroe), and current president John Quincy Adams.

A number of the gold medal recipients had been intimate with the progress of New York's canal efforts. Sending his thanks, John Quincy Adams acknowledged the Erie Canal as "an Event among those most worthy of commemoration, in the progress of human Affairs—an Event equally creditable to the Enterprize and Perseverance of the People of New York; and by the accomplishment of which, in honouring themselves they have reflected honour upon the age and country to which they belong." Adams's vice president, John Calhoun, had tried and failed as a senator to support New York's endeavor as a bond of union; he was already rejecting nationalism for states' rights, becoming the avatar of Southern secession from the Erie-industrialized North.

James Monroe wrote: "The accomplishment of the great work, undertaken by the State of New York, by which the western lakes are united with the Atlantic ocean, through the Hudson river, forms a very important epoch in the history of our great republic. By facilitating the intercourse and promoting the prosperity and welfare of the whole, it will bind us more closely together, and thereby give a new and powerful support, to our free and most excellent system of government." Monroe was inaugurated as president four months to the day before New York State began building its canal and concluded his two terms eight months to the day before New York City celebrated its completion; true to the constitutional scruples of fellow Virginians Jefferson and Madison before him, Monroe had spent those eight years discouraging national improvements, most famously vetoing funding for the Cumberland Road.

James Madison wrote: "As a monument of Public spirit conducted by enlightened Councils, as an example to other States worthy of emulating enterprize, and as itself a precious contribution to the happy result to our country of facilitated communications and inter-mingled interests, bringing nearer and binding faster the multiplying parts of the expanding whole, the Canal which unites the great Western lakes with the Atlantic ocean, is an achievement of which the State of New York may at all times be proud, and which well merited the homage so aptly paid to it by her great commercial Metropolis." It was Madison's stunning veto of John Calhoun's Bonus Bill that had eliminated the prospect of national support for the canal to Lake Erie and emboldened New York to go forward alone.

Jefferson, in the faltering hand of an eighty-three-year-old Founding Father, wrote: "This great work will immortalize the present authorities of New York, will bless their descendants with wealth and prosperity, and prove to mankind the superior wisdom of employing the resources of industry in works of improvement rather than of destruction." Jefferson, of course, had dismissed New York's project as madness, promoted national improvements only so far as they did not benefit New York, and allowed a destructive trade embargo to dim his legacy.

Jefferson wrote on June 8, 1826. A couple of weeks earlier, his fellow ex-president and Declaration of Independence signer, ninety-year-old John Adams, had accepted his medal commemorating what he called "the pride and wonder of the age." On July 1 *Niles Weekly Register* published their letters for the nation's readers. They were the last public thoughts to be heard from the great patriots of Virginia and Massachusetts. Three days later Jefferson and Adams died, on the fiftieth anniversary of the American independence that they had in large part created. It was also the ninth anniversary of New York's own sort of independence, declared at the point of a spade thrust into wet earth near the center of a verging Empire State.

CHAPTER 13

"The Shadowy Remembrance"

[W]hen, by the flow of that perpetual stream which bears all human institutions away, our constitution shall be dissolved and our laws be lost, . . . when the records of history shall have been obliterated, and the tongue of tradition have converted . . . the shadowy remembrance of ancient events into childish tales of miracle, this national work shall remain.

—Gouverneur Morris, 1812

The political coattails of the great Erie celebration were short. The popular outrage over De Witt Clinton's removal from the canal commission in 1824 was exhausted on his triumphant management as governor of the canal celebration. Just days after its conclusion, the state's voters surprised even sanguine Bucktails by returning them to control of the assembly while retaining their senate majority. A rare but calculated accommodation between Clinton and Martin Van Buren subsequently handed important state and local appointments to Clintonians, while Van Buren won statewide political tranquility that served his broader national purposes. When Van Buren forces reportedly had to manipulate election returns in the governor's race the following year to give Clinton a narrow victory over what was supposed to be the nominal opposition of Bucktail William B. Rochester, it was clear that Clinton's political accounts were empty. His 1828 presidential aspirations deflated. Since 1812 Clinton had dreamed of the White House but had always woken up in New York. His political organization now was "entirely dissolved," his most loyal supporters "deserted and destroyed." By the summer of 1827 his rapidly deteriorating health prompted rumors of Clinton's death. He was alleged to be a broken man "disposed to quarrel with his best friends & on good terms only with his decanter." On the snowy Albany evening of February 11, 1828, the heart of the great patron of the Erie Canal finally gave out, and he collapsed dead at his desk. He was only fifty-eight years old.

Clinton's indifference to political organization extended to management of his personal wealth. Scrupulously honest with public money and generous to a fault with his own, he died with substantial debts; the prompt auction of his family's possessions left his wife and four minor children temporarily destitute. A bill to award his estate fourteen years of canal commissioner salary, some $30,000, was thwarted in the assembly by lifelong enemies Erastus Root and Peter Porter, who grudgingly agreed to a $10,000 stipend.

Observances of Clinton's death stretched from the U.S. Congress to the corners of his state, where official business was suspended for a day, followed by elaborate funeral rites in New York City at public expense. No provision was made for a grave, though, and his family could not afford a proper one. Clinton's bones reposed in an Albany cemetery vault for sixteen years, until a private subscription established a permanent burial place and memorial in Brooklyn's prestigious Green-Wood Cemetery.

Before he died, Clinton had the satisfaction of knowing that he had chosen the right side in the Buffalo and Black Rock dispute. Clinton had made Buffalo the scene of the opening celebrations in 1825, but both villages, with their newly completed harbors, anticipated commercial success. Black Rock's hopes began to founder the very next spring. On the last Saturday night in May, a central portion of the stone pier collapsed and was carried away downriver. The *Black Rock Gazette* acknowledged that "[t]his accident [is] the most considerable one that has happened to the harbor" in its short history. The *Buffalo Journal* gleefully reported: "A column of water rushes through the aperture with fearful violence." A steamer that struggled against the turbulence for several hours with full power, auxiliary sails, and ground tackle finally found its way to safety in Buffalo and intended to make future clearances there. The pier was rebuilt and Black Rock's harbor was busy during the 1826 season, but the following April a brutal spring storm caused a major collapse. Lake ice driven by hurricane-force winds piled up in the harbor, demolishing more of the pier and any incentive to make repairs. By June, "not a movement has been made toward repairing the ruins." Porter's Black Rock Harbor Company had "abandoned [its works] and every idea of using the Basin for vessels." Freight forwarders relocated to Buffalo, and Clinton gloated over the ruin he had predicted: "Conceived in sin, fed by ignorance, nourished by cupidity and brought forth in iniquity, it had disappointed no observing man—as long as the Canal lasts, its ruins and history will be subjects of reproach to the projectors."

Clinton did not live to see Porter reproached. In fact, Porter soon became John Quincy Adams's secretary of war and hosted a Washington salon with his "[g]ay, frank, communicative, kind" wife Letitia, "the most popular woman" in capital society since Dolley Madison. In the 1830s, Porter sold his extensive Black Rock land holdings at great profit to Buffalo men, and moved his family to Niagara Falls. Other Black Rock pioneers also cashed out. By the time Porter died in 1844, Black Rock was well on its way to becoming a mere neighborhood of booming Buffalo. In a sense, Black Rock had lost its identity much earlier. In 1825, to facilitate construction of its fated harbor, Black Rock's namesake rock had been blown up. On its site now are the eastern footings of the bridge linking Buffalo and Fort Erie, Ontario, somewhat ironically called the Peace Bridge.

Black Rock disappeared and De Witt Clinton's political legacy was a shadow, but "the Great Clinton Canal" (as some called it) remained vital for generations. It was such a success that it quickly became evident that it was too small.

When the canal opened, a typical thirty-ton barge made the round trip from Albany or Buffalo in sixteen days. By 1841, the trip took the by-then typical seventy-ton barge twenty-two days, slowed by heavy traffic and the canal's minimal dimensions. In 1834 Benjamin Wright, involved with canals and railroads from Canada to Cuba, had admitted that "in the size of our canal . . . we have made great errors, very great indeed." The following year the state decided to enlarge the canal, and work began in 1836, initially under chief engineer John Jervis, by then among the country's leading engineers of canals and railroads.

Enlargement plans bogged down in partisan politics and depression economics. Half a lifetime after his Hercules essays, Jesse Hawley argued pointedly in Albany and the press—under his own name—to let Erie grow:

> No single act—no public measure—except the Declaration of Independence, and the formation of the United States Constitution, has done so much to promote the public prosperity and produce a new era in the history of the country, *as the construction of the Erie Canal.* It is the father of canals in America; and of the State system of internal improvements which has grown up under its benign influences; and that its political influence and importance to the Union, for the construction of the internal improvements *by State funds—as State properties—for State revenues,* on the principle of State Rights, is equal to its commercial values.

Work proceeded fitfully, until the state, somewhat prematurely, finally declared the enlargement complete in 1862, three weeks before Lincoln's Emancipation Proclamation and a year into the Civil War over states' rights. The canal had been reborn as a channel seventy feet wide at the surface, up to fifty-six feet wide at the bottom, and seven feet deep. Thirteen miles had been trimmed from the original 363, and eleven locks from the original eighty-three. All of the locks were enlarged to 110 by 18 feet, most of them doubled to allow two-way traffic.

Hawley called Erie "the father of canals," and it had a substantial paternity. Before Erie there were roughly one hundred miles of American canals. By 1860 there were forty-two hundred miles. With the Erie, Champlain, and ten other canals linked to them or other natural waterways, New York contributed nearly a quarter of the total. Some were important and successful; many, in New York and elsewhere, did not measure up. Dozens of states and developers tried to match Erie's success, only to see their often poorly conceived plans waste millions of public and investor dollars. The Panic of 1837 and the ensuing six-year national depression were caused in large part by fantastic losses in the nascent canal industry. Canals were the country's first technology bubble and bust.

Erie was a father, and a mother too, the so-called "Mother of Cities." The canal birthed Syracuse and Lockport; nurtured the nascent villages of

Rochester and Buffalo; and raised the fortunes of Utica, Albany, and Troy. By 1840 Albany was the ninth largest city in the United States, with Rochester, Troy, Buffalo, and Utica in the top thirty; Syracuse made the list ten years later. Outside of the state, the canal helped make cities of Great Lakes outposts from Cleveland to Detroit to Chicago; Erie was a mecca for settlers and supplies headed west to settle dozens more future cities.

"Surely, the water of this canal must be the most fertilizing of all fluids," wrote an anonymous traveler in 1832, "for it causes towns—with their masses of brick and stone, their churches and theatres, their business and hubbub, their luxury and refinement, their gay dames and polished citizens—to spring up, till, in time, the wondrous stream may flow between two continuous lines of building, through one thronged street, from Buffalo to Albany."

Young Nathaniel Hawthorne "was inclined to be poetical about the Grand Canal" when he boarded a boat in Schenectady, intending to travel the canal to Buffalo and back. "In my imagination, De Witt Clinton was an enchanter, who had waved his magic wand from the Hudson to lake Erie, and united them by a watery highway, crowded with the commerce of two worlds, till then inaccessible to each other." Reality intervened. The canal, in fact, was "an interminable mud-puddle . . . as dark and turbid as if every kennel in the land paid contribution to it. With an imperceptible current, it holds its drowsy way through all the dismal swamps and unimpressive scenery, that could be found between the great lakes and the sea-coast." Dirty boats carried freight and sad families "through a gloomy land and among a dull race of money-getting drudges." In a lonely canal-side tract of "dismal black stumps . . . a sallow-faced woman" appeared at the window of a log cabin: "Lean and aguish, she looked like Poverty personified, half clothed, half fed, and dwelling in a desert, while a tide of wealth was sweeping by her door." The Utica–Syracuse long level, the early pride of its emerging engineers, proved a ghastly nocturnal transit amid forest "decayed and death-struck" by the canal:

Often, we beheld the prostrate form of some old sylvan giant, which had fallen, and crushed down smaller trees under its immense ruin. In spots, where destruction had been riotous, the lanterns showed perhaps a

hundred trunks, erect, half overthrown, extended along the ground, resting on their shattered limbs, or tossing them desperately into the darkness, but all of one ashy-white, all naked together, in desolate confusion.
Thus growing out of the night as we drew nigh, and vanishing as we
glided on, based on obscurity, and overhung and bounded by it, the scene
was ghost-like—the very land of unsubstantial things, whither dreams
might betake themselves, when they quit the slumberer's brain.

Progress itself was the culprit: "The wild Nature of America had been
driven to this desert-place by the encroachments of civilized man. And
even here, where the savage queen was throned on the ruins of her empire, did we penetrate, a vulgar and worldly throng, intruding on her latest solitude. In other lands, Decay sits among fallen palaces; but here, her
home is in the forests." The puritanical New Englander abandoned
canalling at Syracuse.

Hawthorne was among the first of many literary artists to contrast the
image of Erie with its reality. He traveled as a young gentleman tourist
prior to his literary fame. His later, younger, and poorer friend Herman
Melville transited the canal in 1840 looking for work in the west, possibly
hiring onto a canal boat as well, and traveled the canal again in 1847 as
a honeymooner. Four years later, in *Moby Dick* (dedicated to Hawthorne),
Melville offered his own moral judgment:

For three hundred and sixty miles, gentlemen, through the entire breadth
of the state of New York; through numerous populous cities and most
thriving villages; through long, dismal, uninhabited swamps, and afflu-
ent, cultivated fields, unrivalled for fertility; by billiard-room and bar-
room; through the holy-of-holies of great forests; on Roman arches over
Indian rivers; through sun and shade; by happy hearts or broken;
through all the wide contrasting scenery of those noble Mohawk counties; and especially, by rows of snow-white chapels, whose spires stand almost like milestones, flows one continual stream of Venetianly corrupt
and often lawless life. There's your true Ashantee, gentlemen; there howl
your pagans; where you ever find them, next door to you; under the
long-flung shadow, and the snug patronizing lee of churches. For by

some curious fatality, as it is often noted of your metropolitan freebooters that they ever encamp around the halls of justice, so sinners, gentlemen, most abound in holiest vicinities.

A few years later, Melville was inclined to take the longer view: "Advance into knowledge is just like advance upon the Grand Erie canal, where, from the character of the country, change of level is inevitable; you are locked up and locked down with perpetual inconsistencies, and yet all the time you get on."

Even the best writing can pale beside actual fortune and fate. Martha Larson learned this. Twenty years after leading his band of Norwegian Quakers to Western New York, her husband Lars was a leading Rochester shipper and boat builder. Together they had aided in the migration of thousands of Norwegians through New York to what we now call the Old Northwest. In early November 1845 Lars was delivering a load of flour from Buffalo to Albany in a boat newly acquired with a man named Hotaling, who served as captain. At five in the morning on November 13, they were transiting Lock No. 20 just east of Rexford Flats. Crossing the narrow catwalk to operate the lock, Larson fell into the frigid water and drowned. "His body had been in the water about an hour before it was recovered." Martha Larson, widowed with eight children, believed her husband was murdered by his new partner: "[H]e knew if Lars was out of the way he could claim all so we have every reason in the world to think he was pushed into Eternity." A coroner's inquest was requested, but nothing further was reported, and Hotaling apparently laid claim to both cargo and boat. Two weeks later early ice closed the canal for the winter. Twenty Decembers previous, a youthful Lars Larson had reportedly skated the closed canal for 290 miles from Albany to join his young wife, infant daughter, and fellow settlers. Now the canal that had delivered him a prosperous life had taken it, on a cold and friendless night.

For every Erie tragedy, there were many more triumphs. Henry Wells, born in Vermont and raised to make shoes in the Cayuga County settlement called Mentz, turned to shipping after the Erie Canal turned Mentz into Port Byron; in the 1850s he founded Wells Fargo and American Express. George Pullman transformed the canal boats he knew as an

Albion teen into the sleeper cars that revolutionized rail travel. Buffalo merchant Joseph Dart built the world's first grain elevator in 1842, helping to make Buffalo the world's largest grain port seven years later.

In 1854 William Henry Seward called his state's great creation the "imperial Erie canal." He was speaking on the floor of the U.S. Senate about the abrogation of the Missouri Compromise in the Nebraska and Kansas statehood bills. Two decades earlier he had been the land agent for the Holland Land Company, the job originated by Joseph Ellicott. After that he became New York's governor, Clinton's old job. Eventually he became Abraham Lincoln's secretary of state; survived a knife attack in the assassination conspiracy that claimed Lincoln; and arranged the Alaska Purchase, a transaction with Russia that many called folly. Seward knew about imperial power. He knew that New York and the North had gained it, and Virginia and the South hadn't.

The very notion of "Southern" as a sectional identity arose shortly after the completion of the canal. "The southerns will not long pay tribute," observed a Kentucky campaign paper in October 1827, the first published use of the term in a geopolitical context. "A Yankee is a Yankee over the globe," observed a Cincinnati monthly the following year. "The Southerner, too, is such over the whole globe." Two years after completion of the Erie Canal and the same year that New York outlawed slavery, the distinction between North and South was made. A generation later it evolved into open hostility, the North to preserve its economic, political, and perceived moral superiority, the South to escape it. Having joined the industrializing North with the limitless west beyond the Appalachians, the Erie Canal helped to marginalize the economy of the slave plantation South and radicalize its politics.

New York City's advantages were not solely owed to the canal, but its completion was the capstone. The city's rising merchants had been working since the peace with England in 1815 to center the national economy on their port. The existing auction system for disposing of imported goods was revamped to deal effectively with British dumping of its war-delayed commodities; a bill promoted by city auctioneers to slash state auction duties was passed by the legislature on the same day it authorized construction of the Erie Canal in 1817. The following year, regular transatlantic packet service was inaugurated between New York City and Europe, followed four years later by coastal packet service between the city and the southern ports of New Orleans, Charleston, Savannah, and Mobile, creating a "cotton triangle" with New York City at the commercial apex. Whether shipped directly overseas or first to the city, southern cotton and tobacco came under the control of Manhattan bankers and brokers, who provided plantation owners with ready capital for purchases of land, seed, and slaves. As New York port historian Robert Albion observed, city merchants "happily exploit[ed] southern commercial passivity" for nearly half a century before the Civil War finally exploded the arrangement.

Erie completed New York's commercial supremacy over the South and extended it into the west. As early as 1826, the solicitor general of Upper Canada lamented that New York's canal was in use for trade "to an extent that no person could have anticipated." Gradually the mighty Mississippi yielded to the artificial river. In 1835, 62 percent of commodities produced in Ohio, Indiana, Illinois, and Michigan moved downriver to New Orleans, and 24 percent made its way to New York City via the Erie Canal, with the remainder going to eastern ports along the Pennsylvania Mainline, the Pittsburgh Turnpike, or the Cumberland Road. Eighteen years later, 62 percent of western commodities went via the Erie, 29 percent on the Mississippi, and 9 percent on other routes. Migration to the western states and territories, whose population quintupled over three decades to 4.2 million in 1850, was in greatest part along the canal. Merchandise followed: from $10 million worth in 1836 to $94 million in 1853.

The flow of people and goods on the canal made it a stunning financial success. In 1825 toll receipts of half a million dollars exceeded the year's interest on canal loans by $100,000. By 1833 twelve years of toll collection had netted $7.1 million, the cost of building the canal. In 1851 alone the canal brought in $3.3 million in tolls, which had made the collection of assorted taxes for the canal fund unnecessary. When tolls were eliminated on the Erie in 1882, total revenues for its sixty years of operation were $121 million. The original canal and the enlargement had cost $50 million to build and $30 million to repair and maintain, for an extraordinary profit of over $41 million.

The benefit to the state's bottom line was almost beside the point. "The Erie Canal," wrote engineer and engineering biographer Charles Beebe Stuart in 1871, "has exerted an influence and power that beyond computation excels that of any other investment of money ever made in any nation. Not only States that border on the great lakes owe their prosperity, some of them their existence, to this canal, but the States beyond the great River Mississippi must for ever find their markets through its channel to the Atlantic cities."

Stuart's "for ever" understandably did not anticipate interstate trucking and airfreight. But railroads had already signaled the future. At the time when Stuart wrote, rail freight tonnage along lines mirroring the canal had finally exceeded the tonnage carried by canal boats. Taxes on rail freight had artificially delayed the transition; canal freight tonnage peaked in the 1880s and began a steep decline despite the elimination of tolls.

Timing was the key to the advantages New York gained from the canal. If the canal had not been efficiently completed, New York would not have acquired long-term commercial superiority, especially over zealous and jealous Virginia, before railroads made it possible for any eastern state to reach beyond the Appalachian Mountains to the western interior. By completing the canal to Lake Erie in 1825 and establishing trade and travel routes that quickly became permanent before railroads became practical, New York was established as the Empire State, the economic engine and national image of a new global power.

Between 1905 and 1918, the enlarged Erie was replaced entirely by a canal designed for motorized barges. Two hundred feet wide and twelve feet deep with just thirty-six massive electric locks, the inelegantly named New York State Barge Canal used modern technology to canalize the Mohawk, Oneida, and Seneca rivers, a fearsome concept to the builders of the original canal. Trains, trucks, and airplanes ensured that the Barge Canal never reached full utility. Now used almost exclusively by pleasure boaters, the current waterway was renamed in 1992 as the Erie Canal portion of the New York State Canal System, an attempt to attract tourism to what had become a depressed corridor through the center of the state. Built over and around, the original canal exists now in obscure traces, remnants known mostly to canal buffs.

The original Erie Canal turned wilderness into wealth, but by the early 1900s much of the wealth had moved west. Rochester and Syracuse have never equaled the optimism of their long gone days of flour and salt. Buffalo, the country's eighth largest city in 1900, has lost over half its population since 1950; like modern Greece in the long shadows of ancient greatness, Buffalo has had a difficult time becoming something other than the western end of the old Erie Canal. Of all the canal boomtowns, Lockport has found the least else to otherwise recommend it, lamented by native daughter Joyce Carol Oates:

> *eye to eye with the broken windows of warehouses*
> *across the canal*
> *we wait*
> *wait for something to become clear—*
> *but nothing happens*
> *in these meager cities of our childhoods*
> *nothing is declared*

Still, the Erie Canal remains, if not in its original form and relevance, then as enduring evidence of the rise of New York in the nation, and of the nation in the world. The first great bond of American union still resonates in a continental nation that outwardly projects global power while internally dealing with the domestic tensions of empire.

Erie's modern existence is measured in small ways. A favorite activity of school-age children (including mine), beginning in 1999, was collecting state quarters, a nonelectronic game that ran through 2008. In 1999 New York began considering what design it wanted for its quarter, scheduled to be issued by the U.S. Mint in January 2001 as the eleventh in the fifty-coin series released chronologically in order of Constitution ratification or Union entry. From hundreds of designs submitted by New York schoolchildren, coin collectors, artists, and history buffs, Governor George Pataki submitted five concepts to the U.S. Mint: Henry Hudson sailing the *Half Moon* up the river that now bears his name; the British surrender after the Battle of Saratoga, which turned the Revolutionary War in favor of the Americans; the Federal Building on Wall Street, where George Washington was inaugurated as president; a mule pulling a barge along the Erie Canal inside an outline of New York State above the phrase "Gateway to America"; and the Statue of Liberty against a state outline with the phrase "Gateway to Freedom."

Early in 2000, the Mint informed Governor Pataki that the Erie Canal design was "uncoinable," that is, too complicated to depict well on the small area of a quarter. The federal Commission of Fine Arts, meanwhile, had given its nonbinding but influential endorsement to the Saratoga surrender and the Statue of Liberty designs, with a preference for the latter. Sensitive to his upstate constituency, Pataki was said to favor Saratoga, with a final decision to be made in consultations among the governor, the Mint, and the Treasury Department.

Much as the original canal was largely conceived, promoted, and built by upstate New Yorkers, a lobbying campaign by canal supporters from Albany to Buffalo pressed the governor for some recognition of the canal. In July 2000 Pataki formally notified the Mint that he preferred the Statue of Liberty "Gateway to Freedom" design, but with the addition inside the state outline of engraved lines depicting the state's two great waterways: "The Erie Canal and Hudson River spurred the first great westward movement of American settlers, gave access to the rich land and resources west of the Appalachians, and made New York City the pre-eminent commercial city in the United States."

In the following weeks, the Treasury Department gave its formal approval and a Mint engraver set to work on the modified design. On January 8, 2001, Governor Pataki unveiled the new quarter in Albany, officially opening a minting period that produced a billion and a half New York State quarters. In this small way, New York's fifty-third governor preserved the work of the state's fifth governor, the canal's greatest promoter, De Witt Clinton. On the coin of New York's realm, the Statue of Liberty stands out boldly against the familiar outline of the state. The line of the Erie Canal is unnamed but recognizable, especially to those who know its story.

NOTES

ABBREVIATIONS AND SHORT FORMS USED

PB: Paul Busti
Canal Laws: Laws of the State of New York in Relation to the Erie and Champlain Canals
CUL: Columbia University Library
DAB: Dictionary of American Biography
DWC: De Witt Clinton
DWC Papers: De Witt Clinton Papers
TE: Thomas Eddy
JE: Joseph Ellicott
Jefferson Papers: The Thomas Jefferson Papers
JH: Jesse Hawley
MH: Myron Holley
TJ: Thomas Jefferson
JBJ: John Bloomfield Jervis
LOC: Library of Congress
GM: Gouverneur Morris
NYPL: New York Public Library
NYS: New York State
PBP: Peter Buell Porter
RT: Robert Troup
MVB: Martin van Buren
GW: George Washington
BW: Benjamin Wright
SY: Seymour Young

In an effort to minimize the number of notes and citations, an ellipsis after a textual reference generally indicates that the citation covers all quotations up to the next textual reference. Citations to works listed in the bibliography are only by the last name of the author or, for unauthored works, by title short form; where last name appears on more than one work, the citations include the publication year in brackets.

1. AN AMERICAN AMBITION

2 "the United States with veins full . . .": Walt Whitman, *Leaves of Grass* (New York: Penguin, 1986), 8.

2 "Whether we remain in one confederacy . . .": TJ to Joseph Priestly, 19 January 1804, *Jefferson Papers*, LOC.

3 "so abominable": *Register of Congressional Debates*, Senate, 18th Cong., 2nd Sess., 676.

3 "probably the outstanding example . . .": Johnson, 368.

5 "inexhaustible ingenuity . . .": Francis Espinasse, *Lancashire Worthies* (London: Simpkin, Marshall, & Co., 1874), 281, 280.

5 "castle in the air . . .": Smiles, 349, 449.

6 "The building of the Erie Canal . . .": Taylor, 33.

7 "the effusions of a maniac": Hosack, 302.

7 "when all my private prospects . . .": *The* [Rochester] *Telegraph*, 19 July 1825.

7 "a gentleman . . . reflecting mind": *New-York Statesman* (Albany), 2 June 1820.

8 "was too jealous . . .": Roosevelt, 177.

8 "Who is this . . .": Geddes [1880], 292.

11 "a stranger to the western . . .": Hosack, 383.

12 "an indissoluble bond of union": This phrase, often employed in other contexts, was used in relation to an Erie canal by Joshua Forman (Hosack, 346) and De Witt Clinton (*Canal Laws*, 1:140).

2. THE WILDERNESS YEARS

14 "impatient of contradiction . . .": *The Albany Law Journal*, 28 January 1871.

14 "He was a sincere . . .": *Niagara Courier*, 12 January 1842.

18 "It was so dark . . .": Snow et al., 2.

18 "for carrying goods up or down . . .": *Journal of Jasper Danckaerts*, 213.

19 "[A]s this passage . . . at this time": Colden [1747], 34–35.

20 "The *French* . . . Maps and Books": Colden [1747], 28.

22 "[T]he only Way . . .": Pownall, 31.

23 "Prompted by these . . .": GW to Francois Jean, Comte de Chastellux, 12 October 1783, *Fitzpatrick*, 27: 189–90.

24 "The western country is . . .": TJ to GW, 15 March 1784, *Papers of Thomas Jefferson*, 7: 26.

24 "jealousies . . .": GW to TJ, 29 March 1784, Fitzpatrick, 27: 373, 375.

25 "the present juvenile state . . .": GW to Christopher Colles, 25 January 1783, Fitzpatrick, 26: 64–65.

25 "He was wont to say . . .": Francis [1855], 207.
25 "boats of burthen": Clinton [1821], 11.
25 "By this . . .": Colles [1785], 10–11, 13.
26 "An Act . . .": Hosack, 284.
27 "[T]here is a critical juncture . . .": Colles [1785], 12.
27 "No pilgrim . . .": Watson [1856], 278.
28 "I confess . . .": Watson [1856], 281.
28 "a severe cold . . .": Watson [1856], 279.
28 "whole river . . .": Watson [1856], 282.
28 "wholly incompetent . . .": Watson [1820], 74.
32 "Gen. Schuyler . . .": Watson [1820], 75.
32 "my enemy . . .": Watson [1856], 383.
33 "extremely dangerous . . .": *Castorland Journal*, 298.
33 "[N]o mechanical appliances . . .": *Castorland Journal*, 65.
33 "pretended canals": *Castorland Journal*, 66.
33 "which will render . . .": *Castorland Journal*, 198–99.
33 "most popular . . .": Clinton [1821], viii.
35 "the dreadful conditions . . .": JH to "Beloved Jennie," undated letter quoted in Adams [1998].
35 "direct into our country": Hawley [1880], 244.
37 "sat in a fit . . .": *Ontario Messenger*, 27 January 1841, in Shaw [1966], 24.
37 "*there* is the supply . . .": Hawley [1880], 244.

3. "THE EFFUSIONS OF A MANIAC"

39 "great objects": Richardson, 379.
40 "great purposes . . .": Richardson, 409.
40 "I will presume . . .": Hosack, 307, 308.
40 "The trade of this vast country . . .": Cooper [1810], 32–34.
42 "Conversations . . . are getting to be fashionable . . .": Agricola, [5], 24.
43 "of wide information . . .": *DAB*, Forman.
43 "If you wish New-York . . .": *New-York Commercial Advertiser,* 25 June 1807.
44 "best calculated . . .": Turner [1850], 666–68.
45 "in so remote a place . . .": *Hawley Record*, 533.
47 "gratification": PB to JE, March 1802, in Chazanof, 52.
48 "betrayed and defrauded . . .": *Ontario Messenger*, 27 January 1841, in Shaw [1966], 24–25; JH to "Beloved Jennie," in Adams [1998].
48 "[W]e entertain vast ideas . . .": Hosack, 310, 311.
49 "the first hint": Clinton [1821], 19.
49 "to trace any measure . . .": Watson [1820], 67.
49 "to see how it would strike . . .": *Hawley Record*, 533.
50 "In this proposed canal . . .": Hosack, 313, 314.
51 "devoured [it] with greater avidity . . .": *Hawley Record*, 533.

51 "should be calculated . . .": Hosack, 318.

51 "the effusions of a maniac": Hosack, 302.

51 "visionary and impractical": *Hawley Record*, 533.

51 "a man of quiet, unobtrusive habits . . .": Turner [1850], 568.

51 "throwing discredit and ridicule . . .": *Hawley Record*, 533.

52 "my ignorance in the art . . .": Hosack, 319–20.

52 "the trade of almost all . . .": Hosack, 323.

52 "Fifty men associated . . .": Hosack, 325, 326

53 "I hope indeed . . .": Gallatin, 108, 121, 122

53 "in favor of the great subject . . .": TJ to John Barlow, 10 December 1807, *Jefferson Papers*, LOC.

54 "A marine canal . . .": Hosack, 339.

54 "[I]t would be a burlesque . . .": Hosack, 337.

54 "is destined to be . . .": Hosack, 329.

54 "if a canal was ever made . . .": Hosack, 343, 344.

55 "an accurate survey to be made . . .": *Canal Laws*, 1: 7–8.

55 "without much confidence . . .": Hosack, 345.

55 "astonishment of many members . . .": Hosack, 502.

56 "which must appear a bagatelle . . .": Hosack, 345–46.

56 "that it *could do no harm* . . .": Hosack, 346.

56 "I hear it is proposed . . .": George Clinton to DWC, 13 February 1808, DWC Papers, CUL.

57 "in the usual route of communication . . .": *Canal Laws*, 1: 9.

57 "[I]t was expected that something . . .": Simeon De Witt to JE, 13 June 1808, in Severance, 3.

57 "the appropriation will probably . . .": Canal Laws, 1: 11–12.

57 "amongst the fortunate occurrences . . .": Hosack, 265.

58 "Good roads and canals . . .": Gallatin, 8.

59 "will doubtless be much benefited": De Witt to JE, 13 June 1808, in Severance, 3–4.

60 "in case the United States . . .": JE to De Witt, 30 July 1808, in Severance, 15.

60 "will materially change the ideas . . .": De Witt to JE, 24 August 1808, in Severance, 17.

61 "All knowledge of an interior route . . .": *Canal Laws*, 1: 43, 44.

63 "that a canal from Lake Erie . . .": *Canal Laws*, 1: 41.

63 "almost entirely to converse . . .": Hosack, 346, 347.

64 "but nothing was done": Hosack, 302.

64 "indifferent . . .": Cooper [1810], 17, 32, 26.

4. APOLLO RISING

65 "[A]bout 150 years ago . . .": www.imdb.com/title/tt0056085/quotes.

66 "an *immedicable vulnus* in my heart": Bobbé, 225.

66 "of a fine form, and well proportioned . . .": Hosack, 120.

67 "[T]o this change in his habits . . .": Renwick, 256.

67 "was the major issue . . .": July, 43.

67 "On literary subjects . . .": Hammond, 2: 272–73.

68 "a certain coldness and *hauteur* . . .": Hammond, 2: 270, 272.

69 "a liar, a scoundrel . . .": Hammond, 1: 186.

69 "own aggrandizement has been . . .": Adams [1875], 38.

69 "Most of [Clinton's] political work . . .": Roosevelt, 177.

69 "the De Witt Clinton of Illinois": Lamon, 195.

70 "Plymouth Rock landed on *us!*": *The Autobiography of Malcolm X,* with the assistance of Alex Haley (New York: Grove Press, 1965), 201

70 "name a synonym for benevolence": Francis [1858], 83.

70 "had not been trained . . .": New York State Historical Association *Proceedings*, 324, 326.

71 "the would-be Governor": Bobbé, 145.

72 "I had never consulted any person": Hosack, 376.

72 "visionary and extravagant . . .": Hosack, 382.

73 "men of wealth and public spirit . . .": Hosack, 383.

73 "from Hudson's river . . .": Hosack, 98.

74 "[A] man of strong prejudices . . .": *DAB*, "William North."

75 "opening a great navigable canal . . .": *Annals of Congress*, House of Representatives, 11th Cong., 2nd Sess., 1388–1389, 1391.

76 "[T]he violence of party feelings . . .": Campbell, 27.

76 "Be assured Sir . . .": Jonas Platt to DWC, 4 October 1823, in Fox, 154, n.2.

76 "devoted the best powers . . .": Hosack, 384.

5. ERIE RISE AND FALL

77 "to investigate the subject": Hosack, 302.

78 "[W]e have formed sanguine expectations . . .": *American Medical and Philosophical Register*, vol. 1, no.1 (July 1810), 111.

79 "an irreligious and profane man": *Life and Correspondence of Rufus King*, 1: 420.

79 "the promptitude, with which your lively . . .": GW to Morris, 28 January 1792, in Sparks, 218.

79 "Gouverneur is daily employed . . .": John Jay to Robert R. Livingston, 16 February 1779, in Kirschke, 118.

79 "to wish he had lost . . .": John Jay to Robert Morris, 19 September 1780, in Kirschke, 119.

80 "mean village": Campbell, 132.

81 "with the compliments of the commissioners . . .": Hosack, 302.

81 "enraged boatmen": Campbell, 37.

81 "evinced a mutinous spirit . . .": Campbell, 90.

81 "sagacious . . . who understood nothing . . .": Campbell, 99.

81 "continually running the boat zig-zag . . .": Campbell, 102.

81 "dirty and unaccommodating . . .": Campbell, 39, 40.

82 "unnecessary expense . . .": Campbell, 55, 56.

82 "[T]he Senior Commissioner . . .": Campbell, 54.

82 "where Mr. Geddes proposes . . .": Campbell, 111.

83 "great intelligence and talents for business": Campbell, 146.

83 "I am pursuaded [sic]. . .": JE to PB, 9 June 1810, in Shaw [1966], 43.

83 "Montreal will be our market": JE to PB, 11 August 1810, in Shaw [1966], 44.

83 "This year not one . . .": Campbell, 196.

84 "will probably seek Montreal . . .": Campbell, 159.

84 "Does it make any essential difference . . .": Campbell, 164.

84 "singular inconsistency . . .": Clinton [1821], 24.

84 "by far the most important . . .": *Niles' Weekly Register*, 12 March 1812, 46–47.

85 "If our produce once gets into lake Ontario . . .": *American Medical and Philosophical Register*, October 1810, 150–51.

85 "an extensive western canal . . .": *American Medical and Philosophical Register*, January 1811, 374, 378.

85 "[p]ublic expectation . . . on tip toe": Clinton [1821], 24.

85 "Mr. Morris . . .": Clinton [1821], 24.

85 "[W]ith all the greatness of mind . . .": Hosack, 271.

86 "exploded . . .": *Canal Laws*, 1: 48, 49, 51.

86 "Too great a national interest . . .": *Canal Laws*, 1: 68.

87 "that inexhaustible stream . . .": *Canal Laws*, 1: 58–59.

87 "instead of depriving the country . . .": *Canal Laws*, 1: 62.

87 "they, from motives of delicacy . . .": Clinton [1821], 24.

87 "without proper care and deliberation . . .": Hosack, 271.

87 "and read by sensible men . . .": Hosack, 271–72.

88 "to its natural and appropriate objects . . .": Clinton [1821], 24.

88 "I can perceive but vague plans . . .": PB to JE, 17 May 1811, in Severance, 19.

88 "gratuitous suggestion . . .": Clinton [1821], 25.

91 "no part in any of the operations . . .": Hosack, 501.

91 "erroneous": *Canal Laws*, 1: 552.

91 "special benefit . . .": *Canal Laws*, 1: 89–90.

91 "inexpedient . . .": *Canal Laws*, 1: 72, 73.

91 "The characters of the two men . . .": James A. Bayard to Caesar A. Rodney, 22 December 1811, in Carp, 125.

92 "visionary and absurd . . .": Hammond, 1: 302.

92 "We do not assign reasons . . .": *Canal Laws*, 1: 90–91.

92 "an enthusiast as to the advantage . . .": *Canal Laws*, 1: 91.

93 "honorable spirit of enterprise . . .": *Canal Laws*, 1: 95.

93 "in a more prosperous condition . . .": *Canal Laws*, 1: 92.

94 "marks of reluctance were perceptible . . .": *Canal Laws*, 1: 93.

95 "felt the strongest disposition . . .": *Annals of Congress*, House of Representatives, 12th Cong., 2nd Sess., 1078.

96 "hangs back": Morris to DWC, 19 January 1812, DWC Papers, CUL.

96 "These men console themselves . . .": *Canal Laws*, 1: 94.

97 "[T]here can be no doubt . . .": *Canal Laws*, 1: 79.

97 "The life of an individual is short . . .": *Canal Laws*, 1: 81.

98 "[A]s the other commissioners had gained . . .": Hosack, 272.

98 "the course by an inclined plane . . .": *Canal Laws*, 1: 82.

99 "unquestioned . . .": *Canal Laws*, 1: 75.

99 "without hesitation . . .": *Canal Laws*, 1: 82.

100 "[T]he maxims of policy . . .": *Canal Laws*, 1: 72.

100 "sacrifice"; "too much": *Canal Laws*, 1: 87, 101.

100 "the utmost skill of the professional engineer . . .": *Canal Laws*, 1: 85–86.

101 "[T]hese people . . .": JE to PB, 30 March 30 1812, in Severance, 20.

102 "so little expectation . . .": PB to JE, 4 May 1812, in Severance, 22.

102 "satisfactory information from some experienced engineer . . .": *Canal Laws*, 1: 195.

103 "to England for one of the first Engineers there": TE to JE, 10 July 1812, in Severance, 25.

103 "too crooked and serpentine": Hosack, 503.

103 "apprehend a want of water . . .": TE and GM to JE, 14 June 1812, in Severance, 23.

103 "the late declaration of war . . .": JE to TE, 21 July 1812, in Severance, 26–27.

104 "The amount in Land . . .": TE to JE, 10 July 1812, in Severance, 25–26.

104 "It would . . . appear to the public . . .": JE to PB, 21 July 1812, in Severance, 28.

106 "military operations which are not favourable . . .": *Canal Laws*, 1: 103.

107 "the Inhabitants of the two Counties . . .": JE to PB, 21 July 1812, in Severance, 28.

107 "free gift . . .": *Canal Laws*, 1: 104.

107 "He would probably have arrived . . .": *Canal Laws*, 1: 105.

107 "The commissioners were thus frittered down . . .": Clinton [1821], 26.

108 "absent": Clinton [1821], 25.

108 "numerous engagements": Robert Fulton to GM, 22 February 1814, in *Niles' Weekly Register*, 14 May 1814.

109　"strong drink": Alexander, 1: 243.

109　"The canal bubble . . .": JE to PB, 12 August 1815, in Severance, 38.

6. THE CAUSE UNCROWNED

112　"[T]he occasion is a proper one . . .": Richardson, 567.

113　"I could not thus resign . . .": Knapp, 134.

114　"I am perfectly satisfied . . .": TE to RT, 11 November 1815, in Knapp, 232–33.

114　"I place no confidence whatever . . .": RT to TE, 29 December 1815, in Knapp, 236–39.

114　"pressing them to prosecute . . .": Knapp, 154.

116　"which had been unfortunately proposed . . .": Hosack, 385–86.

116　"masterly manner . . .": Knapp, 154–55.

116　"a sagacious discernment . . .": Hosack, 386

117　"It may be confidently asserted . . .": *Canal Laws*, I: 122–43 passim.

120　"the greatest single factor . . .": Miller, 46.

120　"the foundation of the present system . . .": Clinton [1821], 28.

120　"highly important that the west . . .": DWC to JE, 6 January 1816, in Severance, 39.

121　"I think we shall . . .": RT to TE, 11 January 1816, in Knapp, 240.

121　"determined to seize on the canal project . . .": Troup [1822], 1 (of appendix to supplement).

121　"much anxiety," "a remonstrance": JE to DWC, 19 January 1816, in Severance, 39.

121　"It will rest with the Legislature . . .": *Canal Laws*, 1: 116.

122　"gracious manner, affability . . .": *DAB*, "Daniel D. Tompkins."

122　"a tool and a dupe . . .": Clinton [1821], 26.

122　"profoundly ignorant of the subject . . .": DWC to JE, 3 February 1816, in Severance, 41–42.

123　"We have a good cause . . .": DWC to JE, 3 February 1816, in Severance, 42.

124　"many days and nights in Albany . . .": Fox, 44.

124　"[I]f the legislature should not be able . . .": RT to TE, 10 February 1816, in Knapp, 240–42.

124　"a broken reed . . .": RT to DWC, 26 January 1816, DWC Papers, CUL.

125　"sound and intelligent men . . .": Hosack, 432.

125　"Hot-bed Manufactures," "Spinning Jenny, till they are old enough . . .": GM to Moss Kent, 23 January 1816 and GM to Randolph Harrison, 4 March 1816, in Mintz, 239–40.

126　"with respectful observations . . .": Hosack, 272.

126　"I pray you to be persuaded . . .": GM to Canal Commissioners in New-York, 9 March 1816, in *The* (New York) *American*, 7 April 1819.

126　"our own countrymen . . .": *Canal Laws*, 1: 116–18 passim.

127 "the waving plan . . .": JE to Chauncey Loomis, 14 February 1816, in Severance, 46–47.

127 "I would recommend employing . . .": JE to DWC, 21 February 1816, in Severance, 49.

127 "whether clay, loam, sand . . .": JE to DWC, 21 February 1816, in Severance, 49.

128 "the Erie canal . . .": DWC to JE, 27 February 1816, in Severance, 50.

128 "reserved, mysterious, and apparently incapable . . .": Troup [1822], 2 (of appendix to supplement).

128 "Their interviews . . .": Troup [1822], 21 (of supplement).

129 "general view of the difficulties . . .": *Canal Laws*, 1: 146.

129 "had a delicate and difficult . . .": Troup [1822], 1–2 (of appendix to supplement).

129 "put[ting] down the terror . . .": DWC to JE, 15 March 1816, in Severance, 50.

129 "The committee have investigated the subject . . .": *Canal Laws*, 1: 142.

130 "can be improved and completed . . .": *Canal Laws*, 1: 142, 143.

130 "Oh a ditch he would dig . . .": The rhyme appears, among numerous places, in Frank Moss and Henry Parkhurst, *The American Metropolis* (New York: P. F. Collier, 1897), 157.

130 "The Lakes with the Ocean! . . .": *Niles' Weekly Register*, 13 April 1816.

131 "wear the appearance of levity": JE to DWC, 25 March 1816, in Severance, 53.

131 "interesting . . .": DWC to JE, 4 April 1816, in Severance, 56.

132 "directly and eloquently . . .": Hosack, 434–35 passim.

133 "the wisdom of his remarks . . .": Hosack, 436.

133 "with no better success . . .": Troup [1822], 23 (of supplement).

133 "felt assured from his manner . . .": Troup [1822], 3 (of appendix to supplement).

133 "animated debate . . .": Hosack, 437.

134 "might be prejudiced in the public mind . . .": Hosack, 437.

136 "hope deferred": Geddes to DWC, 24 April 1816, DWC Papers, CUL.

136 "The Grand Canal DEFEATED . . .": Severance, 323–26.

136 "not as a positive good . . .": DWC to JE, 4 April 1816, in Renwick, 318.

136 "one of those political revolutions . . .": Hosack, 443.

137 "to the judicious and indefatigable . . .": Clinton [1821], 45.

137 "an active commissioner . . .": JE to DWC, 6 May 1816, in Severance, 57.

137 "the great interest he has taken . . .": JE to TE, 6 May 1816, in Severance, 58–62 passim.

138 "provided the Company has not to pay . . .": JE to JB, 13 May 1816, in Severance, 63. (The Busti quote is in Ellicott's letter.)

139 "to take upon yourself the task . . .": JE to MH, 16 June 1816, in Severance, 64.

140 "child of the people . . .": Clinton [1816], 8, 11, 13.

141 "stout built, quick spoken and cheerful . . .": Young [1909], 344, 345.

141 "upon the fingers of one hand": Wright [1870], 7.

141 "swamp and swale . . .": Young [1909], 333–47 passim. Except where noted, all quotes related to the survey are from this source.

142 "breakfast—chocolate . . .": Lawson, 9.

144 "I feel much pleased with . . .": BW to MH, 4 October 1816, in Erie Canal Museum Newsletter (Spring 2002), 4.

144 "the magnificent scenery of the lake . . .": DWC to Henry Post, 28 July 1816, in Severance, 327.

145 "the great Slope": JE to JB, 15 October 1816, in Severance, 72.

145 "[A]s to passing over extended surface . . .": JE to SY, 24 October 1816, in Severance, 74.

147 "examining the land and the water . . .": DWC to Henry Post, 28 July 1816, in Severance, 327.

147 "the difficult grounds . . .": DWC to JE, 18 August 1816, in Severance, 64, 65.

147 "owing to the loss of one . . .": [Peacock] to JE, 18 August 1816, in Severance, 66.

147 "without a sufficient supply of water . . .": JE to SY, 24 October 1816, in Severance, 75, 76.

148 "[I]n 50 years it will be next to N. York . . .": DWC to Henry Post, 14 August 1816, in Severance, 328, 329.

148 "service to the cause of science . . .": DWC to JE, 18 August 1816, in Severance, 65.

148 "its practicability beyond all manner of doubt.": DWC to JE, 20 September 1816, in Severance, 71.

149 "afforded good pickings . . .": Young, 340–45 passim.

150 "Let *Clinton's* mental pow'rs unfold . . .": William Ray. *Poems on Various Subjects* (Auburn, N.Y.: U. F. Doubleday, 1821), 131–32.

150 "its easy and cheap execution . . .": DWC to John Pintard, 18 August 1816, DWC Papers, NYPL.

151 "We are convinced that the undertaking . . .": *Niles' Weekly Register*, 12 October 1816.

151 "the magnitude of the undertaking . . .": JB to JE, 31 October 1816, in Severance, 78.

151 "a full exposure of the cloven foot . . .": Clinton [1821], 28.

151 "pressing and indispensable importance": Troup [1822], 19 (of supplement).

151 "chilling"; "construed into a settled hostility": Hosack, 439.

152 "the gayety of inexperience . . .": Morris to John Parish, 6 July 1816, *Diary and Letters of Gouverneur Morris*, 2: 601.

152 "a flexible piece of hickory": Rufus King to C[hristopher] Gore, 5 November 1816, in *Life and Correspondence of Rufus King*), 6: 35.

152 "a short but distressing illness": New-York *Evening Post*, 6 November 1816.

7. "THE MOST GIGANTIC UNDERTAKING"

153 "filled a large space . . .": New-York *Evening Post*, 6 November 1816.

154 "I particularly invite again . . .": Richardson, 576.

154 "canals . . . which art finds it . . .": *The Federalist*, 85.

155 "The state of New-York is not unaware . . .": *Canal Laws*, 1: 296.

155 "if the State shall accomplish . . .": JE to Micah Brooks, 30 December 1816, in Severance, 84.

155 "visionary projects": JE to Archibald Clarke, 3 January 1817, in Severance, 87.

155 "canal notions"; "his ignorance . . .": Hosack, 266.

155 "some visionary theorist": JE to Archibald Clarke, 3 January 1817, in Severance, 87.

155 "has had a tendency . . .": Micah Brooks to JE, 16 January 1817, in Severance, 95.

156 "to inquire into the expediency . . .": *Annals of Congress*, House of Representatives, 14th Cong., 2nd Sess., 296.

157 "To legislate for our country . . .": *Annals of Congress*, House of Representatives, 14th Cong., 2nd Sess., 851–58 passim.

158 "fair and unexceptionable standard . . .": *Canal Laws*, 1: 312.

159 "a little uncouth in his manner . . .": Hammond, 1: 371–72.

159 "the Root of all evil": Hopkins [1961], 330.

159 "A South Carolinian or Georgian . . .": *Annals of Congress*, House of Representatives, 14th Cong., 2nd Sess., 861, 862.

160 "yields to the Government . . .": *Annals of Congress*, House of Representatives, 14th Cong., 2nd Sess., 880, 891.

160 "build up the already overgrown . . .": *Annals of Congress*, House of Representatives, 14th Cong., 2nd Sess., 913.

160 "When the Clerk announced the vote . . .": DWC to JE, 14 February 1817, in Severance, 117.

160 "passed the bill to aid . . .": *The Columbian* (New York), 11 February 1817.

161 "[N]ot even an earthquake . . .": *Annals of Congress*, House of Representatives, 15th Cong., 1st Sess., 1371.

161 "existing powers . . .": *Annals of Congress*, House of Representatives, 14th Cong., 2nd Sess., 1060.

161 "he gave a Parthian, parting blow . . .": *The Columbian* (New York), 25 March 1817.

161 "the most exalted station in the union . . .": *Albany Advertiser*, 22 March 1817.

162 "If she wishes to attain that rank . . .": *Northern Whig* (Hudson, NY), 25 March 1817.

162 "After swallowing the National Bank . . .": DWC to Rufus King, 13 December 1817, in Renwick, 320.

162 "reprehensible conduct . . .": Clinton [1821], 44, 45.

163 "intelligence and influence . . .": MH to JE, 11 January 1817; DWC to JE, 21 January 1817; JE to DWC, 20 January 1817, in Severance, 94, 97.

163 "[T]here cannot be a question . . .": JE to DWC, [January 1817], in Severance, 114.

164 "I cannot divest myself . . .": PB to JE, 23 January 1817, in Severance, 98.

164 "not idle in regard to . . .": Hosack, 439.

164 "plain and practical treatise . . .": Young [1817], iii.

164 "not possess the requisite talents . . .": PBP to MVB, 13 February 1817, in Carp, 206–7.

164 "Clinton will certainly be . . .": John Pintard to Eliza Noel Pintard Davidson, 15 February 1817, *Letters from John Pintard*, 1: 56.

165 "was not consulted on the details . . .": *Canal Laws*, 1: 270.

168 "I cannot but believe . . .": MH to JE, 18 February 1817, in Severance, 118.

168 "have immortalized their names . . .": JE to DWC, 16 April 1817, in Severance, 123.

168 "incredulous of its ever be[ing] perfected . . .": PB to JE, 22 February 1817, in Severance, 120.

168 "a good and safe harbor": JB to DWC, 22 February 1817, in Severance, 12.

168 "the jealousy of the Black Rock": PB to JE, 22 February 1817, in Severance, 120.

169 "in the very crisis": Clinton [1821], 44.

170 "very intelligent . . .": *Canal Laws*, 1: 301, 320, 321, 322.

171 "[T]hough little of a rhetorician . . .": Hosack, 439.

171 "vested in some sort of stock . . .": Hosack, 488–92 passim.

173 "was much of the time at Albany . . .": Hosack, 441.

174 "settled conviction . . .": *Canals Laws*, 1: 273–87 passim. Wittingly or not, the committee report substituted "public" for Hamilton's "national" as the penultimate word in the paragraph; see *Annals of Congress*, House of Representatives, 2nd Cong., 1st Sess., 1006.

177 "It was thought most strange . . .": Hosack, 490.

178 "sound judgment [and] practical . . .": Hosack, 440.

179 "no law was ever introduced . . .": *National Advocate*, 31 March 1817.

179 "met with vigorous opposition . . .": Troup [1822], 31 (of supplement).

179 "would never pass": Hosack, 490.

179 "essentially different . . .": Hosack, 492.

179 "tax the people before the Canal . . .": *New-York Daily Advertiser*, 18 April 1817.

180 "most respectable and opulent of her merchants . . .": *Albany Gazette & Daily Advertiser*, 16 April 1817.

180 "materially defective": *The Columbian* (New York), 10 April 1817.

180 "indefatigable"; "out of the house": Hosack, 443.

181 "in a more formidable and determined manner . . .": Hosack, 444.

181 "sterling character . . .": Hosack, 441.

181 "It [is] a principle of equity . . ." *New-York Daily Advertiser*, 16 April 1817.

182 "Who is this James Geddes . . .": Geddes, 292.

183 "language . . . at once persuasive and powerful": Hosack, 448.

183 "the most notable personage": Oliver Wendell Holmes, *The Poet of the Breakfast Table* (Boston: Riverside, 1891), 331.

183 "listened to the great men of Europe . . .": Franklin Ellis, *History of Columbia County, New York* (Philadelphia: Everts & Ensign, 1878), 84.

183 "Will not all the productions . . .": *The Columbian* (New York), 16 April 1817.

185 "[T]he man who will enter into this project . . .": *Albany Gazette & Daily Advertiser*, 16 April 1817.

185 "Now the scene is entirely changed . . .": Hosack, 452.

185 "master spirit": Hosack, 440.

185 "great speech of the session": Hosack, 451.

185 "[W]e have arrived at the point . . .": *New-York Daily Advertiser*, 26 April 1817.

186 "breaking through that reserve . . .": Hosack, 453.

186 "a scoundrel of the first magnitude . . .": DWC to Henry Post, 30 December 1822, in Hanyan, 57.

186 "personal intercourse was very reserved . . .": *Autobiography of MVB*, 85.

187 "I believe our adverse votes . . .": *Autobiography of MVB*, 85.

188 "good behavior . . .": New York State Constitution of 1777, Article 3.

189 "had ever been distinguished . . .": Hosack, 387–88 passim.

191 "In our America we are turning . . .": TJ to Alexander von Humboldt, 13 June 1817, *Jefferson Papers*, LOC.

191 "the powerful weight . . .": DWC to TJ, 25 April 1817; TJ to DWC 14 April 1817, *Jefferson Papers*, LOC.

8. LAYING THE GROUNDWORK

193 "No. 1, True Canal Line": *Memorial of Centennial*, 68.

193 "[W]e [have] the honor of commencing . . .": *Memorial of Centennial*, 56.

194 "The work . . . will diffuse the benefits . . .": Hosack, 455.

194 "the great and glorious undertaking": *Niles' Weekly Register*, 26 July 1817.
194 "[E]ach citizen turned up a clod or two . . .": *National Advocate*, 19 July 1817.
194 "Very likely he did . . .": *Memorial of Centennial*, 56.
194 "derived from the best English engineers . . .": *Canal Laws*, 1: 368.
195 "canals and locks between the Mohawk . . .": *Canal Laws*, 1: 359.
196 "little more than a nominal commissioner . . .": JE to DWC, 25 April 1817, in Severance, 125.
196 "The whole project hangs upon . . .": Young to DWC, 11 August 1817, DWC Papers, CUL.
197 "[a]fter many plans . . .": *Memorial of Centennial*, 68.
197 "superior in length to any summit . . .": *Canal Laws*, 1: 367.
197 "[a]fter a minute and laborious examination . . .": *Canal Laws*, 1: 369.
200 "He is a Quaker . . .": TJ to W. C. C. Claiborne, 24 May 1803, in Barnard, 411.
200 "broken fortune": Isaac Briggs to James Madison, 18 January 1814, *James Madison Papers*, LOC.
201 "all my expectations of advantageous business . . .": Isaac Briggs to TJ, 9 May 1817, *Jefferson Papers*, LOC.
201 "qualifications, industry & integrity . . .": TJ to Isaac Briggs, 18 May 1817, *Jefferson Papers*, LOC.
201 "eminent mathematician": *Canal Laws*, 1: 370.
201 "finances would not long bear it": Isaac Briggs to Joseph Binghurst, 13 May 1817, in Barnard, 415.
202 "bosom friend": *Daily National Intelligencer* (Washington, DC), 10 January 1825.
202 "[T]here are very few men . . .": John Mason to Philip Narbonne Nicholas, 24 May 1818, in Billy Joe Peyton, "To Make the Crooked Ways Straight and the Rough Ways Smooth: The Federal Government's Role in Laying Out and Building the Cumberland Road" (Ph.D. diss., West Virginia University, 1999), 64.
202 "I am induced to believe . . .": Isaac Briggs to TJ, 15 May 1817, *Jefferson Papers*, LOC.
202 "have not yet appointed an engineer . . .": TE to TJ, 16 May 1817, *Jefferson Papers*, LOC.
203 "exile of Erin . . .": Valentine Gill to James Madison, 4 April 1817, James Madison Papers, LOC.
203 "Practical mathematics and mechanics . . .": *Niles' Register*, 29 November 1817.
204 "More lasting the Brass . . .": diary entry, in Way, 47. The translation is of Horace's Ode 30, Book 3.
204 "Mr. Wright is absent . . .": SY to DWC, 11 August 1817, DWC Papers, CUL.

205 "We feel very much dissatisfied . . .": MH to DWC, 9 August 1817, DWC Papers, CUL.

205 "Mr. Briggs is nearly stationary . . .": SY to DWC, 11 August 1817, DWC Papers, CUL.

206 "a decayed settlement . . .": Campbell, 66.

206 "agreeable rather than handsome . . .": Stuart, 104, 108.

207 "entertained the idea . . .": FitzSimons, 22–28 passim.

210 "Go on, Doctor . . .": Earl, 142.

210 "a sprightly, pleasing gentleman . . .": *New-York Statesman* (Albany), 30 June 1820. The quote is from the seventh letter of "Hibernicus," a Clinton pseudonym.

210 "particular pains to call on . . .": *Canal Laws*, 1: 380.

210 "Money is very scarce . . .": DWC to JE, 10 May 1817, in Severance, 125.

211 "There is money in abundance . . .": DWC to W. Steele, 24 June 1818, DWC Papers, CUL.

211 "Some of the most luminous reports . . .": Clinton [1821], 45n.

212 "every alternation in its strata . . .": *Canal Laws*, 1: 368, 369.

212 "Should this Herculean work . . .": JE to PB, 21 June 1817, in Severance, 127, 128.

213 "recently arrived in this country": *Canal Laws*, 1: 403.

213 "men in moderate pecuniary circumstances . . .": *Canal Laws*, 1: 371.

214 "some responsible individual": *Canal Laws*, 1: 372.

214 "men of property and respectability . . .": *Canal Laws*, 1: 373.

214 "safely anticipate . . .": *Canal Laws*, 1: 375.

216 "a man whose responsibility . . .": *Canal Laws*, 2: 514.

216 "[A]mong our first contractors . . .": *Canal Laws*, 1: 375; 2: 516, 518.

218 "very liberal wages": *Canal Laws*, 1: 374.

218 "three-fourths of all the labourers . . .": *Canal Laws*, 1: 403.

218 "Wild Irish bog trotters . . .": Thompson [1979], 222–23.

218 "will afford steady and permanent . . .": *The Exile* (New York), 2 August 1817.

219 "considerable solicitude . . .": *Canal Laws*, 1: 369.

220 "plow and scraper . . .": *Canal Laws*, 1: 405.

220 "to exceed all other maps . . .": "Biographical Sketch of the Late Geographer, John H. Eddy," 13.

9. SECURING THE MIDDLE

223 "It was natural the question . . .": FitzSimons, 28.

224 "the finest invention of the present age": TJ to James Bowdoin, 10 July 1806, *Jefferson Papers*, LOC.

225 "Notwithstanding the unfavorable season . . .": *Canal Laws*, 1: 366.

226 "To join the east to the west . . .": *Canal Laws*, 1: 381.

226 "a luminous and very satisfactory statement . . .": Jediah Prendergast to JE, 12 February 1818, in Severance, 129.

226 "extraordinary": JE to DWC, 6 March 1818, in Severance, 130.

227 "An apparent disposition . . .": John Pintard to Eliza Noel Pintard Davidson, 30 March 1818, in *Letters from John Pintard*, 1:114.

227 "The truth is . . .": DWC to JE, 11, 31 March 1818, in Severance, 131, 133.

227 "The State looks to you . . .": DWC to Ellicott, 24, 31 March 1818, in Severance, 132, 133.

228 "a severe contusion . . .": JE to DWC, 2 April 1818, in Severance, 133, 134, 135, 137.

229 "a safe and commodious harbor . . .": *Canal Laws*, 1: 389.

229 "so well qualified . . .": DWC to Ellicott, 18 June 1818, in *HLC*, 1: 139.

229 "shrewd, self-reliant and diligent . . .": Bagg, 402.

229 "utter want of political tact . . .": Hammond, 1: 452, 495–96.

230 "My regret for your resignation . . .": DWC to JE, 25 September 1818, in Severance, 144.

230 "with my target on my shoulder . . .": FitzSimons, 30, 31, 33.

231 "including all the difficult places": *Canal Laws*, 1: 416.

231 "very backward . . .": Thomas Moore to Isaac Briggs, 7 May 1818, Sandy Spring (Md.) Museum.

231 "I have a son who is about 21 . . .": Thomas Moore to Philip Narbonne Nicholas, 22 May 1818, in Billy Joe Peyton, "To Make the Crooked Ways Straight and the Rough Ways Smooth: The Federal Government's Role in Laying Out and Building the Cumberland Road" (Ph.D. diss., West Virginia University, 1999), 66.

232 "a severe illness . . .": Richmond (Va.) *Enquirer*, 8 October 1822.

232 "a long and painful illness": *Daily National Intelligencer* (Washington, DC), 10 January 1825.

233 "lads and lasses . . .": Watson [1856], 475.

235 "valuable improvements . . .": Watson [1856], 476, 477.

235 "promote the convenience . . .": *Canal Laws*, 1: 401, 402.

237 "appeared to think . . .": *Canal Laws*, 2: 217.

237 "great numbers of wealthy . . .": *Canal Laws*, 1: 403.

238 "a scene of the most animated . . .": *Rochester Telegraph*, 21 July 1818.

238 "will in all human probability . . .": DWC to JE, 25 September 1818, in Severance, 144.

238 "[T]he whole was taken up . . .": *Canal Laws*, 1: 403, 406.

239 "a scientific gentleman . . .": Clark, 2: 65.

240 "It is with extreme diffidence . . .": "Claim of Doct. A. A. Bartow to Canal Commissioners on the Discovery of the Water Lime," ms., n.d., Oneida County Historical Society.

241 "It was supposed Canvass White . . .": JBJ to Samuel Earl, 7 August 1880, in Earl, 131.

242 "a discovery of the greatest importance . . .": *Canal Laws*, 1: 448, 449.
242 "fourth part of the patent": White to Bartow, 16 April 1823, Bartow Papers.
243 "This has so far been . . .": White to Bartow, 12 April 1823, Bartow Papers.
243 "These men may combine . . .": White to Bartow, 16 April 1823, Bartow Papers.
243 "ill success attending the introduction . . .": Bartow to White, 19 May 1823, Bartow Papers.
243 "The reverses experienced . . .": Bartow to White, 28 June 1823, Bartow Papers.
243 "you shall have your portion . . .": White to Bartow, 25 April 1823, Bartow Papers.
244 "In a compromise so far . . .": Bartow to White, 19 May 1823, Bartow Papers.
244 "That decision will be law . . .": White to Bartow, 15 September 1823, Bartow Papers.
244 "appropriate[d] the discovery . . .": *Canal Laws*, 2: 216.
244 "just and equitable . . .": *Canal Laws*, 2: 382.
245 "You will readily perceive . . .": Maurice Wurts to Bartow, 9 December 1825, Bartow Papers.
246 "immovably fastened on the ground": *Canal Laws*, 1: 404.
246 "[T]o see a forest tree . . .": Colden [1826], 55.
246 "[I]f [he] would use a windlass . . .": *Castorland Journal*, 65.
247 "unremittingly employed . . .": *Canal Laws*, 1: 403–4.
247 "my food, drink, and washing . . .": William Thomas to family, 17 August 1818, in Conway, 61.
248 "This country is not . . .": Hugh Jones to parents, 7 September 1818, in Conway, 61–62.
248 "with some great gentleman . . .": David Richard to brother, 11 December 1818, in Conway, 62.
248 "ASTONISHING AND GRATIFYING FACT": Cleveland *Register*, 18 August 1818.
249 "I have every reason for believing . . .": Cleveland *Register*, 25 August 1818.
249 "We know not which to admire . . .": *Charleston Times*, n.d., in Cleveland *Register*, 8 December 1818.
249 "It must be a pleasing reflection . . .": Rochester *Telegraph*, 21 July 1818.
250 "the most sanguine expectations . . .": Albany *Register*, n.d., in Cleveland *Register*, 6 October 1818.
250 "a man of very pleasant manner . . .": FitzSimons, 32–33.
251 "retired to another . . .": Bobbé, 224, 225.
252 "[F]or some time they were loth . . .": *Canal Laws*, 1: 448–49.
252 "pretty well fatigued . . .": FitzSimons, 35, 36.

253 "it stands as a well-designed plan . . .": FitzSimons, 37.

253 "a new and much improved": (advertisement), Palmyra *Register*, 9 February 1820.

254 "from which the muck slid . . .": Wager [1896], 222 (Part One).

254 "far superior to any thing . . .": (advertisement), Palmyra *Register*, 9 February 1820.

254 "region of the rankest vegetable luxuriance . . .": *Canal Laws*, 1: 449–50.

254 "scenes of suffering and distress . . .": Clark, 92.

255 "[A]lthough great exertions were made . . .": *Canal Laws*, 1: 450.

255 "[T]ired of assisting [the poor] in their distress . . .": Eddy to Clinton, 15 February 1817, DWC Papers, CUL.

257 "[B]efore the close of the season . . .": *Northern Whig* (Hudson, NY), 5 October 1819.

257 "The first admission of water . . .": *Utica Patriot*, 26 October 1819, in New-York *Evening Post*, 30 October 1819.

257 "I beheld a sight . . .": *Albany Daily Advertiser*, in New-York *Evening Post*, 30 October 1819.

258 "We sailed from Rome . . .": *Memorial of Centennial*, 66.

259 "But this pressure . . .": *Utica Patriot*, 26 October 1819, in New-York *Evening Post*, 30 October 1819.

256 "From bridge to bridge . . .": *Utica Patriot*, 26 October 1819, in New-York *Evening Post*, 30 October 1819.

260 "The experience of this day's excursion . . .": *Utica Patriot*, 2 November 1819, in *Cherry Valley Gazette*, 9 November 1819.

260 "It was impossible for stupidity itself . . .": Watson [1820], 79.

260 "in a safe and comfortable manner . . .": *Utica Patriot*, 26 October 1819, in *Cherry Valley Gazette*, 2 November 1819.

260 "To no man is the state so much indebted . . .": *Utica Patriot*, 26 October 1819, in *Cherry Valley Gazette*, 2 November 1819.

261 "The spirit which manifested itself . . .": *Niles' Register*, 20 November 1819.

261 "in defiance of the inclemency . . .": *Cayuga Republican*, 15 December 1819.

261 "By the continual passage of boats . . .": *New-York Statesman* (Albany), 23 June 1820.

262 "intention to keep the water . . .": *Canal Laws*, 2: 249.

263 "bluff of hard land . . .": Clark, 2: 10.

264 "The banks of the canal . . .": Onondaga *Register*, 25 April 1820.

264 "only One Line anywhere . . .": Erie Canal Navigation Company, Report to Stockholders, 15 November 1824, in Shaw [1966], 200.

264 "justified in asking toll": *Canal Laws*, 2: 13.

265 "cheaper and more commodious . . .": *New-York Statesman* (Albany), 16 June 1820.

265 "I found its accommodations . . .": Howison, 299–302 passim.

266 "a raft of 440 tons . . .": *New-York Statesman* (Albany), 23 June 1820.

267 "to raise them out of the mud . . .": *Early History of Syracuse*, 21.
267 "It would make an owl weep . . .": Severance, 221.
268 "a most brilliant day dawned . . .": Clark, 2: 98.
268 "Such a spectacle . . .": Hosack, 457.
268 "I have dreaded its progress . . .": Watson [1820], 78, 79, 104n.

10. EASTWARD HO!

269 "there cannot exist a doubt . . .": *Canal Laws*, 1: 394–96 passim.
270 "An unanimity appears to exist . . .": *The* [New York] *American*, 20 March 1819.
271 "He is the political *Ishmael* . . .": New-York *Evening Post*, 1 April 1819.
271 "until the day of his death . . .": Hammond, 1: 497.
272 "The opposition to internal navigation . . .": DWC to Rufus King, 24 January 1819, in *Life and Correspondence of Rufus King*, 6: 196–97.
272 "worthy and respectable men . . .": *Canal Laws*, 2: 517, 518.
273 "I confess myself among those . . .": Nathan Williams to MVB, 9 December 1819, in Shaw [1966], 105.
273 "Tell the people . . .": Carp, 291.
274 "no notice was taken . . .": FitzSimons, 52, 63.
274 "blackguard"; "dastardly accuser": DWC to SY, 25 February 1820, DWC Papers, CUL.
274 "malicious slander": SY to DWC, 20 December, DWC Papers, CUL.
275 "decided opinion . . .": Isaac Briggs to William Darby, 16 January 1819, in Darby, lxiii (of Addenda).
275 "at reasonable prices": *Canal Laws*, 1: 452.
275 "[T]he distresses of the community . . .": *Speeches of the Different Governors*, 166, 168.
276 "the impolitic proceedings": Hosack, 491.
276 "[T]his state can never enjoy . . .": *Canal Laws*, 1: 468.
276 "interfere, in any way . . .": *Canal Laws*, 1: 459.
278 "We have scotched the snake . . .": MVB to Gorham A. Worth, 1 June 1820, in Shaw [1966], 115.
279 "excited a laudable curiosity . . .": *Geneva Gazette*, 15 December 1819, in Clinton [1821], iii.
280 "I felt that some special favor . . .": FitzSimons, 40–41, 45.
281 "In some cases . . .": FitzSimons, 48.
281 "Being economical in my habits . . .": FitzSimons, 49, 59.
282 "eminently upright in purpose . . .": FitzSimons, 81.
282 "In any case of dispute . . .": FitzSimons, 50–51.
283 "Occurrences of this kind are unpleasant . . .": *The* [New York] *American*, 10 August 1822.
284 "correctness": *Canal Laws*, 2: 72.

285 "Mr. Gevins [sic] was a sagacious man . . .": FitzSimons, 53–54.

285 "through the very heart . . .": Spafford, *Gazetteer [1824]*, 473.

285 "Canal when completed . . .": *Our Travels*, 111–12.

286 "to be full of holes . . .": FitzSimons, 54.

287 "complete *hypocritical, lying nincompoop* . . .": BW to JBJ, 9 July 1824, Jervis Papers.

287 "placed at the head": *American Railroad Journal and Mechanics' Magazine*, 15 April 1839.

288 "those supposed improvements . . .": William Bridges, *Map of the City of New-York and Island of Manhattan With Explanatory Remarks and References* (New York: William Bridges, 1811), 25.

289 "the pride and boast of the city": Randel [1864], 848.

289 "I was arrested by the Sheriff . . .": Randel [1864], 848.

289 "while drawing the line . . .": Martha Lamb, *The History of the City of New York, 3 vols.* (New York: A.S. Barnes, 1896), 3: 572.

289 "impassable without the aid of an axe": Randel [1864], 850.

290 "with an accuracy not exceeded . . .": Carey, 7.

290 "no error has ever been discovered . . .": *Manual of the Corporation of the City of New York* (New York: Valentine, 1866), 764.

290 "an eminent mathematician . . .": Carey, 7.

290 "in accordance with the wishes . . .": Randel [1822], [3].

290 "no pecuniary aid . . .": *Albany Gazette & Daily Advertiser*, 27 June 1821.

290 "[H]ow we shall get a line . . .": Henry Seymour to DWC, 16 October 1820, DWC Papers, CUL.

291 "of such importance . . .": *Albany Gazette and Daily Advertiser*, 27 June 1821.

293 "principal object": *Albany Gazette and Daily Advertiser*, 16 July 1821.

293 "re-view and re-examine Mr. Randel's route . . .": *Albany Gazette and Daily Advertiser*, 18 July 1821.

293 "[W]e were informed . . .": *New-York Statesman* (Albany) undated item reprinted in *New-York* (NY) *Spectator*, 7 August 1821.

294 "would be expensive . . .": Randel [1822], 6.

294 "one word heard about crossing the river . . .": [Randel], 11.

294 "the canal can be constructed . . .": *Canal Laws*, 2: 18.

296 "never examined this route": Randel [1822], 5.

296 "no leisure to bestow . . .": Randel [1822], 5.

296 "a new route for the Canal . . .": *New-York Spectator*, 18 December 1821.

296 "devious and almost impracticable direction . . .": *Albany Argus*, 11 January 1822.

296 "an incomprehensible trip across the Mohawk!": *Albany Argus*, 15 February 1822.

297 "the impropriety and ruinous consequences . . .": [Randel], 4, 10, 18.

297 "for the purpose of suppressing it": *Albany Argus*, 5 February 1822.

297 "The termination of the eastern section . . .": *Canal Laws*, 2: 70–75 passim.

299 "crossing the river, in order to pay . . .": [Randel], 12.

299 "[N]otwithstanding the great respectability . . .": *Albany Argus*, 5 March 1822.

300 "shocking oppression and injustice": Carey, title page.

300 "This J.R. is so full of his lies . . .": BW to JBJ, 11 September 1825, Jervis Papers.

301 "stupendous aqueducts . . .": *Canal Laws*, 2: 172.

301 "It had appeared to me . . .": FitzSimons, 113.

301 "Aqueducts with wooden trunks . . .": JBJ to the Canal Commissioners, 24 November 1835, in Larkin [1990], 59.

302 "I had a line continued . . .": FitzSimons, 113.

302 "the route to the opposite side . . .": JBJ to the Canal Commissioners, 20 June 1836, in Larkin [1990], 59.

302 "the desire to gain needed political support . . .": Whitford, 1: 150.

303 "[T]he prices of money . . .": *Canal Laws*, 2: 6.

304 "in a temper . . .": McKelvey [1942], 9.

304 "Ever since the canal was begun . . .": MH to Luther Holley, 20 June 1821, in Shaw [1966], 117.

304 "Our Canals . . . are now safely anchored . . .": DWC to John Pintard, 12 April 1821, DWC Papers, NYPL.

306 "There has been . . . an immense revolution . . .": Adams [1875], 128.

306 "The want of money, in the country . . .": *Canal Laws*, 2: 7.

307 "wild Irish": Mary Archbald to M[argaret] Wodrow, 1 January 1821, in Sheriff, 37.

307 "freeborn Yankees as they are pleased . . .": Mary Archbald to DWC, October [1821], in Sheriff, 40.

307 "Numerous emigrants from the hardy . . .": *Niles' Register*, 29 June 1822.

308 "[S]he looked out of the cabin window . . .": *Hampshire Gazette* (Northampton, Mass), 3 July 1822.

308 "Taken as a whole . . .": *Spafford, Pocket Guide*, 34, 35.

308 "intense and suffocating . . .": "Diary of a Young Girl: The Erie Canal in 1822," Part I, *Rochester History* 62, no. 3 (Summer 2000): 13–17 passim.

309 "obliged to make to each of them . . .": *Our Travels*, 107–10 passim.

309 "New York does not yet feel . . .": Morse to his wife, 27 August 1823, in *Samuel F.B. Morse: His Letters and Journals*, 2 vols. (New York: Houghton Mifflin, 1914), 1: 248–49.

310 "Clinton's big ditch": *Niles' Register*, 29 November 1823.

310 "it would appear as a pitiful exertion . . .": Charles E. Dudley to MVB, 18 January 1823, in Shaw [1966], 166.

310 "The Canal Commissioners have escaped . . .": DWC to Francis Adrian Van der Kemp, 22 April 1823, in Jackson, 277.

310 "Whatever may be our thoughts . . .": Hosack, 80–81.

311 "fine autumnal morning . . .": Colden [1826], 60.

311 "new and superb packet boat . . .": (New York) *Commercial Advertiser*, 11 October 1823.

311 "line of Canal boats . . .": Colden [1826], 60.

311 "many feelings of anxiety . . .": (New York) *Commercial Advertiser*, 11 October 1823.

312 "The banks of the canal . . .": *Albany Argus*, 10 October 1823.

313 "new, rich, and beautiful . . .": (New York) *Commercial Advertiser*, 11 October 1823.

314 "the lock gates were opened . . .": Colden [1826], 61.

314 "deafening peals of applause . . .": Hosack, 458.

314 "public disaster . . .": *Albany Democrat*, 9 July 1824.

314 "For the many errors we have committed . . .": (New York) *Commercial Advertiser*, 11 October 1823.

315 "The *laudari a laudato viro* is more pleasing . . .": DWC to Francis Adrian Van der Kemp, 11 October 1823, DWC Papers, CUL.

315 "[Y]our great canal . . .": TJ to DWC, 12 December 1822, *Jefferson Papers*.

316 "formidable and appalling obstructions . . .": *Canal Laws*, 2: 173–74.

11. HOW THE WEST WAS WON

318 "We are cutting the Ditch . . .": "Canal Digger's Lament," The Dady Brothers, *Songs of the Erie Canal*, compact disc (Landmark Society of Western New York, 2000).

319 "Paddy of the Canal": "Paddy's Song," The Dady Brothers, *Songs of the Erie Canal*, compact disc (Landmark Society of Western New York, 2000).

319 "sickness began to manifest itself . . .": *Canal Laws*, 2: 63.

320 "When these marshes are drained . . .": *Spafford, Pocket Guide*, 39.

320 "the evil": *Canals Laws*, 2: 167.

320 "frequently detained": *Canal Laws*, 2: 250.

320 "It seemed to me like building castles . . .": Webb Harwood to Daniel Terry, 25 November 1821, typescript, Valentown Museum, Victor, N.Y.

321 "The internal concerns of New York . . .": New York *Spectator*, 8 January 1822, in Fox, 302.

321 "by getting a job on the canal . . .": Rochester *Gazette*, 10 October 1820, in Shaw [1966], 119, 121.

322 "to procure an *accurate survey* . . .": *The Following is a statement of such facts as came under the cognizance of the individuals who explored a more southern route for the Grand Canal . . .* (broadside); December 1818, [n.p.], Early American Imprints, Ser. 2, no. 51773.

323 "Economy induced us . . .": *Canal Laws*, 2: 10.

324 "horrible confusion": *Rochester History* 36, no.1 (January 1974), 8.

324 "permanent works . . .": *Canal Laws*, 2: 60.

324 "So far as I understand your plan . . .": Stuart, 95.

325 "impossible to employ as many teams . . .": *Canal Laws*, 2: 102.

325 "This operation is to prevent sudden breaking . . .": Stuart, 96.

325 "much anxiety": *Canal Laws*, 2: 167.

325 "got in the way of the laborers . . .": George H. Woodruff, *History of Will County, Illinois* (Chicago: William LeBaron Jr., 1878), 256.

326 "leaked much less . . .": *Canal Laws*, 2: 167.

326 "watching it unceasingly . . .": *Canal Laws*, 2: 250.

326 "How would the great Brindley . . .": *Canal Laws*, 1: 44.

326 "The country being level . . .": Howison, 288–89.

326 "The Erie Canal—Great! . . .": Rochester *Telegraph*, 9 July 1822, in Shaw [1966], 127.

326 "the greatest mass of mason work": *Canal Laws*, 2: 100.

327 "Who can contemplate without horror . . .": Rochester *Telegraph*, 31 July 1821, in Shaw [1966], 129.

328 "bent down, with the course of the stream . . .": *Canal Laws*, 2: 101.

328 "extremely anxious . . .": Stuart, 96.

328 "It is a structure of admirable solidity . . .": *Canal Laws*, 2: 164.

329 "the most stupendous and strongest . . .": Rochester *Telegraph*, 14 October 1823.

329 "the grandest single feature . . .": *Spafford, Pocket Guide*, 41.

330 "in a state of rapid dilapidation . . .": *Rochester History* 37, no. 3 (July 1975), 6, 7.

331 "The United States—cutting canals . . .": *National Geographic* 178, no. 5 (November 1990), 42.

331 "When the Canal is completed . . .": *Spafford, Pocket Guide*, 43.

332 "Mortified at the result . . .": *Shaft's Complete Lockport Directory* (1861–1862), 8.

332 "Without consulting any one . . .": Stuart, 112; *DAB*, "Nathan Roberts."

332 "I hope you will watch the stone-cutters . . .": Stuart, 95–96.

334 "reasonable exertions . . .": *Canal Laws*, 2: 162.

334 "The Ravine, through which the Canal . . .": *Spafford, Pocket Guide*, 45.

334 "a work of the first magnitude . . .": *Canal Laws*, 2: 245.

334 "a perfect wilderness . . .": *New-York Patriot, n.d.*, in *Middlesex Gazette* (Middletown, CT), 24 July 1823.

334 "regarded as men of business . . .": *Canal Laws*, 2: 98.

334 "It was not therefore . . .": *Canal Laws*, 2: 66.

335 "flies like hailstones . . .": Webb Harwood to Daniel Terry, 25 November 1821, typescript, Valentown Museum, Victor, N. Y.

335 "went on with resolution": *Canal Laws*, 2: 66.

335 "it was perfectly apparent . . .": *Canal Laws*, 2: 98.

335 "to be employed on excavating . . .": *New-York American*, 9 July 1822.

336 "[A]fter getting fairly into their cups . . .": Rochester *Telegraph*, 31 December 1822.

336 "cried out for croppies . . .": "The People v. Moore and Others," *Wheeler's Reports of Criminal Law Cases* (New York: Banks and Brothers, 1860), 3: 83, 86.

337 "a worse description . . .": *Canal Laws*, 2: 160, 161.

338 "gave a flattering test . . .": *Canal Laws*, 2: 243.

338 "sickness prevailed in almost every house . . .": Edward Allen Talbot, *Five Years' Residence in the Canadas: Including a Tour through Part of the United States of America, in the Year 1823*, 2 vols. (London: Longman, Hurst, Rees, Orme, Brown and Green, 1824), 2: 314, 315.

340 "a better site for a great trading Town . . .": Spafford [1813], 141.

340 "grand Imperium of the Western World": Thompson [1966], 152.

340 "western termination at Buffalo": *Canal Laws*, 1: 381.

340 "the mortification & disappointment . . .": Augustus Porter to PBP, 7 November 1815, in Shaw [1966], 143.

341 "There are . . . so many intrigues . . .": JE to PB, 24 August 1818, in Severance, 142.

341 "Buffalo from its local situation . . .": Severance, 154.

341 "The Buffalo harbor will not . . .": David Evans to JE, 13 February 1819, in Severance, 156.

342 "At this place . . .": Thomas [1819], 16–17.

342 "[H]e is a poet and great botanist . . .": Campbell, 176.

343 "The man who wrote that book . . .": Thomas [1888], 44.

343 "giving Items and the expense . . .": BW to David Thomas, 4 January 1821, 16 November 1820, 30 June 1820, in Calhoun, 106–7.

344 "His methods may sometimes . . .": William Richard Cutter, *Genealogical and Family History of Western New York* (New York: Lewis Historical Publishing Company, 1912), 2: 552.

344 "This man was a king among men . . .": *Publications of the Buffalo Historical Society* 5 (1902): 144.

345 "premature . . .": *Canal Laws*, 1: 453.

346 "ungentlemanly, morose, inaccessible . . .": Memorial to Paul Busti, 10 March 1821, in Chazanof, 201.

346 "All well and in high spirits . . .": J. L. Barton to unknown recipient, 9 January 1822, in Shaw [1966], 148.

346 "the canal ought to terminate . . .": *Canal Laws*, 2: 519.

346 "the stress of weather": Severance, 352.

347 "not free from doubt . . .": *Canal Laws*, 2: 79.

348 "in a fair experiment": *Canal Laws*, 2: 95–96.

348 "postpone[d] the ultimate decision . . .": *Canal Laws*, 2: 9.

348 "disregard of truth . . .": Severance, 369–70.

348 "wild and unattainable . . .": Severance, 319.

348 "the machinations of a cold-blooded conspiracy . . .": Black Rock *Beacon*, 24 April 1823, in Shaw [1966], 155.

349 "reasonably safe and permanent": *Canal Laws*, 2: 152.

349 "[T]he extraordinary and unexpected decision . . .": William Peacock to Herman B. Potter, 30 June 1823, in Severance, 176.

349 "As the die is cast . . .": Buffalo *Patriot*, 24 June 1823, in Shaw [1966], 158.

349 "The cause of the quarrel having ceased . . .": Black Rock *Beacon*, 26 June 1823, in Shaw [1966], 158.

350 "All were invited to come . . .": [Hodge], 388, 389.

350 "the citizens partook of a beverage . . .": Severance, 320.

352 "hand-barrows . . .": [Hodge], 389–90.

352 "Buffalo Creek . . . furnishes . . .": Diary of Lewis Roe Overton, photocopy of original, Longwood (N. Y.) Public Library.

352 "a neighbourhood quarrel": Severance, 369.

353 "under all vicissitudes and apprehensions . . .": *Canal Laws*, 2: 212–13.

354 "very reprehensible": DWC to David Thomas, 15 June 1824, DWC Papers, CUL.

354 "If my conduct . . . was reprehensible . . .": MH to Sally Holley, 20 March 1828, in Carp, 347–48.

355 "was received with unmingled . . .": Hosack, 483.

355 "was not an educated man . . .": Hammond, 2: 163.

355 "with difficulty obtained the floor . . .": Hammond, 2: 160.

355 "I hope there is yet a redeeming spirit . . .": Hosack, 484.

356 "one of the deepest finesses . . .": Baltimore *Patriot*, 20 April 1824.

356 "a mere political *ruse de guerre* . . .": *Niles' Weekly Register*, 24 April 1824.

356 "Availing themselves of the supposed unpopularity . . .": Hosack, 482.

357 "The envenomed malignity . . .": New-York *Evening Post*, 15 April 1824.

357 "We cannot believe this most unjust measure . . .": *New-York Daily Advertiser*, 15 April 1824.

358 "a littler act of little minds . . .": reprinted in Rochester *Telegraph*, 27 April 1824.

358 "Political Lunacy . . . as gross and foolish . . .": Boston *Commercial Gazette*, 19 April 1824.

358 "I hope, Judge, . . .": *The Autobiography of Martin Van Buren*, 144.

358 "[A] glorious exit . . .": Francis Adrian Van der Kemp to Clinton, 19 April 1824, DWC Papers, CUL.

358 "Never was there a meaner act": DWC to Henry Post, 15 April 1824, in *Harper's New Monthly Magazine* no. 298 (March 1875): 566.

359 "I am elected governor . . .": DWC to John Jacob Astor, 2 December 1824, in Renwick, 330, 331.

360 "Passing down the canal . . .": Turner [1850], 436, 437.

361 "remarkably beautiful . . .": *Niles' Weekly Register*, 25 June 1825.

361 "Black Rock is destined by nature . . .": *Monroe Republican*, 15 February 1825, in Shaw, 160.

361 "[A]n extremely limpid water . . .": Levasseur, 1: 96.

361 "violent and contrary wind": Levasseur, 2: 186.

362 "a small but handsome port . . .": Levasseur, 2: 188.

362 "saluted by an extraordinary . . .": Levasseur, 2: 191–92.

363 "The mountains have been levelled . . .": Sheriff, 32–34, 193 n. 31.

363 "calculated to bewilder the senses . . .": Ira A. Blossom to H[arm] J[an] Huidekoper, 31 October 1825, in Sheriff, 31.

364 "Here the great Erie Canal . . .": Caroline Gilman, *The Poetry of Travelling in the United States* (New York: S. Colman, 1838), 103.

12. TEN DAYS THAT SHOOK NEW YORK

366 "written when all my private prospects . . .": *The* [Rochester] *Telegraph*, 19 July 1825.

366 "by laborious industry . . .": Hosack, 305.

366 "the grand epoch of uniting the waters . . .": Buffalo *Emporium and General Advertiser*, 29 October 1825.

366 "The firing of heavy cannon . . .": Renwick, 332.

367 "which belching forth its thunder . . .": Orlando Allen to Guy H. Salisbury, 7 April 1863, in "The Erie Canal Gun-Telegraph," *Buffalo Historical Society Publications* 13 (1909): 393–94.

368 "drawn by four grey horses . . .": Colden [1826], 295.

368 "to pass through and take possession . . .": Colden [1826], 296.

368 "rescuing the looks and customs . . .": George Catlin, *Life among the Indians* (London: Gall & Inglis, 1870), vi.

369 "creeping things . . .": Colden [1826], 296.

369 "made by the Aborigines . . .": Colden [1826], 198.

369 "beautifully painted in green . . .": Colden [1826], 196.

369 "most enthusiastic huzzas": Colden [1826], 298.

371 "utter ignorance": Theodore C. Blegen, *Norwegian Migration to America: The American Transition* (Northfield, Minnesota: The Norwegian-American Historical Association, 1940), 611.

371 "a woman of great intelligence . . .": Rasmus B. Anderson, *The First Chapter of Norwegian Immigration* (Madison, Wisc.: author, 1895), 66.

371 "Who comes there?": Colden [1826], 299.

371 "of a superior quality . . .": Colden [1826], 198.

372 "After a revolution of eight years . . .": *Monroe Republican*, 15 November, 27 December 1825, in Carp, 383.

372 "Clinton and the Canal"; "Internal Improvements": Colden [1826], 301.

372 "From the Halls of the Capitol . . .": Lyons *Advertiser*, 2 November 1825, in Carp, 417.

372 "handsomely illuminated . . .": Colden [1826], 302.

373 "two gunners were blown to atoms": Colden [1826], 166.

373 "the offspring of the canal. . . . ": Syracuse *Gazette*, 2 November 1825, in Hosack, 353n.

373 "the first legislative projector . . .": Hosack, 352.

374 "early and decided support . . .": Syracuse *Gazette*, 2 November 1825, in Hosack, 354n.

374 "ruling *genius* . . .": Charles Giles, *The Convention of Drunkards, a Satirical Essay of Intemperance . . . and An Ode of the Completion of the Erie Canal* (New York: Scofield and Voorhies, 1840), 124–26.

375 "deprived of the opportunity . . .": Colden [1826], 306.

376 "There were no cheers . . .": Colden [1826], 307.

376 "banks of the Canal were lined . . .": Colden [1826], 308.

376 "the glory of the nation . . .": Colden [1826], 310.

376 "Such an animating, bright, beauteous . . .": Colden [1826], 313.

377 "like a fleet . . .": Colden [1826], 314.

377 "mild as May . . .": John Pintard to Eliza Noel Pintard Davidson, 5 November 1825, in *Letters from John Pintard*, 2: 196.

378 "benefits of immense importance . . ." Colden [1826], [125].

378 "in a manner suited . . .": Colden [1826], 128.

378 "literally crammed with spectators": New-York *Evening Post*, 5 November 1825.

378 "[T]here will be no limits . . .": *New-York Mirror*, 12 November 1825.

378 "This solemnity at this place . . .": Colden [1826], [272].

379 "Man delights in types and symbols": Colden [1826], 274.

379 "ludicrous exhibition": *New-York Spectator*, 8 November 1825.

379 "piece of ridicule and absurdity": New-York *Evening Post*, 25 October 1825.

380 "one of the most important days . . .": Christopher Prince Diary, 1821–1825, ms., G. W. Blunt White Library, Mystic Seaport Museum.

380 "the largest of the kind ever witnessed . . .": Colden [1826], 324.

380 "compliment paid to the individual . . .": Colden [1826], 245.

381 "'tis done! 'tis done!–The mighty chain . . .": Samuel Woodworth, *Ode for the Canal Celebration . . .*([New York]: Clayton & Van Norden, [1825]).

381 "We have witnessed . . .": Colden [1826], 282.

382 "resort to blows where he could . . .": Bagg, 53.

382 "owing to want of skill . . .": *New-York Spectator*, 8 November 1825.

382 "committed some excesses": New-York *Evening Post*, 5 November 1825.

382 "[N]ot a solitary instance of riot . . .": Colden [1826], 266.

383 "fiery serpents and dragons . . .": Colden [1826], 326.

383 "Take it all in all. . . . ": ElkanahWatson to John James, draft, n.d., in Shaw [1966], 189–90n.

384 "an Event among those most worthy . . .": John Quincy Adams, 23 May 1826, facsimile letter, in Colden [826], [419].

384 "The accomplishment of the great work . . .": James Monroe, 3 July 1826, facsimile letter, in Colden [1826], [418].

385 "As a monument of Public spirit . . .": James Madison, 31 May 1826, facsimile letter, in Colden [1826], [417].

385 "This great work will immortalize . . .": TJ, 8 June 1826, facsimile letter, in Colden [1826], [414].

385 "the pride and wonder of the age.": John Adams, 24 May 1826, facsimile letter, in Colden [1826], [413].

13. "THE SHADOWY REMEMBRANCE"

388 "entirely dissolved . . .": Ambrose Spencer to Jacob Brown, 14 February 1826, in Remini, 122.

388 "disposed to quarrel . . .": William B. Rochester to Henry Clay, 1 August 1827, in *The Papers of Henry Clay*, ed. Mary W. M. Hargreaves and James F. Hopkins (Lexington: University of Kentucky Press, 1959), 6: 837.

388 "[t]his accident . . .": *Black Rock Gazette*, 1 June 1826, in *The Watch-Tower* (Cooperstown, N.Y.), 12 June 1826.

388 "A column of water . . .": *Buffalo Journal*, [30 May 1826], in (Hartford) *Connecticut Mirror*, 12 June 1826.

389 "not a movement has been made . . .": *Buffalo Journal*, 12 June 1827, in *New-York Spectator*, 22 June 1827.

389 "abandoned [its works] . . .": *Rochester Telegraph*, 27 June 1827.

389 "Conceived in sin . . .": DWC to Davis Thomas, 10 June 1827, in Shaw [1966], 162.

389 "[g]ay, frank, communicative . . .": Margaret Bayard Smith to Mrs. [Samuel] Boyd, 6 February 1829, in *The First Forty Years of Washington Society*, ed. Gaillard Hunt, 274 (New York: Charles Scribner's Sons, 1906).

389 "in the size of our canal . . .": Benjamin Wright to William Bouck, 23 December 1834, in Shaw [1966], 241.

390 "[N]o single act . . .": Hawley [1840], 14.

391 "Surely, the water of this canal . . .": [Nathaniel Hawthorne], "The Canal-Boat," *The New-England Magazine* 9 (December 1835): 398–409 passim.

392 "For three hundred and sixty miles . . .": Herman Melville *Moby Dick* (New York: Harper & Brothers, 1851), 278.

393 "Advance into knowledge is just like . . .": Herman Melville *The Confidence-man* (London: Longman, Brown, Green, Longmans, & Roberts, 1857), 268.

393 "His body had been in the water . . .": Rochester *Daily Democrat*, 15 November 1845, in Richard L. Canuteson, "Lars and Martha Larson: 'We Do

What We Can for Them,'" *Norwegian-American Historical Association Publications* 25 (1972): 163–64.

393 "[H]e knew if Lars was out of the way . . .": J. Hart Rosdail *The Sloopers: Their Ancestry and Posterity* (Broadview, Ill.: Norwegian Slooper Society of America, 1961), 120–21.

394 "imperial Erie canal": *Speech of William H. Seward on the Abrogation of the Missouri Compromise in the Kansas and Nebraska Bills* (Washington: Buell & Blanchard, 1854), 4.

394 "The southerns will not long pay . . .": Mitford M. Mathews, *A Dictionary of Americanisms* (Chicago: University of Chicago Press, 1951), 1600, 1601.

395 "happily exploit[ed] southern commercial passivity . . .": Albion, 121.

395 "to an extent that no person . . .": *The Albion* (New York), 21 October 1826.

396 "The Erie Canal . . .": Stuart, 37.

397 "eye to eye with the broken windows . . .": Joyce Carol Oates, "The City of Locks," in *Angel Fire* (Baton Rouge: LSU Press, 1973).

398 "The Erie Canal and Hudson River . . .": George Pataki to Jay W. Johnson, 13 July 2000, copy in author's possession.

BIBLIOGRAPHY

Note: Colden's *Memoir*, Hosack's *Memoir*, and Severance's *The Holland Land Company* are not continuous narratives, but rather unique compendia of an extraordinary number of original letters, reports, documents, essays, and other materials from a variety of writers and other sources, many not available elsewhere in printed or manuscript form. Brevity may not be the soul of citation, but for this book the citations to these volumes are mostly by page number only, regardless of the particular writer or source of the quoted material. Readers are encouraged to discover the remarkable range of information in Colden, Hosack, and Severance. All three are held by major libraries; in recent years, scanned copies of each have appeared online. *Laws of the State of New York in Relation to the Erie and Champlain Canals: Together with the Annual Reports of the Canal Commissioners, and Other Documents Requisite for a Complete Official History of Those Works* compiles, as its title implies, not only relevant laws up to 1825 but also reports, legislative debates and votes, and other original materials, much of it unavailable elsewhere; the *Canal Laws,* as they are generally known, are not easy to find outside of New York and await scanning for researchers working in the digital age.

PRIMARY SOURCES

Adams, Charles Francis, ed., *Memoirs of John Quincy Adams, Comprising Portions of His Diary from 1795 to 1848*, vol. 5. Philadelphia: J. B. Lippincott, 1875.

"Agricola." *A Letter to the Inhabitants of the City and State of New-York; on the Subject of the Commerce of the Western Waters.* New York: S. Gould, [1807].

Andrew A. Bartow Papers, Oneida County Historical Society, Utica, NY.

The Autobiography of Martin Van Buren. Edited by John Clement Fitzpatrick. Washington: GPO, 1920.

Campbell, William W. *The Life and Writings of De Witt Clinton.* New York: Baker and Scribner, 1849.

Castorland Journal: Being a Typewritten Version of the Longhand Translation by Mr. Franklin B. Hough of the Journal Kept in French Recording the Experiences,

Observations, and Events Noted by Simon Desjardins and Pierre Pharoux. . . . Remsen, N.Y.: Remsen-Steuben Historical Society, 1980.

Colden, Cadwallader D. *Memoir: Prepared at the Request of a Committee of the Common Council of the City of New York and Presented to the Mayor . . . at the Celebration of the Completion of the New York Canals.* New York: W. A. Davis, 1826.

[Cooper, Thomas]. *A Ride to Niagara in 1809 by T.C.* 1810; Rochester: George P. Humphrey, 1915.

De Witt Clinton Papers, Columbia University, New York.

Darby, William *A Tour from the City of New-York, to Detroit, in the Michigan Territory, Made Between the 2d of May and the 22d of September, 1818.* New York: Kirk & Mercein, 1819.

The Diary and Letters of Gouverneur Morris, vol. 2. New York: Charles Scribner's Sons, 1888.

The Federalist, on the New Constitution, Written in the Year 1788. Washington, D.C.: Jacob Gideon, June 1818.

Fitzpatrick, John C., ed. *The Writings of George Washington from the Original Manuscript Sources, 1745–1799.* 39 vols. Washington, D.C.: U.S. Government Printing Office, 1931–1944.

FitzSimons, Neil, ed. *The Reminiscences of John B. Jervis, Engineer of the Old Croton.* Syracuse: Syracuse University Press, 1971.

Gallatin, Albert. *Report of the Secretary of the Treasury on the Subject of Public Roads and Canals.* 1808; repr. New York: Augustus M. Kelley, 1968.

Journal of Jasper Danckaerts 1679–1680. Edited by Bartlett Burleigh James and J. Franklin Jameson. New York: Barnes & Noble, 1959 [1913].

Jesse Hawley Papers, New-York Historical Society, New York.

Howison, John. *Sketches of Upper Canada . . . and Some Recollections of the United States of America.* Edinburgh: Oliver & Boyd, 1821.

The Inland Navigation Surveys of the Western and Northern Inland Lock Navigation Companies. [Albany]: New York State Museum, 1992.

John Bloomfield Jervis Papers, Jervis Public Library, Rome, N.Y.

Laws of the State of New York in Relation to the Erie and Champlain Canals: Together with the Annual Reports of the Canal Commissioners, and Other Documents Requisite for a Complete Official History of Those Works. 2 vols. Albany: E. and E. Hosford, 1825.

Letters from John Pintard to His Daughter. 4 vols. New York: New-York Historical Society, 1940.

The Life and Correspondence of Rufus King, Comprising His Letters, Private and Official, His Public Documents, and His Speeches. 6 vols. New York: G. P. Putnam's Sons, 1894–1900.

"Our Travels, Statistical, Geographical, Mineorological, Geological, Historical, Political, and Quizzical": A Knickerbocker Tour of New York State, 1822. Edited by Louis Leonard Tucker. Albany: New York State Library, 1968.

The Papers of Thomas Jefferson. Edited by Julian P. Boyd. 20 vols. Princeton, N.J.: Princeton University Press, 1950–1982. Bobst E302.J463.

Richardson, James D. *A Compilation of the Messages and Papers of the Presidents, 1798–1907*, vol. 1. New York: Bureau of National Literature and Art, 1908.

Severance, Frank H., ed. *The Holland Land Co. and Canal Construction In Western New York; Buffalo-Black Rock Harbor Papers; Journals and Documents.* Buffalo: Buffalo Historical Society, 1910.

Snow, Dean R., Charles T. Gehring, and William A. Starna, eds. *In Mohawk Country: Early Narratives of a Native People.* Syracuse: Syracuse University Press, 1996.

Sparks, Jared. *The Writings of George Washington*, vol. 10. Boston: Russell, Shattuck, and Williams, 1836.

The Speeches of the Different Governors to the Legislature of the State of New-York. Albany: J. B. Van Steenbergh, 1825.

The Thomas Jefferson Papers, Library of Congress.

Troup, Robert *A Letter to the Honorable Brockholst Livingston, Esq., One of the Justices of the Supreme Court of the United States, On the Lake Canal Policy of the State of New-York.* Albany, Packard & Van Benthuysen, 1822.

Troup, Robert, *A Vindication of the Claim of Elkanah Watson, Esq. to the Merit of Projecting the Lake Canal Policy, as Created by the Canal Act of March, 1792: And Also, a Vindication of the Claim of the Late General Schuyler, to the Merit of Drawing That Act, and Procuring Its Passage Through the Legislature.* Geneva, N.Y.: James Bogert, 1821.

SECONDARY SOURCES

Adams, Clarence. "The Erie Canal." Typescript. Niagara County (N.Y.) Historical Society, 1998.

Adams, Samuel Hopkins. *Canal Town.* New York: Random House, 1944.

Albion, Robert Greenhalgh. *The Rise of New York Port 1815–1860.* New York: Charles Scribner's Sons, 1939.

Alexander, De Alva Stanwood. *A Political History of the State of New York.* Vol. 1. New York: Henry Holt and Company, 1906.)

Andrist, Ralph K. "The Erie Canal Passed This Way." *American Heritage* 19, no. 6 (October 1968): 22–30, 77–80.

Bagg, M[oses] M. *The Pioneers of Utica. . . .* Utica: Curtiss & Childs, 1877.

Barnard, Ella Kent. "Isaac Briggs, A.M., F.A.P.S. (1763–1825)." *Maryland Historical Magazine* 7, no. 4 (December 1912): 409–19.

"Biographical Sketch of the Late Geographer, John H. Eddy, of New-York." *American Monthly Magazine and Critical Review* 3, no. 1 (May 1818): 12–14.

Bobbé, Dorothie. *De Witt Clinton.* New York: Minton, Balch & Co., 1933.

Bonomi, Patricia U. *A Factious People: Politics and Society in Colonial New York.* New York: Columbia University Press, 1971.

Brandt, Clare. *An American Aristocracy: The Livingstons.* Garden City, N.Y.: Doubleday, 1986.

Brigham, A. P. "The Eastern Gateway of the United States." *The Geographical Journal* 13, no. 5 (May 1899): 513–24.

Brookhiser, Richard. *Gentleman Revolutionary: Gouverneur Morris, the Rake Who Wrote the Constitution*. New York: Free Press, 2003.

Bush, Charles T. *Hiel Brockway, Founder of Brockport: His Life, His Descendants, His Ancestry*. Brockport, N.Y.: The Western Monroe Historical Society, 1976.

Calhoun, Daniel Hovey. *The American Civil Engineer: Origins and Conflict*. Cambridge, Mass.: Massachusetts Institute of Technology, 1960.

Carey, Mathew. *Exhibit of the Shocking Oppression and Injustice Suffered for Sixteen Months by John Randel, Jun., Esq., Contractor for the Eastern Section of the Chesapeake and Delaware Canal, from Judge Wright, Engineer in Chief, and the Majority of the Board of Directors*. Philadelphia, n.p., 1825.

Casey, Richard P. "North Country Nemesis: The Potash Rebellion and the Embargo of 1807–1809." *NYHS Quarterly* 64, no. 1 (June 1980): 31–49.

Chalmers, Harvey. *The Birth of the Erie Canal*. New York: Bookman Associates, 1960.

Chalmers, Harvey. *How the Irish Built the Erie Canal*. New York: Bookman Associates, 1964.

Chazanof, William. *Joseph Ellicott and the Holland Land Company: The Opening of Western New York*. Syracuse: Syracuse University Press, 1970.

Clark, Joshua V. H. *Onondaga; or Reminiscences of Earlier and Later Times*. 2 vols. Syracuse: Stoddard and Babcock, 1849.

Clinton, De Witt (Tacitus). *The Canal Policy of the State of New-York*. Albany: E. and E. Hosford, 1821.

[Clinton, De Witt]. *Letters on the Natural History and Internal Resources of the State of New York*. New York: E. Bliss & E. White, 1822.

Clinton, De Witt (Atticus). *Remarks on the Proposed Canal from Lake Erie to the Hudson River*. New York: Samuel Wood, 1816.

Colden, Cadwallader. *The History of the Five Indian Nations of Canada*. London: T. Osborne, 1747.

Colles, Christopher. *Proposals for the Speedy Settlement of the Waste and Unappropriated Lands on the Western Frontier of the State of New-York, and for the Improvement of the Inland Navigation Between Albany and Oswego*. New York: Samuel Loudon, 1785.

Condon, George E. *Stars in the Water: The Story of the Erie Canal*. Garden City, N.Y.: Doubleday & Co., 1974.

Conway, Alan. *The Welsh in America; Letters from the Immigrants*. Minneapolis: University of Minnesota Press, 1961.

Cooper, William Cooper. *A Guide in the Wilderness; or the History of the First Settlements in the Western Counties of New York, with Useful Instructions to Future Settlers, in a Series of Letters Addressed by Judge Cooper, of Coopers-town, to William Sampson, Barrister, of New York*. Dublin: Gilbert and Hodges, 1810; facsimile ed., 1986.

Cornog, Evan. *The Birth of Empire: DeWitt Clinton and the American Experience, 1769–1828.* New York: Oxford University Press, 1998.

Crawford, Alan Pell. *Unwise Passions: A True Story of a Remarkable Woman—And the First Great Scandal of Eighteenth-Century America.* New York: Simon & Schuster, 2000.

Dangerfield, George. *Chancellor Robert R. Livingston of New York, 1746–1813.* New York: Harcourt Brace, 1960.

Davis, John Stancliffe. *Essays in the Earlier History of American Corporations.* 2 vols. New York: Russell & Russell, 1965 [1917].

Duncan, John. *Travels through Part of the United States and Canada in 1818 and 1819.* 2 vols. New York: W.B. Gilley, 1823.

Earl, Samuel. "Andrew A. Bartow and the Discovery of Water-Lime in This Country." *Transactions of the Oneida Historical Society at Utica* (1881): 125–43.

Early History of Syracuse. Syracuse: Rose & Miller, 1869.

Edmonds, Walter D. *Erie Water.* Boston: Little Brown, 1933.

Edmonds, Walter D. *Mostly Canallers.* Syracuse: Syracuse University Press, 1987.

Ermenc, Joseph J. "The Great Languedoc Canal." *The French Review* 34, no. 5 (April 1961): 454–60.

Evans, Charles W. *Biographical and Historical Accounts of the Fox, Ellicott, and Evans Families, and the Different Families Connected with Them.* Buffalo: Press of Baker, Jones & Co., 1882.

Evans, Paul Demund. *The Holland Land Company.* Buffalo: Buffalo Historical Society, 1924.

FitzSimons, Neil. "Benjamin Wright: The Father of American Civil Engineering." *Civil Engineering History: Engineers Make History: Proceedings of the First National Symposium on Civil Engineering History.* New York: American Society of Civil Engineers, 1996.

Flexner, James Thomas. *Steamboats Come True.* Boston: Little, Brown, 1978 [1944].

Fox, Dixon Ryan. *The Decline of Aristocracy in the Politics of New York, 1801–1840.* Edited by Robert V. Remini. New York: Harper & Row, 1965 [1919].

Francis, John W. "Reminiscences of Christopher Colles." In *The Knickerbocker Gallery.* New York: S. Hueston, 1855.

Francis, John W. *Old New York; Or, Reminiscences of the Past Sixty Years.* New York: Charles Roe, 1858.

Geddes, George. "The Erie Canal: Origin and History of the Measures That Led to Its Construction." *Publications of the Buffalo Historical Society* 2 (1880): 263–304.

Goodrich, Carter, ed. *Canals and American Economic Development.* New York: Columbia University Press, 1961.

Goodrich, Carter. "The Gallatin Plan after One Hundred and Fifty Years." *Proceedings of the American Philosophical Society* 102, no. 5 (1958): 436–41.

Goodrich, Carter. *Government Promotion of American Canals & Railroads, 1800–1890.* New York: Columbia University Press, 1960.

Gray, Ralph D. *The National Waterway: A History of the Chesapeake and Delaware Canal 1769–1985.* 2nd ed. Urbana and Chicago: University of Illinois Press, 1989.

Gunn, L. Ray. *The Decline of Authority: Public Economic Policy and Political Development in New York State 1800–1860.* Ithaca: Cornell University Press, 1988.

Hager, Robert E. *Mohawk River Boats and Navigation Before 1820.* Syracuse: Canal Society of New York State, 1987.

Haines, Charles G. *Considerations on the Great Western Canal from the Hudson to Lake Erie. . . .* [New York]: Spooner & Worthington, 1818.

Hammond, Jabez D. *The History of Political Parties in the State of New-York.* 2 vols. Albany: C. Van Benthuysen, 1842.

Hanyan, Craig, with Mary L. Hanyan *De Witt Clinton and the Rise of the People's Men.* Montreal: McGill-Queen's University Press, 1996.

Hatcher, Harlan Henthorne. *The Great Lakes.* New York: Oxford University Press, 1944.

Hauptman, Laurence M. *Conspiracy of Interests: Iroquois Dispossession and the Rise of New York State.* Syracuse: Syracuse University Press, 1999.

Hawley, Jesse. *Essay on the Enlargement of the Erie Canal.* Lockport: Published at the Courier Office, 1840.

Hawley, Merwin S. "The Erie Canal: Its Origin, Its Success and Its Necessity." *Publications of the Buffalo Historical Society* 2 (1880): [305]–34.

Hawley, Merwin S. "Origin of the Erie Canal." *Publications of the Buffalo Historical Society* 2 (1880): [227]–61.

The Hawley Record. Compiled by Elias S. Hawley. Buffalo: E. H. Hutchinson & Co., 1890.

Haydon, Roger, ed. *Upstate Travels: British Views of Nineteenth-Century New York.* Syracuse: Syracuse University Press, 1982.

Hislop, Codman. *The Mohawk.* [1948]. Syracuse: Syracuse University Press, 1989.

"Historical Writings of Judge Samuel Wilkeson, Prefaced with a Biographical Sketch by his Son, the Late Samuel Wilkeson, Jr." *Publications of the Buffalo Historical Society* 5 (1902): 135–214.

[Hodge, William]. "How Buffalo Dug the Canal." *Publications of the Buffalo Historical Society* 13 (1909): 387–90.

Hopkins, Vivian C. "The Governor and the Western Recluse: De Witt Clinton And Francis Adrian Van Der Kamp." *Proceedings of the American Philosophical Society* 105, no. 3 (September 1961): 315–33.

Hosack, David. *Memoir of De Witt Clinton: With an Appendix, Containing Numerous Documents, Illustrative of the Principal Events of His Life.* New York: J. Seymour, 1829.

Hubbard, J. T. W. *For Each, the Strength of All: A History of Banking in the State of New York.* New York: New York University Press, 1995.

Jackson, Harry F. *Scholar in the Wilderness: Francis Adrian Van der Kemp.* Syracuse: Syracuse University Press, 1963.

John, Paul E. *A Shopkeeper's Millennium: Society and Revivals in Rochester, New York, 1815–1837.* New York: Hill and Wang, 1978.

Johnson, Paul. *A History of the American People.* New York: HarperCollins, 1998.

July, Robert William. *The Essential New Yorker: Gulian Crommelin Verplanck.* Durham: Duke University Press, 1951.

Kapsch, Robert J. *Canals.* New York: Norton, 2004.

Kass, Alvin. *Politics in New York State 1800–1830.* Syracuse: Syracuse University Press, 1965.

Kirby, Richard Shelton, "William Weston and His Contribution to Early American Engineering." *Newcomen Society Transaction* 16 (1935–1936): 11–130.

Kirschke, James J. *Gouverneur Morris: Author, Statesman, and Man of the World.* New York: St. Martin's Press, 2005.

Knapp, Samuel L. *The Life of Thomas Eddy.* New York: Conner & Cooke, 1834.

Koeppel, Gerard. "Andrew Bartow and the Cement That Made the Erie Canal." *New-York Journal of American History* 66, no. 1 (Spring–Summer 2005): 52–60.

Lamon, Ward H. *The Life of Abraham Lincoln; From His Birth to His Inauguration as President.* Boston: James R. Osgood and Company, 1872.

Langbein, W. B. *Hydrology and Environmental Aspects of Erie Canal (1817–99).* Geological Survey Water-Supply Paper 2038. Washington, D.C.: U.S. Government Printing Office, 1976.

Larkin, F. Daniel. *John B. Jervis: An American Engineering Pioneer.* Ames: Iowa State University Press, 1990.

Larkin, F. Daniel. *New York State Canals: A Short History.* Fleischmanns, NY: Purple Mountain Press, 1998.

Larson, John Lauritz. *Internal Improvement: National Public Works and the Promise of Popular Government in the Early United States.* Chapel Hill: University of North Carolina Press, 2001.

Lawson, Dorris Moore. *Nathan Roberts: Erie Canal Engineer.* Utica, N.Y.: North Country Books, 1997.

Levasseur, A[uguste]. *Lafayette in America in 1824 and 1825.* 2 vols. Philadelphia: Carey and Lea, 1829.

Long, John H., ed. *New York: Atlas of Historical County Boundaries.* Compiled by Kathryn Ford Thorne. New York: Simon & Schuster, 1993.

Lord, Philip L., Jr. *The Neck on Mohawcks River-New York's First Canal.* n.p.: The Canal Society of New York State, 1993.

Marx, Leo. *The Machine in the Garden.* New York: Oxford University Press, 1964.

McIlwraith, Thomas. "Freight Capacity and Utilization of the Erie and Great Lakes Canals before 1850." *Journal of Economic History* 36, no. 4 (December 1976): 852–77.

McKelvey, Blake. "The Erie Canal, Mother of Cities." *New-York Historical Society Quarterly* 35 (January 1951): 55–71.

McKelvey, Blake. "Rochester and the Erie Canal." *Rochester History* 11, nos. 3 & 4 (July 1949): 1–24.

McKelvey, Blake. *Rochester on the Genesee: The Growth of a City.* 2nd ed. Syracuse: Syracuse University Press, 1993.

McKelvey, Blake. "Water Power City Overflow: Leaves from an Historian's Notebook." *Rochester History* 4, no. 2 (April 1942).

McNamara, Brooks. *Day of Jubilee: The Great Age of Public Celebrations in New York 1788–1909.* New Brunswick, N. J.: Rutgers University Press, 1997.

Memorial of Centennial Celebration of the Turning of the First Shovelful of Earth in the Construction of the Erie Canal, Held at Rome, N.Y., July 4th, 1917. . . . Rome: Rome Sentinel Co., 1917.

Miller, Nathan. *The Enterprise of a Free People: Aspects of Economic Development in New York State during the Canal Period, 1792–1838.* Ithaca: Cornell University Press, 1962.

Miller, Nathan. "Private Enterprise in Inland Navigation: The Mohawk Route Prior to the Erie Canal." *New York History* 31 (October 1950): 398–413.

Mintz, Max M. *Gouverneur Morris and the American Revolution.* Norman: University of Oklahoma Press, 1970.

Moore, Thomas. *An Essay on the Most Eligible Construction of Ice-Houses. Also, A Description of the Newly Invented Machine Called the Refrigerator.* Baltimore, Md.: Bonsal & Niles, 1803.

Murphy, Joseph Hawley. "The Salt Industry of Syracuse—A Brief Review." *New York History* 30 (July 1949): 304–15.

Mushkat, Jerome. *Tammany: The Evolution of a Political Machine, 1789–1865.* Syracuse: Syracuse University Press, 1971.

New York State Historical Association. *Proceedings* 14 (1915).

Olenick, Andy. and Richard O. Reisem. *Erie Canal Legacy: Architectural Treasures of the Empire State.* Rochester: Landmark Society of Western New York, 2000.

Palmer, Richard F. "The Forwarding Business in Oswego 1800–1820." *Inland Seas* 41, nos. 2 & 3 (1985): 100–11, 175–84.

Pownall, Thomas. *A Topographical Description of the Dominions of the United States of America.*, Edited by Lois Mulkearn. New York: Arno Press, 1976 [1776].

Randel, John. "City of New York, north of Canal Street, in 1808 to 1821." *Manual of the Corporation of the City of New York.* New York: Valentine, 1864.

Randel, John. *Description of a Direct Route for the Erie Canal, at Its Eastern Termination: With Estimates of Its Expense, and Comparative Advantages.* Albany: G. J. Loomis & Co., 1822.

[Randel, John]. *An Examination of the Line of the Great Erie Canal as Adopted by the Commissioners, from Schoharie Creek to Its Final Destination at the Tide Waters of the Hudson River: Contrasted with a More Safe, Direct and Practicable Line, and Exhibiting Some of the Reasons Why the Latter Ought to Be Preferred.* Albany?: s.n., 1822.

Rapp, Marvin A. *Canal Water and Whiskey: Tall Tales from Erie Canal Country.* Buffalo: Heritage Press, 1992.

Remini, Robert. *Martin Van Buren and the Making of the Democratic Party.* New York: Columbia University Press, 1959.

Renwick, James. *Life of Dewitt Clinton.* New York: Harper & Bros., 1840.

Ristow, Walter W., ed. *A Survey of the Roads of the United States of America 1789 By Christopher Colles.* Cambridge, Mass.: Harvard University Press, 1961.

Ritchie, William A. *The Archaeology of New York State.* Fleischmanns, N.Y.: Purple Mountain Press, 1994 [1965].

Roosevelt, Theodore. *New York.* New York: Longman, Green, 1891.

Sale, Kirkpatrick. *The Fire of His Genius: Robert Fulton and the American Dream.* New York: The Free Press, 2001.

Seelye, John. *Beautiful Machine: Rivers and the Republican Plan, 1755–1825.* New York: Oxford University Press, 1991.

Seelye, John D. "Rational Exultation: The Erie Canal Celebration of 1825." *American Antiquarian Society Proceedings* 94, pt. 2 (October 1984): 241–67.

Shaw, Ronald E. *Canals for a Nation: The Canal Era in the United States, 1790–1860.* Lexington: University of Kentucky Press, 1990.

Shaw, Ronald E. *Erie Water West: A History of the Erie Canal, 1792–1854.* Lexington: University of Kentucky Press, 1990 [1966].

Sheriff, Carol. *The Artificial River: The Erie Canal and the Paradoxes of Progress, 1817–1862.* New York: Hill and Wang, 1996.

Shorto, Russell. *The Island at the Center of the World.* New York: Vintage, 2004.

Smiles, Samuel. *Lives of the Engineers.* London: John Murray, 1861.

Spafford, Horatio Gates. *A Gazetteer of the State of New-York: Carefully Written from Original and Authentic Materials, Arranged on a New Plan, in Three Parts. . . .* Albany: H.C. Southwick, 1813.

Spafford, Horatio Gates. *A Gazetteer of the State of New-York, Embracing an Ample Survey and Description of Its Counties, Towns, Cities, Villages, Canals, Mountains, Lakes, Rivers, Creeks and Natural Topography. Arranged in One Series, Alphabetically: With an Appendix.* Albany: B.D. Packard, 1824.

Spafford, Horatio Gates. *A Pocket Guide for the Tourist and Traveller Along the Line of the Canals, and the Interior Commerce of the State of New York.* New York: T. and J. Swords, 1824.

Stagg, J. C. A., "Between Black Rock and a Hard Place: Peter B. Porter's Plan for an American Invasion of Canada in 1812." *Journal of the Early Republic* 19, no. 3 (Fall 1999): 385–422.

Stuart, Charles B. *Lives and Works of Civil and Military Engineers of America.* New York, D. Van Nostrand, 1871.

Svejda, George J. *Irish Immigrant Participation in the Construction of the Erie Canal.* Washington, D.C.: Division of History, Office of Archeology and Historic Preservation, National Parks Service, U.S. Department of the Interior, 1969.

Swerdlow, Joel L. "Erie Canal: Living Links to Our Past." *National Geographic* 178, no. 5 (November 1990): 39–65.

Sydnor, Charles. "The One-Party Period of American History." *American Historical Review* 51, no. 3 (April 1946): 439–51.

Tanner, Henry S. *A Description of the Canals and Railroads of the United States.* [1840]; New York: Augustus M. Kelley, 1970.

Tarkov, John. "Engineering the Canal." *American Heritage of Invention and Technology* (Summer 1986): 50–57.

Taylor, George Rogers. *The Transportation Revolution.* New York: Harper & Row, 1951.

Thomas, David. *Travels through the western country in the summer of 1816. . . .* Auburn, N.Y.: David Rumsey, 1819.

Thomas, J[ohn] J[acob]. "Memoir of David Thomas." *Collections of Cayuga County Historical Society* no. 6 (1888): 39–53.

Thompson, Harold W. *Body, Boots, & Britches: Folktales, Ballads and Speech from Country New York.* 1939; Syracuse: Syracuse University Press, 1979.

Thompson, John, ed. *Geography of New York State.* Syracuse: Syracuse University Press, 1966.

Turner, O[rsamus]. *History of the Pioneer Settlement of Phelps & Gorham's Purchase, and Morris' Reserve. . . .* Rochester: W. Alling, 1851.

Turner, O[rsamus]. *Pioneer History of the Holland Purchase of Western New York.* Buffalo: Jewett, Thomas & Co., 1850.

Wager, Daniel E. *Our City and Its People: A Descriptive Work on the City of Rome, New York.* 1896; Deansboro, N.Y. : Berry Hill Press, 1996.

Wager, Daniel E. *Our County and Its People: A Descriptive Work on Oneida County, New York.* Boston: The Boston History Company, 1896.

Watson, Elkanah *History of the Rise, Progress, and Existing Condition of the Western Canals in the State of New-York. . . .* Albany: D. Steele, 1820.

Watson, Winslow C., ed. *Men and Times of the Revolution; or, Memoirs of Elkanah Watson. . . .* 2nd ed. New York: Dana and Company, 1856.

Way, Peter. *Common Labor: Workers and the Digging of North American Canals, 1780–1860.* Baltimore, Md.: Johns Hopkins University Press, 1997 [1993].

Whitford, Noble E. *History of the Canal System of the State of New York, Together with Brief Histories of the Canals of the United States and Canada.* 2 vols. Albany: Brandow Printing Company, 1906.

Wright, Benjamin H. *Origin of the Erie Canal: Services of Benjamin Wright.* Rome: Sandford & Carr, 1870.

Wright, Elizur. *Myron Holley; and What He Did for Liberty and True Religion.* Boston: Printed for the author, 1882.

Wyckoff, William. *The Developer's Frontier: The Making of the Western New York Landscape.* New Haven, Conn.: Yale University Press, 1988.

Wyld, Lionel D. *Low Bridge: Folklore and the Erie Canal.* Syracuse: Syracuse University Press, 1962.

[Young, Samuel]. *A Treatise on Internal Navigation.* Ballston Spa [N.Y.]: U.F. Doubleday, 1817.

Young, William C. "Reminiscences of Erie Canal Surveys in 1816–1817." *Publications of the Buffalo Historical Society* 13 (1909), 333–47.

DISSERTATIONS

Carp, Roger Evan. "The Erie Canal And The Liberal Challenge to Classical Republicanism, 1785–1850." Ph.D. dissertation, University of North Carolina, 1986.

Grande, Joseph Anthony. "The Political Career of Peter Buell Porter, 1797–1829." Ph.D. dissertation, University of Notre Dame, 1971.

Harrison, Joseph Hobson, Jr. "The Internal Improvement Issue in the Politics of the Union, 1783–1825." Ph.D. dissertation, University of Virginia, 1954.

Roland, Daniel Dean. "Peter Buell Porter and Self-Interest in American Politics." Ph.D. dissertation, Claremont Graduate School, 1990.

Turcott, Jean Marie. "Waiting for the Erie Line: Property, improvement, and market revolution in the Southern Tier of New York State, 1790–1850." Ph.D. dissertation, State University of New York at Buffalo, 2001.

REFERENCE WORKS

Dictionary of American Biography. New York: Charles Scribner's Sons, 1936.

Encyclopedia of the New American Nation: The Emergence of the United States, 1754–1829. 3 vols. Detroit: Thompson Gale, 2006.

The Encyclopedia of New York City. New Haven, Conn.: Yale University Press, 1995.

The Encyclopedia of New York State. Syracuse: Syracuse University Press, 2005.

ACKNOWLEDGMENTS

Thousands of people created the Erie Canal. It seems as if nearly as many had a hand in this book.

Of those who helped in various ways with research materials or guidance on specific subjects or the canal generally, I thank these people in particular: Bill Carr, Daniel Carr, Jackie and Marc Cheves, Bill Hecht, Dwight T. Pitcaithley, Max Mintz, Robert E. Wright, F. Daniel Larkin, Craig Hanyan, David Minor, Carol Sheriff, John Seelye, John I. Garver, John J. Gara, Robert J. Kapsch, Philip Lord, Scott Monje, George J. Svejda, Bill Starna, Charles Gehring, and Craig Williams. Special recognition to Jane Dieffenbacher, the historian of the Town of Fairfield in Herkimer County, New York, for making me aware of and happily sharing her research on Andrew Bartow. And special thanks to Valerie Paley at the *New-York Journal of American History.*

These institutions, and many people at them, helped me immensely: the Hawley Society (which preserves that family's extensive history); the Sandy Springs (Maryland) Museum; the Rochester Historical Society, the Rochester Public Library, the Buffalo and Erie County Historical Society; the Oneida County Historical Society, in Utica; the Remsen-Steuben Historical Society, in Remsen, New York; the Niagara County Historical Society in Lockport; the Jervis Public Library in Rome; the Adirondack Museum, Blue Mountain Lake, New York; the Great Lakes Historical Society, Vermilion, Ohio; the American Canal and Transportation Center, York, Pennsylvania; the New York Public Library, the New-York Historical Society Library; the Columbia University Library; the New York State Library; the Princeton University Library; the University of Michigan Special Collections Library; the Library of Congress; and the New York State Archives.

Among many who helped in the tedious, time consuming, and not inexpensive process of image collection, I especially thank Clayton Lewis at the University of Michigan's William L. Clements Library, Bob Graham in the Great Lakes Historical Collections of the Bowling Green State Library, and Tom Lisanti at the New York Public Library.

Among many good friends who read and responded to early drafts of sections of this book, Dennis Powell deserves singular mention: he read the original manuscript very closely, reworking pages and pages of material that wasn't fit to print, drawing out ideas obscured by dense research. Thanks for gracious assistance with much of that research goes to Emily Wiedemann, Matthew Bresler, Amber Scherf, and Neha Dubli.

This book was born by chance at an editorial meeting attended by my agent Russ Galen; he's the best partner in the book world that this writer could have. This book took a late turn toward Da Capo but it seems as if Bob Pigeon and I have been friends for years; every serious writer deserves such a dedicated editor. Renee Caputo at Perseus kept the project on its tight deadlines, cheerfully. My thanks also to Lissa Warren, Trent Knoss, and others at Perseus who have had a hand in this book's fortunes.

My mother Elinor Koeppel turned me toward writing at an impressionable age; my father Bevin Koeppel has always stressed the importance of details, essential to any book of history. I write now with the constant support and editorial advice of my wife, Diane, and our children, Jackson, Harry, and Kate, who hopefully will all turn out to be better (and quicker) at writing than I am.

INDEX